Lo[illegible]
at G[illegible]sburg

Longstreet at Gettysburg

A Critical Reassessment

Cory M. Pfarr

Foreword by Harold M. Knudsen

McFarland & Company, Inc., Publishers
Jefferson, North Carolina

Library of Congress Cataloguing-in-Publication Data

Names: Pfarr, Cory M., 1989– author. | Knudsen, Harold M., writer of foreword.
Title: Longstreet at Gettysburg : a critical reassessment / Cory M. Pfarr ; foreword by Harold M. Knudsen.
Description: Jefferson, North Carolina : McFarland & Company, Inc., Publishers, 2019 | Includes bibliographical references and index.
Identifiers: LCCN 2019002680 | ISBN 9781476674049 (paperback : acid free paper) ♾
Subjects: LCSH: Gettysburg, Battle of, Gettysburg, Pa., 1863. | Longstreet, James, 1821–1904—Military leadership.
Classification: LCC E467.1.L55 P43 2019 | DDC 973.7/349—dc23
LC record available at https://lccn.loc.gov/2019002680

British Library cataloguing data are available

ISBN (print) 978-1-4766-7404-9
ISBN (ebook) 978-1-4766-3499-9

Front cover: James Longstreet, 1863 (courtesy HistoryInFullColor.com)

Printed in the United States of America

McFarland & Company, Inc., Publishers
Box 611, Jefferson, North Carolina 28640
www.mcfarlandpub.com

For God; my wife, Michelle;
my children, Anita, David, and Abigail;
and the rest of my family.

Acknowledgments

First and foremost, I would like to thank my wife, Michelle, for her constant encouragement and support throughout the entirety of this four-year project and for reading and offering suggestions on multiple drafts of this book. Her and my children's patience and understanding when I sometimes spent hours at a time in my study researching, writing, or editing was greatly appreciated. I would also like to thank Dr. Charles F. Ritter for his advice and guidance throughout the writing and editing process. Dr. Ritter always made himself available to answer any question or concern I had in a timely manner. Lastly, I would like to express gratitude to the McFarland editorial team for making the publication experience so pleasant and efficient.

Table of Contents

✦ Day Three ✦

Maps

Maps by Hal Jespersen

Foreword
by Harold M. Knudsen

Upon the death of Robert E. Lee in 1870, several of General James Longstreet's contemporaries who sought to discredit him for his postwar politics took aim at his war record in order to accomplish their character assassination. This led to a century-and-a-half-long assault from many writers in different periods who invented one falsehood after the next on why Lee was defeated at Gettysburg. Nearly all these falsehoods attributed the defeat to Longstreet for one reason or another. For the first time ever, a writer has taken on the considerable task of looking at every single one of these charges against Longstreet regarding Gettysburg, analyzing them for their motive, for their plausibility, and then showing why they are false. Cory Pfarr's work is a powerful broadside that demolishes each one.

From the first books written in the decades after the war, to the Lost Cause era that gained full steam generally in the 1890s through the 1930s, and on to the second generation of Lost Cause writers like Douglass Southall Freeman in the 1940s, these groupthink narratives about Gettysburg were continuously reinforced and repeated from one book to the next. Audiences were trained to believe what writers said as gospel, rather than educated to examine the true records. Perhaps in the 1960s the historical novel *The Killer Angels* provided the first respite from the negativity about Longstreet that at least showed him in a fictional setting as a consummate professional who cared about helping Robert E. Lee. From this came a few later books and magazine articles that began to re-evaluate and re-educate the public on Longstreet slowly into the 2000s and out to today. None, however, have addressed Longstreet at Gettysburg solely like this fine work has.

From all of Longstreet's interactions with Lee, to his battle preparations and his execution of the plans, Pfarr shows a mastery of thorough research: how to use historical primary sources to debunk incorrect secondary source historiography. All three days of Gettysburg get a full treatment in this work through a unique angle. It is truly a fresh and original look at Gettysburg, and anyone who cares about the truth of Longstreet's place in the record that is Gettysburg should read this *tour de force* of historical method.

Harold M. Knudsen, a retired Army lieutenant colonel, is the author of General James Longstreet: The Confederacy's Most Modern General. *He lives in Alexandria, Virginia.*

Prologue: Abandoned by History

"The faithful historian of the future will assign him his due"
—John H. Leathen

Gainesville, Georgia, mid–1890s: After enduring a sixteen-hour trip in a Pullman Car, Hamlin Garland, the turn of the twentieth century American essayist and novelist, walked through a town "so distinctively of the mountain south," it engendered a sense of having "entered another world." Meandering his way along dirt roads, he imagined a "large, old-fashioned southern place, with pillars wide and tall" as his final destination, but instead found a tree with a board nailed to it, reading "Wine for Sale." Across the road was a sizable vineyard and as he walked on, he came upon a "lean, farmer-like person," who pointed him toward "an ordinary story and a half [*sic*] farm house, such as a northern carpenter might build."

"You'll find him in his vineyard," said the man.[1]

Garland moved along until he happened upon the person he sought to meet, "a big old man, stooping a little low now, and slow of gait," with "scissors in hand, busily pruning his vines." The young journalist was now face-to-face with former Lieutenant General James Longstreet, Commander of the Army of Northern Virginia's First Corps and senior subordinate to General Robert E. Lee, Commander of the Army of Northern Virginia, who referred to Longstreet as "my old war-horse" and "the staff in my right hand" while serving by his side from 1862 to 1865.[2]

Hamlin Garland, 1890s (courtesy Keith Newlin).

During the wartime years, Longstreet had cut the physical appearance of a soldier in the prime of his life. The men who served under Longstreet described him in many admiring ways and came up with different nicknames; "the best fighter in the whole army," "a bully general," a "real bulldog fighter," "Old Peter," and the "Bull of the Woods" after his commanding performance at the Battle of Chickamauga in September 1863. According to Thomas Goree, a First Corp aide-de-camp, Longstreet stood nearly six feet tall, was said to have weighed about 200 pounds, had light-brown hair and blue eyes, and wore "a large, heavy set of whiskers and moustache, which hides the lower part of his face." Goree further described his chief as "exceedingly punctual and industrious," while "when he dresses up in his uniform and mounts his horse, I think that he presents a better appearance than any other man in the Army. The ladies all say that he is the handsomest." Gilbert Moxley Sorrel, another First Corp aide-de-camp, wrote similarly of the General, describing him as "a soldier every inch, and very handsome, tall and well-proportioned, strong and active, a superb horseman and with an unsurpassed soldierly bearing." On Longstreet's temperament, Goree deemed him "one of the kindest, best hearted men I ever knew," who was happiest "in the presence of ladies ... at the table ... [and] on the field of battle," while admitting that "those not well acquainted with him think him short and crabbed." On the battlefield, Longstreet was, according to Goree, "a man of but very few words, and keeps at all time his own counsels ... very reserved and distant toward his men, and very strict, but they all like him." Sorrel also described Longstreet as "reserved" and "very serious," particularly after he lost three children to scarlet fever within one week's time in the winter of 1862. After that personal tragedy, Longstreet was, according to Sorrel "a changed man," where "later years" and time only "lightened the memory of his sorrow."[3]

Years later, Hamlin Garland was encountering a very different man. He immediately noticed Longstreet's physical infirmities. The General's voice was faint and his right arm largely crippled—both ailments caused by a nearly mortal wound received at the Battle of the Wilderness in May 1864. The latter ailment would plague him the rest of his life. Upon Longstreet's return to the army in October 1864, Gilbert Moxley Sorrel noted, "His right arm was quite paralyzed and useless." By May 1875, Longstreet informed Thomas Goree he was currently in Hot Springs, Arkansas, "on a visit to try the effect of these waters on my crippled arm and shoulder." Though it was reported in July 1888 at the 25th anniversary of the Battle of Gettysburg that Longstreet was "a tall soldierly-looking man with white hair and flowing gray whiskers," it was also written that "Longstreet does not look strong, and his 67 years bear heavily on him. His enfeebled condition attracted attention, and he was induced to sit down. He sank into his chair with a sigh." Three years later in January 1891, Goree visited Longstreet in San Antonio, Texas, where he found his former

James Longstreet, prior to the war (Library of Congress).

Chief "very feeble, and is so deaf that it is hard to converse with him." By the time Garland met Longstreet in the 1890s, the General's hair appeared "white as wool," his skin "ruddy," and he was "quite deaf in one ear."[4]

James Longstreet, 1890s (*From Manassas to Appomattox*).

To better hear the young journalist, Longstreet welcomed Garland into his house, "small and plainly furnished." When Longstreet first moved to Gainesville from New Orleans in 1875, he had purchased and lived in a much larger two-story house, described as "richly furnished," replete with wartime memorabilia and numerous books, while the structure was surrounded by farmland, orchards and vineyards. However, misfortune struck in 1889 when Longstreet's uninsured home burned to the ground, taking with it nearly all his wartime memorabilia and correspondence. He could not afford to rebuild the two-story home, so he moved into the quaint cottage that had been a former outbuilding. The General had also been the owner of the Piedmont Hotel in town, which was a three-story, two-wing, white-columned structure complete with 36 guest rooms. Longstreet and his family typically spent the winter months at the Piedmont. Though the establishment never proved very profitable for Longstreet, a *New York Times* correspondent who sojourned there in the winter of 1888—just a year before the General lost his home—wrote of the then sixty-seven year old, "He is the very embodiment of good humor. He tries to make everyone comfortable, and as his hotel commands the best breeze from the Blue Ridge, he usually succeeds. He will mount three flights of steps to carry an apple to some little fellow who learns to know and love the bronzed face and white hair of this Southern veteran."[5]

Once inside the cottage, Garland found that though Longstreet's physical being had grown infirm since the wartime years, his mental acuity and integrity remained fully intact as Longstreet recalled with Garland one of his favorite topics, his lifelong friendship with the then-late General and ex-President Ulysses S. Grant. Late in life, Grant demonstrated, as claimed, that he knew Longstreet "very well," writing that "He was brave, intelligent, a very capable soldier, subordinate to his superiors, just and kind to his subordinates, but jealous of his own rights, which he had the courage to maintain." As Longstreet reminisced, Garland scribbled "remarkable personality ... not merely a great solider ... thinker of unusual originality ... brave, high-minded citizen ... liberal-minded, honorable man." On the whole, Garland summarized his impression of Lee's Warhorse—"He talked like a philosopher, a gentleman and a lover of the whole America. He made a powerful impression upon me." Despite the great hardships and despair Longstreet had experienced in the late 1880s and early 1890s Longstreet proved capable of making a remarkable impression on Garland. Within mere months of losing his house to fire, Longstreet endured the loss of his first wife, Louisa, to whom he had been married for 42 years and bore him ten children, five of whom lived to adulthood. Coupled with these losses, Longstreet continued to shoulder physical infirmity in his right arm and throat. He was forced to write with his left hand, while his voice, which had bellowed on the battlefield years ago, was reduced to a mere whisper at times. Osmun Latrobe, formerly of Longstreet's wartime staff, relayed some telling correspondence from Longstreet in an 1890 letter: "I received a letter from him [Longstreet] a few days ago; in it he said: 'My arm is paralyzed; my voice that once could be heard all along the lines, is gone; I can scarcely speak above a whisper; my hearing is very much impaired, and sometimes I feel as if I wish the end would come What a change!'"[6]

Although noticing Longstreet's poor physical state was likely inevitable, Garland seemed to look beyond it and touch on a subtle, yet powerful quality about the old soldier. While expressing clear admiration for Longstreet, the young journalist interspersed smaller hints of a much more omnipresent issue in the General's postwar life, writing that "He steadily upheld every measure which in his judgment would restore the Union and peace and harmony soonest, no matter what his critics might say. It does not appear in General Longstreet's talk that he holds any bitterness towards his detractors." In spite of Garland's presumption, Longstreet's letter to Latrobe seemed to give a different account and alluded to another war that Longstreet had been continually fighting for years after Appomattox: "I have some misrepresentations of my battles that I wish to correct, so as to have my record correct before I die." Garland, who was just an infant when Longstreet had offered his services to the Confederacy in 1861, surely erred in his claim that the General held no "bitterness toward his detractors." For certainly, behind Longstreet's calm façade was a man who had been affected deeply by the verbal attacks hurled at him by these so-called critics and detractors since the late 1860s. Indeed, both of Garland's loaded statements about Longstreet's critics and detractors, seemingly mentioned only in passing in his newspaper article, hint at two overshadowing issues that enveloped the General's postwar life, and ultimately coalesced into one, main controversial topic.[7]

* * *

Garland's first statement on Longstreet's critics alluded to a series of political decisions the General made after the war and postwar Southern leaders' reaction to them. Garland refrained from much additional commentary about his observation, perhaps so as not to hamper his article with controversial issues about a man he almost immediately came to respect and esteem. For the first couple of years after the war, Longstreet was largely a lesser known figure when compared to the likes of Lee, Thomas "Stonewall" Jackson, Pierre Gustave Tutant (P.G.T.) Beauregard, and Joseph Johnston, but was nonetheless well-liked, looked upon favorably, and garnered a great deal of respect from Southern historians. One contemporary historian, Edward Pollard, called Longstreet "conspicuous," "brilliant," and "trusted, faithful, diligent, a hardy campaigner, a fierce obstinate fighter, an officer who devoted his whole mind to the war." Another historian, James McCabe, wrote in 1870 that Longstreet was Lee's "most trusted lieutenant," and gave him high marks for his performance at Gettysburg, and even criticized Lee's actions there. That said, from 1865 to 1867, Longstreet was largely eclipsed by other actors in the war, namely the Virginians Lee, Jackson, and James Ewell Brown (J.E.B.) Stuart.

While Longstreet was often described as a dependable and capable subordinate and, along with Jackson, part of Lee's star squad in 1862 and early 1863, he never received the attention and accolades Jackson did. As in John Esten Cooke's *Wearing of the Gray*, written shortly after the war, Longstreet's role in battles was usually either minimized or completely absent. Cooke, like a number of modern historians, went as far as to suggest that Jackson was Lee's senior subordinate, when in fact Longstreet had been. Even so, Longstreet was respected, even if misrepresented.[8]

The first visible spark of controversy about Longstreet surfaced in 1867 following a series of letters the General wrote to the editor of the Democrat Party-leaning newspaper, the *New Orleans Times.* In the first few articles, Longstreet addressed postwar Reconstruction and recommended the South accept their defeat, cooperate, and reconcile with the North, believing this strategy would hasten Reconstruction recovery in the South. More controversially, by June 1867, Longstreet not only recommended Southern acceptance, but advised cooperation with the leading Northern political party, the Republicans. Longstreet wrote, "The war was made upon Republican issues, and it seems to me fair and just that the settlement should be made accordingly." Longstreet contended that Republican principles were now the law of the land. "The sword has decided in favor of the North, and what they claimed as principles cease to be principles, and are become law. The views that we hold cease to be principles because they are opposed to law. It is therefore our duty to abandon ideas that are obsolete and conform to the requirements of law," Longstreet wrote unabashedly. These pronouncements should not be misconstrued and misinterpreted, as they were by many at the time, to mean he outright supported the Republican Party; rather, more realistically, Longstreet sought amelioration and an opportunity to retain some vestiges of the old Southern order through this cooperation with the North and Republican Party. For instance, on the issue of blacks being granted the right to vote in the South, Longstreet wrote, "Since the negro has been given the privilege of voting, it is all important that we should exercise such influence over that vote, as to prevent its being injurious to us, & we can only do that as Republicans." As another historian aptly put it, "Longstreet sought to control the black vote." Longstreet expressed his stance on Republicans in a personal letter, not in his public articles, where he made such statements as "Hence it becomes us to insist that suffrage should be extended in all of the States, and fully tested. The people of the North should adopt what they have forced upon us; and if it be proved to be a mistake, they should remove it by the remedy under republican principles of uniform laws upon suffrage."[9]

Even though Longstreet's Uncle Augustus forthrightly expressed to his nephew his misgivings about Longstreet's June 1867 article, writing, "It will ruin you, son, if you publish it," Longstreet proceeded with publication. While Longstreet justified his views with an honest desire to ensure Southerners "save the little that is left of us, and go to work to improve that little as best we may," declaring "I think that the time has come for peace and I am not willing to lose more blood or means in procuring it," many in the South called the General's calls for cooperation with the dominant Northern political party a blatant betrayal, an anathema to everything for which they had fought and been dealt at the hands of the "Black Republicans" during the war. To make matters more difficult and suspect, in what should have otherwise been a moment of reprieve, Longstreet received an official Federal pardon on June 19, 1867, only days after making his controversial appeal to Southerners. Coupled with Longstreet's public pronouncements, he subsequently took public action and endorsed his lifelong friend, Republican Ulysses S. Grant, for President in 1868 and was consequently appointed as surveyor of the port of New Orleans. A few years later in 1872, Republican governor William Kellogg of Louisiana appointed him major general of militia and state police forces in New Orleans. While holding that position in September 1874, Longstreet was shot in the leg when his leadership of a black militia force instigated a clash with the White League, which opposed the "carpetbagger" Republican governor. By 1880, Longstreet served as Ambassador to the Ottoman Empire and deputy collector of internal revenue during the administration of President Rutherford B. Hayes. Continuing to serve Republicans, he functioned as U.S. Commissioner of Railroads from 1897 to 1904, under the William McKinley and Theodore Roosevelt presidencies. Perhaps not surprisingly, while many Southerners reacted vehemently to Longstreet's politics, many Northerners lauded Longstreet's call to assimilate and accept defeat. Major General Daniel Sickles' praise of Longstreet just after the General's death exemplified this contrast:

> Longstreet's example was the rainbow of reconciliation that foreshadowed real peace between the North and South. He drew the fire of the irreconcilable South. His statesmanlike forecast blazed the path of progress and prosperity for his people, impoverished by war and discouraged by adversity. He was the first of the illustrious Southern war leaders to accept the result of the great conflict as final. He folded up forever the Confederate flag he had followed with supreme devotion, and thenceforth saluted the Stars and Stripes of the Union with unfaltering homage. He was trusted servant of the republic in peace, as he had been its relentless foe in war. The friends of the Union became his friends, the enemies of the Union his enemies.[10]

Undoubtedly, Longstreet received his fair share of blistering condemnation for his politics, even from former comrades and friends. His old subordinate, Daniel Harvey (D.H.) Hill, who had defended the General's center at Antietam's "Bloody Lane" during the Army of Northern Virginia's September 1862 invasion of the North, called his former chief a "scalawag," which in the South was code word for a white southerner who not only supported, but personally benefited from Republican political rule. Robert Toombs, another subordinate who had commanded a small force that held Longstreet's right flank at Antietam's "Burnside's Bridge" wrote simply, "I would not have him tarnish his own laurels." Jubal Early, also a former officer in the Army of Northern Virginia and subsequently one of Longstreet's harshest postwar critics, wrote, "All the Confederates here have been much distressed at the course pursued by Longstreet. He has very much obscured the fame won by him during the war." At a time when many ex-Confederates were rallying to the banner of the Lost Cause, celebrating the memory of Southern Armies' valiant acts under a perceived just and righteous cause, Longstreet was calling for reconciliation with the North and acceptance of Reconstruction under Republican yoke. A few short months after his June 1867 publication, Longstreet left the Episcopal Church (he later became a Catholic)—typically the denomination of choice for military men in the North and South—gave up his business venture with the Owens' brothers, William and Edward, and moved to Lynchburg, Virginia, for the summer. Historians have cited other valid reasons explaining why Longstreet made these changes in the summer of 1867, and no evidence exists to support these actions were a direct result of the public backlash he received in Louisiana, though it is probably safe to guess that all of them were.[11]

Throughout the years and amidst all of this controversy, Longstreet consistently showed minimal interest in discussing political differences, even in personal correspondence. Although he held a number of political posts after the war, he was never passionate about political particulars. In May 1867, in the midst of writing his controversial *New Orleans Times* articles, he clarified his political intentions to his then business partner in a cotton brokerage, William Owen: "I am not a politician or office seeker" he wrote, "but I think it my bounden duty to assist the people." And when Thomas Goree, a former aide and postwar Democrat, pledged his personal good feelings to Longstreet despite their political differences, the General replied that he did not wish to spark a controversy, and that "the difference in our politics is not so great as it appears, if sifted to the bottom. The end that we seek, I know, is the same, the restoration of the Southern people to their natural and proper influence. The best and speediest means of arriving at this end has been [the] only difference." He repeated a similar theme to Goree in 1892, when he observed that "I am glad at times to feel that I am not in politics. In 1867, when the Reconstruction Acts passed, I was anxious to keep the South out of the troubles that she has passed through since, and that was about the extent of my interest in affairs of state." These private declarations, and others similar to it, contradict former Chief Historian for the Fredericksburg and Spotsylvania National Military Park Robert Krick's rather off-the-cuff statement that "As Longstreet fell into steadily greater disfavor after the war, he adopted the expedient of blaming his difficulties on individuals hostile to him because of political considerations and his other unpopular postwar traits." On the contrary, Longstreet's postwar writings contain very little mention of politics or political differences whatsoever when addressing other's attacks on his military record. There is little evidence that Longstreet used his postwar Republican politics as a crutch.[12]

Even as a palpable Longstreet critic, Robert Krick rightly points out the tendency of Longstreet's "modern supporters [to] believe that whole-souled admiration for the general only faded after the war for irrelevant reasons," namely that Longstreet was vilified by many after the war simply for his Republican stripe. To the contrary, the chief consequence of Longstreet's postwar political decisions was that it yielded a fertile environment for the growth of additional criticism of the General at a time when the Southern "Lost Cause" faction was congealing. This faction was largely made up of former Confederate officers dedicated to protecting and enshrining the military prowess of Robert E. Lee, or as Jubal Early admitted in the postwar years, "My sole purpose has been to vindicate the fame of the great commander of the Army of Northern Virginia and the truth of history." In short, because Longstreet became a Republican and that political party was viewed with almost universal contempt in the South during and after the war, any additional criticism by his critics, even of the General's wartime record, was more easily accepted and perpetuated as truth.[13]

Garland's second assertion referring to Longstreet's "detractors" is more open-ended, but also much more significant as it succinctly alludes to what became—and still remains—the heart of the controversy: Longstreet's actions at the July 1863 Battle of Gettysburg. In the minds of many Southerners, "If Longstreet was a traitor after the war, he might well have been a traitor during it, particularly at Gettysburg—he had disobeyed Lee's orders; he had obstructed and delayed; his defeatism had caused defeat," mid-twentieth century historian George Stewart so succinctly and aptly outlined the rationale behind attacking Longstreet in the postwar years.[14]

Shortly after Robert E. Lee's 1870 death, Lost Cause advocates sought to forever enshrine the General as a marble, infallible man. Coupled with that objective, Lost Cause proponents crafted a narrative that made the Battle of Gettysburg the most important battle of the war, and the high-water mark for the Confederacy. They believed that if the Confederates had won at Gettysburg, the South may have won the war. "Gettysburg, not so directly or immediately, but practically, decided the fate of the Confederacy," maintained one member, John B. Gordon. They also recognized that Lee's judgment had been questioned most in the postwar years over that specific battle, and that, as previously mentioned, Longstreet had actually done so publicly in journalist William Swinton's *Campaigns of the Army of the Potomac* in 1866, albeit indirectly via feedback he provided the author in an interview. Further, Longstreet's adoption of Republican politics after the war meant that he was already reviled by many Southerners as a turncoat, and therefore, pinning any blame on the non–Virginian scalawag for losing the all-important Battle of Gettysburg would stick fairly easily. And so, within just a few months after Lee's death (and significantly, not before), Longstreet was made the convenient scapegoat for the Gettysburg failure. It became common occurrence in the postwar years for Lost Cause enthusiasts to state outright the complete fabrication, "General Lee died believing that he lost Gettysburg ... by Longstreet's disobedience of orders." They mercilessly attacked Longstreet over their version of his actions at Gettysburg, ultimately resulting in well over a century's worth of debate concerning the General's military worth, bearing, and judgment. Postwar Longstreet detractors' writings about Longstreet as it relates to Gettysburg have proven by far the most enduring in defining his overall reputation as both a general and a man in history books.[15]

Robert E. Lee, postwar (Library of Congress).

Jubal Early, a Second Corps division commander at Gettysburg, initiated the opening salvo against Longstreet in January 1872, most famously including rhetoric of Lee's First Corps' "Sunrise Attack" plan—a long-since debunked Lost Cause myth. In January 1873, William Pendleton, who had been the Army of Northern Virginia's deficient Chief of Artillery at Gettysburg, joined Early in his attempt to obliterate Longstreet's reputation. Early and Pendleton both alleged that Lee had intended for two divisions within Longstreet's corps to attack the Federal left flank at sunrise on July 2. This allegation was universally disproven in the 1870s, largely a result of Longstreet's receipt of a number of letters from former Confederate officers present at Gettysburg, who collectively stated they had no knowledge of such a plan. But Longstreet's detractors were not finished. Armistead Lindsay (A.L.) Long, formerly of Lee's staff during the war, soon joined the anti–Longstreet group and broadened the critique of Longstreet's actions at Gettysburg from the mythical "sunrise attack" to a more imprecise, but enduring accusation that Longstreet launched his attack on July 2 much later than Lee had expected. Walter Taylor, another Lee staffer, quickly echoed Long's argument. In other words, the strategy to scapegoat Longstreet immediately shifted to the accusation that he intentionally delayed the second and third days' battles because he disagreed with Lee's tactical approach at Gettysburg. They claimed he turned to sulking, and like one modern historian astoundingly branded it, played a "little game" to sabotage the Army of Northern Virginia's chance for victory. Variations of this interpretation have persisted into a sizable portion of twentieth and twenty-first century historical scholarship. By the late 1870s, the anti–Longstreet partisans had completed their first campaign against Longstreet's alleged actions at Gettysburg, and tellingly of the vicious and incessant war against him, faction member the Reverend John William Jones wrote William Pendleton in 1878: "I suspect that Longstreet is very sick of Gettysburg before this. Certainly there has not been left 'a grease spot' of him."[16]

Now, well over 100 years since Longstreet's death, large pieces of the Lost Cause brief against the General endure, especially about his actions at Gettysburg. Longstreet once branded these advocates the "Knights of the quill," who "have consumed many of their peaceful hours in publishing, through books, periodicals, and newspapers, their plans for the battle, endeavoring to forestall the records and to find a scapegoat." Historian George Stewart wrote in 1959 that the decades-long controversy "had a profound effect upon the historical tradition, apparently because of the common belief that where there is so much smoke there must be some fire." The lasting historical interpretation of those who aimed to singe Longstreet's record directly contrasts how his peers and contemporaries thought history would portray and understand Lee's Warhorse. The outpouring from the latter group began at 11 a.m. on January 6, 1904, the day of Longstreet's funeral.[17]

The bishop presiding at Longstreet's funeral, who had served under his command for four years during the war exclaimed, "We who knew him forty odd years ago ... we know what a tower of strength Longstreet was to the noblest knight who has graced tented field since the peerless Bayard passed from the earth, Robert E. Lee; we feel and know today that neither boundless praise nor fullest words of gratitude can exaggerate the worth of James Longstreet or pay him what we owe." In contrast to how many modern historians typically describe Longstreet, the Vicksburg, Mississippi *Herald* aptly wrote, "Longstreet was Lee's right hand.... How highly he was held at headquarters and the war department was shown in his being made the senior lieutenant general, even over Jackson, after the 1862 test by fire." In similar fashion, the Bainbridge, Georgia *Searchlight* asserted "Perhaps in point of military ability he ranked next to the great Lee himself." The *New York Journal* predicted, "After a while Southern capitals will be adorned with statues of Longstreet."[18]

These statements contrast sharply with some modern historians' dubious conclusions. Popular historian Stephen Sears in *Gettysburg* poses the odd question, "How would

Longstreet handle his new position as Lee's senior lieutenant?" with respect to the reshuffling of corps in the Army of Northern Virginia after Jackson's death in May 1863. In another instance, Sears writes similarly, "With the death of Stonewall Jackson, Lieutenant General James Longstreet was not only Lee's senior lieutenant but by default his senior advisor." Sears never mentions that Longstreet was promoted to the rank of lieutenant general on October 9, 1862, a day before Stonewall Jackson. Similarly, academic historian Glenn LaFantasie inaccurately portrays Longstreet as inferior to Jackson among Lee's advisors: "With the death of Stonewall Jackson after Chancellorsville, Longstreet at age forty-two had assumed the mantle of Lee's most trusted lieutenant."

The fact is when Lee first assumed command of the Army of Northern Virginia just before the Seven Days Campaign in 1862, and then successively through the Second Manassas, Sharpsburg, and Fredericksburg campaigns, Longstreet consistently demonstrated his solid, capable, and dependable qualities as principal subordinate to Lee. Lee often sought Longstreet's council and regularly camped with his "Old Warhorse" well before Jackson's death. Gilbert Moxley Sorrel clearly described the General's good standing in the army and partnership with Lee: "Longstreet was second in command and it soon became apparent that he was to be quite close to Lee. His camps and bivouacs were nearby the General's." Lee appreciated Longstreet's aptitude for careful planning, exhaustive preparation, precise organization, and of course his seemingly innate ability to manage large numbers of troops, coordinate a stout defense, and deliver a crushing counterattack against the enemy. Sorrel asserted that Longstreet's dogged resolve and coolness during the most chaotic scenes of battle were hallmarks of his generalship: "Such efficiency on the field as I may have displayed," Sorrel wrote, "came from association with him and the example of that undismayed warrior. He was like a rock in steadiness when sometimes in battle the world seemed flying to pieces." Above all, Lee seemed to appreciate and trust Longstreet's council because it often offered a different tactical perspective on events, perhaps often contrary to his own. Thomas Goree, another Longstreet aide, wrote of their unique relationship: "Genl. Lee needs him not only to advise with, but Genl. Longstreet has a very suggestive mind and none of the other Lt. Genls. have this." The Houston, Texas, *Chronicle* echoed these sentiments:

> If any man or woman doubts or calls into question the record of James Longstreet as a soldier, let him or her ask the veteran Southern soldier who followed him ... what they think of him, and with one voice they will say, "He was Lee's 'warhorse.'" When we heard Longstreet was in the lead or in command, or was coming, we knew that victory would follow the fighting; we trusted him; Lee trusted him; the army trusted him.[19]

Since Longstreet's death, some historians have expressed agreement with these and similar statements. George Stewart maintains that both Lee and Longstreet were "large-minded enough to appreciate the capacities of the other, different though they might be." In other words, the dichotomy between the generals created a diverse combination of strategic and tactical vision that served the army well. Lee was very often a natural risk taker, while as popular historian Jeffry Wert points out, Longstreet's maxim was that "risks had to be measured by costs."[20]

The press and those who paid their respects to Longstreet in 1904 seemed to direct their thoughts on the General to future historians, believing that in time scholars would accurately and fully represent the General's wartime accomplishments. It is clear that

James Longstreet's grave, Gainesville, Georgia (author's collection).

the Atlanta, Georgia *Constitution* had the inflammatory postwar writings about Longstreet's actions at Gettysburg in mind when it contended, "Hereafter truth will take hold upon the pen of history and rewrite much that has been miswritten of this great son of the South." The New York *Tribune* succinctly predicted, "We do not think that history will sustain the contentions of General Longstreet's critics.... He will certainly be classed hereafter by open-minded critics as one of the ablest and most intelligent of commanders who fought under the South's flag." J.W. Matthews of the Macon, Georgia *Telegraph* said, "Longstreet's war record, like that of Stonewall Jackson's, needs no defense.... Impartial history will ever link the names of Lee, Jackson, and Longstreet upon the brightest page of history of the incomparable Army of Northern Virginia." Captain John H. Leathen, formerly of the Second Regiment Virginia Infantry "Stonewall Brigade," believed that "his fame is securely fixed, and the faithful historian of the future will assign him his due and fitting place in the annals of his age."[21]

A number of groups made up of ex-Confederate soldiers also expressed similar convictions regarding the future treatment of Longstreet. The Hattiesburg, Mississippi Camp wrote on February 6, 1904, "History will be incomplete without according him her brightest page." The John A. Green Camp of Dickens, Texas thought "History will hand down his name to posterity as one of the great generals of the South." Other examples abounded from across the South, "History in time will give to him that which is due"; "when history shall be gathered and cast into final form, honorable will be the place assigned to our great general"; "That in the remotest history his achievements will be appreciated."[22]

Some individuals even mentioned future historians' treatment of Longstreet as it specifically related to his actions at the Battle of Gettysburg. The Pat Cleburne Camp in Texas held that "When the true facts are known, an admiring and grateful people will place him second only to the immortal Lee, who, though all the facts were known to him, exonerated Longstreet from blame, saying, 'The fault is mine,'" in reference to Lee's infamous words after the failure of Pickett's Charge on the third day of the battle. John T. Callaghan, the Vice President of the Confederate Association wrote, "Future history will vindicate his character in his course on that field and everywhere else where duty called him during the eventful period for '61 to '65." And finally, both the Pat Cleburne and Walker Camps put forth the exact same resolution:

> *Resolved,* That the war that has been and is being waged on the military record of James Longstreet for failure to do his duty at the Battle of Gettysburg is not in keeping, in our opinion, with the record as it is made up from the reports of General Lee, commander-in-chief of the Confederate army in that conflict. If General Longstreet had failed to execute the orders of General Lee, and been the cause of the defeat of the Confederate army, as is charged, we believe he would have been court-martialed and dismissed from the service instead of being retained and trusted on down to Appomattox, as he was.[23]

But "future history" has not fairly represented James Longstreet, especially his actions at Gettysburg. Since his death, historians have largely fallen far short of fully doing him justice. Over the years, many have presented blatantly biased accounts packed with emotional arguments, conjecture, and half-truths, oftentimes based on a seemingly casual reading of source material. Some authors have come closer to presenting an impartial vision of Longstreet's actions at Gettysburg, but for one reason or another, several crucial connections have not been made, consistencies and inconsistencies in certain source materials have not been pointed out, and in general, as one author has maintained, a "penetrating analysis" has not yet been integrated into a single, succinct examination. Indeed, even after all the books written and published about the battle over the years, this is the first full-length work on Longstreet's Gettysburg performance and the resultant controversy originating from it which still continues to this day. Other historians have touched on this particular subject in an article, chapter, or perhaps over the course of a full-length book on the battle itself, but never more directly or as exhaustively as this book.[24]

Furthermore, while this book analyzes works previously examined by multiple historians who have written about Longstreet, such as Glenn Tucker and William Garrett Piston, these works have never been scrutinized to such an extent or depth, especially in the context of the major controversial moments involving Longstreet at Gettysburg.

This book significantly addresses Longstreet critics and historians who wrote about Gettysburg prior to 1965 because those parties largely created the biased and often misinterpreted source material used by many modern historians. In most cases, pre-1965 critic or historian references are juxtaposed against modern historian claims, and often both assertions are found to be tainted with similar Lost Cause falsehoods that have stood the test of time with little or no supporting evidence. In other words, it was deemed not to be prudent, or actually possible, to discuss modern historians' treatment of Longstreet's Gettysburg performance without also discussing older critics and historians. With that said, the main focus of this work is certainly on how old, erroneous Lost Cause claims about Longstreet at Gettysburg persist into many modern historians' accounts.

It is also important to note that historians mentioned in this book are a representative sample of modern writings. Likewise, all specific criticisms of Longstreet's actions addressed in the book are a representative sample of the most significant and persistent critiques of Longstreet since the postwar years. The book seeks to address every major and repeatedly encountered critique leveled against Longstreet's Gettysburg performance in dozens of studies on the Gettysburg battle. The sampling of prominent historians mentioned provided ample opportunity to bring every significant critique of Longstreet's actions at Gettysburg to the fore, allowing them to be addressed in a detailed manner. More statements made by other modern historians could surely have been found and incorporated, but they very likely would not have significantly added to or enhanced the content and purpose of this book. In fact, adding more may have bloated the work, changing the appeal of the text from adequate to irritating.

This book addresses, and ultimately uses, specific criticisms of Longstreet's Gettysburg performance as a lens into his overall battle performance, especially since those criticisms span all three days of the battle. Indeed, even though the book's main focus is on a number of specific controversial topics related to Longstreet, any glaring gaps between those specific topics are filled with narrative and commentary about what is known about his physical movements, decisions, and actions. As it turns out, in writing the book this way, Longstreet's overall performance during the Gettysburg Campaign *is* analyzed and covered to an extent not yet seen in any published work on the topic to date.

1

The Quibbling of Historians

"Offensive in strategy, but defensive in tactics"
—James Longstreet

A focus on Longstreet's behavior at Gettysburg may seem a historical cliché in 2019. Yet, that three-day encounter turned out to be the single most important event in Longstreet's life. In 1997, *Gettysburg Magazine* contributor Daniel Laney declared that Longstreet "was destined to be one of the most controversial figures of the war, and much of that reputation would spring from the three days at Gettysburg." Indeed, Gettysburg came to define both James Longstreet the General and the man, because the battle did not end for him in July 1863, but continued into the postwar era, pulling in and involving numerous Confederate and Federal officers, who all gave their accounts in a contentious debate that sought to address why the Army of Northern Virginia lost. Longstreet's contributions to William Swinton's 1866 book and his subsequent writings about the battle between the late 1870s and late 1890s ignited a firestorm engulfing a number of Confederate officers whose sole ambition was to defend General Robert E. Lee's decisions at Gettysburg. Longstreet, who questioned Lee at Gettysburg (and became a postwar Southern Republican to boot), was the scapegoat.[1]

While a close reading of Longstreet's writings on Gettysburg reveals that their core assertions are both reasonable and consistent, his modern critics have been harsh in their judgment. Typical of the critique, academic historian Gary Gallagher has described Longstreet's writings as "'Old Pete's' clumsy rejoinders," where he showed "poor judgment" and "defended himself against his tormentors ineptly, launching indiscreet counterattacks that often strayed widely from the truth." Jeffry Wert contends that "factual errors, misstatements, omissions, and criticisms of other officers, including Lee, marked his writing and subjected him to further criticism," and in another account, describes them as "intemperate, critical writings." Gettysburg College historian Peter Carmichael's impression of the First Corps commander's writings is simply that "Longstreet was his own worst enemy. He wildly exaggerated his contributions to the Army of Northern Virginia, often at the expense of Lee and his fellow officers." Robert Krick, Longstreet's harshest modern critic by far, writes that "Longstreet launched a steady flood of attacks against his former Confederate colleagues, often straying from the demonstrable truth and regularly contradicting his own accounts from one article to the next." And Virginia-born historian Clifford Dowdey, most active as a writer during the 1950s and 1960s and perhaps the most scathing Longstreet critic to date believes Longstreet "invented things that never happened, distorted recorded incidents, told outright lies apparently without realizing it, and contradicted himself in his various accounts." Similar negative opinions were first expressed by several ex-Confederate officers in the postwar years. One of those officers was Cadmus Wilcox, who was enlisted by Jubal Early in 1875 to join the anti–Longstreet faction and soon thereafter argued that Longstreet's writings "have been shown to abound in misstatements, gross exaggerations and to savor somewhat of self-laudation."[2] Contrary to these assertions, modern academic historian William Garrett Piston has advanced a more evenhanded judgment, contending that "While his account of the battle was not without errors, it was essentially accurate. Indeed, his writings might have won considerable approval had he taken into account, when composing them, that Lee had become a saint." Mid-twentieth century popular historian Glenn Tucker put it best when he chided modern scholars' typical treatment of Longstreet's writings in his 1968 work, *Lee and Longstreet at Gettysburg*, asserting that "Dwelling on the minor variations smacks of pettifoggery."[3]

Like any other officer during the war, Longstreet made mistakes and blunders in other battles; however, a close analysis reveals that he made very few at the Battle of Gettysburg. In truth, and as the common saying goes, historians have largely made a mountain out of a molehill when it comes to Longstreet's actions at Gettysburg. Of all Lee's corps commanders at that battle in the summer of 1863, Longstreet was by far the most reliable and subordinate, despite his tactical reservations. Contrary to what many modern Longstreet critics would admit, if supported properly during the second day's battle, the First Corps commander's assault would likely have broken the Federal line. Even though many historians admit that Lee's two other corps commanders, Richard Ewell and Ambrose Powell (A.P.) Hill, were to blame for many of the Confederate failures at Gettysburg, analysis focused on Longstreet's actions always prove most protracted and pedantic. In some cases, their writings have exuded a palpable vindictiveness present in some of the more prominent anti–Longstreet writers' accounts of the late nineteenth century. A number of historians have widely used, and therefore trusted, some of the most agenda-driven postwar writings, or simply cherry-picked information from sources to support their claims, while ignoring contradictory parts of those same sources. These are illogical fallacies, all fulfilling an agenda that has almost imperceptibly transitioned from defending Robert E. Lee's decisions at Gettysburg to taking every opportunity to denigrate Longstreet's record and further bolster the now almost mythological status of Thomas "Stonewall" Jackson. Certainly at this point, Peter Carmichael's belief that Longstreet exaggerated the role he played in the Army of Northern Virginia can be redirected and applied to scholars' modern exaggeration of Jackson's omnipresent role in the army, especially at the expense of Longstreet. In his book about the third day's battle at Gettysburg, academic historian Earl Hess promotes this biased modern historical tendency when he writes, "[Lee] wanted Longstreet to be his right-hand man, as Stonewall Jackson had done on so many battlefields. Jackson had died less than two months earlier as a result of wounds received at Chancellorsville, and Lee was hoping Longstreet would fill his shoes." Further on in his narrative, he advances this false partiality again, writing, "When Longstreet rushed his troops back to Lee immediately after Chancellorsville, Jackson was out of the picture, and he now had to shoulder the responsibility of becoming Lee's right-hand man." Likewise, mid-twentieth century academic historian Edwin Coddington minced no words and wore the Jackson partiality on his sleeve when outright alleging in his Gettysburg narrative that "Longstreet in no way replaced the dead Jackson."[4]

Thomas "Stonewall" Jackson, wartime (Library of Congress).

At the same time, more sympathetic modern accounts of Longstreet's actions at Gettysburg have often been deficient in a careful and skeptical reading of specific source materials, ultimately resulting in narratives that lack a precise analysis of his actions at some of the most controversial points in the battle. They have neglected to address arguments raised by Longstreet's critics. They have also compromised too much with the anti–Longstreet group, oddly seeming to take them at their word in some instances, perhaps so as not to create too many waves in the academic community. All of these decisions have resulted in barren accounts that make little headway in better understanding Longstreet at Gettysburg. A fresh reading of the source material versed in, but liberated from, previous academic interpretation is necessary.

* * *

One issue numerous historians have muddied for decades is the pre-campaign meetings between Lee and Longstreet that took place in Fredericksburg, Virginia, in May 1863. After returning from spring foraging in Suffolk, North Carolina, on May 9, Longstreet engaged in conversation with Lee over the course of three days (May 11–13) about the Army of Northern Virginia's prospective summer campaign. At first, under the impression that Lee was to remain in a defensive posture in Virginia, Longstreet proposed a western concentration scheme that he believed would ultimately relieve the pressure Federal General Ulysses S. Grant was then putting on Vicksburg, Mississippi. Longstreet suggested that two divisions from his corps—commanded by George Pickett and John Bell Hood—combine with General Braxton Bragg's army at Tullahoma, Tennessee, while General Joseph Johnston's army also shifted to join them. Collectively, Longstreet, Bragg, and Johnston would first assail the Federal force commanded by General William S. Rosecrans, then move north into Kentucky and Ohio to threaten the Northern heartland. The goal was to turn Grant's attention away from Vicksburg and further east. According to Longstreet, Lee agreed with his subordinate only in part, "believ[ing] the idea of an offensive campaign was not only important, but necessary";

however, he remained opposed to dividing his Virginia army and instead countered with proposals for an offensive strategy northward into Maryland and Pennsylvania. Longstreet expressed that he thought a "campaign in thoroughly Union states would require more time and greater preparation than one through Tennessee and Kentucky"; though, upon recognizing that Lee was "determined that he would make some forward movement" north from Virginia, the discussions turned to the strategic and tactical outlines of a Pennsylvania campaign.[5]

From here, the historical misrepresentation begins. Many historians unfairly charge that Longstreet's postwar accounts of this meeting lack consistency. In a letter to his Uncle Augustus, written only three weeks after the battle on July 24, 1863, Longstreet revealingly wrote, "The battle was not made as I would have made it. My idea was to throw ourselves between the enemy and Washington, select a strong position, and force the enemy to attack us," and further, "So far as is given to man the ability to judge, we may say, with confidence, that we should have destroyed the Federal army ... had we drawn the enemy into attack upon our carefully-chosen position in its rear." Longstreet continued, "I fancy that no good ideas upon that campaign will be mentioned at any time, that did not receive their share of consideration by General Lee. The things that he might have overlooked himself, were, I believe, suggested by myself." In this early letter, Longstreet clearly revealed that he believed Lee had erred in his decision to employ the tactical offensive at Gettysburg against the Federal army's strong Cemetery Ridge line. He further emphasized that he had advocated for a tactical defensive approach whereby the Confederate army maneuvered to a strong position of their own and let the Federals attack them. Additionally, Longstreet insinuated that Lee had "overlooked" some ideas; ideas that he alleged he had made clear to Lee during the battle. After all, to Longstreet, this kind of reciprocal relationship and open dialogue with Lee was nothing new. "I consider it a part of my duty to express my views to the commanding general," he revealed.[6]

By 1866, just a year after the war had ended, William Swinton interviewed Longstreet for his book, *Campaigns of the Army of the Potomac*, and details about the General's recollections of his pre-campaign meetings with Lee were included. Like the 1863 letter to his Uncle, Longstreet insisted that he and Lee had planned to use the tactical defensive in any general battle north of the Potomac. Longstreet again referred to "things" he suggested to Lee that the commanding general "might have overlooked himself" at Gettysburg. Swinton wrote, "[Lee] was far from expecting or desiring to take upon himself the risk of a general battle, at a point so distant from his base. He was willing to do so only in case he should, by maneuvering, secure the advantage of the defensive." The author continued, "Indeed, in entering upon the campaign, General Lee expressly promised his corps commanders that he would not assume a tactical offensive, but force his antagonist to attack him." Instead of focusing on the real relevance of what Longstreet told Swinton, namely that a general battle was not to be fought using the "tactical offensive" during the campaign, nearly all historians have harped over two words: "expressly promised." Granted, if Longstreet did indeed allege that Lee made such a "promise" to his corps commanders—something he never overtly admitted elsewhere in the postwar years—surely that was an exaggeration. The evidence suggests that Lee and Longstreet very likely planned to not use the tactical offensive, but surely there was no "promise." With that said, historians have given the two words "expressly promised" their own great and exaggerated importance, taking away from the larger and more important point about the guiding tactical approach for the campaign.[7]

On July 25, 1873, shortly after Longstreet's actions at Gettysburg were first publicly challenged by William Pendleton and others, he wrote a private letter to his former subordinate and division commander at Gettysburg, Major General Lafayette McLaws. McLaws had just written to his old Chief, informing him of Pendleton's recent speech alleging that Longstreet was generally insubordinate at Gettysburg and, more specifically, had failed to carry out Lee's plan for a "sunrise" attack on the morning of July 2. The importance of Longstreet's 1873 response to McLaws is fourfold. It was a private letter, which is typically more revealing and candid than one's public writings; it was written by him as opposed to a ghostwriter; it was his first real analysis of the Pennsylvania campaign since the war had ended; and lastly, it was written very early in the controversy, or in other words, before the General had a chance to become more defensive and bitter about the steady and constant barrage of attacks he faced in the 1880s and 1890s.

On the subject of his discussions with Lee in May 1863, Longstreet told McLaws that between "the 10th of May '63—until the battle" they had "firmly fixed in [their] minds" that "the ruling ideas of the [Pennsylvania] campaign" were to "under no circumstances ... give battle, but exhaust our skill in trying to force the enemy to do so in a position of our own choosing." The former First Corps commander maintained that, in short, he proposed "Napoleon's advice to Marmot at the head of an invading army. 'To make the enemy fight him in his own position.'" In recalling this "advice," he frankly admitted that "I don't know that I give Napoleon's own words, but I believe that I give in substance, his meaning." Longstreet informed McLaws that he and Lee "agreed that this was a good maxim, and particularly applicable to the Confederate army," in reference to their manpower "losses" being "so heavy when we attacked that our Army must soon be depleted to such extent that we should not be able to hold a force in the field sufficient to meet our adversary." Longstreet further held that he and Lee also conversed about how each army corps would be employed in this general plan: "The 1st corps to receive the attack and fight the battle. The other Corps, to then fall upon and destroy the Army of the Potomac." Later in the letter, Longstreet again maintained and stressed that over the course of those weeks, he and Lee frequently "discussed our previous battles, and fruitless victories," namely the battles of First and Second Manassas, Fredericksburg,

James Longstreet, probably late 1860s (Library of Congress).

and Chancellorsville, "and had concluded that even victories such as these were consuming us, and would eventually destroy us, so that a fruitless victory for us was about the equivalent of a defeat to the Federals, and only left the result to time."[8]

Longstreet's first public postwar account of the strategic and tactical approach he advocated during the Pennsylvania campaign was included in a November 1877 article titled "Lee in Pennsylvania," which was printed in the *Philadelphia Weekly Times*. Again, the language of the then fifty-six year old was a bit different, but the idea remained the same. After Longstreet found that Lee had decided on a "forward movement" into Pennsylvania:

> I finally assented that the Pennsylvania campaign might be brought to a successful issue if he could make it offensive in strategy, but defensive in tactics. This point was urged with great persistency. I suggested that, after piercing Pennsylvania and menacing Washington, we should choose a strong position, and force the federals to attack us.... I was never persuaded to yield my argument against the Gettysburg campaign, except with the understanding that we were not to deliver an offensive battle, but to so maneuver that the enemy should be forced to attack us—or, to repeat, that our campaign should be one of offensive strategy, but defensive tactics. Upon this understanding my assent was given.[9]

Ten years later in February 1887, Longstreet again gave his account of his and Lee's pre-campaign understanding on tactics in the *Battles and Leaders of the Civil War* series, whereby after explaining how Lee did not want to divide his army and send two divisions out West, he wrote:

> I then accepted his proposition to make a campaign into Pennsylvania, provided it should be offensive in strategy but defensive in tactics, forcing the Federal army to give us battle when we were in strong position and ready to receive them. One mistake of the Confederacy was pitting force against force. The only hope we had was to outgeneral the Federals.... We talked on that line from day to day, and General Lee, accepting it as a good military view, adopted it as the key-note of the campaign. I suggested that we should have all the details and purposes so well arranged and so impressed upon our minds that when the critical moment should come, we could refer to our calmer moments and know we were carrying out our original plans.[10]

And finally, in Longstreet's memoirs, *From Manassas to Appomattox*, published in 1895, he again went into very similar detail about his May 1863 discussions with Lee:

> His plan or wishes announced, it became useless and improper to offer suggestions leading to a different course. All that I could ask was that the policy of the campaign should be one of defensive tactics; that we should work so as to force the enemy to attack us, in such good position as we might find in his own country, so well adapted to that purpose, which might assure us of a grand triumph. To this he readily assented as an important and material adjunct to his general plan.[11]

Over the years, historians have gone to great lengths to argue that Longstreet's series of accounts were not only inconsistent and arrogant, but fanciful. Yet in his statements on the issue, Longstreet repeatedly said essentially the same thing: that he and Lee had come to an understanding that the campaign should be one of offensive strategy and defensive tactics. And further that the Army of Northern Virginia should maneuver so as to get between the Federal army and Washington, select a strong defensive position, and receive the enemy's attack. Historians' tangential focus on some of the language Longstreet chose to use, deeming it egotistical, such as his use of "I then accepted" or "to this he readily assented" misses the real point and only serves to merely perpetuate an emotional agenda claiming, as one modern historian does, that Longstreet was actually false, misrepresentative, and "disloyal" to Lee for "thirty years after [his] death." In the postwar years, Longstreet critics like Cadmus Wilcox expressed similar sentiments. "General Longstreet represents the plan adopted to have been what he styles offensive in strategy and defensive in tactics. We are to believe from his representations that these conditions were exacted of General Lee before he would yield his assent to the movement," Wilcox wrote. In the 1950s, Clifford Dowdey wrote that Longstreet's use of the word "assent" or "consented ... by a corps commander shows the depth of his delusion about the equality of the collaboration" with Lee. Robert Krick picks up where Wilcox and Dowdey left off in criticizing Longstreet's use of language with more apparent emotion than reason, exclaiming, "That a corps commander would use words of that sort in describing the decisions of his army's head reveals a phenomenal degree of cocky disrespect."[12]

Historians' arguments that Longstreet's accounts of the pre-campaign planning were simply fanciful are a serious charge, and one they have time and again sought to support with two primary sources. In his biography on the General, Jeffry Wert cites a May 13, 1863, letter from Longstreet to Texas Senator Louis Wigfall, where the former wrote in guarded terms about the prospects of an offensive movement across the Potomac River and insisted that if indeed that were the settled-upon plan, "we should want everything that we had and all that we could get." Wert concludes that "Nowhere in the correspondence with Wigfall is a cornerstone of Longstreet's postwar analysis, namely that Lee agreed to use the tactical defensive in an engagement," as if Longstreet was undoubtedly obliged to go into specific details with the Senator about tactical particulars he had discussed with his commanding general. In fact, Longstreet's letter to Wigfall provided very little detail about Lee's plans beyond "There is a fair prospect of forward movement" for a reason, which the General explicitly mentioned. At the beginning of the correspondence, Longstreet informed Wigfall that he wished not to confide "Some of these matters by me to anyone beyond Gen. Lee and yourself." Contrary to Wert's conclusion, Longstreet's failure to mention that he and Lee had discussed defensive tactics, does not mean they never discussed them. In another essay on Longstreet at Gettysburg, Wert again employs this letter and writes, "In this contemporary private letter, then, Longstreet endorsed Lee's strategic offensive across the Potomac River, contrary to his later published assertions." This statement is inaccurate. Longstreet consistently asserted in the postwar years that he agreed to the Pennsylvania campaign "provided it should be offensive in strategy but defensive in tactics."[13]

Like Wert, Edwin Coddington sought to use the Wigfall letter to maintain that Longstreet's writings around the time of the campaign were at variance with his postwar contentions. On Longstreet's assertion that he and Lee had agreed upon a strategic offensive and tactical defensive campaign plan, Coddington believed that "there is every reason to doubt its validity." Coddington guessed that "Very possibly in reviewing the campaign he [Longstreet] conceived the idea that if he had exacted such a promise from Lee, the outcome might have been different," and "The more he thought of this possibility, the more his conviction grew that he had suggested defensive tactics when in fact he had not done so." Despite Coddington's conjecture, there is nothing in the Wigfall letter that discounts the likelihood that Longstreet suggested the army pursue defensive tactics during the forthcoming campaign. The First Corps commander's suggestion would likely have been born out of his own unique observations and experiences in battles under Lee's command over the past year. It was no secret that Longstreet thought battles like Second Manassas or Fredericksburg were more advantageous to the army than those like the Seven Days or Chancellorsville. Coddington's argument, like many other twentieth century historians,' appears to be preemptively swayed by the alluring allegations of the postwar anti–Longstreet partisans, particularly in claiming to know what Longstreet "thought" and how the General came to pathologically believe his own claims. Perpetuating the anti–Longstreet sentiments of the Lost Cause, Coddington presents students of the war with Longstreet the charlatan who conjured up his own tall tales and convinced himself to believe them.[14]

The second and more widely employed source that has found its way into almost every narrative that delves into the Longstreet-Gettysburg controversy is an 1868 interview of Robert E. Lee, conducted by Colonel William Allan. During the war, Allan had served on the staffs of Thomas "Stonewall" Jackson, and later, Jubal Early, Longstreet's biggest postwar critic. After the war, Lee invited Allan to teach mathematics at Washington College in Lexington, later known as Washington and Lee College. As some have suggested, the Colonel was "a man of high principle but one of Lee's most devoted followers for whom the commanding general could make no mistake." There can be little doubt that Allan was a Lost Cause subscriber and wished to support Lee. Allan's postwar writings about Gettysburg are glaringly subjective. Yet, historians have accepted Allan's interview without hesitation and usually quote this passage to support their argument against Longstreet:

> He [Lee] referred to a reported conversation of Longstreet, in which the latter was reported to have said that General Lee was under a promise to the Lieutenant General not to fight a general battle in Pennsylvania. General Lee said he did not believe this was ever said by Longstreet. That the idea was absurd. He never made any such promise and never thought of doing any such thing.[15]

This passage from Allan's account of the interview is in response to Allan's question of whether Lee had made "a promise to the Lieutenant General not to fight a general battle." This question had no basis because Longstreet never made any such claim. On the contrary, Longstreet said that he and Lee had come to an understanding that "he was willing to" fight a general battle "only in case he should, by maneuvering, secure the advantage of the defensive." And further, Longstreet mentioned that Lee had made a promise "that he would not assume a tactical offensive" which says nothing of a promise "not to fight a general battle." In fact, Lee wrote in his January 1864 after-battle report that "It had not been intended to deliver a general battle so far from our base unless attacked." Douglas Southall Freeman attempted to spin Lee's statement by ignoring those two words, "unless attacked." Freeman wrote lamely, "He [Lee] had never contemplated a campaign without the possibility of a battle, and he certainly had made no pledge concerning that or the strategy or tactics to be employed." Yet in his after-battle report, Lee clearly expressed that he did not wish "to deliver a general battle ... unless attacked." Clearly, Lee went into the campaign looking to avoid a certain kind of battle.[16]

Furthermore, in the same Allan source, historians have either missed or neglected to use some other quotes that further confirm this critical point. Allan wrote, "As for Gettysburg—First, he did not intend to give battle in Pennsylvania if he could avoid it.

The South was too weak to carry on a war of invasion, and his offensive movements against the North were never intended except as parts of a defensive system," and additionally, "He expected therefore to move about, maneuver, and alarm the enemy, threaten their cities, hit any blows he might be able to deliver without risking a general battle, and then, towards fall, return and recover his base." Offensive movements within a defensive system, maneuvering and threatening the North's core cities, hitting any blows "without risking a general battle," all sound eerily similar to traditionally accepted classic Longstreet doctrine, with a mixed bag of tactical characteristics reminiscent of Lee's victories at Second Manassas and Fredericksburg, and more generally, any instance where the Army of Northern Virginia was not involved in a slugfest with the Federals.[17]

It is surprising then to note how often historians have misconstrued Allan's erroneous question as proof that Lee never planned to guide his campaign decisions by the tactical defensive. Jeffry Wert writes, "In April 1868, when asked if he had consented to fight a defensive battle in Pennsylvania, Lee replied that 'the idea was absurd...,'" when in point of fact, Allan never even posed the question in that fashion. Likewise, Stephen Sears, in his one-volume account of the battle, makes the same erroneous evaluation of the Allan source, writing, "Longstreet implied that Lee promised him he would fight tactically only a defensive battle in Pennsylvania.... That of course was nonsense.... Lee said as much when asked about it after the war. He 'had never made any such promise, and had never thought of doing any such thing,' was his reply." Glenn LaFantasie contends similarly, "Longstreet argued that he had only agreed to an offensive in the spring of 1863 in return for Lee's promise to assume the tactical defensive in the campaign.... Lee himself later vehemently denied that he had ever made such a promise. 'The idea,' said Lee in an 1868 interview, 'was absurd.'" All these historians, and others, have either misread or flat-out misrepresented Allan's question to Lee.[18]

Beyond General Lee's assertion in his after-battle report that a general battle was not intended "unless attacked" by the Federals, there were other Confederate participants in the battle who confirm Longstreet's statements regarding the intended use of the tactical defensive for the campaign. One of these men was Edward Porter (E.P.) Alexander, whose works, *Military Memoirs of a Confederate* and *Fighting for the Confederacy*, have been heralded universally by historians as being two of the most disinterested and impartial postwar accounts of the war. Gary Gallagher writes of Alexander, "Students have known for decades that only a handful of books by participants possess the enduring value of *Military Memoirs*; as an exercise in dispassionate analysis, it simply has no peer. *Fighting for the Confederacy* will redouble the debt owed to Porter Alexander." In another essay, Gallagher sings Alexander's praises, writing that he "stood in noble contrast to the emotional approach of many former Confederates," and that he is "easily the most astute military analyst among Lee's lieutenants." Similarly, Jeffry Wert has asserted that Alexander "became perhaps the most astute student of the army's operations among former members." Alexander's writings are certainly informative; however, contrary to Gallagher and Wert's universal endorsement of Alexander, the artilleryman's accounts can, at times, be just as self-serving and muddled as any other postwar writing. With that said, like Longstreet, Alexander did demonstrate the same basic consistency in his works when discussing the Army of Northern Virginia's intended tactical approach for the summer 1863 campaign.[19]

In *Military Memoirs*, Alexander wrote of the pre-campaign discussions, "[Lee] finally decided upon an invasion of Pa.... In the discussion with Longstreet, it was assumed that the strategy of the campaign should be such as would force the enemy to attack our army in position" and later, in the same chapter, "Lee's plan had long been formed to concentrate his own army somewhere between Cashtown and Gettysburg, in a strong position where it would threaten at once Washington, Baltimore, and Philadelphia. The enemy, he hoped, would then be forced to attack him." In *Fighting for the Confederacy* he echoed those statements, albeit in a more unreserved manner, asserting "On the first day we had taken the aggressive," but "I think it must be frankly admitted that there was no real difficulty, whatever, in our taking the defensive the next day; & in our so manouvring [*sic*] afterward as to have finally forced Meade to attack us." Alexander's conclusion was that the pursuit of the tactical aggressive was actually never the Confederates' objective; rather, strategic maneuvering coupled with the tactical defensive was the intended approach for the campaign, which he believed could still have been pursued even after the first day's clash. Alexander's assertion that Lee intended "to have finally forced Meade" to attack further supports the opinion that, based on his understanding of the pre-campaign plans, Lee would have been looking for any and all opportunities to extricate himself from a slugfest and to instead occupy a strong defensive position from which to receive a Federal attack.[20]

A letter from Alexander to anti–Longstreet faction member the Reverend John William Jones, written in March 1877, much earlier than his two books, further confirms Longstreet's claim of an intended tactical defensive. In the letter, Alexander described how he was personally uncertain if Lee had accounted for any objections to his Pennsylvania campaign (presumably referring to Longstreet's initial Kentucky Invasion Plan), but then admitted, "even if he did, I can imagine his confidence in defeating the enemy in a decisive battle, by forcing them to attack us, as so great, and as based on such reasonable grounds, as to fully justify the movement." A few sentences later, Alexander pondered whether the Army's chances for victory would have been greater in Virginia or Pennsylvania, only to again maintain, "Bear in mind that the great condition to assure its defeat was to force it to attack General Lee." More reminiscent of Longstreet's contentions than ever since accredited with, Alexander concluded "but yet I think [Lee] could easily have manoeuvred [*sic*] as to force Meade to attack him.... They could have been forced to attack us, and they never had driven us from a field since the war began. Excellent positions also were to be found everywhere in that section....

E.P. Alexander, postwar (from *Military Memoirs*).

So much for the general plan of the campaign." Like his narration in *Fighting for the Confederacy,* Alexander also hinted that Lee's end goal for the Gettysburg campaign had always been to maneuver so as to fight defensively. In this letter, he even held that Lee could have transitioned to the defensive even after the Second Day's battle, writing, "It was possible to have withdrawn from the offensive and taken the defensive, and forced Meade to assault us, and to have given him a crushing defeat." In sum, Alexander's position was clear; the general plan of the campaign was to maneuver to a strong defensive position and force the Federal army to attack. Like Longstreet, Alexander believed the candle of opportunity to fulfill that general plan remained lit even after the Army had pursued multiple days of the tactical aggressive at Gettysburg.[21]

Yet another source by a close participant in the battle that confirms Longstreet's statements about the intended use of the tactical defensive was Colonel Walter Taylor's "The Campaign in Pennsylvania," written well before his more often quoted memoirs. Taylor was one of Lee's principal aides during the war and also proved to be one of his biggest defenders after the war. Taylor was not one of those Lost Cause members who alleged that Lee had wanted to use Longstreet's corps to lead a "Sunrise Attack" on the second day at Gettysburg. While he was critical of Longstreet's actions at other points in the battle, he does state specifically that "[Lee's] design was to free the State of Virginia ... from the presence of the enemy, to transfer the theatre of war to Northern soil, and, by selecting a favorable time and place in which to receive the attack which his adversary would be compelled to make on him, to take the reasonable chances of defeating him in a pitched battle." In this instance, Taylor pointed out that given the way events unfolded prior to July 1, referring to the unintended absence of Lee's cavalry chief, J.E.B. Stuart, the commanding general did not take one of those "reasonable chances" and should never have expected to deliver any kind of effective and informed tactical offensive movement at Gettysburg. He wrote that "An army without cavalry in a strange and hostile country is as a man deprived of his eyesight ... he may be ever brave and strong, but he cannot intelligently administer a single effective blow." In another account, Taylor notes that "The first great disadvantage experienced by General Lee was the unexpected absence of his cavalry." Longstreet echoed this contention in one of his *Battles and Leaders* accounts, asserting bluntly, "I do not think there was any necessity for giving battle at Gettysburg. All of our cavalry was absent, and while that has been urged by some as a reason why battle should have been made at once, to my mind it was one of the strongest reasons for delaying the battle until everything was well in hand."[22]

2

The Indispensable J.E.B. Stuart Roams East

"From him alone could information be expected"
—Henry McClellan

"On the morning of the [July] 1st," Longstreet recalled, "General Lee and myself left his headquarters together, and had ridden three or four miles, when we heard heavy firing along Hill's front. The firing became so heavy that General Lee left me and hurried forward to see what it meant. After attending to some details of my march, I followed." Thus began Longstreet's experience at the Battle of Gettysburg.[1]

Longstreet's journey to that moment had begun nearly a month earlier, when on June 3, 1863, Lafayette McLaws and John Bell Hood's First Corps divisions marched out of Fredericksburg, Virginia, en route to Culpeper Court House, which they reached on June 8. George Pickett's division would not catch up with the rest of the First Corps at Culpeper until June 11, having been delayed waiting for Lee and Secretary of War James Seddon to make a decision about two of his brigades positioned north of Richmond. On the 8th, Lee's most trusted cavalry commander J.E.B. Stuart held a grand parade at Brandy Station near the Orange and Alexandria Railroad to show off his horsemen. Lee wrote of the affair to his wife, "I reviewed the cavalry in this section yesterday. It was a splendid sight.... Stuart was in all his glory." All of this pomp and circumstance, although customary during those times, occurred while Stuart was supposed to be ensuring Second Corps commander Richard Ewell's and Longstreet's right flank was guarded from any Federal encroachment. Historians have not stressed the Stuart problem enough; a problem that dogged the entire campaign and was largely self-inflicted by Lee. Stuart's cavalier handling of his cavalry force and Lee's acquiescence to such handling were evident at Brandy Station. The day after the second grand parade, Stuart was caught off-guard when Alfred Pleasanton's Federal cavalry attacked his unprepared and scattered forces. One of Stuart's staff members, Captain Charles Minor Blackford wrote of the battle, "The cavalry fight at Brandy Station can hardly be called a victory. Stuart was certainly surprised and but for the supreme gallantry of his subordinate officers and the men in his command it would have been a day of disaster and disgrace." Though the superior numbers of the Confederates repulsed the Federals in an all-day battle, it embarrassed Stuart and induced him to soon thereafter ask Lee for permission to execute an unnecessary ride around the Federal army, reminiscent of what he had done the previous year during the Seven Days Campaign. But this round beheld fatal repercussions.[2]

While Ewell's corps proceeded into the Shenandoah Valley west of the Blue Ridge Mountains and captured Winchester on June 15, Longstreet left Culpepper Court House on the same day, and by the 17th and 18th, his divisions were skirting along the east side of the Blue Ridge, assisting Stuart's cavalry to hold the range's passes—Manassas Gap, Ashby Gap, and Snickers Gap. For the time being, A.P. Hill's Third Corps trailed behind Longstreet. The First Corps commander proved to be very attentive to his divisions' progress, reportedly staying up until near midnight on one occasion to survey and inspect his lines. One of his aides, Major Raphael Moses suggested to Longstreet that he must be exhausted, whereby Lee's Warhorse rebutted, "No, I have never felt fatigue in my life." Just days later, British observer Arthur Fremantle confirmed Longstreet's apparent stamina: "The iron endurance of General Longstreet is most extraordinary: he seems to require neither food nor sleep." Moses also later remembered how Lee and Longstreet were often together throughout the march northward, meeting frequently and camping close to one another. Moses suggested that "I think he [Lee] relied very much on Longstreet." Likewise, Fremantle immediately noticed that "He [Longstreet] is never far from Lee, who relies very much upon his judgment." Longstreet himself revealed that he and Lee's discussions "almost always" proved to be "of severe thought and study"; not the typical superior-subordinate relationship of orders and assent. On the contrary, Lee regularly sought out Longstreet's thoughts and recommendations. General D.H. Hill believed that to Lee, Longstreet was a "confidential friend, more intimate with him than anyone else." Perhaps as a result of Lee and Longstreet's continual dialogue as the army moved north, the army commander wrote Confederate President Jefferson Davis on June 25, again citing his intention to maneuver the army to a selectively chosen position of their liking to invite battle. "It seems to me that we cannot afford to keep our troops awaiting possible movements of the enemy, but that our true policy is, as far as we can, so to employ our own forces as to give occupation to his at points of our own selection.... It should never be forgotten that our concentration at any point compels that of the enemy," he reflected, in seeming accord with Longstreet's later statements about the guiding tactical principles for an impending general battle.[3]

For fives day prior to writing Davis, Lee was dealing with another matter; a matter that became one of the most significant of the campaign: J.E.B. Stuart. Even though Stuart had been fending off Federal cavalry probes at Aldie on June 17 and 18, Middleburg on June 18, and Upperville on June 21 and 22, the cavalry chief expressed in his after-battle report his profound desire to "look for some other point at which to direct an effective blow." Longstreet later contended that Stuart was seeking "something better than the drudgery of a march along our flank." One of Lee's military secretaries reported that Stuart had a "conversation" with Lee and Longstreet near Ashby Gap on June 20, which is likely when the cavalry officer first pitched his idea for a raid. Stuart wanted to keep "a brigade or so in my present front, and passing through Hopewell or some other gap in Bull Run mountain, attain the enemy's rear, passing between his main body and Washington, cross into Maryland, joining our army north of the Potomac." Lee's dependence on Stuart's reconnaissance and his paranoia about being surprised by enemy

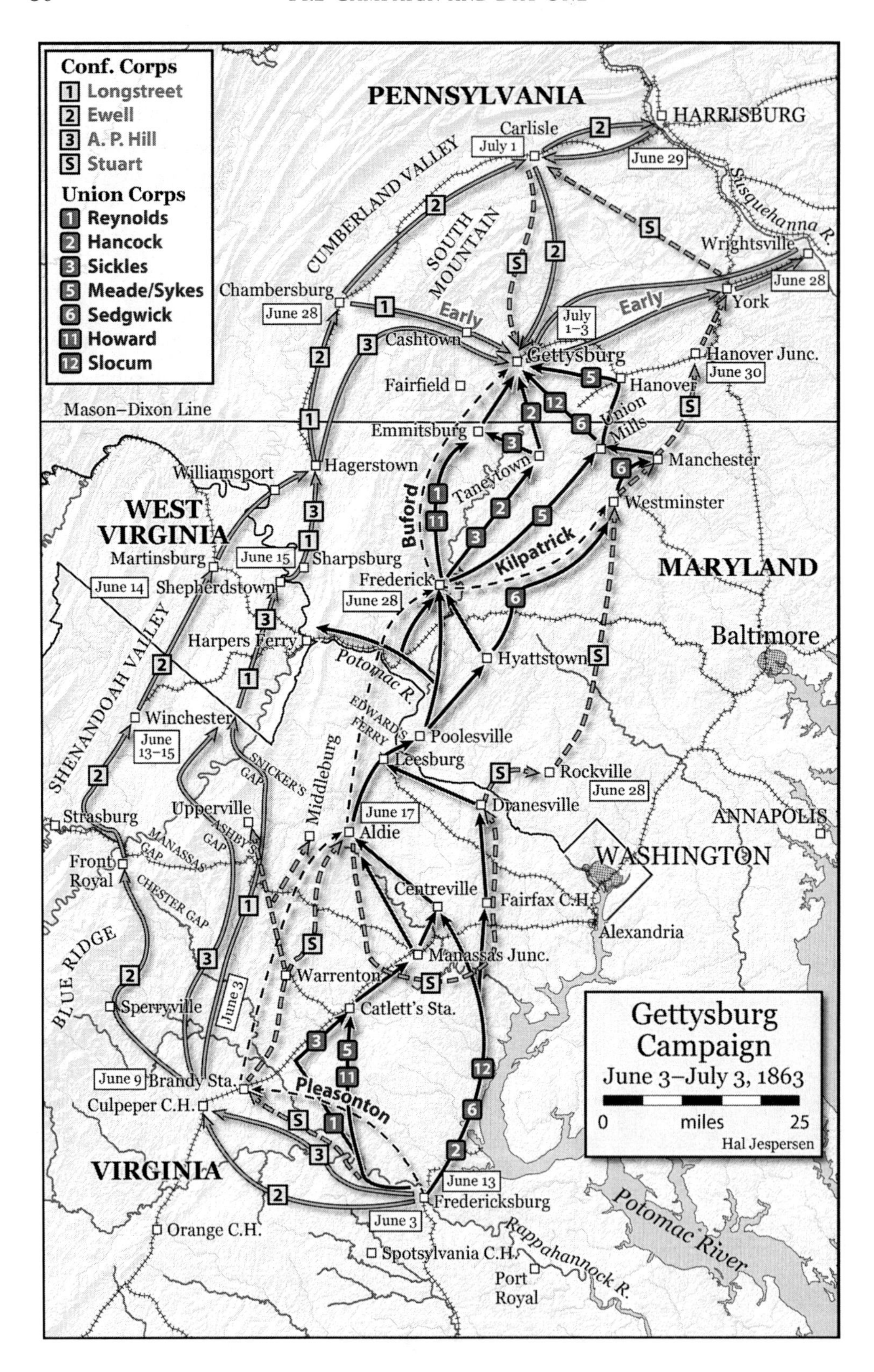

Conf. Corps
1 Longstreet
2 Ewell
3 A. P. Hill
S Stuart
Union Corps
1 Reynolds
2 Hancock
3 Sickles
5 Meade/Sykes
6 Sedgwick
11 Howard
12 Slocum
PENNSYLVANIA
HARRISBURG
Carlisle
July 1
June 29
CUMBERLAND VALLEY
SOUTH MOUNTAIN
Susquehanna R.
Wrightsville
June 28
York
Chambersburg
June 28
Early
July 1–3
Cashtown
Gettysburg
Hanover Junc.
June 30
Fairfield
Hanover
Mason–Dixon Line
Emmitsburg
Union Mills
Taneytown
Manchester
Hagerstown
Williamsport
Westminster
Buford
Kilpatrick
WEST VIRGINIA
Martinsburg
June 15
Sharpsburg
Frederick
MARYLAND
June 14
Shepherdstown
June 28
SHENANDOAH VALLEY
Harpers Ferry
Potomac R.
Hyattstown
Baltimore
EDWARD'S FERRY
Winchester
June 13–15
Poolesville
Leesburg
SNICKER'S GAP
Middleburg
Rockville
June 28
Dranesville
Strasburg
Upperville
June 17
Aldie
ANNAPOLIS
ASHBY'S GAP
MANASSAS GAP
Front Royal
WASHINGTON
CHESTER GAP
Centreville
Fairfax C.H.
Alexandria
BLUE RIDGE
Manassas Junc.
Warrenton
June 3
Catlett's Sta.
Sperryville
Gettysburg Campaign
June 3–July 3, 1863
0 miles 25
Hal Jespersen
June 9
Brandy Sta.
Pleasonton
Culpeper C.H.
VIRGINIA
June 13
Fredericksburg
June 3
Orange C.H.
Spotsylvania C.H.
Rappahannock R.
Potomac River
Port Royal

movements are evident in his letters to the cavalry officer, yet, despite his undoubted reservations, he ultimately agreed to grant Stuart's petition. Some historians and Civil War enthusiasts over the years have argued that whatever the case, and before the campaign even began, Lee had it in mind to deliver a knockout blow against the Federals in one grand tactical offensive battle. This theory does not bear scrutiny. Halfway through the march north, Lee allowed his cavalry chief and principal intelligence arm to ride off un-tethered to the main army, while concurrently asking where General Joseph Hooker, commander of the Army of the Potomac, was located and what he was doing. This decision was certainly not one that would be made by a commander focused on soon inviting any kind of general battle with the Federal army, especially any kind of offensive battle that would require even more timely and accurate information on the enemy's whereabouts and dispositions. The decision demonstrates some ambivalence about campaign objectives, lends some support to what Longstreet later said about the tactical defensive, and corresponds with what Lee wrote to Davis on June 25 about controlling the initiative and patiently selecting positions or "points of our own selection."[4]

That said, Lee did impose limitations on Stuart's plan, or perhaps Stuart had not originally presented his plan to Lee in the way he later characterized it in his August 1863 battle report. Lee wanted Stuart to leave two brigades to continue guarding the Blue Ridge passes and then directed that he move "into Maryland, and take position on General Ewell's right ... guard his flank, keep him informed of the enemy's movements, and collect all supplies you can for the use of the army." Lee also informed Ewell of what he should expect from Stuart, which was "to march with three brigades across the Potomac, and place himself on your right, and in communication with you, keep you advised of the movements of the enemy."[5]

Lee's June 22 letter was first sent to Longstreet, who was told to forward it to Stuart if he thought the cavalryman's services "can be spared from my [Longstreet's] front, and provided I think you [Stuart] can move across the Potomac without disclosing our plans." Longstreet proceeded to forward Lee's letter to Stuart, while informing the commanding general that he had included a "suggestion that he [Stuart] pass by the enemy's rear, if he thinks that he may get through." Longstreet also wrote a separate letter to the cavalryman with commentary that indicated the First Corps commander already had additional correspondence with Lee regarding Stuart's raid: "He [Lee] speaks of your leaving via Hopewell Gap, and passing by the rear of the enemy." Stuart's headquarters was then located at Rector's Crossroads, which was about ten miles east of Ashby Gap; therefore, any move "via Hopewell Gap" meant that Stuart would not be riding north, but rather southeast. And of course, any movement to pass behind the enemy's rear meant Stuart would be heading east, away from the army, and nowhere near the proper position to guard Ewell's flank in a timely manner.[6]

As postscripts, Longstreet offered his own opinion of Stuart's use of Hopewell Gap and his passing behind the rear of the enemy: "If you can get through by that route, I think that you will be less likely to indicate what our plans are, than if you should cross by passing to our rear." Longstreet believed that the alternate proposal for Stuart to follow the First and Third Corps to the Potomac and cross behind them would reveal where the Army of Northern Virginia's actual center of mass was located and allude to its intentions and objective. Longstreet added in summation, "You had better not leave us, therefore, unless you can take the proposed route in rear of the enemy." Longstreet critics will point out that he concurred in Lee's "proposed route" for Stuart to pass in rear of the enemy. Even though Longstreet later recognized that "Stuart should never have been permitted to leave the main route of march," undoubtedly, the evidence is overwhelming that he subscribed and encouraged the plan at the time, believing that Stuart's eastward movement would better obscure the intentions of the army's larger movement.[7]

With that said, Lee unilaterally provided Stuart with a supplementary order on June 23 that proved to be concurrently more restrictive and more discretionary. Lee directed that "If General Hooker's Army remains inactive you can leave two brigades to watch him, and withdraw the three others." In other words, if the Federal army remained idle, Stuart could commence his eastward movement. On the other hand, Lee wrote, "should he [Hooker] now appear to be moving northward, I think you had better withdraw this side of the mountains tomorrow night, cross at Shepherdstown next day, and move over to Fredericktown." Put simply, if the Federal army was on the move, Stuart should, as Longstreet put it the day before, "cross by passing to our rear" at Shepherdstown, pivot toward Frederick, and then race northward to cover Ewell's right flank, as Lee's orders previously directed. Lee also gave Stuart alternate instructions: "You will, however, be able to judge whether you can pass around their army without hindrance, doing them all the damage you can, and cross the river east of the mountains. In either case, after crossing the river, you must move on and feel the right of Ewell's troops, collecting information, provisions, etc." While Lee retained Stuart's ultimate objective as getting on the right of Ewell's corps to protect its flank, he had now provided his subordinate with a discretionary opening to "pass around their army," which was a step further than crossing the Potomac "in rear of the enemy." Whereas in the more conservative option (if he found Hooker moving north), Lee named "Shepherdstown" as the specific place for Stuart to cross, in his pass around the Federal army option he named nowhere except for a vague reference to "east of the [Blue Ridge] mountains," which realistically could be anywhere from just east of Harper's Ferry to Washington, D.C. Lee's staff officer, Charles Marshall later indicated that by east of the mountains, Lee actually meant "immediately east of the mountains, so as to be close to the right flank of the army"; however, Lee wrote no such specific thing to Stuart on June 23. On this subject, Longstreet said in his memoirs that Stuart's crossing point east of the Blue Ridge "was not determined between the Confederate commander and his chief of cavalry, there being doubt whether the crossing could better be made" between the Blue Ridge and the Federal army, or rather between the Federal army and Washington.[8]

And so, on June 24 with his discretionary order in hand, Stuart arranged the three cavalry brigades of Wade Hampton, Fitzhugh Lee, and John Chambliss for the movement eastward. On the 25th, he led his 4,900 men out and almost immediately ran into "hindrance"; however, Stuart would not be deterred from his desire to "pass around their army." The cavalry column ran into Federal General Winfield Scott Hancock's Second Corps near Haymarket. The next day, the 26th, Hancock moved north and crossed the Potomac, while Stuart continued to ride east. Since Stuart had already experienced "hindrance" and had undoubtedly understood that Hooker was "moving northward" and not idle, Stuart should have immediately defaulted to Lee's orders, instructing him to "cross at Shepherdstown next day, and move over to Fredericktown," or at the very least to find the closest Potomac crossing due northward. But Stuart did not do that, and instead continued on to within just a few miles of Washington, D.C. By the 28th, he had little idea where Lee or the Second Corps divisions were located, and had managed to lose all sight of his principal objective of finding and guarding Ewell's right. Consequently, Stuart was unavailable to provide his usual screening and intelligence services, the approach from Emmitsburg to the Gettysburg vicinity was left wide open, and the left wing of the Federal army could sweep north looking for the Confederate army.[9]

Though Longstreet told Stuart to order the very capable Wade Hampton to take charge of the troopers still guarding the mountain passes and to trail the army's right and rear as Federal forces pressed northward, Stuart instead assigned the brigades of Beverly Robertson and William "Grumble" Jones to that task. He also ordered Robertson to "instruct General Jones from time to time as the movements progress, or events may require, and report anything of importance to Lieutenant-General Longstreet, with whose position you will communicate by relays through Charlestown." Robertson and Jones ultimately failed in all of these duties and stayed put in the mountain passes for days after the Army of the Potomac crossed the Potomac River. As word from Stuart fell silent and his absence continued, Lee also failed to take advantage of the cavalry troops he did possess in Robertson, Jones, and John S. Mosby. Not until June 29 did Lee call on Robertson to join the army, and the cavalryman did not complete that movement until July 3, the last day of the Gettysburg battle. Mosby was apparently given no assignment, and in the absence of orders moved into Pennsylvania west of the main army to raid and plunder. In short, since taking command, Lee had solely depended on Stuart and now wanted only Stuart. Even with other resources available, Lee waited for Stuart and consequently groped forward in the dark without him. Stuart's chief of staff, Major Henry McClellan, best characterized Lee's sole dependence on Stuart: "It was the absence of Stuart himself that he felt so keenly.... It seemed as if his cavalry were concentrated in one person, and from him alone could information be expected."[10]

J.E.B. Stuart, wartime (Library of Congress).

3

Lee Hesitates Without Stuart

"The want of cavalry had been and was again seriously felt"
—A.P. Hill

Throughout June 25 and 26, Longstreet's corps forded the Potomac River at Williamsport and the army pushed on through Maryland, reaching and crossing the Mason-Dixon Line the night of June 26. On June 27, the bulk of the Army of Northern Virginia filtered west of Gettysburg into Chambersburg, Pennsylvania. Lee and Longstreet set up camp together in a grove of trees called Shatter's Woods. There, on the evening of June 28, Longstreet's scout, the Tennessean, "ragged, weather-beaten" Henry Thomas Harrison, returned to him with intelligence that the Federal Army had also crossed the Potomac and marched northwest to Frederick City, now known as Frederick, Maryland. The news surely startled Longstreet and he immediately sent his aide, Major John Fairfax, to inform Lee of the spy's report. Soon thereafter, Lee spoke with Harrison in-person. Though the commanding general was initially skeptical of the scout's news, always having relied on the absent J.E.B. Stuart for such intelligence, he was indeed surprised by the information and took it seriously. For his shrewd use of Harrison, Longstreet was even praised by Douglas Southall Freeman, who wrote, "Credit, then, was due Harrison, and indirectly, Longstreet. Corps commanders seldom employed spies, but Longstreet, with his usual care for detail, saw to it that his spies were well-chosen and diligent." In reaction to Harrison's intelligence, over the course of that night and early morning hours of June 29, Lee changed his strategic plan from a move toward Harrisburg, Pennsylvania, instead ordering a concentration of the army near Cashtown or Gettysburg in preparation for potential engagement with the enemy. Lee's after-battle report clearly reflects his unease at the time: "In the absence of the cavalry it was impossible to ascertain his intentions; but to deter him from advancing farther west, and intercepting our communication with Virginia, it was determined to concentrate the army east of the mountains."[1]

On June 30, Lee and Longstreet learned that General Joseph Hooker had been replaced with General George G. Meade as commander of the Army of the Potomac. Longstreet recalled spending the majority of the day with Lee, while Ewell's corps marched west and southwest as rapidly as possible from Carlisle and York to rejoin the army, and Hill's men blocked up the road toward Cashtown in the First Corps' front. This traffic jam forced Longstreet to camp at Greenwood. Years later, Longstreet recollected of that evening: "General Lee spent the night with us, establishing his headquarters, as he frequently did, a short distance from mine."[2]

* * *

So, on the morning of July 1, Lee and Longstreet initially rode east together across South Mountain toward Cashtown and Gettysburg. Later, Longstreet recalled that Lee seemed to be "in his usual cheerful spirits" on the eight-mile ride. The First Corps' divisions of Lafayette McLaws and John Bell Hood began their march out of Greenwood, while George Pickett's division stayed behind at Chambersburg to guard the army's wagon trains and rear—traditionally duties of a cavalry unit. Likewise, Evander Law's brigade of Hood's division was placed on picket duty at New Guilford, a small town east of Chambersburg and 24 miles from Gettysburg. While Longstreet's men encountered serious bottlenecks on their way toward Gettysburg—running into Major General Edward Johnson's division of Ewell's corps coming down from Shippensburg—A.P. Hill's leading division under Major General Harry Heth precipitated a general engagement with John Buford's Federal cavalry division, and subsequently, Major General John Reynolds' Federal infantry on the northwest outskirts of Gettysburg. Units from another division of Hill's corps commanded by Major General William Pender also engaged, and the battle further escalated as Ewell's Second Corps smashed into the Federal Eleventh Corps commanded by Major General Oliver Howard north of Gettysburg. Eventually the leading units of the Army of the Potomac were sent streaming through Gettysburg and onto high ground just south of the town known as Cemetery Hill.[3]

Throughout the early morning hours, Lee seemed unsure of what to make of the initial clash. When the commanding general first heard the rumblings of artillery to the east, three to four miles into his ride with Longstreet, and received no immediate word as to what was going on, a member of his staff, Colonel Armistead Long, recollected that "This caused Lee some little uneasiness." Lee left Longstreet to attend to the advance of his corps and rode forward to investigate. Without J.E.B. Stuart's assistance, Lee repeatedly demonstrated he was in the dark as to the events taking place in his front. E.P. Alexander believed that Stuart's absence was the principal reason the Confederates stumbled into battle on July 1 and greatly contributed to Lee's misunderstanding of the day's happenings. "The absence of Stuart, with the bulk of the cavalry, does seem to cut some figure. Had they been with us Gen. Lee would doubtless have been too well informed of the enemy's exact location to have permitted two divisions to blunder into an attack upon two corps & a division of cavalry," Alexander later wrote. Many times during the day, Lee told Hill, Ewell, and other subordinates that he did not want to bring on a general engagement, but even as he said these words, a general engagement had clearly already begun. At 12 noon, Lee was with Major General Richard Anderson, a division commander in Hill's corps, who later recollected "I found General Lee intently listening to the fire of the guns, and very much disturbed and depressed. At length he said, more to himself than to me, 'I cannot think what has become of Stuart. I ought to have heard from him long before now.... In the absence of reports from him, I am in ignorance as to what we have in front of us here.'" Lee guessed, "It may be the whole Federal Army, or it may be only a detachment. If it is the whole Federal force, we must fight a battle here." And finally, rather strangely, Lee concluded, "If we do not gain a victory, those defiles and gorges which we passed this morning will shelter us from disaster." This account confirms that Lee was ignorant of the situation without Stuart, yet even in that state, he seemed resolutely determined that the army must fight a pitched battle if the whole Federal army was present, while simultaneously anticipating the necessity of depending on the mountains to the west if his army was to experience defeat. In short, Anderson witnessed Lee in confused stream of consciousness. His account suggests that the commanding general was suffering from a deep bout of uncertainty, resulting from a dearth of intelligence.[4]

Later in the day, this uncertainty was further demonstrated after Hill's two divisions of Heth and Pender, along with Ewell's divisions under Robert Rodes and Jubal Early had pushed the Federal First and Eleventh Corps south of Gettysburg to regroup on elevated ground at Cemetery Hill. Even if these four divisions were deemed completely unusable for further fighting that day, Lee soon had, at the very least, two fresh divisions under Richard Anderson and Edward Johnson on hand to push the attack. Longstreet later wrote of this opportunistic moment in the battle, "the crushing defeat inflicted on the advance of the Federal Army in the casual encounter on the 1st ... should have been pushed to extremities, that occasion furnishing one of the few opportunities ever furnished for 'pursuit pell-mell.'" General Fitzhugh Lee, a cavalry officer during the war, nephew of Robert E. Lee, and postwar Longstreet critic even agreed with this contention, stating, "Had we known it at the time, the position on the heights fought for on the 2nd could have been gained on the afternoon of the 1st by continuing without delay the pursuit of the Federals." Without a doubt, as A.P. Hill bluntly put it in his after-battle report, "The want of cavalry had been and was again seriously felt." Even after all the fighting north and west of town and the subsequent retreat of multiple Federal Corps through Gettysburg, Lee could not see that a general engagement had already begun and that if he did not act decisively at that critical moment, the Federals would seize the initiative simply as a result of gaining the strong defensive position on Cemetery Hill. This view was reflected in his own after-battle report, where in recollecting where he thought the rest of the Federal army was located after 4 p.m. on the first day, he asserted, "Without information as to its proximity, the strong position which the enemy had assumed could not be attacked." Yet, even in the midst of this obvious uncertainty, Lee vaguely ordered "General Ewell ... to carry the hill occupied by the enemy, if he found it practicable, but to avoid a general engagement until the arrival of the other divisions of the army."[5]

Lee attributed his hesitancy in attacking Cemetery Hill that evening to the "weakened and exhausted" divisions of Heth, Pender, Rodes, and Early, along with the Federal army's "overwhelming numbers of fresh troops." After attacking aggressively in the morning hours and instigating a general engagement, A.P. Hill wrote that "prudence led me to be content with what had been gained"; that his troops were "exhausted and necessarily disordered"; and, "fresh troops of the enemy were available." Likewise, Ewell explained his inability to act on Lee's "if practicable" orders as resulting from his "inability to bring artillery to bear" on Cemetery Hill, and that "the troops with me were jaded by twelve hours' fighting and marching." Lee did not mention the express availability of Anderson or Johnson in his after-battle report, but Hill and Ewell did in theirs. Hill underscored that Anderson "had just come up," while Ewell maintained "General Johnson's division (the only one of my corps that had not been engaged) was close to the town." Longstreet also recollected later that as he rode to the front to meet with Lee around 5 p.m., he saw that "Anderson's division was then filed off along the ridge, resting."[6]

John Bachelder, a preeminent historian on the battle in the late nineteenth century underscored the Confederates' missed opportunity at this juncture most adeptly: "The best chance for a successful attack was within the first hour, and unquestionably the great mistake of the battle was the failure to follow the Union forces through the town, and attack them before they could reform on Cemetery Hill." Bachelder went through the available units for such a push toward Cemetery Hill. "[James] Lane's and [Edward] Thomas' brigades, of Pender's division, and [William] Smith's of Early's division, were at hand for such a purpose, and had fired scarcely a shot. [George] Dole's, [Robert] Hoke's, and [Harry] Hays' brigades were in good fighting condition, and several others would have done good service."[7]

Lee's hesitancy to provide direct orders to his two new corps commanders—exemplified most noticeably in not pushing his subordinates to at least use fresh brigades from Anderson and Johnson's divisions—was directly attributable to his lack of general awareness, but also to a lack of leadership at such a critical moment. Most historians have held that Lee was known to issue discretionary orders, letting subordinates, like Longstreet and Jackson (in the past) exercise their own judgment; however, this explanation is a convenient and ultimately fanciful overture when it comes to Gettysburg. Lee must have recognized that Ewell and A.P. Hill would require extra supervision, especially considering how events had unexpectedly unfolded during the morning hours of July 1 against his wishes. Ewell and Hill would need clearer and more direct orders than Lee had been accustomed to issuing to the likes of Longstreet and Jackson. The mere necessity for two new commanders to replace one underscores Lee's recognition that neither could fill Jackson's shoes. Academic historian Allen Guelzo advances this argument well with respect to Lee's actions on the afternoon of July 1: "Perhaps in the end" he writes, "it was the great mistake of Robert E. Lee at Gettysburg that, having had to reach past his corps commanders to direct operations that afternoon, he did not keep reaching past them. Whatever blame attaches to Ambrose Powell Hill in the twilight of July 1st also attaches to Robert E. Lee for not overriding them." Yet, surprisingly, the overwhelming majority of historians have given Lee a pass for not "overriding them," contending that Lee simply did not command that way. This general absolution of wrongdoing is even more unusual when considering Lee's lack of decisive leadership at such an opportune moment meant the Confederates allowed the Federals to coalesce around the best ground at Gettysburg, Cemetery Hill, without a fight. It further meant that Lee set up his army to carry out bloody attacks against that very same, albeit reinforced and more established position for two more days.[8]

Lee's imbalance as a commanding general at Gettysburg originated from his deficiency of timely and accurate information as to the whereabouts of the Federal army and a lack of cavalry screening. When asked in 1868 why he lost at Gettysburg, Lee wrote, "Its loss was occasioned by a combination of circumstances," and the first one that came to mind was that "It was commenced in the absence of correct intelligence." In an interview with William Allan, Lee went further, stating outright that "Stuart's failure to carry out his instructions forced the battle of Gettysburg." Indeed, Longstreet attributed the entire first day's events to the want for cavalry reconnaissance, writing, "Owing to the absence of our cavalry, and our consequent ignorance of the enemy's whereabouts, we collided with them unexpectedly." In another account, on Lee having to seemingly grope forward in the dark, he asserted similarly "As he advanced towards his adversary, the eyes and ears of his army were turned afar off.... There is no doubt it greatly disturbed General Lee's mind." Again, Fitzhugh Lee confirmed Longstreet's contentions, "It is well known that General Lee loitered, after crossing the Potomac, because he was ignorant of the movements and position of the antagonist. For the same reason he groped in the dark at Gettysburg. From the 25th of June to July 2nd, General Lee deplored Stuart's absence, and almost hourly wished for him." Brigadier General Cadmus Wilcox of Anderson's division later insisted that "the absence of the cavalry was seriously felt and greatly embarrassed General Lee.... It was the want of information due to the absence of the cavalry that brought about the second day's battle at Gettysburg." Captain Justus Scheibert wrote similarly, "General Lee was very much concerned and restless about General Stuart, of whom he had heard and seen nothing for several days, and whom he could have used well on this and the preceding day," in reference to July 1 and 2. Gilbert Moxley Sorrel also confirmed the formidable negative effect Stuart's absence had on Lee, asserting, "He was the eyes and ears and strong right arm of the commander, and well may he have missed him. All through the marches [Lee] showed it." Perhaps E.P. Alexander put it most aptly when he claimed Stuart's absence directly led to the July 1 "blunder" of "two divisions" of Confederate infantry initiating an "attack upon two corps & a division of cavalry." Historians have often drawn much attention to Lee's frustration and unease at Gettysburg, often naming Longstreet's consistent and forthright tactical reservations and alleged general "slowness" as the root cause for these emotions on the evening of the first day and during the last two days of the battle. There is no reliable evidence to support such an argument. A more reasonable and justifiable conclusion is that any anxiety Lee experienced at Gettysburg was first and foremost derived from Stuart's absence.[9]

4

Lee and Longstreet Deliberate Tactical Offensive

"We could not call the enemy to position better suited to our plans"
—James Longstreet to Robert E. Lee

Just as Lee was staring at the Federal army's rallying point on Cemetery Hill, Longstreet rode up and dismounted. It was around 5 p.m. He drew his glasses and began "noting movements of detachments of the enemy on the Emmitsburg road, the relative positions for maneuver, the lofty perch of the enemy, and the rocky slopes from it, all marking the position clearly defensive." Longstreet then turned to Lee and said matter-of-factly, "We could not call the enemy to position better suited to our plans. All that we have to do is file around his left and secure good ground between him and his capital." In another postwar account, Longstreet held that he stated very similarly, "I urged that we should move around by our right to the left of Meade, and put our army between him and Washington, threatening his left and rear, and thus force him to attack us in such position as we might select." Thinking in terms of the tactical approach he and Lee had discussed previously for a general battle during the campaign, Longstreet's statements suggest he thought the commanding general was already contemplating such a move.[1]

Characteristically, Clifford Dowdey described the First Corps commander's suggestions to Lee on the evening of July 1 as nothing less than an "insubordinate harangue." Dowdey, who often resorted to telling readers his interpretation of battle participants' thoughts and feelings, believed Longstreet was, at that moment, in a "strangely disturbed state of mind" as someone who "had convinced himself that since Jackson's death he had replaced Stonewall as Lee's collaborator." Dowdey clearly demonstrated he was yet another twentieth-century subscriber to the early Lost Cause myth that Jackson had been Lee's most trusted subordinate. Further, the Virginian historian claimed that once Lee initially rejected Longstreet's tactical defensive plan on the evening of July 1, it shattered what Longstreet believed to be his "equal partnership" with Lee. In Dowdey's words, that "partnership existed only in his mind" and "Longstreet simply could not accept the repudiation of the relationship as he had conceived it." Resultantly, on one page alone of his 1958 work, *Lee & His Men at Gettysburg*, Dowdey characterized Longstreet at that moment in the battle in a whole host of negative ways. Longstreet possessed an "intense jealousy of Jackson's fame," had an "unreflective mind," turned to "glumly brooding" and "muttering," and demonstrated that he was "puzzled," "agitated," and "evasive."[2]

James Longstreet, 1863 (HistoryInFull Color.com).

Bruce Catton, a journalist who wrote a three-volume history of the war in the 1950s and 1960s, also weighed in on Longstreet's July 1 proposal. Catton, like Douglas Southall Freeman and Clifford Dowdey, among others, perpetuated the erroneous taint and mythical falsehoods of the Lost Cause movement well into the twentieth century. An influential author at an influential time, Catton's works in particular were written and devoured by millions of readers just before, during, and immediately after the centennial years when Civil War history was extremely popular in the United States. His analysis of the war and its participants, along with Freeman's and Dowdey's, was inculcated into the generation of academic and popular historians that followed. Catton wrote confidently on the First Corps commander's suggestion to Lee on the evening of July 1, "Longstreet, to be sure, proposed that the army circle to its right to get into Meade's rear, but Lee quickly dismissed the idea." Catton then presented what he believed to be the principal reason for why Lee rejected Longstreet's suggestion: "He no longer had Stonewall Jackson, the one man who could have led such a move." Specifically, in this case, Catton perpetuated the myths of the Lost Cause generation and erroneously believed there was no evidence Lee considered Longstreet's proposal throughout the night of July 1. He also maintained outright that Lee's go-to, senior, and most trusted subordinate was Jackson, who was dead in July 1863 and therefore could not be relied upon.[3]

Catton imposed this central tenet of the Lost Cause ideology on his narrative, renewing the fiction that the commanding general only thought Jackson could be trusted to execute such a flanking maneuver, while concurrently implying the falsehood that Lee thought Longstreet slow, incapable of celerity of movement. One of the originating sources for this claim was Lost Cause believer the Reverend John William Jones who alleged he had spoken to Lee in Lexington before his death, where upon the former commanding general's "reading a letter making some inquiries of him about Gettysburg," he slammed his hand down on the table and exclaimed, "If I had had Stonewall Jackson.... I would have won that fight, and a complete victory there would have given us Washington and Baltimore, if not Philadelphia, and would have established the independence of the Confederacy." Jones' story, recounted in numerous postwar publications, reeks of Lost Cause fabrication—all the way from the hero-worshipping amplification of Jackson to the overemphasis on the importance of the Gettysburg battle.[4]

Historians have paid insufficient attention to Longstreet's clear explanation of the logic behind his July 1 flanking proposal or have discredited it as self-serving. Reflecting back on this critical moment in the battle, Longstreet contended that if the Confederates had executed such a turning movement as he suggested on the night of July 1 "we should either have been attacked—the very thing we had been hoping and mourning for—or we should have dislodged Meade from his position without striking a blow." The First Corps commander then described the outcomes of each option. "If we had been attacked, we should have certainly repulsed it," he argued. It is not unreasonable to assume Longstreet was reflecting back on the Army of Northern Virginia's complete and utter defensive victory at the Battle of Fredericksburg in December 1862, where Lee's army suffered only a 6 percent casualty rate. Of the other possibility, he wrote, "Had Meade deserted his position without striking a blow in its defense, the moral effect in our favor would have been tremendous." Longstreet concluded his explanation with an astute and often ignored realization about other options open to the Confederate army at the time, regardless of whether his flanking proposal did not result in Meade's decision to attack or vacate his position at Gettysburg. "The thirteen days that elapsed between our first recontre and our recrossing of the Potomac would have surely given time and opportunity for different work and greater results than were had at Gettysburg." Again, Longstreet was referring to his belief that even if Lee's tactical aggressive had succeeded after July 1 in forcing Meade from his Cemetery Ridge position, the accomplishment would not have outweighed the great loss of Confederate manpower. Longstreet did not want to engage in a fruitless victory.[5]

Captain Justus Scheibert later wrote that he agreed with Longstreet's July 1 tactical suggestion: "In my opinion it would not have been difficult at Gettysburg to maneuver General Meade out of his formidable position either by marching vigorously to the north or east ... or ... by advancing upon Frederickstown and threatening Washington." Further, a message sent from General Meade to General Halleck before the July 2 battle suggested the Federal army commander was worried about such a turning move and his reaction would have been to abandon the Cemetery Ridge position at Gettysburg had the Confederates chosen to maneuver that way. "If not attacked, and I can get any positive information of the enemy which will justify me in doing so, I will attack. If I find it hazardous to do so, and am satisfied that the enemy is endeavoring to move to my rear and interpose between me and Washington, I shall fall back on my supplies at Westminster," Meade wrote. Similarly, General Winfield Scott Hancock, commander of the Federal Second Corps, believed the Cemetery Ridge position "was a very strong one, and advantageous for a defensive battle, having for its only disadvantage that it might be turned." Longstreet's proposal was not only in accordance with what he and Lee's tactical intentions had been for the campaign, but was also the maneuver the Federals feared the Confederates might perform on the evening of July 1.[6]

Even so, on July 1, Lee reacted to Longstreet's turning suggestion with some "impatience," and "striking the air with his closed hand," said "If he is there tomorrow I will attack him." If this was indeed how Lee presented his July 2 tactical plan to Longstreet, it would have undoubtedly repelled, worried, and surprised Longstreet all at once. In fact, Longstreet later told his subordinate Lafayette McLaws that Lee's response elicited all of those reactions: "You will now understand my surprise at finding all of our previously arranged plans so unexpectedly changed, and why I might wish and hope, to get the Gen., to consider our former arrangements." Longstreet was not the kind of general to make a hasty decision, especially when it portended toward the employment of outright aggressive tactics against a quality defensive position. Historian Glenn Tucker accurately described Longstreet's persona, writing, "He is not emotional and regards that trait in others a weakness. He does not try to force his cards when they are running against him. Longstreet liked to win.... If the odds were not in his favor, he would wait for a fresh deal. Eventually he would hold the aces." Likewise, George Stewart held that Longstreet had a predilection to "weigh the evidence," was "a realist," and frequently sought "to base his judgments upon determined fact, and then stubborn to maintain them." Tucker and Stewart's characterizations are similar to what Adeline Baum, an early twentieth century member of the United Daughters of the Confederacy, wrote of Longstreet right after his death: "True to his convictions, he acted always after careful consideration as his judgment has shown him was best." Indeed, Longstreet was not alone in his opinion of Lee's decision on the evening of July 1. E.P. Alexander later dubbed Lee's choice to continue the tactical offensive at Gettysburg after the first day's fight his fatal mistake. "I think it a reasonable estimate," he wrote, "to say that 60 percent of our chances for a great victory were lost by our continuing the aggressive." The artillerist believed Lee had unburdened Meade of making a tough decision in how he should react to the Confederate's victory on July 1. In line with Longstreet's information to Lee about having forced the Federals into a position well-suited to the original campaign plans, Alexander later wondered what the outcome would have been had "Lee ... been satisfied with his victory of the first day; & then taken a strong position & stood on the defensive.... For I am impressed by the fact that the strength of the enemy's position seems to have cut no figure in the consideration [of] the question of the aggressive."[7]

Robert E. Lee, wartime (Library of Congress).

In his after-battle report, Lee justified his insistence on the tactical offensive after the first day's fight. First, he wrote, "to withdraw through the mountains with our extensive trains would have been difficult and dangerous," and secondly, "we were unable to await an attack, as the country was unfavorable for collecting supplies in the presence of the enemy." William Swinton, who interviewed Longstreet in 1866, characterized Lee's "main motive for giving battle" aggressively at Gettysburg as "an excuse that can hardly be considered valid." Swinton then outlined two familiar and additional options that Lee had on the evening of July 1, namely to maintain a defensive posture on the Seminary Ridge position, or execute a turning movement around the Federal left as Longstreet had suggested. On the first option, Swinton contended

"A considerable part of the trains had not yet been advanced to the east of the mountains, and he could readily have withdrawn all under cover of his line of battle; and then retired his army over the same routes—the Cashtown and Fairfield roads—over which he ultimately retreated." On the second option, Swinton described how with Longstreet's flank "securely posted on the Emmettsburg road," the Confederate army could have filed off the Federal left toward Frederick to get between Meade and Washington, D.C. If nothing else, Swinton added, it would have forced the Federals to relinquish the strong Cemetery Ridge position at Gettysburg.[8]

Longstreet and Swinton were not alone in their skepticism of Lee's rationale for continuing the tactical offensive at Gettysburg after July 1. E.P. Alexander reminded students of the war that "we stayed three days longer on that very ground, two of them days of desperate battle, ending in the discouragement of a bloody repulse, & then successfully withdrew all our trains & most of the wounded through the mountains." Regarding Lee's second justification for assuming the tactical offensive (the army's inability to collect necessary supplies), Alexander cited the Confederate retreat from Gettysburg: "Finding the Potomac too high to ford, protected them all & foraged successfully for over a week in a very restricted territory along the river, until we could build a bridge." Alexander concluded that "it does not seem improbable that we could have faced Meade safely on the second at Gettysburg without assaulting him in his wonderfully strong position." Alexander also underscored the possibility of maintaining a defensive posture on Seminary Ridge ("it could never have been successfully assaulted"), along with the option to fall back east toward Cashtown and fight a defensive battle in the "mountain passes," forcing "Meade to take the aggressive." William Oates, a brigade commander in Longstreet's corps, and hardly a Longstreet fan after the war, wrote of Lee's decision and Longstreet's proposed alternative, "It may have been best for Lee to have flanked Meade out of his strong position and have forced him to attack and thus to have acted on the defensive.... Lee, with all his robust daring and adventurous spirit, should not have ordered the impossible, as was apparent to a skilled observer." As Oates should have readily recognized, Longstreet was that "skilled observer" on the evening of July 1 making that exact tactical defensive suggestion, while simultaneously cautioning against Lee's "impossible" tactical offensive plan.[9]

Longstreet was undoubtedly taken by surprise at Lee's intentions for July 2. In responding to his commander's "I will attack him tomorrow" statement, Longstreet emphasized that "If he is there, it will be because he is anxious that we should attack him—a good reason, in my judgment, for not doing so." Popular historian Noah Trudeau mischaracterizes Longstreet's interjection as a "welled up ... rare burst of insubordinate testiness," which completely ignores Lee and his corps commanders' well-documented open and frank relationship. The British observer Arthur Fremantle saw this affinity immediately. "The relationship between him [Lee] and Longstreet are quite touching—they are almost always together.... It is impossible to please Longstreet more than by praising Lee."[10]

According to Longstreet, Lee pushed back on his proposal and remained "impressed with the idea that, by attacking the Federals" on the next day, he could "whip them in detail." "They are there in position, and I am going to whip them or they are going to whip me," Lee said. In another account of this discussion, Longstreet recalled also saying, perhaps upon recognizing Lee's fixation on the tactical aggressive for the next day, "If that height has become the objective, why not take it at once? We have forty thousand men, less the casualties of the day; he cannot have more than twenty thousand."[11]

Whether Longstreet actually said that last bit is unknown, as we only have his account to go on. Longstreet critic Douglas Southall Freeman accepted Longstreet's claim: "He [Longstreet] argued that if Lee intended to attack, he should do so immediately." As did mid-twentieth century novelist and historian Shelby Foote, who wrote, "He [Longstreet] was still opposed to the attack, he said, but if it was going to be made at all, it had better be made at once." Nevertheless, the logical significance of Longstreet's alleged statement remains essential. If Lee's intention at that point in the battle was to attack the Cemetery Hill position and "whip them in detail," however contrary it was to the original plan to carry out a tactical defensive battle, why wait until the next day to do it? Again, we return to Lee's after-battle report when he recalled of this moment, "The remainder of that army, under General Meade, was approaching Gettysburg." Lee wrote as if he actually had possessed the intelligence at that time in the battle to know that only a portion of Federal army had retreated to and was then positioned on Cemetery Hill. Yet, he then admitted, "Without information as to its proximity, the strong position which the enemy had assumed could not be attacked." In another section, he wrote just the opposite, "It had not been intended to deliver a general battle so far from our base unless attacked, but coming unexpectedly upon the whole Federal army." Lee's after-battle report shows his logic and decision-making processes at that moment on July 1 were strikingly muddled and contradictory. In one statement, he acknowledged knowing the whole Union army had not yet joined the remnants of two Federal Corps on Cemetery Hill, and that he would only be, then, facing a portion of the enemy's force. In another statement, he claimed knowing he was up against "the whole Federal army." Nevertheless, he expressed that he did not then have enough knowledge about the rest of the Federal army's location to press the attack right then and there. What had happened to Lee's characteristic audacity?[12]

Instead, even in Lee's state of apparent uncertainty, he insisted confidently and with alleged impatience to Longstreet, "If he is there to-morrow I will attack him." Lee had decided that he would rather attack the whole Federal army in their "strong position" on July 2, than attack an outnumbered portion of it in that same position on July 1. Lee also seemingly assumed he would regain J.E.B. Stuart on the following day to better understand the battlescape. If his eyes and ears of the army did not return, did Lee not realize he would be pursuing the tactical aggressive against that same strong, albeit more complex defensive position with a more potent and prepared Federal army occupying it? Longstreet remembered pressing this point to Lee: "I reminded him that if the Federals were there in the morning, it would be proof that they had their forces well in hand, and that with Pickett in Chambersburg, and Stuart out of reach, we should be somewhat in detail." Yet, on the evening of July 1, Lee was on a completely different wavelength, as evidenced by some statements he made to Austrian hussar and observer Fitzgerald Ross after the Confederate army had been defeated at Gettysburg and was retreating to the Potomac River. Ross recalled Lee asserting that "Had he [Lee] been aware that Meade had been able to concentrate his whole army ... he certainly should not have attacked him"; however, he had been "led away, partly by the success of the first day," believing that "Meade had only a portion of his army in front of him, and seeing the enthusiasm of his own troops, he had thought that a successful battle would cut the knot so easily and satisfactorily, that he determined to risk it." In short, Lee admitted to Ross that he had been possessed by an overconfidence born out of the results of the first day's battle (and very likely, previous battles). Lee claimed he had actually been uninformed as to exactly what was in his front, and despite that reality, he made a conscious decision to gamble with the army and press the tactical offensive on July 2.[13]

* * *

While Longstreet was present, Lee sent his infamous "if practicable" order to Ewell, directing the Second Corps commander to assess the possibility of an attack and seizure of the high ground, namely Cemetery and Culp's Hill. Lee again oddly cautioned Ewell to "avoid a general engagement until the arrival of the other divisions of the army," in apparent refusal to acknowledge that a general engagement had been ongoing since the initial clash at 7:30 in the morning. Many years later, in 1905, James Power Smith, a member of Ewell's staff, recalled that he approached Lee at that moment with word that Second Corps division commanders Jubal Early and Robert Rodes believed Cemetery Hill could be taken if support were provided from A.P. Hill's sector. Strangely, Lee said nothing of Hill's men, but instead, according to Smith, turned to Longstreet, who was then "dismounted, and with glasses inspecting the position of the south of Cemetery Hill," and asked if his men were up and available to support such an attack. Of course, Longstreet's men were still miles away because of the long holdup in letting the remainder of Hill's corps, Johnson's division, and the Second Corps wagon train precede McLaws and Hood's divisions. Longstreet allegedly told Lee, "General, there comes the head of my column where you see that dust rising," which was about "three or four miles in our rear"; though he did offer trying to push up his two leading brigades with all possible haste, if necessary. After Longstreet informed Lee of the status of his corps, namely that McLaws' division remained miles away, Smith alleged that Lee told him to inform Ewell "he regretted that his people were not up to support him on the right, but he wished him to take Cemetery Hill if it were possible." Again, it is important to note that Lee bizarrely said nothing of the availability of fresh units from A.P. Hill's corps to "support him [Ewell] on the right."[14]

A number of modern historians have framed Smith's recollection of Lee's allegations at that encounter as some sort of valid rebuke of Longstreet not having his divisions present at that moment; however, Lee must have known and understood that the Chambersburg Pike had been in bottleneck shape the entire day. In fact, Lee played a large role in clogging the road from Cashtown, once again, as a result of his ignorance of the Federal army's precise location. Upon deciding to concentrate the army during the last days of June, Lee had issued a discretionary order to Ewell, telling him to either march to Cashtown or Gettysburg. Unfortunately, Ewell initially chose Cashtown. Once he learned of the battle unfolding at Gettysburg, Ewell was able to divert Robert Rodes' division directly to Gettysburg, while Jubal Early's division marched southwest from

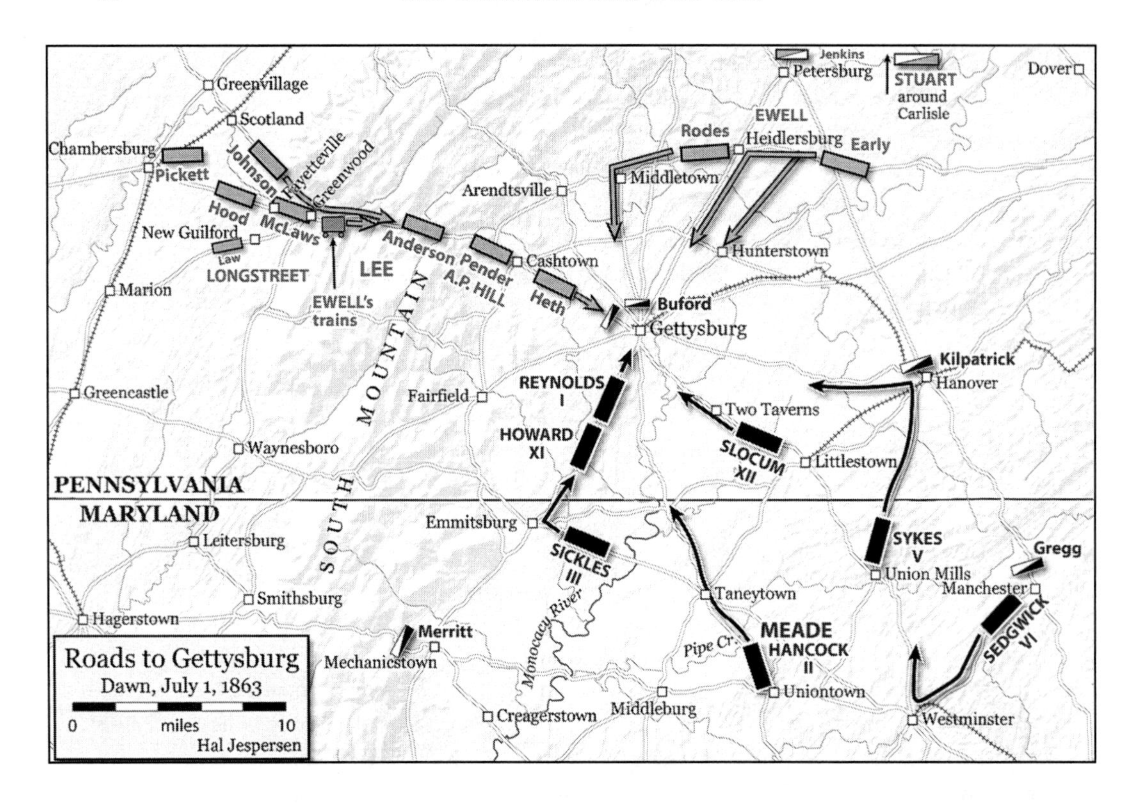

Heidlersburg; however, since Edward Johnson's division was already much further along toward Cashtown, it and the Second Corps wagon train were forced to move eastward toward Gettysburg on the Chambersburg Pike. When Lee was riding with Longstreet during the morning hours of July 1, both generals noticed the head of Johnson's division at an intersection. Probably wanting to expedite the concentration of Ewell's corps as quickly as possible, Lee instructed Longstreet to give Johnson's division the right-of-way on the road and halt the First Corps divisions until Johnson passed. As a result, Hill's corps, Johnson's division of Ewell's corps, the whole Second Corps wagon train (purportedly, some fourteen miles in length), and Longstreet's two divisions lurched along the same road on July 1. This quandary on the Chambersburg Pike resulted in a several-hours-long delay for Longstreet's two divisions, whereby McLaws' division was unable to reach Marsh Creek, about three and a half miles from the battlefield, until near the midnight hour, while Hood's division filtered into the same bivouac soon thereafter.[15]

In discussing Smith's alleged meeting with Lee on the evening of July 1, Gary Gallagher has advanced some misleading conclusions. "Lest Smith's reading be deemed suspect because of his well-known antipathy toward Longstreet," he says "it is important to note that a trio of witnesses friendly to the First Corps chief also sketched a man deeply upset about the prospect of attacking on July 2nd." Though Smith's alleged interaction with Lee was entirely about the potential accomplishments of that evening with Longstreet's divisions, for some reason, Gallagher uses the staff officer's account to pivot to a separate topic: Longstreet's misgivings about attacking on July 2. The historian then uses an infamous quote from First Corps aide Gilbert Moxley Sorrel, discussed in more detail later, some recollections from First Corp commissary officer Raphael Moses, and statements made by British army officer and observer Lieutenant Colonel Arthur Fremantle, to argue that Longstreet possessed "deep misgivings" about Lee's intention to attack the next day. Of course, Longstreet had misgivings about attacking the Federal's strong position on July 2 and readily voiced them that evening and the next morning; however, the issue with Gallagher's historical approach in this instance is that none of these accounts from Sorrel, Moses, or Fremantle have anything to do with Longstreet's informing Lee that his divisions were neither available nor present for battle at 5:30 p.m. on July 1, which is what "Smith's reading" was all about. Above all, Smith's recollections about Longstreet's unavailability at that moment in the battle were patently obvious, and therefore, completely insignificant. Longstreet was simply reporting to Lee the truth that his divisions were delayed on the Chambersburg Pike.[16]

Once Longstreet reported the status of the First Corps divisions, Lee apparently did not recognize he had fresh and semi-fresh divisions on hand from both Hill's and Ewell's corps to precipitate or support an attack on Cemetery Hill—namely Early, Johnson, Pender, and Anderson. Historian Edwin Coddington, who was often critical of Longstreet, concluded on this topic, "Responsibility for the failure of the Confederates to make an all-out assault on Cemetery Hill on July 1 must rest with Lee." When the commanding general discussed Johnson's fresh division in his after-battle report, he oddly stated of Ewell, "He decided to await Johnson's division"; however, Johnson's division, according to Ewell's report, was "close to the town" and available. Apparently, just after sunset, Ewell instructed Johnson to take Culp's Hill, an adjoining elevation he thought commanded the Cemetery Hill position, if unoccupied; however, the Second Corps commander left the decision to act entirely in Johnson's hands and never followed up with him until after midnight (five hours later) to see if the order had been carried out.[17]

Lee also had Anderson's division of Hill's corps and portions of Pender's and Early's divisions. Around the sunset hour, Ewell queried Jubal Early (before he tapped Johnson) if two of his brigades, Hays and Avery, could immediately occupy Culp's Hill, but the contentious division commander demurred, citing how his men "had been doing all the hard marching and fighting and was not in condition to make the move." Additionally, General William "Extra Billy" Smith, commanding Early's reserve brigade, sent an aide to Ewell to report that "a heavy force was ... moving up in their rear." Ewell did not believe this information, but it was enough for him to "suspend movements until I can send & inquire into it." Ewell continued his streak of malleability and accepted Early's objections; however, if Lee wanted either one of his new corps commanders to attack, as commanding general, he could have easily ordered it done. Lee's lax approach in not pressing Ewell or Hill demonstrated he was unsure himself as to what course was best. This contention is confirmed during a conversation Lee had with Isaac Trimble at Ewell's headquarters on the following morning, July 2, where he admitted "The enemy have the advantage of us in a shorter and inside line and we are too much extended. We did not or could not pursue our advantage of yesterday and now the enemy are in good position." Lee's statement is puzzling when considering that both he and Longstreet had assessed the Federal position to be at the very least, "good," at their 5 p.m. meeting, even with only a portion of the Union army then occupying it. As far as the responsibility of whether "we did not or could not pursue" the advantage of the first day, this failure ultimately rested with the uncertainties of the commanding general, not the hesitancies of his green subordinates, Ewell and Hill. E.P. Alexander made this observation most explicitly: "There could not be a more striking illustration, either of the danger of giving any important orders in any conditional form, or of failing to follow up all such orders with some supervision. When the firing gradually died out instead of being renewed, Lee took no action."[18]

In one of his essays on Lee's actions at Gettysburg, Gary Gallagher contends that Walter Taylor's postwar writings confirm "Lee was unhappy" with "Ewell's failure to press his assaults," as if Lee were powerless as commanding general to make sure those assaults were indeed pressed. Gallagher uses a passage from Taylor's postwar memoirs, *Four Years with General Lee*, that oozes with Lost Cause rhetoric to make the argument that the supposedly powerless Lee would have been much more aggressive had he been in Ewell's position: "The prevailing idea with General Lee was, to press forward without delay; to follow up promptly and vigorously the advantage already gained." In reality, it was well within Lee's power to make this "prevailing idea" happen without delay during those few opportune hours on July 1; however, he neither issued Ewell a direct order nor followed up with him to make sure his vague order was carried out. For years after the battle even Ewell understood "I have been blamed by many for not having pressed my advantage the first day at Gettysburg"; however, he also laid much of the responsibility on Lee, writing, "General Lee came upon the ground before I could have possibly done anything, and after surveying the enemy's position, he did not deem it advisable to attack."[19]

5

An Unfortunate Position Considered ... and Reconsidered

"No reasonable probability of his accomplishing any good"
—E.P. Alexander

On the night of July 1 Lee considered his options. Gary Gallagher says that throughout the night Lee was worried about depending on Longstreet and began to lose faith in his Warhorse's ability to lead an attack the next day. In general terms, this claim seems to be in harmony with the allegation that, on the evening of July 1, Lee told several subordinate officers on the Confederate left, in an uncharacteristically vocal manner, that "If I attack from my right, Longstreet will have to make the attack. Longstreet is a very good fighter once he gets in position and gets everything ready, but he is so slow." Longstreet directly addressed this alleged comment in the postwar years, asserting, "He [Lee] is credited with having used uncomely remarks concerning me, in the presence of a number of subordinate officers, just on the eve of battle." Longstreet discounted such rumors: "It is hardly possible that any one acquainted with General Lee's exalted character will accept such statements as true. It is hardly possible that any general could have been so indiscreet as to have used such expressions under such circumstances." However, Gallagher implies that Lee's fixation on Ewell's position on the Confederate left and his constant inquiry into whether an attack could be launched from that position were indicators of his reluctance to depend on Longstreet. "It is reasonable to assume," Gallagher concludes, "that Lee did not relish the prospect of entrusting his assaults on July 2 to a man obviously opposed to resuming the offensive."[1]

This is a far-fetched assumption. It is more likely that Lee's predilection for worry and doubt which continued throughout the night of July 1 and well into the morning of the second day, was fueled by other people and other situations. Lee's actions that night support this contention. Something about Ewell's position on the Confederate left, just south and outside the town of Gettysburg, bothered Lee. E.P. Alexander emphasized how poor Ewell's position was on the Confederate left: "It was an awkward place, far from our line of retreat ... & not convenient either for re-inforcing others or being reinforced.... This part of the enemy's position was strongest & it was practically almost unassailable." Ewell's account on this issue also underscores Lee's uncertainty about the Second Corps position: "I received orders soon after dark to draw my corps around to the right, in case it could not be used to advantage where it was; that the commanding

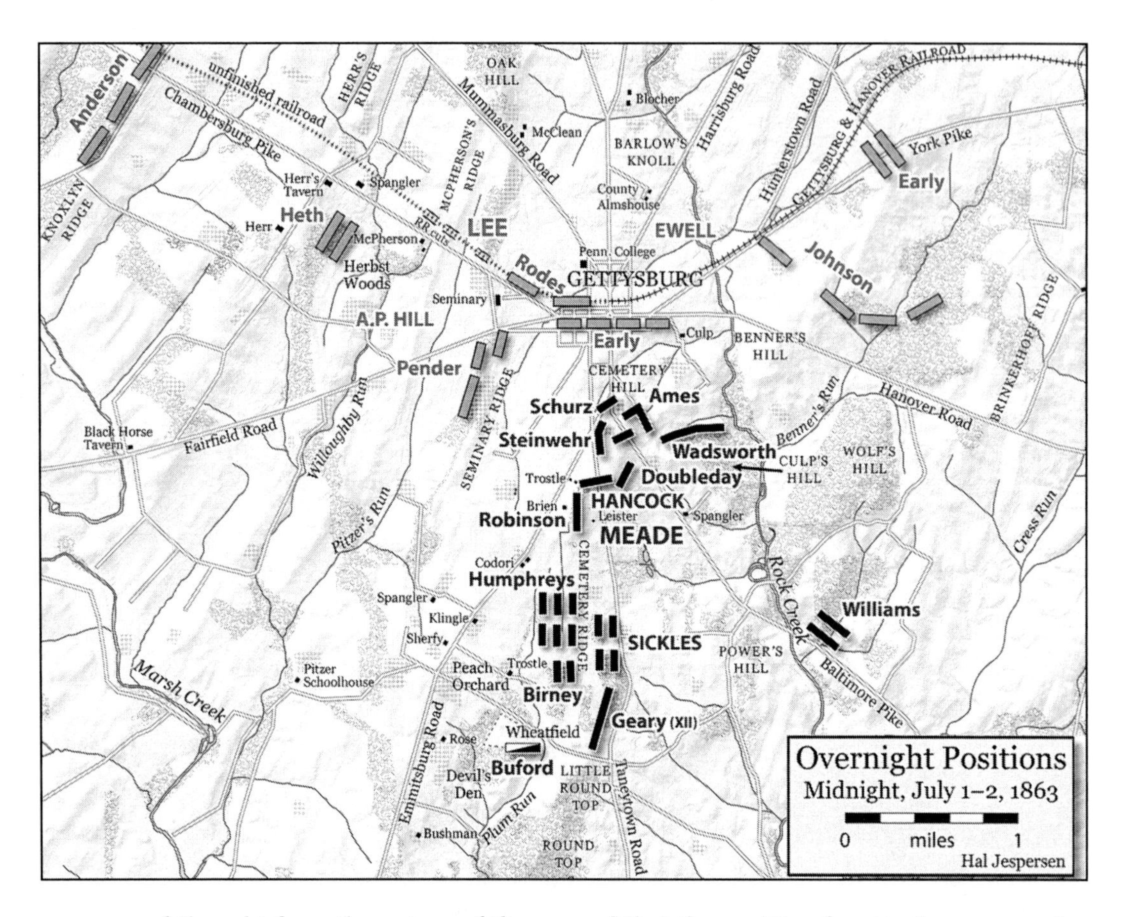

general thought from the nature of the ground that the position for attack was a good one on that side." Soon thereafter, probably around 6 p.m., Lee decided to ride over to Ewell's headquarters at the Blocher Farm, where he met with Ewell, Early, and Rodes to further discuss the possibility of launching a general attack from the Second Corps' front the next day. If that were not possible the question remained whether the corps should be moved around to the right to support an attack or maneuver further. Subsequent accounts of this meeting suggest that Early dominated the conversation and answered "no" to both questions, pointing to the Federal left as the most opportune target for an attack the next day and that the Second Corps should remain where it was. Ewell and Rodes concurred with this judgment. For some reason, Ewell oddly never informed Lee of the orders he issued just prior to their meeting, instructing Johnson to take Culp's Hill, if unoccupied.[2]

E.P. Alexander thought that Lee erred badly in leaving Ewell in the position north of Cemetery Hill. "Yet the orders to come out from the awkward place he [Ewell] was in—where there was no reasonable probability of his accomplishing any good on the enemy's line in his front & where his artillery was of no service—were never renewed & he stayed there till the last," he maintained. In another account, Alexander again underscored Lee's failure to extricate Ewell's corps: "No one ordered the division to be carried back to the right, where it could have been of much service in subsequent operations, and where Lee had intended it to be. It was far too weak to attack the strong position of the enemy on Culp's Hill, and its communication with the rest of the army was long, roundabout, and exposed to the enemy's view." The young artillerist also expressed later how he found it odd that Lee was seemingly persuaded to attack the Federal left the next day by officers who had never even seen the left: "Ewell, Early, and Rodes ... urged, instead, that Longstreet should attack the enemy's flank. Not one of those present had more than a very vague idea of the character and features of the enemy's line, and it is therefore not surprising that this advice, though very plausible in view of the success of former flank movements, was here the worst possible." Confirming Alexander's observations, military historian Edward Bonekemper III notes that Ewell's poor location contributed greatly to the Army of Northern Virginia's inferior position as a whole in comparison to the Federals' strong one by the morning of July 2: "They [the Federals] had superior numbers, an imposing defensive position, and the advantage of interior lines, which permitted them to move soldiers quickly to threatened points in their lines. Meade had twenty-seven thousand men per mile along a three-mile inverted-fishhook line, while Lee had ten thousand men per mile along a five-mile semi-circle. That disparity augured ill for Lee's army."[3]

Gary Gallagher has rightly discounted Jubal Early's postwar allegations that during this 6 p.m. meeting with Lee the commanding general vocally expressed concern in entrusting Longstreet with a July 2 attack. Gallagher maintains that "This assertion, with its claim of precise accuracy nearly fifteen years after the alleged quotation was uttered, reeks of Lost Cause special pleading and lacks support from evidence closer to the event." However, Gallagher then infers that Lee's "facial expression may well have indicated as much [concern] to Early and others." It is unclear how Gallagher knows about Lee's facial expression. The issue is Early's statement that Lee said he had lost confidence in his Warhorse, a statement Gallagher rejects. Furthermore, Lee had many reasons to be frustrated that evening, least of which was Longstreet's ability to lead an attack the next day.[4]

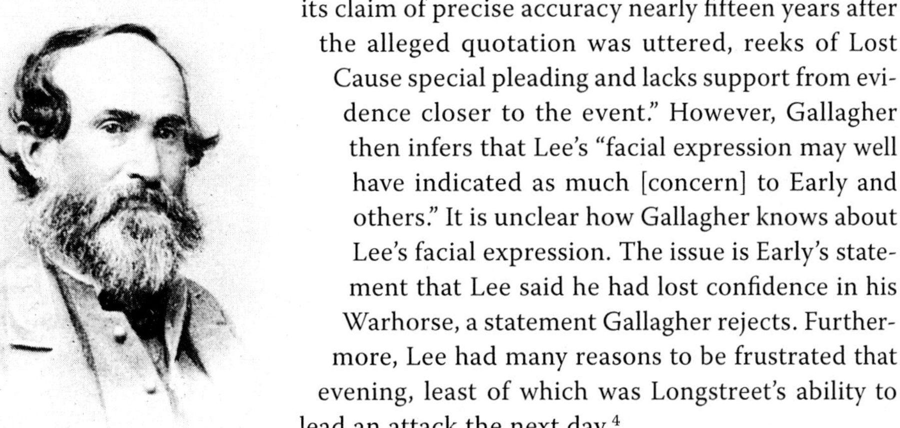

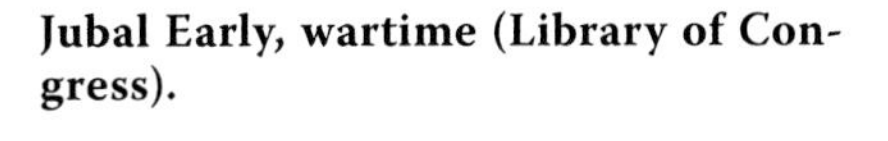

Jubal Early, wartime (Library of Congress).

Later in the evening of July 1, still fretting about his left, Lee changed his mind and sent a staff officer, Colonel Charles Marshall, to inform Ewell of his decision to move the Second Corps around to the right. Ewell again consulted with Rodes and Early and personally rode to Lee's headquarters to argue the directive. Once more, a deliberation ensued regarding a possible attack from Ewell's front and the merit of swinging around to the right. At this second meeting, Ewell informed Lee he thought the army had an opportunity against Culp's Hill—a feature that "commanded their [the Federals'] position and made it untenable"—and had earlier ordered Johnson's division to seize it, if unoccupied. Lee apparently acquiesced; however, when Ewell returned to his front and checked on Johnson for the first time since sunset, he found that his division commander had been inactive, failing to carry out orders issued five hours earlier to capture Culp's Hill if no Federals were present. Johnson finally sent out a reconnaissance party after midnight to see if this hill was occupied, but near the crest they ran into gunfire from Federal Brigadier General Lysander Cutler's First Corps regiment, the 7th Indiana. The reconnaissance party suffered a few casualties and withdrew. The Federals had occupied Culp's Hill, and as a result, the bungled effort was dropped for now.[5]

Ultimately, in these late night encounters with Lee, the Second Corps officers seemed to agree with Longstreet's earlier statements to Lee regarding the vulnerability of the Federal left: "His [Meade] weak point seemed to be his left, that we might threaten it if we intended to maneuver, or attack it if we determined upon a battle." The First Corps chief believed the whole army maneuvering to a strong position beyond the Army of the Potomac's left flank or executing a wide-ranging flank attack with multi-corps support against its left were the Confederates' best options if Lee persisted in his desire to fight at Gettysburg. Lee's acquiescence in letting Ewell remain north of Cemetery Hill, even while obviously very uncertain about the prudence of that decision, further demonstrated Lee's ambivalence toward his main objective at Gettysburg and the best way forward in accomplishing it. His consistent contemplation on moving Ewell's corps around to the right indicates Lee may have had Longstreet's suggestions in mind for drawing off the Federal left to get between them and Washington D.C., or to execute a massive flank attack with Longstreet's two divisions of Hood and McLaws spearheading the assault, with two additional corps in support.[6]

Historian Jeffry Wert thinks otherwise, wholly believing Lee never considered Longstreet's July 1 proposal to move off the Federal left and had ample reason not to do so that evening. "Longstreet's proposal of a vague flank movement was impractical, and Lee rightly dismissed it at the time. Without Stuart's cavalry, he could not agree to a movement into the unknown," Wert argues. Yet, Lee's multiple meetings with Ewell and Second Corps division commanders and staff that evening, where he suggested moving a third of the army to the right indicates otherwise. Was Lee fully aware of the Confederate left's poor position north of Cemetery Hill? Did he consider executing a turning movement on the right, in line with Longstreet's earlier proposal? Lee's conversation that evening with another of Ewell's aides, George Campbell Brown, implies as much when he told the aide to inform Ewell "not to become so much involved as to be unable readily to extricate his troops.... I have not decided to fight here and may probably draw off my right flank ... so as to get between the enemy & Washington & Baltimore, & force them to attack us in position." Wert's argument that Lee was hampered in his movements without Stuart is certainly a valid point; however, it begs to question why Lee would seriously contemplate extricating an entire corps from its position north of Cemetery Hill in the dark, overnight hours without Stuart. Even Stuart's absence did not seem to deter Lee from considering such a complex move.[7]

Gary Gallagher contends that as Lee settled in for the evening at his headquarters, he "spent a long night working out details for the next day's fighting," and that "lack of enthusiasm among his subordinates for continuing the tactical offensive must have grated on him." Considering that Longstreet was the only subordinate who expressed reservations about continuing the tactical offensive, Gallagher's statement seems aimed at the First Corps commander. In a response to Longstreet's 1883 articles on the Battle of Gettysburg, Colonel William Allan, the Second Corps staff officer who interviewed Lee after the war and who was a great admirer of the commanding general, was one of those individuals who initially perpetuated this myth of Lee working frantically throughout the night to iron out all the intricate details for an early morning attack on Meade's army. Allan wrote confidently of Lee, "On the night of the 1st (not on the forenoon of the 2d, as General Longstreet has it) he decided, after a conference with Ewell and his division commanders, to make the attack early next day from his right with Longstreet's two divisions that were within reach, this attack to be supported by Hill and Ewell."[8]

Allan believed that accounts from other Lost Cause writers and members of the anti–Longstreet group, "Generals Fitz Lee, Pendleton, Early, Wilcox, and many others" confirmed his opinion that during the overnight hours of July 1, Lee had definitively decided that he would attack early the next day with Longstreet from his right, and the other two corps would provide the supporting role. In short, Allan believed in the "sunrise attack" theory, or that Lee had expected Longstreet to execute an early morning attack. One of the names Allan mentioned was Cadmus Wilcox, who concluded similarly on this issue, "To have renewed the battle at the earliest possible hour the next day was what as a military man he [Lee] should have done.... Without personal knowledge in the matter, I am constrained to believe that as it was General Lee's purpose to renew the battle early the next morning, he did issue orders to that effect." Wilcox admitted that he possessed little knowledge on the matter, but unsurprisingly gave Lee the benefit of the doubt in being "a military man" so, naturally, he concluded the commanding general must have issued orders to attack early on July 2. Wilcox never saw fit to delineate with any degree of specificity as to how Lee wished Longstreet to renew the Confederate attack the following morning, and his argument seems to unwind upon reading his succeeding paragraph, which discussed how during the morning hours, not the night before, it was "determined to make the attack, on the right and with Longstreet."[9]

Historians subsequently perpetuated these falsehoods well into the twentieth century. In his four-volume *R.E. Lee* published in 1934 and 1935, Douglas Southall Freeman held that Lee provided Longstreet with no "positive order to attack at any particular point the next morning." However, he also contended that "Longstreet must have known that Lee wished the First Corps brought up as rapidly as possible." Freeman then advanced a series of conclusions of dubious credibility, namely that "Lee intended to attack as soon as it [the First Corps] arrived," that he made this plan completely apparent in-person to Longstreet sometime during the overnight hours, and that "toward midnight" he had specifically instructed Ewell to be ready to attack simultaneously with Longstreet in the morning, but not until "he heard Longstreet's guns open."[10]

On the contrary, Lee spent the night not frittering away time on tactical details, but rather trying to decide more generally where he should initiate an attack for the next day's fight, obsessing over Ewell's position, and fretting about Stuart's whereabouts. Harry Pfanz, a former Chief Historian for Gettysburg National Military Park, wrote accurately about Lee on the night of July 1, contending that "Although Lee was determined to attack the next day, he seemed undecided still about how that attack should be made." Lee spoke with his secretary, Colonel Armistead Long, and continued to show the ambivalence that had plagued his actions and decisions for the entire day. "Colonel Long," Lee pondered, "do you think we had better attack without the cavalry? If we do, we will not, if successful, be able to reap the fruits of victory." Stuart's absence was still front and center in Lee's mind, just ahead of his fixation on Ewell's poor position. Right before Lee met with Ewell for the second time that evening at his headquarters, the General had sent a group of about 10 men led by James D. Watters to find his chief cavalry commander. They carried sealed, written orders directing Stuart to rejoin Lee and the army immediately. Lee did not want to grope forward in the dark for the next day's actions, as he had on July 1, and he would especially require Stuart's services if he intended to deliver a more complex and coordinated offensive action against the strong Federal position.[11]

* * *

Longstreet succinctly and accurately described where Lee left him on the night of July 1. "When I left General Lee on the night of the 1st," he recalled, "I believed that he had made up his mind to attack, but was confident that he had not yet determined as to when the attack should be made." Lee's Warhorse then rode back to his two division's encampment at Marsh Creek, with the troops continuing to filter in past midnight. Longstreet was aware Lee wanted to stay at Gettysburg and attack the Federal position, but he had received neither additional nor more specific clarifying orders during the overnight hours. He stated clearly, "On the night of the 1st I left him without any orders at all." E.P. Alexander confirmed Longstreet's recollection, writing succinctly, "No orders whatever were given Longstreet that night." Even so, recognizing some kind of action would take place the next day, Longstreet instructed George Pickett's division in Chambersburg and Evander Law's brigade of Hood's division in New Guilford to begin their march at once to Gettysburg.[12]

Douglas Southall Freeman described what he believed to be Longstreet's state of mind on the evening of July 1: saying he "was eating his heart away in sullen resentment that Lee had rejected his long-cherished plan of a strategic offensive and a tactical defensive." Freeman also expressed his opinion that Longstreet had already determined to obstruct Lee's July 2 offensive plans: "When Old Pete left army headquarters late in the evening, he was sure of Lee's intention to attack.... For his part, Longstreet was determined to prevent, if he could, an attack he believed to be unwise." Freeman's prejudice toward Longstreet was palpable in these accounts and in many others, where he often downplayed Longstreet's contributions and amplified either Stonewall Jackson's or Lee's. Freeman often portrayed Longstreet as overly ambitious, constantly seeking independent command, slow, moody, and prone to sulking (hence why, according to Freeman, Lee always felt compelled to camp near Longstreet). The Virginia-born historian also consistently portrayed Jackson as Lee's senior, principal, and most trusted lieutenant, a trend that continues to this day in many Civil War publications. Freeman's characterization of Longstreet in this manner became the historical norm in the early to mid-twentieth century. Freeman, more than anyone else, shaped and influenced not only the content, but the tone of subsequent critical examinations of Longstreet's actions at Gettysburg for decades to come, effectively serving as the bridge between the postwar anti–Longstreet group's myths and exaggerations and many modern historians' continued perpetuation of those exaggerations.[13]

More realistically, and less dramatically, on the evening of July 1, Longstreet, like Lee, did feel uneasy, albeit for different reasons than the commanding general. Dr. Dorsey Cullen, the First Corps medical director wrote to Longstreet after the war and remembered that with respect to the first day's successes, the First Corps commander had not shared the "same cheerful view of it that I did and presently you remarked that it would have been better had we not fought than to have left undone what we did." Cullen further recalled Longstreet commenting on the strong Federal position "that it would take the whole army to drive them from [it], and then at a great sacrifice." Lieutenant Colonel Arthur Fremantle, a British army officer who observed the battle from the Confederate perspective and encamped with the First Corps throughout the contest wrote of Longstreet, "At supper this evening, General Longstreet spoke of the enemy's position as being 'very formidable.' He also said that they would doubtless intrench [*sic*] themselves strongly during the night." Longstreet's comments were most likely spoken with Lee's "If the enemy is there, I will attack him" statement in mind, and they plainly indicate he remained unimpressed with the idea of employing the tactical aggressive against a stronger and better reinforced Federal position the next day. The First Corps commander further and even more importantly recognized that the realities of the Federal's defensive position predestined that the Confederates could only win a "fruitless victory" at best.[14]

> If we had made the move around the Federal left, and taken a strong position, we should have dislodged Meade without a single blow; but even if we had been successful at Gettysburg, and had driven the Federals out of their stronghold, we should have won a fruitless victory, and returned to Virginia conquered victors. The ground they occupied would have been worth no more to us than the ground we were on. What we needed was a battle that would give us decided fruits, not ground that was of no value.[15]

In another account, Longstreet wrote similarly about his belief "that, even if we carried the heights in front of us, and drove Meade out, we should be so badly crippled that we could not reap the fruits of victory," and further that "the heights of Gettysburg were, in themselves, of no more importance to us than the ground we then occupied, and that the mere possession of the ground was not worth a hundred men to us." In short, Longstreet later summed up in simple terms what he was trying to tell Lee on the evening of July 1: "That Meade's army, not its position, was our objective." Captain Justus Scheibert also echoed Longstreet's sentiments about the Confederate army's goal being a victory that proved strategically and politically fruitful, not just a victory with great loss of life. "It probably would have been possible to win a victory after heavy sacrifices with a strong concentration of all corps, but the main purpose, the conquest of the North, and thereby the forcing of peace, would have been unrealized," Scheibert said. The Captain then quoted some of Lee's own sentiments on this topic, sentiments that would probably have fallen on deaf ears had anyone said them to Lee on the evening of July 1. "'I cannot sacrifice one more man without decisive results.... My soldiers are too valuable for that. It is peace for which we are fighting!'" Lee allegedly told Scheibert. Indeed, the difference between Lee's and Longstreet's mindset on the evening of July 1, a difference that would continue throughout the remainder of the battle, was

Longstreet thought "a battle that would give us decided fruits" was still possible by way of maneuvering the army to a strong defensive position to receive a Federal attack, while looking for a tactical opportunity to execute a counterstroke. Conversely, Lee believed he had to fight some kind of offensive battle at Gettysburg despite the palpable indecision he had shown against the Cemetery Hill position on the evening of July 1 and with the continued absence of Stuart. Lee's subsequent immovable resolve demonstrated his determination to do just that for two more bloody days.[16]

6

The Seething Disagreement and Apparent Apathy That Weren't

"No, General, I wish it placed just perpendicular to that"
—Robert E. Lee to James Longstreet

Longstreet was up early on the morning of July 2; sometime around 3 a.m. "The stars were shining brightly ... when I reported at General Lee's head-quarters and asked for orders," he recollected. In Douglas Southall Freeman's first major historical narrative, *R.E. Lee*, he alleged that when Longstreet joined Lee the latter was expecting the First Corps divisions to be forming for an attack "along the slope from which they were to advance." Freeman inaccurately continued in dramatic fashion: "But they were not there, not a man of them. Was the opportunity to be lost because of Longstreet's slowness?" Clifford Dowdey contended that as Longstreet rode up to Lee he possessed a "strangely disturbed mind" and was suffering from an "inner agitation over the burst bubble of his dream of sharing a partnership with Lee," which "showed in his impassive, heavily bearded face." In Dowdey's conception of events, Longstreet was "pondering ways of bringing Lee around to his own preferred plan of action." In popular historians David Schultz and Scott Mingus' more recent study of the July 2 battle, they initially perpetuate, albeit less emotionally, these same vague conjectures: "It is reasonable to assume he [Lee] believed Longstreet would be up and moving his divisions before dawn, in time to situate themselves for whatever was required as early as possible." Two sentences later, the authors then essentially invalidate their earlier statement, admitting that at the time Longstreet reported to Lee on the early morning of July 2, "Everything planned thus far relied upon vague information presented by men who had no real idea of what was transpiring east of the Emmitsburg Road." Still later, Schultz and Mingus expand on their second argument, underscoring the fact that "Lee knew the enemy was out there somewhere east of the Emmitsburg Road along Cemetery Ridge, but that was about the extent of his initial working knowledge of the tactical situation south of the Copse of Trees." They continue, "He [Lee] had no solid intelligence about the enemy's current forces on the field and their disposition," while indicating that the commanding general "lacked a solid grasp of the terrain and how many other Union forces were converging on his army."[1]

Realistically, upon reporting to Lee's headquarters—located in a shaded area on Seminary Ridge, near the Lutheran Seminary building—Longstreet again examined the

Federal Cemetery Ridge position and advised against attacking it, while for the second time proposing they perform a broad turning movement around Meade's left flank to get between the enemy and Washington, D.C., select a strong defensive position, and await a Federal attack. According to John Bell Hood, that morning Lee had "coat buttoned to the throat, sabre-belt buckled round the waste, and field glasses pending at his side.... He seemed full of hope, yet, at times, buried in deep thought." Though Lee had yet to decide on a plan of attack, or for that matter, from where he wanted to initiate an attack, it quickly became apparent to Longstreet that the commanding general was resolved to continue the tactical offensive at Gettysburg. Shortly after the battle, in a letter to his friend and Texas Senator Louis Wigfall, Longstreet explained he believed Lee's rationale at that moment was "due I think to our being under the impression that the enemy had not been able to get all his forces up. Being under this impression Gen. Lee thought it best to attack at once."[2]

Historians David Schultz and Scott Mingus claim, without any supporting evidence, that at that moment and throughout the morning hours "He [Longstreet] was adamant—some writers suggest insubordinate—in his open disagreement with Lee in front of others. After lengthy discussions, during which sketches were drawn in the dirt, Longstreet finally relented." Schultz and Mingus seem to suggest Longstreet was continually and openly challenging Lee and his tactical approach on the morning of July 2. In a 1996 issue of *Gettysburg Magazine*, Kevin O'Brien advanced this opinion outright, alleging that "Lt. Gen. James Longstreet argued all morning with Lee about the wisdom of any attack on the Union position at Gettysburg." Yet, the actual historical record shows only that after Longstreet realized very early on that Lee's mind was made up to attack the Federal position, he dropped the subject. The First Corps commander later remembered that he and Lee then "discussed the probable results," and "observed the position of the Federals, and got a general idea of the nature of the ground." The Federal "fishhook" battle line, then extending from Culp's Hill down to the northern base of a rocky hill later known as Little Round Top, again made a great impression on Longstreet, who recalled, "There was formed a field of tremendous power upon a convex curve, which gave the benefit of rapid concentration at any point or points. The natural defences had been improved during the night and early morning." Longstreet believed that the Confederate army was in no position to launch any sort of concerted and coordinated attack on such a strong position, writing, "The cavalry was not yet heard from. The line so extended and twisted about the rough ground that concentration at any point was not possible." Gilbert Moxley Sorrel later reaffirmed Longstreet's observations: "The situation on the morning of the 2nd was far from favorable to us. First of all, our position, comparable to the enemy's, was not good. It may be said to have been decidedly inferior. We were the outer line, he held the inner. We were the cord to the arc on which his heavy columns were massed."[3]

Most likely, within the first hour of Longstreet's arrival at Lee's headquarters, and with J.E.B. Stuart's continued absence still in mind, the commanding general issued two orders. The first order was to direct Captain Samuel Johnston, an engineer officer on Lee's staff, to reconnoiter and examine the Federal left. Longstreet also sent his own engineer, Major John J. Clarke, to accompany Johnston. This reconnoitering party likely set out around 4 a.m. The second order instructed Colonel Charles Venable of Lee's staff to ride to Ewell's corps to reexamine if that part of the army should be moved to the right and, if not, to determine if there was an opportunity to initiate the day's main assault from that position. Venable later described how "About sunrise on the 2d of July I was sent by General Lee to General Ewell to ask him what he thought of the advantages of an attack on the enemy from his position. (Colonel Marshall had been sent with a similar order on the night of the 1st.)" In short, both of these orders were given in hopes that the resultant intelligence would provide Lee with an answer as to where and how to attack the Union position.[4]

It is at this point on the morning of July 2 that First Corp division commander Lafayette McLaws often bursts onto the scene in most history books. After dealing with the slow bottleneck march toward Gettysburg on July 1, McLaws' division reached Marsh Creek, a few miles from Gettysburg, toward the midnight hour. His and Hood's division resumed their march toward the battlefield before dawn, with Hood reaching the field around sunrise and McLaws around 8:30 a.m. In McLaws' postwar account about Gettysburg, he described the sequence of events, writing, "The march was continued at a very early hour, and my command reached the hill overlooking Gettysburg early in the morning. Just after I arrived General Lee sent for me ... and I went at once and reported." McLaws recollected how he found Lee "sitting on a fallen tree with a map beside him." According to the division commander, Lee then pointed out a position on the map to McLaws and said "I wish you to get there if possible without being seen by the enemy." As if Lee knew at that moment exactly where he wanted a division of his army placed, McLaws described the nature and location of that position: "The place he pointed out was about the one I afterwards went to, and the line he marked out on the map for me to occupy was one perpendicular to the Emmitsburg Road." Lee allegedly then asked McLaws "Can you get there?" To which the division commander replied that he "knew of nothing to prevent me," but wanted to "go in advance and reconnoiter." Most curiously, McLaws then threw a wrench in his narrative. In response to his reconnoiter request, he remembered Lee saying, "Major Johnston, of my staff, has been ordered to reconnoiter the ground, and I expect he is about ready." McLaws allegedly replied, "I will go with him."[5]

Lafayette McLaws, wartime (Library of Congress).

With the exception of a few historians, many have accepted and utilized McLaws' sequence of events without question and as incontrovertible gospel. The truth of the matter is that McLaws' account should be questioned. In the first place, engineers Johnston and Clarke left on their reconnaissance mission sometime around 4 a.m., and McLaws was nowhere near General Lee at that time. McLaws related as much earlier in his narrative. "Some time after my arrival [at Marsh Creek] I received orders from General Longstreet to continue the march at four a.m., but the order was afterwards countermanded, with directions not to leave until sunrise," he remembered. It has been established that Johnston and Clarke returned sometime between 7 and 8 a.m., and if McLaws set out for Gettysburg at sunrise, it stands to reason that he did not meet with Lee until after the reconnaissance party had returned. Furthermore, if we are to believe McLaws' notion that Lee pointed to specific places on a map and identified exactly how he wanted the division commander to place his men, common sense dictates Lee had already received Johnston's intelligence report and felt confident enough in his understanding of the ground to relate where he wanted McLaws placed. Therefore, McLaws' recollection of Lee stating that Johnston was then "about ready" to reconnoiter, and his reply that he would like to "go with him," were both either misremembered or disingenuous. A more accurate arrival time for McLaws would be sometime around 8:30 a.m., after Johnston returned, not before.[6]

Part two of McLaws' narrative picks up after he made his confusing request to accompany Johnston on a reconnaissance mission that had already been completed. McLaws then recalled that Longstreet denied his reconnaissance request, and two subsequent requests (one to have McLaws' engineer Lieutenant Thomas Montcuve join Johnston), saying, "No, sir, I do not wish you to leave your division." Considering that Johnston and Clarke were in fact not just starting out, but had returned from their reconnaissance, Longstreet's denials were reasonable since Major Clarke had already accompanied the scouting party as First Corps representative, and undoubtedly reported those details to him. In any case, McLaws claimed that soon thereafter he "reconnoitered myself for my own information," despite Longstreet's reservations. McLaws also remembered that during his morning meeting with Lee, Longstreet had also pointed to the map and recommended a different placement for the division than Lee had directed, saying "I wish your division placed so." McLaws recalled Longstreet tracing a position with his finger that was parallel to the Emmitsburg Road, which prompted Lee to respond, according to McLaws, "No, General, I wish it placed just perpendicular to that." Many historians have contended that Lee and Longstreet's disagreement on the tactical placement of McLaws' division represented the outward manifestation of a larger disagreement about general tactics for the day's attack. They insinuate definitively that Longstreet disagreed with Lee over McLaws' placement because he was still smarting over Lee's choice to pursue the tactical aggressive against the strong Federal position. They contend that Longstreet was acting in a petulant way and seizing any opportunity to disrupt Lee's plans. These historians should consider the possibility that Longstreet and Lee simply disagreed on where to place McLaws' division based on their knowledge of the ground as reported by engineers Johnston and Clarke. McLaws' statement that "General Longstreet appeared as if he was irritated and annoyed" at that moment more likely resulted from Lee's tactical meddling in his division's placement. As those same historians have abundantly pointed out over the decades, Lee typically left such tactical decisions to his corps commanders, and so they should be the first to agree that Longstreet would have had reason to be somewhat miffed. With Longstreet on-hand and present, it would have been very unusual behavior for Lee to reach down past the corps commander and deal directly with a division-level officer.[7]

Lee's uncharacteristic behavior did not end there, nor go unnoticed by numerous people that morning. Captain Justus Scheibert of the Prussian Royal Engineers, who was present on Seminary Ridge as an observer, perceived "Lee was not at his ease, but was riding to and fro, frequently changing his position, making anxious inquiries here and there, and looking care-worn.... This uneasiness ... was contagious to the army, as will appear from the reports of Longstreet, Hood, Heth, and others, and as also appeared to me from the peep I had of the battlefield." In writing to Longstreet after the war, First Corps division commander John Bell Hood remembered that Lee "walked up and down in the shade of large trees near us, halting now and then to observe the enemy. He seemed full of hope, yet at times, buried in deep thought.... General Lee was seemingly anxious you should attack that morning." Hood based this last assertion on Lee's seemingly paranoid statement to the division commander sometime that morning, "The enemy is here. If we don't whip him, he will whip us." Hood also recalled that Longstreet had even said to him sometime that morning, "The General is a little nervous this morning; he wishes me to attack; I do not wish to do so without Pickett. I never like to go into battle with one boot off." Longstreet later described Lee's nervous behavior as a "subdued excitement, which occasionally took possession of him when 'the hunt was up,' and threatened his superb equipoise." The potential causes for Lee's uncharacteristic behavior that morning were clearly numerous, ranging first and foremost from the continued absence of J.E.B. Stuart's cavalry, along with a lack of timely and accurate intelligence about the Federal position, to his prolonged indecision about what to do with Ewell's corps, and even to allegations he was suffering from frequent bouts of diarrhea.[8]

Longstreet critics will argue that Lee was most bothered and irritated by Longstreet. They allege that he had all-of-the-sudden lost confidence in his Warhorse's ability to carry out whatever attack plan he had in mind and was perturbed at his corps commander's repeated petition to maneuver the army around the Federal left. Subscribing to this view, Edwin Coddington wrote that along with "the loss of Jackson and the absence of Stuart, and the uncertainty about Meade's intentions.... Much of Lee's uneasiness undoubtedly rose from Longstreet's rather truculent attitude and obvious unwillingness to attack." Realistically, Coddington would only have been able to support two of these assertions with actual evidence, those being Stuart's absence and his uncertainty about Meade's intentions. There remains absolutely no proof beyond conjecture that Lee was uneasy on the morning of July 2 because of "the loss of Jackson" or because of Longstreet's alleged "truculent attitude and obvious unwillingness to attack." Yet, Coddington continued in this vein to hold that Longstreet displayed "violent objections to his [Lee's] proposals," which the historian believed "must have come as a shocking surprise" to the commanding general. Coddington charged that Lee was "disturbed" by Longstreet's alleged "violent objections"; however, he "nevertheless kept his temper." The uncorroborated and misleading residue of both the postwar Lost Cause movement and the anti–Longstreet group is easily observable in Coddington's narrative. Similarly, Robert Krick claims that some of Longstreet's "series of conferences with Lee" on July 2 were "turbulent," a word that misleadingly suggests anger, chaos, and confusion. Despite the fact that most historians admit that the Confederate army's path to attack readiness on July 2 was complex and necessarily protracted throughout the morning hours, Krick believes that "Longstreet faced the simple fact that he must move to the right and attack." He then visualizes Longstreet as "accept[ing] that responsibility in the poorest possible grace." It is interesting and curious that Krick decides to employ the term "responsibility" instead of "order." Indeed, it would not have been Longstreet's responsibility to, in Krick's terms, "move to the right and attack," until Lee ordered it so. He further suggests it is reasonable to support all these claims using a description of Longstreet made by First Corps aide Major Thomas Goree from December 1861. Amazingly, Krick actually haphazardly contends that because Goree once observed of Longstreet when "something has not gone to suit him ... [he] merely looks grim," this observation essentially proves Longstreet was acting in just such a manner on July 2, and his supposed "grimness" was foremost to blame for any and all delay leading up to the Confederate attack.[9]

Another historian, Stephen Sears, has even said Lee and Longstreet's working relationship had by the morning hours of July 2 become consumed by "what was now a seething disagreement"; however, this contention is little more than an exaggeration supported by one quote uttered in Moxley Sorrel's postwar memoirs. Referring to Longstreet's postwar accounts of the battle, Sorrel wrote, "We can discover that [Longstreet] did not want to fight on the ground or on the plan adopted by the General-in-Chief. As Longstreet was not to be made willing and Lee refused to change or could not change, the former failed to conceal some anger. There was apparent apathy in his movements. They lacked the fire and point of his usual bearing on the battlefield." When historians use this quote in their narratives they never seem to point out exactly where Sorrel placed this observation in his own account. Even though the staff officer presented this now-infamous quote at the very beginning of his chapter on Gettysburg as a general observation, not in reference to any particular moment during the battle, historians always inject this comment in their sections about Longstreet's actions on the morning of July 2 as irrefutable proof that the corps commander was acting up.[10]

Historians have universally employed Sorrel's quote by itself without ever delving into the nature of the "apathy" to which the First Corps staff officer was referring or the timing of this demonstrated behavior. In all actuality, Sorrel initially followed up his quote rather lamely and vaguely, writing, "His [Longstreet's] plan may have been better than Lee's, but it was too late to alter them with the troops ready to open fire on each other"; however, later in the chapter, Sorrel hinted at when he observed this "apparent apathy." He wrote, "We were too late on our right. An attack, powerful indeed, at 4 p.m. was quite different from the commanding General's expectation of one in the forenoon." He recollected that the attack was "long-deferred," but admitted it "was done in smashing style by McLaws's and Hood's divisions and a few of Hill's troops, Longstreet personally leading the attack with splendid effect." Likewise, Sorrel judged that "We gained ground rapidly and almost carried Round Top, but the morning delay was fatal. It had been heavily reinforced while we were pottering around in sullen inactivity. Undoubtedly Lee's intention was to make the attack in the forenoon and support it with strong movements from Hill and Ewell." Therefore, we see here that Sorrel uttered absolutely no criticism of Longstreet's actions once the battle commenced in the afternoon hours, but rather described them as "smashing" and "splendid." Instead, Sorrel relegated his censure about "apathy" and "sullen inactivity" to his own mistaken belief that his Chief had delayed Lee's intention of launching a morning attack.[11]

In short, Sorrel's comments were fueled by inaccurate details about what actually happened on the Confederate side to prevent the execution of a morning attack on

July 2. And since his "apparent apathy" quote was uttered with these erroneous details in mind, it should hold little water. Lee may have wanted to attack on the morning of July 2, but at no time was he ready to deliver an attack. As we will see, Lee was hampered by numerous factors: J.E.B. Stuart's absence, multiple reconnaissance missions, indecision about what role Ewell's corps would play in the day's actions, Anderson's division of Hill's corps (on Longstreet's left) not fully in position until 12 noon, and Lee giving his express consent to wait for Law's brigade to join Hood's division. All these events, and others, prior to 12 noon happened under the commanding general's eye and were therefore stamped with his approval. In discussing Lee's temperament on the morning of July 2, E.P. Alexander did not "get the impression that General Lee thought there was any unnecessary delay going on," and the young artillerist likely had this intuition because, in reality, Lee and Longstreet were moving as quickly as events and circumstances allowed.[12]

7

Intelligence Woes, Indecision and an Unfortunate Position Re-Reconsidered

"There was little to be hoped for from any immediate attack then possible"
—E.P. Alexander

Before Lee spoke with McLaws sometime between 7 and 9 a.m., he had received an encouraging, albeit inaccurate intelligence report from Captain Johnston upon his return from examining the Federal left. Johnston later held that when he rode up he found, "Generals Lee, Longstreet, and A.P. Hill sitting on a log near the seminary" and then "[Lee] looked up, saw me and at once called me to him, and on the map which he was holding I sketched the route over which I had reconnoitered." In intimating where he had been and what he had seen, Johnston "was not interrupted" and informed "the three Generals" that he had only run into "three or four Union cavalrymen," had "gotten up on the slopes where I had a commanding view, then rode along the base of round top," and claimed to have seen no significant body of Federal troops anywhere south of Cemetery Hill. Lee "was surprised" at Johnston's "getting so far" to "the extreme right" and, according to Johnston, while pointing to Little Round Top on the map, asked "'did you get there?" Johnston "assured him I did."[1]

Contrary to Douglas Southall Freeman's contention that "the early morning reconnaissance of Captain S.R. Johnston was accurate—so far as he went," Johnston's report was a complete and utter wash. The captain's mistaken claim that there were no Federal troops south of Cemetery Hill was extremely significant in shaping Lee's inaccurate view of the Union position. What is clear is that at the time Johnston conducted his reconnaissance several Federal units were indeed south of Cemetery Hill. Buford's Federal cavalry was posted at the Sherfy Peach Orchard along the Emmitsburg Road. Two regiments of General John Geary's division occupied the north face of Little Round Top from late on July 1 until the early morning of July 2, before being siphoned off to Culp's Hill. General Daniel Sickles' Federal Third Corps arrived throughout the morning hours via the Emmitsburg Road, taking up position on the southern end of Cemetery Ridge. In addition, General Winfield Scott Hancock's Federal Second Corps marched up the Taneytown Road behind Little and Big Round Top, taking up position between Sickles' Corps and Cemetery Hill. Also by 9 a.m., two Federal Fifth Corps divisions were located on the Granite Schoolhouse Lane, a small roadway that linked the Baltimore Pike and Taneytown Road, just 1100 yards behind Sickles' line on Cemetery Ridge. There was certainly no dearth of Federal activity south of Cemetery Hill during the morning hours of July 2; however, Johnston's erroneous report to Lee induced the belief that the Union left ended on Cemetery Hill and was vulnerable to flank attack. In discussing Federal troop activity on the "southern stretches of Cemetery Ridge," Douglas Southall Freeman stated that "By the time McLaws and Hood arrived, that part of the ridge was held by strong, well-placed troops." Because of this fact, Freeman actually admitted "much of the criticism of Longstreet evaporates."[2]

Johnston's reconnaissance information coincided with what others had been telling Lee since the previous evening. Colonel Armistead Long of Lee's staff alleged he told Lee during the night, "At present only two or three corps of the enemy are up, and it seems best to attack before they are greatly strengthened." Long's counsel and Johnston's reconnaissance report proved extremely misleading, however, and as E.P. Alexander noted, by 8 a.m. on July 2, during the time of Johnston's intelligence mission, "practically the whole of both armies was upon the field except Pickett's division and Law's brigade of the Confederates, and the 6th Corps of the Federals." In short, throughout the morning hours of July 2, Lee had fashioned an attack plan based on erroneous intelligence.[3]

Brigadier General William Pendleton, Lee's Chief of Artillery, claimed in his official battle report that he accompanied Johnston during the morning reconnaissance, but soon after its conclusion, "Returned to an elevated point on the Fairfield road, which furnished a very extensive view, and dispatched messengers to General Longstreet and the commanding general. Between this point and the Emmitsburg road, the enemy's cavalry were seen in considerable force, and, moving up along that road towards the enemy's main position, bodies of infantry and artillery, accompanied by their trains." Pendleton was seeing Sickles' Corps continue to file into their Cemetery Ridge position just north of Little Round Top. Charles K. Graham's Federal Third Corps brigade did not finish their march to Gettysburg until sometime around 9 a.m. Pendleton's observations contrasted sharply with what Johnston had earlier reported, namely that there were no Federal troops south of Cemetery Hill; however, it appears that the Artillery Chief never presented this information to Lee and Longstreet.[4]

Soon after Pendleton observed the enemy filing along the Emmitsburg Road toward Cemetery Ridge, the First Corps artillerist E.P. Alexander was arriving at the front. He later recollected that he was about a mile away from Seminary Ridge at 9 a.m. when Colonel James Walton, Longstreet's Chief of Artillery, rode ahead to report the reserve artillery's presence on the field, comprised of the Washington Artillery and Alexander's battalion. Alexander recalled that about a half hour later, Walton returned and said that Longstreet wished to see him. Arriving on Seminary Ridge sometime between 9 and 10 a.m., Alexander found Lee, Longstreet, many other generals and staff officers, and large bodies of infantry nearby. "In Gen. Lee's presence," Alexander remembered, "Longstreet pointed out the enemy's position & said that we would attack his left flank." The First Corps commander directed Alexander to "take command of all the artillery on the field, for the attack," and to ride ahead, examine the ground, and then bring up his battalion. With that said, Longstreet cautioned Alexander, under orders from Lee, to be sure to remain unseen by the enemy "signal station whose flags," according to the artillerist, "we could see wig-wagging on Little Round Top." Reflecting years later on that morning, Alexander described how futile he believed Lee's attack plan to be: "When, at nine o'clock, the arrival of Longstreet's reserve artillery was reported, it must be admitted that there was little to be hoped for from any immediate attack then possible. Lee had however decided to make one." Even so, now having orders from Longstreet, Alexander recollected that within 10 minutes' time he was "off to examine all roads leading to the right & front, & get an understanding of the enemy's position & how and where we could best get at it."[5]

Around this time, Lee once again began fretting about his other flank, the Second Corps' position, and from where the main attack should commence. "Not fully appreciating the strength of the enemy's position, and misled by the hope that a large fraction of the Federal army was out of reach, Lee had determined to strike, and only hesitated as to the best point of attack," E.P. Alexander later wrote of Lee's indecision on the morning of the 2nd. Indeed, Lee had sent Colonel Charles Venable around 7 a.m. "to confer with the commander of the Second Corp as to opportunity to make battle by his left" or to move the corps around to the Confederate right, but had yet to hear back from his staff officer. Therefore, Lee decided to ride to Ewell's position himself. "He was still in doubt whether it would be better to move to his far-off right," Longstreet later asserted. Venable confirmed the accuracy of Longstreet's claim in a postwar letter to the General, writing, "General Lee came himself to General Ewell's lines.... General Lee was explicit in saying that the question was whether he should move all the troops around on the right and attack on that side." Historian Harry Pfanz echoed Longstreet's statement, writing, "It seems unlikely that the plan for the day's assault had really matured at that time."[6]

On the contrary, Jeffry Wert criticizes Longstreet's actions at this juncture. Wert contends that when Lee rode over to Ewell's headquarters around 9 a.m., "Lee had not issued specific orders to Longstreet to begin the movement, but undoubtedly Longstreet understood that McLaws' and Hood's divisions and First Corps' artillery batteries would be involved with an assault along the Emmitsburg Road. Lee, too, undoubtedly expected Longstreet to begin preparations, if not begin the march, while he conferred with Ewell." Wert's critiques seem forced. Wert uses the word "undoubtedly," as if to say that he knows for certain that Longstreet completely understood Lee's attack plan by 9 a.m. He again employs the word "undoubtedly" when arguing that Lee expected Longstreet to initiate detailed preparations and even begin the march while he met with Ewell. Lafayette McLaws provided modern scholars with a critical recollection on this topic that is not quoted often. The First Corps division commander remembered that during his "brief interview" with Lee and Longstreet, the former "did not appear to be particularly anxious that Longstreet should occupy the left. He certainly was in no hurry for it.... My information at the time was that he was not decided positively as to the main point of attack." Indeed, Lee specifically rode over to the Confederate left to confer with Ewell about the possibilities of either moving his corps to the right or initiating the day's attack from their current position north of Cemetery Hill. In other words, Lee had not yet made up his mind about the general plan of attack for the day. Would the Second Corps remain where it was? Would Ewell or Longstreet initiate the attack? If Longstreet began the attack, how would Ewell provide support? Wert also neglects to mention that Law's brigade of Hood's division had not yet arrived by 9 a.m. and that numerous reconnaissance missions were ongoing until 1 p.m. to further clarify the contours of the Federal position and to find a way to march unseen by Federal signalmen.[7]

Over on the Confederate left, Lee met initially with Major General Isaac Trimble and then with Ewell, Venable, Long, and probably Early. Ewell again persuaded Lee to let the Second Corps remain where it was and advocated for the main attack to be made against Meade's left. Therefore, with that issue finally resolved, the commanding general gave the Second Corps commander his orders: "To make a simultaneous demonstration upon the enemy's right, to be converted into a real attack should opportunity offer." Lee then returned to the right of his battle line to issue Longstreet's orders.[8]

Years later, Armistead Long alleged that it was during this ride back to Longstreet's divisions that Lee appeared frustrated with his Warhorse and went so far as to express his disappointment openly with the staff officer, exclaiming "What *can* detain Longstreet? He ought to be in position now!" Douglas Southall Freeman carried Long's dubious recollection into the twentieth century, when claiming that "Lee was hoping that Longstreet would soon open the attack, and as the minutes passed in silence all along the front, he began to get restless.... The chances of a successful attack were fast slipping away." Edwin Coddington echoed Freeman, also expressing complete confidence in Long's recollections: "This account [Long's] was offered as evidence of Lee's impatience with the slow-moving Longstreet. Doubtless Lee was impatient not only with Longstreet himself...."[9]

In another equally dubious account, Long claimed that around 10 a.m., "General Lee's impatience became so urgent that he proceeded in-person to hasten the movement of Longstreet." In a confusing description of events, Long alleged that before Lee made it to Longstreet's corps he received "welcome tidings that Longstreet's troops were in motion." Long then claimed that Lee stopped, found a "convenient point," and "waited a reasonable time for Longstreet to reach his destination, and then set out to meet him, but, on arriving at the point of action, it was found that Longstreet was still absent." Simply put, Long's recollections show obvious Lost Cause fabrication, since Lee had by that time not issued Longstreet any orders.[10]

Another even more prolific Lost Cause writer, Jubal Early, who wrote with great vehemence against Longstreet in the postwar years made similar claims about Lee's supposed intentions on the morning of July 2. In one case, Early stated emphatically that "it was intended by General Lee that the attack from his right flank on the enemy's left should commence at a very early hour on the morning of the 2d." And yet it is clear that Long's and Early's recollections were born of agenda to defend Lee's decisions and actions at all costs by blaming Longstreet. As has been established, Lee never issued orders on the night of July 1 and spent the majority of the morning on July 2 gathering intelligence about the Federal position, while trying to decide where he should initiate an attack. Early was presented with this argument in the postwar years and the former division commander's reaction was surprising. "If that was the case," he wrote, "then he [Lee] exhibited a remarkable degree of indecision and vacillation, and the responsibility for the procrastination and delay that occurred must rest on him, and him alone." Then immediately, as if he had conceded his argument too much in a momentary slipup, Early reverted back to his defense of Lee: "There is one thing very certain, and that is that either General Lee or General Longstreet was responsible for the remarkable delay that took place in making the attack. I choose to believe that it was not General Lee, for if anyone knew the value of promptness and celerity of military movements, he did." The amount of evidence confirming Lee took considerable time on the morning of July 2 to formulate a full-bodied plan is colossal, but "choosing to believe" something else based on nothing but the general's accustomed military temperament was simply the way of the Lost Cause faction and anti–Longstreet group.[11]

Gary Gallagher has included Early's thoughts on Longstreet's July 2 actions in many of his writings about Gettysburg. Gallagher has sometimes framed Early's argument misleadingly for students of the war, writing in one instance that "Lee expected the attacks to begin at dawn, insisted Early (a charge Longstreet easily proved to be untrue—though Lee certainly wanted the attacks to start as early as possible)." Gallagher concedes that Early's view had no merit and that Longstreet was in the right, but then doubles back in vacillation to claim Lee "certainly" wanted to attack early. The fact is it does not matter if Lee intended or wanted to attack "as early as possible." The historical record shows that on the morning of July 2, Lee was not comfortable with issuing Longstreet an attack order until at least 11 a.m., after he had returned from Ewell's front.[12]

Gallagher also references E.P. Alexander when discussing this same topic, contending that "Lee bore a major portion of responsibility for the late opening of the attacks by Alexander's reading of the evidence." Indeed, like Early, Alexander also advanced the oft-familiar and ineffectual statement that "Gen. Lee much desired" for Longstreet's attack "to be made very much earlier." Yet unlike Early, Alexander did not simply cite Lee's predilection for audacity as proof that Longstreet must have been to blame, but instead proceeded to highlight the many justifiable reasons for delay. After all, Alexander asserted, Lee was there with Longstreet throughout most of the morning hours and was "apparently consenting to the situation from hour to hour." Helen Longstreet, the General's second wife who adamantly defended her husband's wartime record for years after his death, echoed Alexander's inclinations: "Matters on the morning of July 2 were not awaiting Longstreet's movements. All that long forenoon everything was still in the air, depending upon Lee's personal examinations and final decisions," and again, "At sunrise of the 2d, General Lee himself did not know where to attack. He did not know as late as ten or eleven o'clock. His mind was not fully made up until after he came back from Ewell's front ... and had made the final examination on the right." Even Douglas Southall Freeman who typically took every opportunity to cast Longstreet as the villain wrote on this subject, "Lee's one positive order was that delivered at 11 o'clock for Longstreet to attack."[13]

8

A Misconceived Attack Plan Set in Motion

"This was impossible until I occupied that road"
—Daniel Sickles

Once Lee arrived back near Seminary Ridge at 11 a.m., he had finally decided that Longstreet's two divisions of McLaws and Hood, supported by Anderson's division of Hill's corps (in Pickett's absence) would execute the day's main attack. "He ... informed me," Longstreet recalled, "that it would not do to have Ewell open the attack. He, finally, determined that I should make the main attack on the extreme right." For the first time on July 2, Lee issued Longstreet his orders. "I received instructions from the commanding general to move, with the portion of my command that was up, around to gain the Emmitsburg road, on the enemy's left," Longstreet wrote in his after-battle report. Upon completing the march, Hood's division was to be placed to the right of Anderson, and McLaws's division to the right of Hood, with McLaws opening the attack. Lee ordered Captain Johnston, who had headed the misleading early morning reconnaissance, to act as a guide for McLaws' and Hood's divisions during their march to the far Confederate right. Most especially, Lee wanted Johnston to escort the divisions along a route that would ensure they remain unseen by the enemy. Once placed, Lee believed that Longstreet's corps would be "partially enveloping the enemy's left, which he was to drive in." Other battle reports provide additional insight into Lee's initial plan against the Federal left. Richard Anderson wrote that Longstreet's "line would be in a direction nearly at right angles with mine; that he would assault the extreme left of the enemy and drive him toward Gettysburg." A.P. Hill stated that "Longstreet was to attack the left flank of the enemy, and sweep down his line." In a postwar letter to Longstreet after the war, John Bell Hood succinctly described Lee's general plan, writing that he was directed "to proceed to our extreme right, and attack up the Emmettsburg road..." and again, "The instructions I received were to place my division across the Emmettsburg road, form line of battle, and attack."[1]

In short, Longstreet was to execute a flank attack sweeping up the Emmitsburg Road toward the Federal left flank thought to be anchored on Cemetery Hill. To Longstreet's left, Anderson's division of Hill's corps was to "co-operate" with the First Corps divisions and "threaten the enemy's center, to prevent reinforcements being drawn to either wing." Ewell's corps was to initiate a "simultaneous demonstration upon

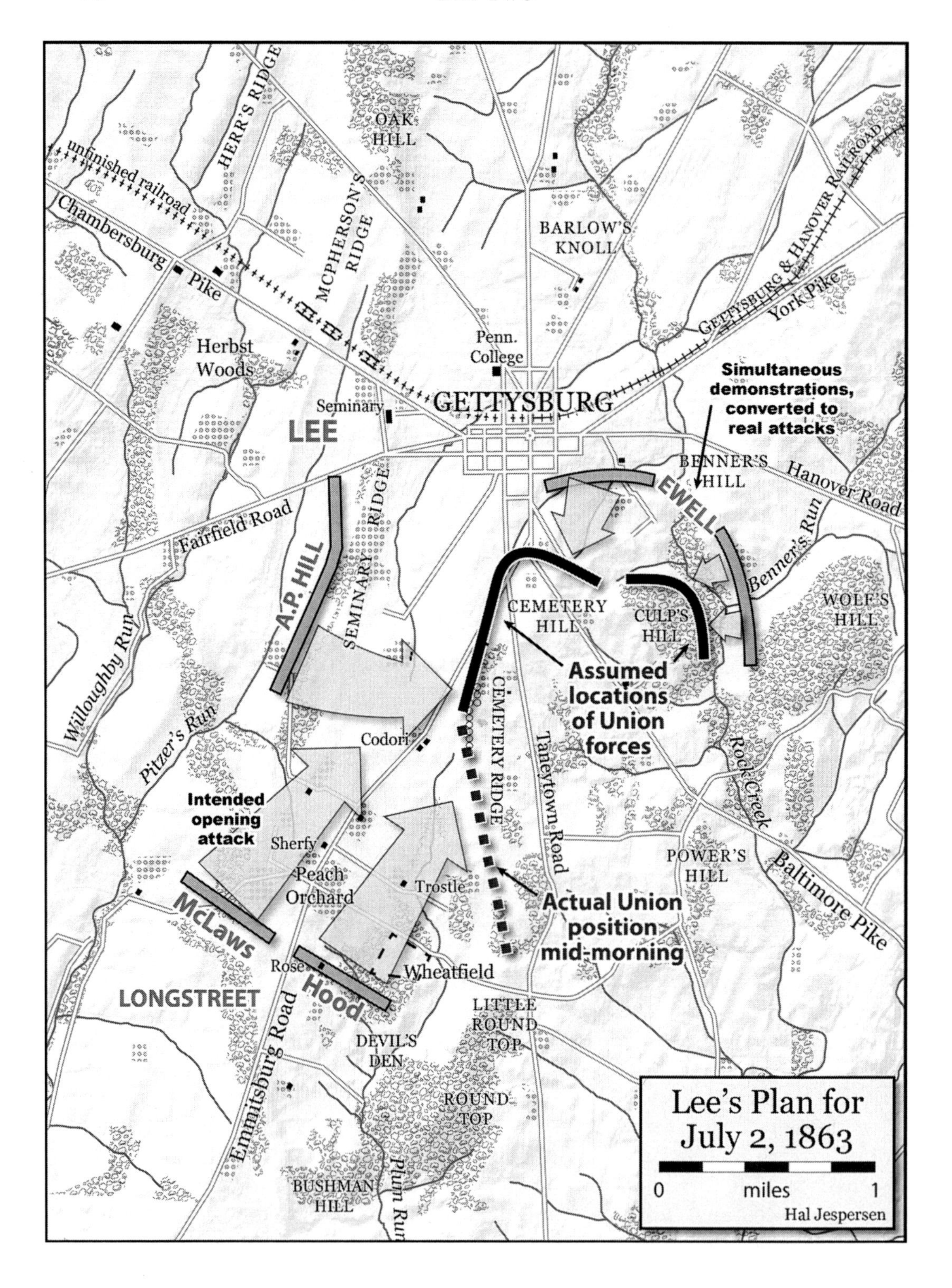

HERR'S RIDGE
OAK HILL
unfinished railroad
Chambersburg Pike
MCPHERSON'S RIDGE
BARLOW'S KNOLL
GETTYSBURG & HANOVER RAILROAD
York Pike
Herbst Woods
Penn. College
Seminary
GETTYSBURG
LEE
Simultaneous demonstrations, converted to real attacks
BENNER'S HILL
Hanover Road
EWELL
Fairfield Road
A.P. HILL
SEMINARY RIDGE
Benner's Run
CEMETERY HILL
CULP'S HILL
WOLF'S HILL
Willoughby Run
Assumed locations of Union forces
CEMETERY RIDGE
Taneytown Road
Codori
Pitzer's Run
Rock Creek
Intended opening attack
Sherfy
Peach Orchard
Trostle
POWER'S HILL
Actual Union position mid-morning
Baltimore Pike
McLaws
Rose
Wheatfield
Hood
LONGSTREET
LITTLE ROUND TOP
DEVIL'S DEN
Emmitsburg Road
ROUND TOP
BUSHMAN HILL
Plum Run
Lee's Plan for July 2, 1863
0 miles 1
Hal Jespersen

the enemy's right," transitioning to a "real attack should the opportunity offer." Of course, Ewell's actions, whether to be a "demonstration" or a "real attack," were designed to lock several Federal corps in place so Meade could not shift them against Longstreet.[2]

Hypothetically, if Longstreet had somehow found a way to attack between 9 a.m. and 3 p.m. on July 2, before Sickles' Federal Third Corps moved out to the Peach Orchard salient, his men, in attacking "up the Emmettsburg [*sic*] Road," would have actually been moving perpendicular with flank exposed to several Federal corps then positioned on Cemetery Ridge. Indeed, Lee's entire initial plan was one big misconception in that if Longstreet's divisions had formed "on the right of Hill" prior to Sickles' move, he would have "enveloped" nothing, and in executing an attack up the Emmitsburg Road would have "drove in" little but air. Only a few participants in the war and historians since have drawn attention to this reality. Longstreet alluded to this common sense flaw in Lee's original July 2 plan in his postwar writings. In addressing comments Walter Taylor made about "the manner in which General Lee would have fought" or attacked on July 2, Longstreet maintained, "He says that General Lee ordered that the column should go to the attack with its right flank exposed to the enveloping forces on the Federal left." Daniel Sickles, in his introduction to Helen Longstreet's book about her then-late husband, contended similarly that "The only order of battle announced by General Lee on July 2 of which there is any record was to assail my position on the Emmitsburg Road, turn my left flank (which he erroneously supposed to rest on the Peach-Orchard), and sweep the attack 'up the Emmitsburg Road.' This was impossible until I occupied that road.... This we have seen, was not done until towards three in the afternoon." In another instance, the Federal Third Corps commander declared that "These often repeated orders of General Lee to "attack up the Emmitsburg road" could not have been given until near three in the afternoon of July 2, because before that hour there was no Union line of battle on the Emmitsburg road." Yet, influenced by what his staff officers had been telling him since the previous evening and what Captain Johnston had reported that morning, Lee's initial assault plan was indeed to attack up the Emmitsburg Road, where realistically, there were no Federal troops until approximately 3 p.m. in the afternoon.[3]

* * *

Upon receiving orders to move around 11 a.m., Longstreet requested that Lee allow him to wait for the arrival of Brigadier General Evander Law's brigade of Hood's division before commencing the march. Lee consented to this delay of approximately 40 minutes. Law had set out for Gettysburg around 3 a.m.; his men setting a grueling pace to reach the battlefield by noon. In the years after the war, many Confederate participants in the battle and historians since have sought to criticize Longstreet for this request, with some stating that it was the last card he could have played to purposefully delay an attack he did not want to make. Douglas Southall Freeman believed that the sole reason Lee issued Longstreet a direct order at 11 a.m. was because "it was manifest Longstreet was endeavoring to delay." Further, on the topic of Law's men, Freeman never saw fit to mention the fact Lee had consented to Longstreet's request to wait for the brigade. Rather, in his opinion, Lee rode off to "make a further reconnaissance" after issuing his

11 a.m. orders, and then returned only to find "that officer [Longstreet] had seen fit to wait about forty minutes for Law's brigade to come up."[4]

Modern historian Robert Krick also believes that Longstreet purposefully delayed, writing, "Evander M. Law's brigade of Alabama troops, one of eight brigades scheduled for the march was not yet up. Longstreet insisted on waiting for its arrival." Krick suggests Longstreet was imprudent to request waiting for one more brigade to enlarge his force by one-eighth, as if another brigade would not make a difference in the strength of the First Corps attack, already inhibited by the absence of Pickett's division. Notably absent in Krick's analysis is Lee's complicity in the decision to wait for Law's brigade. Walter Taylor also omitted this fact when he wrote in the postwar years, "Fearing that his force was too weak to venture to the attack, *he [Longstreet] delayed* until Law's Brigade joined its division about noon on the 2d. In this, General Longstreet clearly admits that he assumed responsibility of postponing the execution of the orders of the commanding general." Similarly, Lost Cause partisan the Reverend John William Jones made the blanket statement that Lee "did not hesitate to say in the intimacy of private friendship that he lost the battle of Gettysburg mainly because of *Longstreet's disobedience of orders*." Taylor and Jones neglected to mention that by Lee giving his consent, the commanding general agreed with Longstreet as to the necessity of waiting for Law. E.P. Alexander also believed Longstreet's request and Lee's consent had merit. "The history of the battle," Alexander contended, "seems to justify this delay (Longstreet calls it 30 minutes), as without Law's brigade our first attack must have been dangerously weak."[5]

Beyond simply criticizing Longstreet in waiting for the arrival of Law's brigade, Krick advances his opinion further, suggesting that, so as to minimize added delay, Longstreet should have begun the march while Law was racing to join the First Corps divisions. It appears Edwin Coddington would have agreed, asserting in his own narrative that "he [Longstreet] ... insisted upon Law's appearance before starting to move his men to the right. He never explained why Law could not have found the rest of Hood's division just as easily near the Emmitsburg road as on the Chambersburg Pike." Similarly, David Schultz and Scott Mingus contend, "There was no viable reason, however, for Longstreet to keep his men he had on hand marking time, and yet that is precisely what he did. His divisions under Hood and McLaws did not march a step toward their jump-off position." In stating that Longstreet's decision to wait for Law before commencing the march "ticked off moments potentially golden for the South," and that "Longstreet simply was dragging his feet," Krick neglects to point out that the Confederates were then operating under the mistaken impression that the Federal flank was anchored on the Emmitsburg Road and therefore any attack up that road would land squarely on their flank. An attack as planned around Krick's so-called "golden moments" of the 12:30 to 1 p.m. timeframe would have very likely been confusing since the Federal army's flank was not then positioned on the Emmitsburg Road. In fact, no major Federal force was posted there until just before Longstreet's actual attack a few hours later.[6]

In this version of events, Lee appears to be absolved of any responsibility for causing this alleged unnecessary delay. As commanding general, Lee could have pushed Longstreet along if he felt that time and circumstance required it. In response to this argument, Krick and other historians have contended that Lee was a hands-off general and seldom meddled with subordinates' tactical decisions. Yet, had Lee not overridden

Longstreet's earlier order to McLaws with respect to where to place his division? Above all, Longstreet was not acting in a vacuum in the late morning hours of July 2. There were a number of other pieces involved and they were still moving into place.

Indeed, the wait for Law's brigade was not the only cause for delay after 11 a.m. Around the time Lee spoke with McLaws in the mid-morning hours, he also directed A.P. Hill to bring up Anderson's division to support Longstreet's attack in Pickett's absence. That division was then positioned on Herr's Ridge to the west. Cadmus Wilcox's brigade of Anderson's division, the unit that was to connect with Longstreet's left flank, did not take its position along Seminary Ridge until 12 noon. Given that Longstreet's divisions were to form to the right of Anderson's division, Longstreet would naturally have had to wait for those brigades to be in place before the First Corps could be positioned properly for the attack. Furthermore, historian Harry Pfanz has pointed out that Anderson positioned Wilcox in a defensive manner, "rather than the deployment needed for their later assault," and the division commander "at that time was thinking in defensive and not in offensive terms." Even Longstreet critic Clifford Dowdey saw fit to criticize Lee's orders for Anderson on July 2—"to cooperate ... in Longstreet's attack"—calling them "the vaguest he ever gave. He did not specify whether Anderson was to act under the orders of Longstreet, commanding the attack, or of Hill, his new corps commander, or Lee's own." Shortly after taking position in Pitzer's Woods, Anderson's defensive posture had to be altered when General Daniel Sickles ordered Hiram Berdan's sharpshooters toward the vicinity of where Wilcox's brigade was posted. This probe precipitated a brief firefight just after 12 noon, where Wilcox's brigade was forced to engage and clear the enemy from the woods.[7]

Additionally, before and after the Wilcox-Berdan skirmish, several Confederate reconnaissance missions were ongoing. Chief of Artillery William Pendleton mentioned in his after-battle report that prior to 12 p.m. Captain Samuel Johnston examined the front again, this time in the company of another engineer, Colonel William P. Smith. It seems a number of historians are either unaware of Johnston's second reconnaissance or they simply neglect to include it in their analysis of July 2. Noah Trudeau never mentions Johnston's continued scouting efforts to find a concealed route to the right and contends, "In an omission that would never be explained, neither Longstreet nor McLaws had detailed any officer of [E.P] Alexander's caliber to scout the way." Trudeau also advances a typical anti–Longstreet group mode of conjecture to buttress his argument: "A partial explanation for Longstreet was that his failure to persuade Lee to attempt a much wider flanking move had left him visibly agitated and not sufficiently focused on the myriad of small details that a corps commander had to handle."[8]

William Pendleton, wartime (Library of Congress).

On the contrary, reconnaissance efforts, including Johnston's, abounded around the midday hours. According to Pendleton, Longstreet "about midday ... arrived and viewed the ground." The artillery commander also provided insight into how he met and helped E.P. Alexander get "the best view he then could of the front," whereby he "conducted the colonel to the advanced point of observation previously visited" (likely the position Pendleton had been to around 9 a.m.). Pendleton then described the dangers of this observation point with threats from enemy sharpshooters and the ensuing clash between Wilcox and Berdan nearby. After that fight concluded, Pendleton believed that "some view of the ground" beyond Pitzer's Woods and "much farther to the right than had yet been examined, seemed practicable." Curiously, Pendleton, and probably Alexander, then "rode in that direction, and, when about to enter the woods, met the commanding general, *en route* himself for a survey of the ground." After meeting with Cadmus Wilcox and riding with Colonel Armistead Long, Pendleton then reached the "farm house at the summit" of a ridge, "where the cross-road from Fairfield, &c., emerges," and "noticed the field and the enemy's batteries." Simply stated, Pendleton recalled that between 11 a.m. and, at least, 1:30 p.m., additional Confederate reconnaissance of the ground was conducted by numerous officers ranging from Johnston, Smith, and Alexander, to, probably on a more limited basis, Longstreet and Lee.[9]

Colonel Armistead Long was also present during this hodgepodge of Confederate reconnaissance missions. As stated previously, Long's later recollections are regularly cited by historians as proof that Lee was frustrated with Longstreet throughout the morning and early afternoon of July 2. Long's Lost Cause agenda consistently defending Lee and blaming Longstreet again makes an appearance at this juncture in the narrative. Long alleged that around 1 p.m. Lee "observed that the enemy had occupied the Peach Orchard" with Sickles' entire corps, which apparently stirred renewed impatience with Longstreet for not having already occupied that position. Long's recollections were erroneous. No substantial Federal force was present at the Peach Orchard at 1 p.m.—certainly not Sickles' command—but historians have not gone out of their way to dismiss and challenge Long's claims with the same fervor in which they criticize Longstreet's postwar statements. Lafayette McLaws dismissed Long's claims outright, writing that Lee's secretary was spewing "but the story of an ignorant and prejudiced person." To McLaws, Long was simply "not telling us the events which came under his own observation." McLaws contended, accurately, that at 1 p.m., there simply were not any considerable Federal units in the area. Indeed, after Meade ordered Buford's cavalry back to Westminster, leaving the Federal left without a cavalry screen, Third Corps Brigadier General David Birney ordered the 3rd Maine regiment and a company of Colonel Hiram Berdan's U.S. Sharpshooters through the Peach Orchard area between 11 a.m. and noon "with directions to feel the enemy." After those units clashed with Wilcox's brigade in Pitzer's Woods for about 20 minutes, they withdrew toward the Federal line before 2 p.m. Beyond scattered skirmishing, that quarter remained unoccupied until sometime around 3 p.m. when Sickles' whole corps moved forward to the Peach Orchard.[10]

9

The First Corps March Conundrum

"Guided as he was by General Lee's staff officer"
—Lafayette McLaws

"At length—my recollection is that it was 1 p.m.—Major [*sic*] Johnston, of General Lee's staff, came to me and *said he was ordered to conduct me on the march.* My command was at once put in motion—Major Johnston and myself riding some distance ahead," Major General Lafayette McLaws later wrote of Lee assigning Captain Johnston, the engineer who had conducted the misleading early morning reconnaissance, to lead the First Corps divisions covertly into attack position. As early as his after-battle report, written less than a month after the engagement, Longstreet echoed McLaws' testimony, writing, "Engineers, sent out by the commanding general and myself, guided us." Further, in his postwar accounts, Longstreet consistently described Johnston's role during the march, asserting that "General Lee ordered Colonel Johnston, of his engineer corps, to lead and conduct the head of the column. My troops, therefore, moved forward under guidance of a special officer of General Lee, and with instructions to follow his directions"; "[Lee] ordered the march, and put it under the conduct of his engineer officers, so as to be assured that the troops would move by the best route and encounter the least delay in reaching the position designated by him for the attack ... at the same time concealing the movements then under orders from view of the Federals"; and again, "General Lee ordered his reconnoitering officers to lead the troops of the First Corps and conduct them by a route concealed from the view of the enemy." Postwar critics of Longstreet, like Colonel William Allan, often downplayed Johnston's role and criticized how Longstreet described the engineer's function. Johnston "had been sent to give information, not command his corps," Allan declared. Likewise, Fitzhugh Lee posited, "Colonel [*sic*] Johnston did not even know where General Longstreet was going. He supposed he had been ordered to ride with him [Longstreet] simply to give him the benefit of his reconnaissance." Douglas Southall Freeman perpetuated these dubious testimonies in the twentieth century, contending that "He [Longstreet] left the direction of the van entirely to S.R. Johnston, the reconnaissance officer Lee had put at his disposal." Similarly, Clifford Dowdey asserted that "This engineering officer assumed no more authority than would, say, a friendly local civilian who offered merely his knowledge of the country." In Freeman and Dowdey's accounts, Johnston was cast merely as a resource Longstreet could choose to use, as opposed to the officer Lee had ordered to conduct the First Corps' concealed march.[1]

Noah Trudeau and Robert Krick echo William Allan, Fitzhugh Lee, Douglas Southall Freeman, and Clifford Dowdey's opinions and solely use Johnston's postwar recollections in their analysis. They cite Johnston's postwar claim that he "had no idea that I had the confidence of the great Lee to such an extent that he would entrust me with the conduct of any army corps moving within two miles of the enemy's line." Trudeau endorses Johnston's claims, writing, "To the end of his days, Longstreet would remain convinced that Lee had appended Samuel Johnston to the expedition as its guide, while that young officer himself understood his duties as being solely advisory." Krick also accepts Johnston's testimony as truth and asserts with great confidence that "Lee suggested that Captain Johnston join Longstreet's column on its march; any other use of the man best informed about the ground would have been criminally negligent. The army commander of course gave his staff captain no special authority." Krick believes that Lee merely "suggested" that Johnston, "the man best informed about the ground," was only to accompany the column, not guide it along a concealed route over ground he had personally reconnoitered multiple times in the morning. Indeed, Johnston was the best informed man and so would have been the logical choice to guide the marching column. On this topic, Krick also accuses Longstreet of being exceedingly difficult and intentionally vindictive:

> Longstreet decided to *play an ugly game with the misguided Lee*—and with thousands of unfortunate soldiers and the destiny of a mighty battle—by taking the ludicrous position that Sam Johnston really commanded the march. He was Lee's man on the spot, and this wholly silly march and attack were Lee's idiotic idea so let him have his way and then we'll just see who really knows best![2]

Lafayette McLaws' testimony on the issue of Johnston's intended role during the march is especially revealing and noteworthy. Krick, who characterizes McLaws as "among the most pointed detractors Longstreet ever earned," states emphatically that "McLaws provides key testimony about his chief at Gettysburg." And yet, on the topic of the First Corps divisions' march, Krick chooses not to use McLaws' "key testimony" at all. McLaws confirmed Longstreet's written statements as to Lee's employment of Captain Johnston to find a concealed route to the right and lead the First Corps column along that concealed path into position. McLaws recounted that at some point during the morning hours "Genrl Lee then remarked that he had ordered a reconnaissance for the purpose of finding out a way to go into position without being seen by the enemy and I must hold myself in readiness to move." Lee's insistence on marching the column to its attacking point without being seen by the Federals was later dubbed by McLaws as a "millstone" around Longstreet's "neck," and a major factor in further delaying the attack.[3]

Contrary to the adamant opinion of postwar Longstreet critics like Fitzhugh Lee, who held that besides Captain Johnston's 4 a.m. reconnaissance "NO OTHER ORDERS HE [Johnston] RECEIVED," the engineer did in fact carry out additional reconnaissance activities on the morning of July 2, as confirmed by Pendleton's after-battle report. It is initially unclear which reconnaissance activity McLaws referred to in his account. That said, Johnston's initial examination of the Federal left took place from around 4:30 a.m. to 7:30 a.m. and was ordered with the intention of discovering fundamental information about the Federal position. Conversely, McLaws' recollection references a

Johnston-led reconnaissance specifically conducted to "find out a way into position without being seen by the enemy"; a mission that would most logically be carried out *after* knowing basic information about the enemy's whereabouts. Indeed, in the postwar years, Johnston explicitly admitted to Lafayette McLaws that he reconnoitered for potential concealed routes, writing that he examined "the roads over which our troops would have to move in the event of a movement on the enemy's left." In a decision likely made to avoid diffusing their arguments, it is worth noting that prominent Lost Cause writers and modern historians, such as Fitzhugh Lee and Robert Krick, neglect to mention Johnston's other scouting activities on the morning of the July 2. Noah Trudeau also neglects to expand beyond Johnston's early morning reconnaissance in his analysis: "Johnston's scout this morning had been undertaken not to locate a route sufficient for a corps, but to reconnoiter the enemy line."[4]

Sometime between 12:30 and 1 p.m.—McLaws says 1 p.m. in one account, and even 2 p.m. in another—the Confederate First Corps column of 14,500 men and three battalions of artillery started out. "Major Johnson [*sic*] came to me," McLaws recalled, "and said that he was ready to conduct my division; within ten minutes it was in motion and Major Johnson [*sic*] and myself went ahead of it some 200 yards." McLaws later recollected that, at the time, he saw no evidence Lee was irritated or annoyed with Longstreet. He described Lee "as calm and cool as I ever saw him and evidenced nothing in his manner to make me think for a moment that he had been thwarted in any movement by any delay on the part of anyone or from any other cause." McLaws believed Longstreet had been, as he put it, "resting under the eye of General Lee" the entire morning on July 2, and "General Longstreet, acting under the orders of General Lee, and guided as he was by General Lee's staff officer, could not have attacked before 2 o'clock, on the 2nd, and it is yet to be shown that he could have attacked before 4, when he did make the assault."[5]

Included in Clifford Dowdey's analysis of the beginning of the First Corps march is an open speculation on what he believed Longstreet was thinking and feeling at the time. "His usually immobile face," Dowdey pronounced, "was reflecting the torments of his frustration and outrage. He had been rejected as 'another Jackson' in council, his advice had been finally dismissed with a brusque order.... His native stubbornness gave him the capacity to turn himself into something like an automaton." To Dowdey, Longstreet proceeded "dully, in the self-imposed stupidity of renouncing all initiative." Yet, Dowdey admitted, perhaps unwittingly, that all his judgments of Longstreet would have gone totally unnoticed to those around him on July 2: "Longstreet had given no hint that his bad humor reflected a disturbance so profound that he would be reduced to a state of incompetence for command." Longstreet "had given no hint" of his alleged state of mind, yet Dowdey seemed to take it upon himself to fill blanks in the historical record. Dowdey's commentary on this topic demonstrates the extent to which historical conjecture has been advanced when analyzing Longstreet's actions at Gettysburg.[6]

Once the First Corps column lurched forward, Longstreet rode along with Lee for some time "until the line had stretched out on the march." Lee's Warhorse then stayed in the middle of the column with Hood's division, which trailed McLaws. A South Carolina officer claimed to see Longstreet "once or twice" during those fleeting moments, recalling that "he had his eyes cast to the ground, as if in a deep study." If Lee was con-

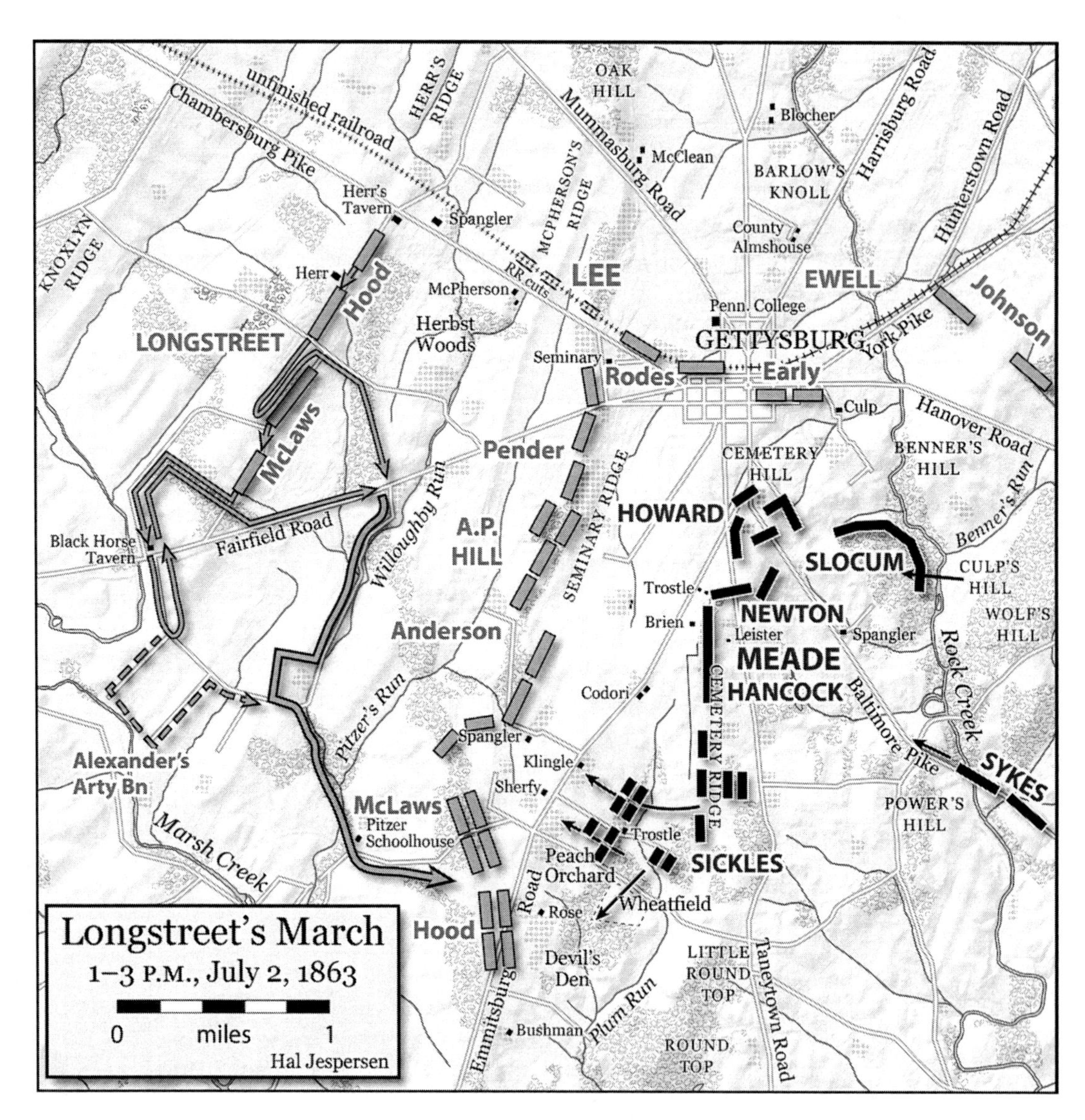

Longstreet's March
1–3 P.M., July 2, 1863

cerned about where Longstreet was located, where the column was headed, or possessed little confidence in who was leading the column at that time, his initial ride in the trailing division with Longstreet bears little evidence to support that theory. Surely, if Lee disapproved of how Longstreet was conducting his corps, as commanding general, he would have said so, or as the First Corps commander put it in the postwar years, "If the movements were not satisfactory in time and speed of moving, it was his power, duty, and privilege to apply the remedy.... If he failed to apply the remedy, it was his fault." Additionally, if Longstreet's after-battle report assertion that Johnston "guided us" was inaccurate, surely Lee would have insisted it be struck from the official record.[7]

While Lee once again rode over to Ewell's front, Longstreet's column moved southwest along Herr Ridge, then skirted along roads running parallel to Marsh Creek until it reached Black Horse Tavern. Here, at the direction of McLaws and Johnston, the column halted. They realized if the column continued up a small rise located at the tavern, they would expose themselves to Federal signalmen on Little Round Top. Robert Krick has claimed, again based only on Johnston's checkered postwar account that the Captain actually warned Longstreet prior to reaching the small rise that they would be exposed, and in Krick's words, "Longstreet had no comment. He watched as the column went over the crest into the view of the Federals and halted." There is no other source record suggesting Johnston was with Longstreet before the column reached Black Horse Tavern. In fact, on the contrary, McLaws said that he was with Johnston at the head of the column. Furthermore, there is no evidence to corroborate the assertion that the column continued forward "over the crest." Conversely, the evidence suggests that the divisions halted prior to the crest upon recognizing that if they carried on they would be exposed to the Federals. Krick also neglects to point out that the Confederate column was seen before it even reached Black Horse Tavern. Indeed, Gilbert Moxley Sorrel expressed afterwards how absurd he thought Lee's entire idea was with respect to insisting the column march unseen by Federal signalmen. "We were seen from the start and signaled constantly," Sorrel declared, while "much valuable time was lost by this trial, with which better knowledge of the ground by General Lee's engineers would not have been attempted." It is clear that attempts made in the morning to find an approach route concealed from the enemy had failed. Either Johnston never actually found a concealed route during his reconnaissance activity, or simply made a mistake during the march and led the column down the wrong path.[8]

McLaws remembered of this frustrating moment at Black Horse Tavern that he "sent back and halted my division and rode with Major [*sic*] Johnston rapidly around the neighborhood to see if there was any road by which we could go into position without being seen." McLaws found no way around the predicament and upon returning to the column found Longstreet present. A dialogue, as recounted by McLaws, ensued:

"What is the matter?" asked Longstreet.

"Ride with me," McLaws replied, "and I will show you that we can't go on this route, according to instructions, without being seen by the enemy."

Both generals rode to the crest of the hill, clearly visible to enemy signalmen on Little Round Top. Longstreet later wrote, "Looking up toward Round Top I saw that the signal station was in full view."

"Why this won't do. Is there no way to avoid it?" Longstreet inquired.

McLaws alleged he then told Longstreet of the private reconnaissance he had conducted in the morning hours while waiting for Confederate attack plans to fully mature and Johnston to return from his mission to find a concealed route to the right.

Upon hearing of McLaws' earlier reconnaissance, Longstreet asked, "How can we get there?"

"Only by going back—by countermarching," McLaws answered.

Being "very impatient at this delay," Longstreet ordered the countermarch. The First Corps commander suggested allowing Hood to lead the countermarch since he was positioned behind McLaws' division; however, McLaws insisted he lead the column.

"General, as I started in the lead, let me continue so," requested McLaws.

"Then go on," Longstreet ordered and rode off.[9]

It is at this scene on July 2 that Armistead Long, whose recollections are frequently quoted by Longstreet critics, resumed his dubious postwar narrative about the First Corps commander's "delay," writing that "It was now after one o'clock, and General Lee's impatience again urged him to go in quest of Longstreet. After proceeding about a mile, we discovered Hood's division at a halt; it was said, waiting for McLaws, whose divisions had taken a wrong direction." Contrary to Long's allegations, the historical record shows Lee left Longstreet during the early part of the First Corps march and again rode over to Ewell's position on the Confederate left. Conversely, Long alleged that he and Lee were only "about a mile" away when Longstreet began to execute his countermarch; yet, there are no other accounts that corroborate that claim.[10]

Further, from pro–Longstreet Jeffry Wert to anti–Longstreet Robert Krick, many modern historians' common critique of Longstreet at this juncture involve the recollections of E.P. Alexander, who in the postwar years briefly inserted himself into this frustrating scene at Black Horse Tavern. Alexander described the route he took, probably closer to 1:30 p.m. or so, to get his own artillery battalion down near Pitzer's Schoolhouse in preparation to support the infantry attack, writing, "I had come there by a short & quite direct road, which at one point passed over a high bare place where it was in full view of the Federal signal station. But I avoided that part of the road by turning out to the left, & going through fields & hollows, & getting back to the road again a quarter mile or so beyond." Alexander then explained his encounter with McLaws' column as it was halted at Black Horse Tavern shortly thereafter. "Then I recall riding back for something, & finding the head of one of our divisions of infantry standing halted in sight of the signal station. It had been put on that road to march, but told, as I had been, to keep out of view." What follows are the critical details of Alexander's account: "Finding that the road brought them into view they halted & sent back for orders or a guide. Finally, after a delay which must have been much over an hour, orders came, and, I believe, a guide to lead them by 'Black Horse Tavern.'" Alexander also contended, solely in his *Fighting for the Confederacy* account, that he even "told the officers at the head of the column of the route my artillery had followed—which was easily seen—but there was no one with authority to vary the orders they were under, & they momentarily expected the new ones for which they had been sent & which were very explicit when they came after the long, long delay."[11]

E.P. Alexander, wartime (from *The Photographic History of the Civil War in Ten Volumes: Volume Five, Forts and Artillery*).

The latter part of Alexander's account is exceedingly confusing and the artilleryman's multiple accounts of this scene do not corroborate in many of their lesser and more significant details. Among his irregularities were his accounts of artillery movements near Pitzer's Schoolhouse. For instance, in his *Fighting for the Confederacy* narrative, Alexander said he had his own battalion near Pitzer's Schoolhouse and was waiting for the infantry and Cabell's and Henry's batteries before he began "riding back for something"; however, in his *Military Memoirs*, he contended he had placed "my own, Cabell's, and Henry's ... in the valley of Willoughby Run awaiting the arrival of the infantry," and that he rode back explicitly "to learn the cause of their non-arrival." Though referring to the same event, in one account, Alexander contended that only his battalion had made it to Pitzer's Schoolhouse before he rode back and had no recollection of the reason he rode back. In the other, all three batteries were present at Pitzer's and he claimed to have returned to discover why the infantry had not arrived.[12]

More significantly, Alexander correctly pointed out that his artillery had earlier avoided the elevated hill at Black Horse Tavern by taking a path off to the left and cutting across fields. With that said, the critical question becomes: which person of authority was informed of this revelation by the artilleryman? Robert Krick skirts this noteworthy question altogether, merely asserting "When he [Alexander] noticed the infantry not only failing to follow his example but also halted in clear view of Little Round Top—thus canceling *both* secrecy and speed—he was astonished. The infantry never did follow Alexander's simple and convenient route." In Krick's version, Alexander rode up, was surprised, shook his head, and rode away in disgust. Daniel Laney has also written contemptuously of Longstreet with respect to his non-use of Alexander's artillery route, "Apparently on this day that simple and efficient maneuver was beyond Longstreet and he elected a countermarch that would cost two to three precious hours." Jeffry Wert's account of Alexander's alternate route is equally questionable and incomplete. Wert does not see fit to mention Alexander's short physical presence on the scene, only writing that "Hours earlier Porter Alexander had faced the same problem at the rise and detoured through the fields without exposing his batteries to Union view. The tracks of the artillery wheels must have been visible, but Longstreet and McLaws chose not to follow them, which would have saved valuable time." On the contrary, Alexander unveiled in one of his accounts that he had actually "told the officers at the head of the column of the route my artillery followed."[13]

Who were these officers, and why were they never named? Were they McLaws and Johnston, who, as McLaws recounted, were "riding some distance ahead," and in another account even said they went ahead of the column "some 200 yards," therefore obviously arriving at the Tavern predicament first? By McLaws' account, once the column was forced to stop at the Tavern, he and Johnston searched for options to avoid the elevated crest, but found nothing promising. Were McLaws and Johnston riding in search of that alternate route at the exact moment Alexander arrived? McLaws neither mentioned speaking with nor seeing Alexander, nor wrote about an alternate path across fields. When McLaws returned, he found Longstreet already at the head of the column wondering why the march had stopped. Had Alexander also missed Longstreet, not sticking around long enough with those unidentified officers to make his case to his Chief? A statement Alexander made in his *Military Memoirs* subtly insinuated that the artilleryman did indeed make his appearance between the time McLaws and Johnston were riding and when Longstreet arrived. "Riding back presently to learn the cause of their non-arrival, the head of the column was found halted ... while messages were sent to Longstreet, and the guide sought a new route." Even if this were the case, why had "astonished" Alexander not stuck around to at least point out his artillery path to Johnston, McLaws, or Longstreet?[14]

Like McLaws, Longstreet never once mentioned seeing Alexander at Black Horse Tavern, nor did he ever refer to hearing alternate suggestions to take a path across fields. Johnston, in the postwar years, claimed he had suggested to Longstreet that the column march across fields, perhaps, at first glance, signifying that he may have spoken to Alexander and was passing on the information to the corps commander on his behalf. Douglas Southall Freeman appeared to believe Johnston outright, asserting the Captain "notified Longstreet that if the troops continued along the road ... their presence would be disclosed to the enemy. Johnston pointed out a shorter, concealed route across a nearby field." Jeffry Wert has also taken Johnston at his word, apparently without noticing the time at which Johnston alleged he spoke with Longstreet. Wert states misleadingly, "Johnston claimed that he recommended to Longstreet that the troops skirt the hill by marching across fields, but the general 'preferred the road.'" A close examination of the source reveals the Captain actually maintained he had spoken to the First Corps commander before the column reached the crest at the Tavern; in other words, at a time when Longstreet was located nowhere near Johnston. "When we reached the bend of the road," Johnston recollected, "I called General Longstreet's attention to the hill over which he would have to pass, in full view of the enemy, and also to a route across the field, shorter than the road and completely hidden from the enemy's observation." Johnston claimed Longstreet then told him he "preferred the road." Johnston's account is even more suspect since E.P. Alexander neither mentioned speaking to the Captain nor verified his claim as to why Longstreet allegedly chose to countermarch instead of using the field route. Rather Alexander stated in an 1877 letter, "For some reason, which I cannot now recall, they would not turn back and follow the tracks of my guns."[15]

Alexander's *Fighting for the Confederacy* account is also confusing when cross-referencing it with Brigadier General Joseph Kershaw's version of the events during the march. Kershaw was one of those officers "at the head of the column, which was halted at the end of the lane leading to the Black Horse Tavern, situated some five hundred yards to our right." Just before Kershaw's brigade reached the rise in the road near the Tavern, they were "halted by General McLaws in person, while he and General Longstreet rode forward to reconnoiter. Very soon those gentlemen returned, both manifesting considerable irritation, as I thought." It stands to reason that if Alexander had talked to "officers at the head of the column," Kershaw must have been one of them, or was at least very close by; however, like McLaws and Longstreet, the brigade commander neither mentioned Alexander in his account, nor any other person, for that matter, suggesting the column move by a path off to the left.[16]

For all intents and purposes, Alexander's appearance on the scene proved of little significance because there is no evidence he talked to anyone of importance to press his point about taking the path across fields. Captain Johnston, the designated guide who had led the column down the wrong road (or a road he had never been on) in the first place, claimed he recommended the cross-fields path to Longstreet *before* the column stopped at the crest, though there is absolutely no evidence Johnston was anywhere near Longstreet at that particular moment. In fact, McLaws consistently puts Johnston with him at the head of the column, which is not where Longstreet was located when the divisions approached Black Horse Tavern. Further, Alexander never recollected talking to Johnston once the column had stopped, and no one else said anything about what Johnston allegedly suggested. For some reason, Alexander did not stick around long at Black Horse Tavern, and never spoke to Longstreet. Assuming Johnston did speak to Longstreet on Alexander's behalf, which is uncorroborated, why would Longstreet continue to put his trust in a man who had misled the column thus far and demonstrated he did not know where he was going, or as Longstreet put it in his after-battle report, one who "guided us by a road which would have completely disclosed the move"? Jeffry Wert contends that Longstreet and McLaws "never gave their reasons" for choosing to countermarch instead of following Alexander's path across fields. Wert uses Johnston's suspect testimony again and concludes that "perhaps Johnston was correct—Longstreet thought it better to stay on the roads." But in fact, reasons were provided in McLaws' account of the episode. In short, the historical record suggests that Longstreet consulted McLaws, almost exclusively, about what should be done at Black Horse Tavern and the division commander affirmed that based on a personal reconnaissance he had conducted earlier in the day, there was another route which required a countermarch, prompting Longstreet to order the countermarch.[17]

10

McLaws Ordered to Attack an Occupied Road

"General Lee was with General Longstreet"
—Lafayette McLaws, Osmun Latrobe

In the postwar years, Lafayette McLaws described the nature of the alternate and concealed route he had suggested to General Longstreet on the afternoon of July 2: "After very considerable difficulty, owing to the rough character of the country in places and the fences and ditches we had to cross, the countermarch was effected." Sometime between 2 p.m. and 4 p.m., McLaws' and Hood's columns retraced their steps to their starting position on Herr Ridge near the Adam Butt House, and upon reaching the Hagerstown Road, marched northeast until they intersected a road that ran parallel to Willoughby Run. General Pendleton later described this road as "the ravine road," which, according to McLaws, had "fences on the side not giving room enough for a company front, making it necessary to break files to the rear." It was at that moment Pendleton apparently saw fit to have members of his staff aid the First Corps divisions in their course toward Pitzer's Schoolhouse, and in general, "to remedy, as far as practicable, the delay." The column, with Kershaw's brigade of McLaws' division still in front, turned left at the Schoolhouse junction and marched due east toward their attack positions at the intersection of Seminary Ridge and the Wheatfield Road.[1]

As the column approached the intersection, Longstreet was riding with Kershaw's brigade and soon after making the left turn at Pitzer's Schoolhouse, spoke in-person with Kershaw, directing him to "attack the enemy at the Peach Orchard ... turn the flank of that position," and then "extend my line along the road ... with my left resting on that road." Longstreet then rode forward to speak with McLaws.

"How are you going in?" Longstreet queried his division commander.

McLaws responded, "That will be determined when I can see what is in my front."

"There is nothing in your front"; Longstreet retorted, "you will be entirely on the flank of the enemy."

McLaws understood his orders, replying, "Then I will continue my march in columns of companies, and after arriving on the flank as far as is necessary will face to the left and march on the enemy."

"That suits me," Longstreet answered and then rode off.[2]

Longstreet's dialogue with both Kershaw and McLaws demonstrated he and Lee, who was undoubtedly in close proximity, were still under the mistaken impression there were little to no Federal troops positioned south of the Confederate's objective, Cemetery Hill. Longstreet was carrying out Lee's orders to place McLaws' division in a manner so as to quickly maneuver into position perpendicular to the Emmitsburg Road. But, as Kershaw's brigade moved forward and "emerged from the woods" sometime between 3 and 3:30 p.m., the situation was found to be entirely different from what was expected.[3]

Indeed, for the entire day leading up to the attack, the Confederate high command had possessed a mistaken belief about the strength and nature of the Federal position. For many years after the war, E.P. Alexander held that "Not only was the selection [of the point of attack] about as bad as possible, but there does not seem to have been any special thought given to the matter. It seems to have been allowed almost to select itself as if it was a matter of no consequence." Alexander's sense that the Confederates seemed to have been improvising as they went along on July 2 was further explained by Lafayette McLaws, who ascribed the army's problems leading up to the attack to "the want of proper reconnaissance having been made before the general plan of attack had been determined on ... from hasty reports, made probably by persons not skilled in such matters, that there was not much to overcome, and this erroneous opinion was never corrected." Apparently unknown to the Confederates was that, by mid-morning the Federal line stretched all the way down Cemetery Ridge, with its left flank anchored just north of Little Round Top. As already suggested, if Lee and Longstreet had found some miraculous way to attack in the morning hours, their advance up the Emmitsburg Road would have required significant "real-time" alterations in alignment and direction, or such a movement would have invited a sure counterstroke against their right flank by elements of at least two Federal corps. As it would turn out, Longstreet's attack required last-minute alterations at the 3 p.m. hour, in reaction to a much different battlescape than the Confederates had expected. General Daniel Sickles' Federal Third Corps had advanced from its position on Cemetery Ridge to the Sherfy Peach Orchard sometime toward the middle of Longstreet's march. By the time Kershaw readied for the attack around 3 p.m., Sickles' corps stretched along the Emmitsburg Road, pivoted at the Peach Orchard, and then bent back toward Little Round Top. Sickles' Peach Orchard salient had been established.[4]

McLaws was initially dumbstruck with what he saw in his front, writing later "The view presented astonished me, as the enemy was massed in my front and extended to my right and left as far as I could see." The division commander continued on, "Thus was presented a state of affairs which was certainly not contemplated when the original plan or order of battle was given, and certainly was not known to General Longstreet a half hour previous." McLaws was correct, although in fact, Lee's original plan of battle never reflected the actual state of affairs on the Federal left. All the reconnaissance efforts throughout the morning and early afternoon had failed to produce an accurate representation of the Federal position south of Cemetery Hill.[5]

In reaction to the Federals' advance position, Confederate attack plans had to be altered, but not surprisingly, these modifications did not happen instantaneously. There was a transition period when the high command had to first recognize and acknowledge the different "state of affairs" in their front and modify tactics accordingly. Postwar accounts suggest it took some time for the high command to even understand how the

Federal Third Corps was positioned, not along or parallel with the Emmitsburg Road, but instead at an angle that arched back into Plum Run Valley and Devil's Den. Indeed, the Federal left flank was not on the Emmitsburg Road to "partially envelop" or "drive in."

And so it was that Longstreet, with considerable proof that Lee was present, issued orders for McLaws to commence the attack. Evidence from the day's events suggests that Lee intended in his initial plan for McLaws to open the attack. In their early morning conference, Lee had spoken with McLaws personally and was most insistent that he position his division perpendicular to the Emmitsburg Road. McLaws' division had also led the march and countermarch, and therefore Longstreet's order to attack sometime between 3:30 and 4 p.m. likely came as little surprise to McLaws had it not been for what he was then seeing in his front. McLaws later recollected this confusing juncture in the battle, when 'an order came from General Longstreet, borne by Major Latrobe ... asking why I did not charge, "there was no one in my front but a regiment of infantry and a battery of artillery."' McLaws then described how he told Latrobe there was much more than that in his front and he would "charge so soon as my division was formed for it." After the order was allegedly repeated, McLaws argued again that the "enemy was so strong in my front that it required careful preparation for the assault, or it necessarily would be a failure," and suggested Longstreet come look for himself.[6]

In analyzing this moment in the battle, many historians over the years have written as if Lee was not present with Longstreet. They allege Longstreet was stubbornly ordering McLaws to attack without examining or acknowledging the unexpected position of the Federal line. Clifford Dowdey declared that "Old Pete, having finally reached the point of attack designated by Lee, had his mind set on sending those troops in precisely as Lee had ordered hours before.... No message was sent to Lee." Likewise, in his *Battle Cry of Freedom,* academic historian James McPherson writes of this moment in the battle, "Finding the Union left in an unexpected position, Longstreet probably should have notified Lee." David Schultz and Scott Mingus claim that "instead of [McLaws] sending a rider to inform Longstreet that Yankees were not where they were supposed to be, decided to report in person. He found the corps commander." On the contrary, McLaws provided no commentary suggesting he rode over in-person to see Longstreet. Initially, Schultz and Mingus also describe the scene with an absent Lee: "McLaws tried reasoning with the general about alternate options, but Old Peter refused his entreaties." However, several pages later they admit that "Longstreet was in consultation with Lee when both McLaws and Hood formally requested amendments to the stated plan to attack up the Emmitsburg Road."[7]

Other historians have even gone so far as to say Longstreet was unilaterally issuing these orders out of spite toward Lee, to show him his tactical offensive plan was doomed to fail. "Longstreet abdicated ... responsibility and insisted that Lee's plan, now long stale and necessarily only a general guide in any event, be rigidly honored," contends Robert Krick. Krick also advances his opinion that Longstreet was actually playing a game with Lee and his men on July 2, writing, "It had become apparent that Lee knew far less well than Longstreet how to win a battle, and here was an irresistible opportunity to prove it to him."[8]

Contrary to these assertions, Longstreet was not by himself. McLaws recalled that it was evident Lee was present with Longstreet. "Not long after the order came peremptorily for me to charge, *the officer representing that General Lee was with General Longstreet, and joined in the order*." Osmun Latrobe confirmed Lee's presence with Longstreet, when stating "General Lee was with General Longstreet and was impatient that the charge was delayed." Likewise, Austrian eyewitness Fitzgerald Ross observed of this moment that Lee and Longstreet "held a conference on horseback," and the latter rode "up the line and down again, occasionally dismounting, and going forward to get a better view of the enemy's position." Therefore, given that the attack order had Lee's stamp of approval, McLaws said he would advance within five minutes; however, sometime within that five-minute period "a courier dashed up with orders for me to wait until Hood got into position." McLaws' account suggests that after Lee initially ordered the division commander to commence the attack or joined in Longstreet's order, he observed the true state of the Federal position and was forced to formulate an alternate attack plan. This new plan would feature Hood's division opening the attack on McLaws' right. Hood, who had been behind McLaws during the divisions' entire march to the staging area, was directed to skirt past McLaws' division and extend the First Corps' front further to the right in an attempt to find the actual location of Meade's left flank. John Oeffinger alleges misleadingly of these alterations that "Sickles's action caused Longstreet to rethink a part of the attack," again leaving Lee out of the scene. Likewise, Edwin Coddington noted the involvement of Osmun Latrobe during these communications between Longstreet and McLaws, while concurrently overlooking Latrobe's frank confirmation that Lee was present with Longstreet at that moment. Coddington wrote with certainty of a Lee-less scene, "At the last minute he [McLaws] received an order from Longstreet to hold off until Hood could get into position. Longstreet's blind insistence that he push ahead before he was ready annoyed McLaws." Despite these assertions, McLaws, Latrobe, and Ross' accounts confirm Lee was indeed present with or in close proximity to Longstreet at the time the attack plan was modified. Therefore, should Lee not be held equally responsible in any allegations that initial attack orders were issued prematurely or that last-minute alterations caused additional delay?[9]

11

Hood's Proposition

"General Lee's orders are to attack up the Emmitsburg Road"
—James Longstreet to John Bell Hood

Major General John Bell Hood did not want to attack the Federal position as ordered. As his troops filed off McLaws' right and took position on Warfield Ridge, he sent scouts to determine if there was a more opportune way to attack by sweeping around the Round Tops, in lieu of assaulting the Federals head-on. In writing later about the location of the Federal left flank, Hood recollected that his scouts "soon reported to me that it rested upon Round Top mountain; that the country was open and that I could march through an open woodland pasture around Round Top and assault the enemy in flank and rear." Once he arrived at his attacking position, Hood also confirmed the Federal flank was located well to the left of where he had been informed it would be anchored. He remembered "plac[ing] one or two batteries in position and opened fire. Fire from the enemy's guns soon enveloped his lines. His left rested on or near Round Top." If he was to have any chance of "partially enveloping the enemy's left," as Lee had directed, Hood realized the attack could not be carried out as planned, that is to say "up the Emmitsburg Road."[1]

Hood discovered the ground over which his division would be forced to attack under Lee's plan was less than desirable. "I should have first to encounter and drive off this advanced line of battle; secondly, at the base and along the slope of the mountain, to confront immense boulders of stone, so massed together as to form narrow openings, which would break our ranks and cause the men to scatter whilst climbing up the rocky precipice," he later recollected. Resultantly, Hood informed Longstreet of his observations and proposed an alternate attack, deeming it "unwise to attack up the Emmitsburg Road, as ordered." For the first time, Hood sent a staff officer to Longstreet, urging his Chief "to turn Round Top and attack the enemy in flank and rear." According to Hood, he received a prompt reply from Longstreet, who repeated the original order: "Gen'l Lee's orders are to attack up the Emmetsburg [*sic*] road." Hood recalled he immediately sent another staff member to relay he "feared nothing could be accomplished by such an attack, and renewed my request to turn Round Top." Longstreet again replied, "Gen'l Lee's orders are to attack up the Emmetsburg [*sic*] road."[2]

It was at this critical moment Hood became cognizant of the predicament Longstreet had warned Lee about the night before. Without reservation, Hood believed the strength of the Federal position was impressive: "I knew that if the feat was accomplished it must be a most fearful sacrifice of as brave and gallant soldiers as ever engaged in battle.... I could not reasonably hope to accomplish much by the attack as ordered. In fact ... the enemy occupied a position by nature so strong—I may say impregnable.." One of Hood's brigadier generals, Evander Law, was equally impressed with the Federal position on July 2, writing later "That the great natural strength of the enemy's position in our front rendered the result of a direct assault extremely uncertain." Law echoed Longstreet's concerns about achieving a fruitless victory. Even if the Confederates succeeded in breaking the Federal's Cemetery Ridge line, Law asserted "the victory would be purchased at too great a sacrifice of life, and our troops would be in no condition to improve it." Further, Law contended that he supported "the occupation of Round Top during the night [of July 1] by moving upon it from the south, and the extension of our right wing from that point across the enemy's left and rear, being not only practicable, but easy." This plan was Longstreet doctrine, and if there be any doubt, Law finished up with a statement that could have been pulled from any of Longstreet's writings—"Such a movement would compel a change of front on the part of the enemy, the abandonment of his strong position on the heights, and force him to attack us in position."

John Bell Hood, wartime (Library of Congress).

Based on Longstreet's statements leading up to his attack on July 2, it is reasonable to assume he agreed with Hood's negative assessment of the battlescape; however, it is equally reasonable to suggest he recognized the timing was not opportune to entertain major tactical alterations with one division. That time had passed. Evaluating the merit of Hood's proposal in the postwar years, E.P. Alexander asserted, "It is not likely that the movement proposed by Hood would have accomplished much. Already our line was dangerously extended, and to have pushed one or two divisions past the 3d corps and around the mountain would have invited their destruction."[3]

Hood tried a third time to make his case to Longstreet, who again responded "Gen'l Lee's orders are to attack up the Emmettsburg road." The corps commander then sent a member of his own staff, Major John Fairfax, to repeat the order again. Soon thereafter, according to Hood, Longstreet himself rode up and heard in-person his subordinate's reservations against the attack as ordered, but the First Corps commander merely said, "We must obey the orders of General Lee."[4]

Longstreet critics have held that even at this moment, just prior to his corps' attack on July 2, he was still smarting over Lee's early morning dismissal of his tactical proposal to move the army around to the right to avoid having to execute these very kinds of overtly aggressive attacks. Cadmus Wilcox made this argument, contending "General Longstreet would have us believe from his conduct towards General Lee at Gettysburg that their understanding was in the nature of a contract, and General Lee having, in his opinion, disregarded it, he (Longstreet) was thereby absolved from all obligation to obey his orders." Likewise, Douglas Southall Freeman asserted scathingly: "Determined, apparently, to force a situation in which his [Longstreet's] plan would have to be adopted in spite of Lee, he delayed the attack on the right until Cemetery Ridge was crowded with men, whereas if he had attacked early in the morning, as Lee intended, he probably could have stormed that position and assuredly could have taken Round Top. Longstreet's slow and stubborn mind rendered him incapable of the quick daring and loyal obedience that had characterized Jackson.... It was Lee's misfortune at Gettysburg that he had to employ in offensive operations a man whose whole inclination was toward the defensive."[5]

A number of historians still perpetuate Freeman's opinion. They often pivot off of Moxley Sorrel's infamous "apparent apathy" quote, previously discussed, and argue Longstreet was discomposed; his military judgment and bearing deeply affected by his alleged "seething" disagreement with Lee. Glenn LaFantasie writes characteristically on this matter, "Lieutenant General James Longstreet, all surly and bearish to everyone around him ... on July 2, simply did not want to make the flank attack against the Union left." Some even insist Longstreet, like a petulant child who did not get his way, dragged his feet purposefully, sulked, and only told Hood to follow Lee's orders in attacking up the Emmitsburg Road to show the commanding general how flawed his plan was and how he knew better. Clifford Dowdey, on this topic, dramatically compared Longstreet's repeated directives to Hood—"General Lee's orders are to attack up the Emmitsburg Road"—to the disciple Peter's three denials of Jesus Christ. Likewise, Shelby Foote alleged "All that was lacking to complete the symbolism was a cockcrow." In his biography of Lee, Emory Thomas declares "Longstreet acted out his prolonged pout on July 2 and attacked Meade's flank only after giving the Federals enough time to accumulate and implant ample defenders." On the Longstreet-Hood dialogue specifically, Daniel Laney believed "By now, Longstreet would hear none of it," claiming to know how the corps commander felt during those moments. "He was still suffering from his rebukes from General Lee and was unwilling or unable to exercise the vaunted discretion heretofore the trademark of Lee's trusted lieutenants," Laney postulated. In this same fashion, Robert Krick has described Longstreet's reasoning behind his refusal of Hood's flanking petition as fueled by spite against Lee: "To alter [Lee's plan] would be to impair the lesson Lee needed to learn.... Longstreet refused to go look for himself or consider any alternatives. To do so would have been to exercise corps command, and he was not yet ready to climb off his high horse."[6]

Krick's statements echo mid-twentieth century historians Hamilton J. Eckenrode and Bryan Conrad's assertions in their 1936 biography, *James Longstreet: Lee's War Horse.* Like Douglas Southall Freeman, Eckenrode and Conrad believed one of the principal struggles for the Confederates at Gettysburg, and even throughout the course of the war, was a war of wills between Lee and Longstreet, whereby they held that the latter was always trying to assert his dominance and prove he knew better than the commanding general. The biographers speculated "[Longstreet] was beside himself with thirst and hunger for fame and high position.... Always he sought to push himself forward, not over-careful as to the means; ever he was discontented at being under Lee, thinking himself to be the better man, seeing in his mind's eye movements that would demonstrate his superiority. That itching of his colored all of his generalship." Krick's assertions also correspond with what Ben Williams, Longstreet's great nephew, wrote about his Great Uncle's military personality in his best-selling 1947 novel, *House Divided.* In the novel, Williams has Longstreet saying things like "If there's anything I hate worse than stupidity, it's opposition"; "I can never do, wholeheartedly, what someone else tells me to do when I'm sure he's wrong"; and, "But even when I'm wrong, I'm right, because I do better work when I think I'm right. A wise superior will never insist that I do something I think is a mistake." Likewise, Krick's opinion echoes Clifford Dowdey, who held that "sometime in the early morning he [Longstreet] made the—probably unconscious—decision to shift from words to action to get his own way. He began to procrastinate as a means of obstructing the execution of Lee's strategy." Krick's statements about Longstreet's desire on July 2 to not "impair the lesson Lee needed to learn" and his constant assertions that Longstreet was actively and purposefully playing a "little game" with Lee and his men falls right in line with Eckenrode and Conrad's, Williams', and Dowdey's pronouncements in the 1930s, 40s, and 50s. Paradoxically, Longstreet critics have therefore claimed that the General both disobeyed and adhered too much at Gettysburg.[7]

The progression of events on July 2 was very likely a lot less dramatic. For Lee and Longstreet, the day had already been a long one. In summary, it had taken Lee almost the entire morning to formulate an attack plan; riding back and forth between Ewell's and Longstreet's corps on several occasions to ascertain who should initiate the day's attack. On the other hand, Longstreet had braved a long countermarch ordeal, which according to Joseph Kershaw resulted in Longstreet's "manifesting considerable irritation." Reaping the fruits of J.E.B. Stuart's crucial absence, the Confederate high command put all of its stock in misleading multi-party reconnaissance of the ground and the Federal position throughout the morning and early afternoon. Lee's engineer and designated guide, who had supposedly seen no troops south of Cemetery Hill and found a concealed way forward for the First Corps, led the divisions down an unconcealed path, forcing Longstreet to take McLaws' advice to countermarch. Then, once Longstreet completed his march, he found Federals all over the ground south of Cemetery Hill, forcing the Confederates to produce an altered attack plan that commenced with Hood's, rather than McLaws' division. Attributing Lee's and Longstreet's probable frustrations at that point in the day to their tactical disagreement in the early morning, after they had spent the last several hours trying to actively carry out Lee's 11 a.m. orders, pushes the bounds of historical credibility. Taking that argument another step forward and speculating that Longstreet was actively trying to sabotage the attack or seeking to teach Lee a lesson and attain some kind of "I told you so" moment is pure conjecture.

Compared to many modern historians, Federal General Daniel Sickles' postwar thoughts on Longstreet's conduct leading up to his July 2 attack were much more substantiated. Longstreet's rejection of Hood's Round Top flanking plan signaled to Sickles "the firm adherence of Longstreet to the orders of General Lee. Again and again, as Hood plainly points out, Longstreet refused to listen to Hood's appeal ... always replying, 'General Lee's orders are to attack up the Emmitsburg Road.'" In short, evidence suggests that not only did Longstreet recognize Hood's plan would take way too long to develop in the waning afternoon hours, but his multiple refusals to consider the plan suggest he was trying to carry out Lee's orders.[8]

Another thing that should be known about this juncture in the battle is that when Hood was pressing Longstreet to allow him to strike around the Round Tops, Lee was at least in close proximity. Contrary to what Douglas Southall Freeman wrote on this topic, namely that "of all this, of course, Lee knew nothing," Lee was indeed either with or very close to Longstreet for the majority of the time between the end of the march and when Hood's division attacked. McLaws, as shown, confirmed this contention when he stated that before receiving orders to "wait until Hood got into position," he had received an order for his own division to attack, and it was evident Lee had "joined in that order." Since Lee was indeed present when Longstreet first ordered McLaws to commence the attack, it is extremely likely he was also present or nearby when Hood expressed his reservations about attacking "up the Emmitsburg Road." The British observer Fitzgerald Ross' recollections support this assertion. Ross clearly recalled that Longstreet engaged in a "long consultation with the Commander-in-Chief" at that moment.[9]

Longstreet's repeated instructions to Hood stemmed as much from the latency of the idea as from Lee having a very precise view of the main objective and how to obtain it. Therefore Longstreet seemed left with little choice but to repeat to Hood to abide by General Lee's orders to attack up the Emmitsburg Road. Many officers after the war misleadingly alleged that very early in the day, Lee recognized the supreme importance of the Round Tops and made seizing them his primary goal. One such example was when Gilbert Moxley Sorrel wrote inaccurately, "Round Top and his high shoulders were on our right, and held by us would be everything. This Lee quickly saw and tried for. They made the key for the position, and with it dangling at our girdle the lock would have yielded and the door opened." Contrary to now-popular belief, Lee never designated Little Round Top as the objective for Longstreet's attack. Rather, Lee had his sights on gaining a foothold on Cemetery Ridge. Crushing and seizing Sickles' Peach Orchard position along the Emmitsburg Road was thought to be a vital first step in accomplishing that goal. Lee stated as much in an after-battle report he wrote three weeks after the engagement: "In front of General Longstreet the enemy held a position from which, if he could be driven, it was thought our artillery could be used to advantage in assailing the more elevated ground beyond, and thus enable us to reach the crest of the ridge. That officer [Longstreet] was directed to carry this position.... After a severe struggle, Longstreet succeeded in getting possession of and holding the desired ground." Indeed, as Helen Longstreet succinctly declared over 100 years ago, 'Longstreet was ordered to attack a specific position "up the Emmitsburg road," which was not Little Round Top.'[10]

Critics of Longstreet also say the Federal position would not have looked the way it did to Hood, so formidable, if the First Corps had been in position to attack in the morning hours, which they claim was exactly what Lee had intended. "Had Longstreet attacked not later than 9 or 10 a.m., as Lee certainly expected, Sickles's and Hancock's corps would have been defeated before part of the Fifth and Sixth corps arrived. Little Round Top ... would have fallen into Confederate possession," insisted William Allan. General Fitzhugh Lee wrote similarly, "an attack made upon the Federal position ... any time before 12 o'clock ... would have embraced many elements of success; and from all I have heard and believe, such an attack was ordered." John B. Gordon claimed to know that "General Lee distinctly ordered Longstreet to attack early the morning of the second day ... but Longstreet delayed the attack until four o'clock in the afternoon, and thus lost his opportunity of occupying Little Round Top, the key to the position, which he might have done in the morning without firing a shot or losing a man." Even Gilbert Moxley Sorrel apparently bought into some of these opinions, writing, "An attack, powerful indeed, at 4 p.m., was quite different from the commanding General's expectation of one in the forenoon.... Undoubtedly Lee's intention was to make the attack in the forenoon and support it with strong movements by Hill and Ewell."[11]

At times, E.P. Alexander also wrote of his support for these dubious beliefs. "It has since appeared," the former artillerist asserted, "that if our corps had made its attack even two or three hours sooner than it did, our chances of success would have been immensely increased.... By ten, or eleven o'clock at latest, it was entirely practicable for us to have delivered our attack in good shape." Like Allan and Early, Alexander emphasized that Little Round Top, "the key to the whole position" could have easily been taken in the morning hours. In one account, he even seemed to single out Longstreet as to blame for any delay, asserting his belief that "Longstreet did not wish to take the offensive. His objection to it was not based at all upon the peculiar strength of the enemy's position for that was not yet recognized, but solely upon general principles." In yet another example, the editor of Captain Justus Scheibert's recollections of the war includes a footnote in the second day at Gettysburg section that is equally misleading. In response to Scheibert's observation that "Not until 4:30 o'clock in the afternoon did General Lee order General Longstreet to attack," the editor apparently believed the foreign observer put too much responsibility on Lee and alleges that "Scheibert tactfully omits mention of Lee's grave concern over Longstreet's delaying in attacking the enemy."[12]

Jeffry Wert, whose views are typically more favorable and supportive of Longstreet's performance at Gettysburg, offers a summary of the General's actions on the morning of the second day that is actually very comparable to Allan's and Early's statements. "Longstreet's performance during the morning deserves criticism," Wert writes. "Had he attended to the details that were his responsibility and not allowed his disagreement with Lee to affect his judgment and effort, the afternoon assault would have begun sooner, but not several hours earlier." Similarly, historian James McPherson, in his widely read, one-volume history of the Civil War *Battle Cry of Freedom*, writes of Longstreet's pre-attack actions on July 2, "Longstreet's state of mind as he prepared for this attack is hard to fathom.... But Longstreet did seem to move slowly at Gettysburg. Although Lee wanted him to attack as early in the day as possible, he did not get his troops into position until 4:00 p.m." McPherson is reasonable in his analysis and does advance some "reasons for this delay," but then ventures into conjecture, surmising that "Longstreet may have been piqued by Lee's rejection of his flanking suggestion, and he did not believe in the attack he was ordered to make. He therefore may not have put as much energy and speed into its preparation as the situation required."[13]

In arguing this position, Wert and McPherson actually align themselves with the somewhat toned-down but still scathing mode of attack Douglas Southall Freeman employed against the General in his three-volume work, *Lee's Lieutenants*, published in 1943. In these books, Freeman softened earlier arguments he made in *R.E. Lee* wherein Longstreet was solely to blame for the Confederate defeat, tried his best to force his tactical suggestions on the commanding general, and when that did not work, deliberately tried to sabotage Lee's plans through delay. Instead, Freeman altered his line of reasoning in the 1940s to allege that once Lee turned down Longstreet's proposals on the evening of July 1 and morning of July 2, the corps commanders simply lost the judgment, effort, energy, and strength to carry out his orders efficiently and effectively. "In plain, ugly words, he sulked. The dissent of Longstreet's mind was a brake on his energies," Freeman believed. In another section, Freeman wrote similarly, "There can be no escaping the conclusion that his behavior was that of a man who sulked because his plan was rejected by his chief." Shelby Foote echoed Freeman's assertions in his own Gettysburg narrative: "Renewing his [Longstreet's] plea for a withdrawal this morning, the burly Georgian had been rebuffed again: whereupon he turned sulky. Though he had of course obeyed all orders given him, he had not anticipated them in the best tradition of the Army of the Northern Virginia, with the result that he was partly to blame for the delays encountered." Therefore, like Foote and Freeman's later work, Wert and McPherson do not subscribe to the claim that Longstreet actively and deliberately tried to sabotage Lee's tactical plans, but rather that he lost (in McPherson's case, he uses the more suspect "may have") all of his keenness, fervor, and passion as a military leader once Lee declined to pursue the tactical defensive. As a result of Longstreet losing his military bearing, according to these historians, Confederate preparation for and execution of the July 2 attack suffered.[14]

These and similar critiques have been addressed previously; however, a good summary is in order. Lee may have intended and wanted many things, but the fact of the matter is he simply was never ready to provide Longstreet with attack orders until around 11 a.m. Major Thomas Goree, Longstreet's aide-de-camp articulated this point most effectively in an 1875 letter to his former Chief, writing, "On the 2d and 3d days of the battle before the fighting commenced, I know that Genrl. Lee was constantly with you, and that any movement that you made, as well as all delays, was with his advice or concurrence." Indeed, necessary and approved delays ensued throughout the morning, followed by the unfortunate countermarch ordeal, which was largely precipitated by Lee's insistence that Longstreet's column march completely unseen by the enemy and be initially guided by an officer who did not know where he was going.[15]

Furthermore, even if Longstreet had been able to attack sometime during the mid-morning hours, Sickles' entire Third Corps was on the south end of Cemetery Ridge sometime between 9 and 10 a.m. Therefore, Lee's original plan to attack up the Emmitsburg Road toward Cemetery Hill would have met flanking fire from multiple Federal corps as Longstreet's divisions strafed northeastward in their front. Wert admits this much elsewhere in his narrative: "The attack plan ordered by Lee—an attack up the Emmitsburg Road—had little chance of success if Union general Daniel Sickles kept his corps on Cemetery Ridge." Sickles himself wrote persuasively on this exact topic after the war, asserting, "If he [Longstreet] had attacked in the morning, as it is said he should have done, he would have encountered Buford's division of cavalry, five thousand sabres, on his flank, and my corps would have been in his front, as it was in the afternoon." Sickles made a good point; however, based on the Confederates' misbegotten plan to attack up the Emmitsburg Road, his Federal Third Corps would have been on Longstreet's flank, not his front, if the Southerners had assaulted in such a manner earlier in the day. Curiously, in E.P. Alexander's *Military Memoirs*, the artillerist seemed to hold a different point of view altogether regarding the alleged effectiveness of a Confederate attack made earlier on the right. "43 of the 51 Federal brigades of infantry were upon the ground at 8 a.m.," Alexander wrote, "and occupying the strong position already described.... When, at nine o'clock, the arrival of Longstreet's reserve artillery was reported, it must be admitted that there was *little to be hoped for from any immediate attack then possible.*" In this account, Alexander clearly held that an earlier attack would have made little difference as far as results were concerned.[16]

In a similar vein, historian Glenn Tucker persuasively contended that Longstreet launched his attack at the most opportune time on July 2: "In many respects it seems that Longstreet's attack was delivered, fortuitously more than by intent, at exactly the right moment, because it was at the only time he was likely to catch Sickles' Third Corps so grievously exposed." Edwin Coddington agreed with Tucker: "It so happens that Longstreet could not have hit the Union left flank at a more inopportune moment for Meade.... Before his [Sickle's] men could dig in and Meade could shift the Fifth Corps from right to left, Longstreet opened his attack."

On the topic of Little Round Top, contrary to Alexander, Allan, and Early's belief, Lee never designated "Round Top Hill" as an objective during the morning hours of July 2. The Confederates' fight for Little Round Top occurred less purposefully, and more out of happenstance when a portion of Hood's division veered off toward the elevated ground in the early stages of Longstreet's attack.[17]

Alexander's suggestion that "Longstreet did not wish to take the offensive" at Gettysburg was accurate in the general sense, but his allegation that the First Corps commander was intentionally dragging his feet is supposition and contrary to historical evidence. Furthermore, his belief that Longstreet had not recognized the "peculiar strength of the enemy position" leading up to the July 2 attack is equally unsubstantiated, since Longstreet demonstrated in his conversation with Lee as early as the evening of July 1 that he understood the strength of the Federal position. Even more confusingly, as is rather common with Alexander's writings, he contradicted his critical commentary on Longstreet's actions during the morning hours at other points in the same narrative. Indeed, in another section, Alexander wrote that Lee "was present on the field all the time, & was apparently consenting to the situation from hour to hour. Longstreet is bitterly blamed for asking for delay.... But it seems to me that ... it ... must be modified by the fact that Gen. Lee's granting the request justified it as apparently prudent, at the time."[18]

12

Longstreet According to McLaws

"The plan of battle, so far as his forces were concerned, could not be carried out"
—Lafayette McLaws

Lafayette McLaws did not appreciate, as he described it, James Longstreet's excessive meddling in his division's affairs on July 2. In a letter to his wife written just five days after the battle, he lambasted Longstreet and seemed to put all the blame on his Chief. "Genl Longstreet is to blame," seethed McLaws, "for not reconnoitering the ground and for persisting in ordering the assault when his errors were discovered." Getting to the heart of his frustration with Longstreet, McLaws alleged that "During the engagement he was very excited, giving contrary orders to every one, and was exceedingly overbearing. I consider him a humbug—a man of small capacity, very obstinate, not at all chivalrous, exceedingly conceited, and totally selfish. If I can it is my intention to get away from his command." Over the years, Longstreet critics have employed this quote as evidence that the General had selfish motivations on July 2, his actions directly affected by his disagreement with Lee over tactics. For example, Robert Krick writes of McLaws' statement, "The misbegotten tendency to flick away attacks on Longstreet's behavior as the work of a dishonest postwar cabal just will not stand up in considering McLaws' most pointed description of July 2." Historians like Krick contend that Longstreet's judgment was clouded by the tactical reservations he held against Lee's attack plan, which they believe affected his military bearing and handling of the First Corps' attack. Likewise, John Oeffinger, editor of McLaws' letters, asserts that at Gettysburg, Longstreet did not permit "McLaws to do what McLaws felt was rightfully his duty on July 2," and furthermore that Longstreet's generalship hindered the assault, despite its success, writing, "Longstreet's uncoordinated action and micromanagement of the division's attack did not deter McLaws's men from delivering one of their best assaults for the Confederacy."[1]

Yet, once again, if we look just beneath the surface of McLaws' post-battle comments about Longstreet, it seems it would have been more suitable for the division commander to direct his frustration at General Lee. Indeed, in that same section of the letter, McLaws stated "I think the attack was unnecessary and the whole plan of battle a very bad one." This assertion could just as easily have been present in any of Longstreet's after-battle and postwar writings. But instead of acknowledging General Lee had made the decision to attack and was the architect of the "whole plan of battle," McLaws immediately began his already-quoted diatribe against Longstreet. The charge that Longstreet himself did not sufficiently reconnoiter the ground has already been addressed. In the absence of J.E.B. Stuart, numerous reconnaissance were conducted during the morning and early afternoon, including one by McLaws himself, which according to him, facilitated the First Corps' countermarch. Furthermore, also as related previously, General Pendleton noted that "about midday" General Longstreet himself "arrived and viewed the ground." It is reasonable to assume Longstreet also received intelligence from his engineer, Major Clarke, and like General Lee, put his trust in Captain Johnston's multiple reconnaissance missions. Longstreet had also sent out E.P. Alexander and two lieutenants from the 1st South Carolina Cavalry to gain a better understanding of the ground off to the right in preparation for the attack.[2]

As for "persisting in ordering the assault when his [Longstreet's] errors were discovered," the errors were more attributable to the commanding general. Moreover, they were less "errors" than deficiencies in accurate intelligence. In short, the absence of a good understanding of the Federal position was continually evident on July 2. Throughout the morning, the Federal left was positioned well south of Cemetery Hill and east of the Emmitsburg Road. Seemingly by chance, it just so happened that by the time the Confederate First Corps completed its march, the Federal Third Corps had moved forward and was positioned near the Emmitsburg Road, even if its left flank was not anchored there. McLaws and Osmun Latrobe confirmed Lee's presence with Longstreet in the hour or so previous to the attack. Latrobe further stated that "General Lee ... was impatient that the attack was delayed." These allegations that Lee was impatient at that point, given the day's late hour, were confirmed by his actions. Initially, he pushed, through Longstreet, for McLaws to commence the attack almost immediately upon arrival without addressing the obviously altered Federal position. Then, he made his only modification to the original attack plan, having it begin with Hood's rather than McLaws' division. Otherwise, it is clear he simply wanted the attack to begin. When Hood discovered the Federal left was located well back from the Emmitsburg Road, Lee pushed, again through Longstreet, for his orders to be carried out and for the attack to begin "up the Emmitsburg Road." It is reasonable to assume Lee was insistent because his goal, as confirmed through his first after-battle report, was to seize the Peach Orchard and use it as a foothold to gain Cemetery Ridge—his principal objective. But as expected, initially Hood, and later Evander Law (after the former was wounded during the early stage of the attack) had to acknowledge the existence of these Federal troops, resulting in the division's attack effectively splitting in two—one part progressing through Devil's Den, the other toward Little Round Top.

Historians rarely contrast McLaws' post-battle letter with his postwar statements, which perhaps offer a less-emotionally charged account of July 2. Five days after the battle he charged Longstreet with "persisting in ordering the assault when his errors were discovered," while in his postwar narrative of the battle he was more circumspect. In describing Longstreet's comportment during the hour before the attack commenced, McLaws wrote:

> I have no doubt but that when General Longstreet became suddenly aware of the true state of affairs, that instead of the head of his column debauching from the woods on the flank of the enemy (recollect the head of the column was conducted by General Lee's staff officer), they were suddenly confronted with superior forces, in position and ready for the fight; and besides

> extending far away to his right, he was very much disconcerted and annoyed, principally because it was evident at a glance that the plan of battle, so far as his forces were concerned, could not be carried out.[3]

Interestingly, here McLaws attributed Longstreet's distress and irritation at this point in the battle to the existence of an unexpected and extensive Federal battle line, rather than to general tactical reservations against the attack. Following this passage, he indicated that after Longstreet discovered the Federal line extended further to the right than expected, the General was forced to conduct an attack more parallel than perpendicular to the Emmitsburg Road. In McLaws' estimation, it was then that the First Corps commander was faced with a "question":

> Was it General Longstreet's duty, or would he have been justified, when he became aware that General Lee's order could not be obeyed, that the reconnaissance on which they were based had been faulty, and that he had therefore given, those orders under mistaken or false information, to have halted his command, and going back to General Lee, inform him of the true status of the enemy, and that his order of attack should be changed, as it was not the best under the circumstances?[4]

In this passage, McLaws openly described the Confederate reconnaissance as "faulty," and Lee's orders as simply based on "mistaken or false information." As discussed and proven already, the Confederate high command would have found these underlying issues to be true, whether Longstreet attacked at 10 a.m. or 4 p.m. Yet, following these statements, McLaws shifted his attention back to Longstreet, questioning if his Chief should have "gone back to General Lee" to "inform him of the true status of the enemy." Confusingly, McLaws made this statement as if Lee was not present at this juncture in the battle, contradicting his earlier narrative asserting Lee was present with Longstreet when the latter initially ordered him to attack. In short, it would seem that McLaws formed this question while under the mistaken impression that Lee was not able to see the Federal corps' forward position along the Emmitsburg Road, arching back toward the Round Tops, with his own eyes, and was uninformed of the "true status of the enemy."

McLaws' misunderstanding of Lee's awareness of the changed battlescape is confirmed when later in his narrative he alleged that "General Lee did not think the enemy's left was occupied so strongly as it was, even at that late hour, and was not made aware of the great natural strength of the enemy's position." He continued to once again make Longstreet a culprit and Lee an absentee non-entity, asserting, "If General Longstreet had taken the responsibility to report that the positions in his front were naturally so strong and were strongly occupied that his force could not accomplish the important results that were expected, and insisted on a delay.... I do not think the battle would have been fought at all." McLaws then strangely closed his argument with many hypotheticals, alleging that if Longstreet had delayed; if he had been allowed time to concentrate his whole corps, including George Pickett's division; and, if a "more thorough examination" was made of the Federal position, "General Lee would have manoeuvred [*sic*] to force an attack upon himself." From McLaws' point of view, if only Longstreet had exercised more of those seemingly negative qualities he attributed to his Chief only five days after the battle—obstinacy, conceit, and selfishness—in his dealings with Lee on the afternoon of July 2, Lee's Warhorse might have had the chance to employ the tactical defensive after all.[5]

On the contrary, Lee was indeed in control and aware of the situation. McLaws explicitly admitted elsewhere in his narrative, "It is true he [Longstreet] could have waited, but he was, as I understood it, urged to the assault." Lee was present with Longstreet when deciding to alter the attack to have it commence with Hood's division, as he likely was also present when Longstreet insisted that Hood follow Lee's orders to "attack up the Emmitsburg Road." Lee could have changed "his order of attack," as McLaws put it, but given the late hour, his growing impatience at the attack's delay, and his true objective being Cemetery Ridge, not Little Round Top, he insisted it be carried out as ordered. To keep Lee's point of attack and principal objective in mind, Longstreet's two divisions would have to make tactical alterations in reaction to the Federal position as the battle unfolded.[6]

More confusingly, it is only later in McLaws' narrative he contradicted most, if not all, of his earlier points, stating he did not believe "General Longstreet is to be blamed for not disobeying orders to attack when he became aware that, contrary to expectations, the enemy was in great force in his immediate front." The former Major General then once again remembered, "For, as I understood Major Latrobe, General Lee was with him [Longstreet] when the enemy had opened on my division, thus disclosing their immediate presence, and but a short while after Hood's reports must have been received." McLaws further conceded that if "Longstreet had not engaged" at that time and not followed Lee's directive to attack up the Emmitsburg Road, "some ... in the army ... would have ascribed his conduct to the worst of motives." In short, it has been established that Lee was there and Longstreet had his orders. Longstreet was a professional soldier and knew the time for any disagreement had passed hours ago. He would carry out Lee's orders as directed to the best of his ability, or as McLaws stated of how Longstreet recognized his duty on the afternoon of July 2, "his orders were positive" and it was "imperative ... upon an officer's honor to do his best to carry it out."[7]

McLaws' other assertion in his post-battle letter to his wife referring to Longstreet's issuing "contrary orders" and being "very excited" and "exceedingly overbearing" on July 2 were likely in reference to his belief that Longstreet took too heavy a hand in the direction of his division. Years later, McLaws provided a specific example, describing how while preparations were being made to attack, Longstreet rode over to McLaws and asked, "'Why is not a battery placed here?'" According to McLaws, Longstreet "pointed to the place where the road by which we marched reached the edge of the open space in front." McLaws then allegedly replied, "General, if a battery is placed there it will draw the enemy's artillery right among my lines formed for the charge and will of itself be in the way of my charge, and tend to demoralize my men." Despite McLaws' reservations, Longstreet was said to have ordered the battery placed there anyway, and so it was, which was said to have "at once drew the enemy's fire of artillery upon it, cutting the limbs of trees in abundance, which fell among around my men, and the bursting shells and shot wounded or killed a number whilst in line formed for the advance, producing a natural feeling of uneasiness among them."[8]

This particular account is presented in almost every anti–Longstreet narrative as irrefutable evidence that Lee's Warhorse was acting out of deep frustration on the afternoon of July 2; however, Harry Pfanz has explicitly pointed out there exists no record of artillery being placed in the position referenced by McLaws, writing that besides the division commander's story, "There seems to be no other mention of a battery's having been in the road itself. Alexander did not mention it." Sifting through Alexander's post-war letters and memoirs, there is indeed no mention of said battery, and no testimony elsewhere to confirm or refute McLaws' account.[9]

McLaws' charge in his post-battle letter that Longstreet had paid the most attention to his division on July 2 was substantiated. Longstreet's reasoning for doing so are found in a curious letter he wrote to McLaws just a month before the battle on June 3. "You spoke of going South the other day. If you wish to go I expect that I may make the arrangement for you I was speaking of for myself," Longstreet reassured McLaws. He then described the proposed arrangement: "That is for you to go there and let Beauregard come here with a Corps. We want everybody here that we can get and if you think of going south one must agree to send us every man that you can dispense with during the summer particularly." Longstreet assured McLaws he could make this transfer happen "if it is desirable to you." The superficial reason for Longstreet broaching this subject was a request from Lee to have his corps commander inquire about McLaws' physical health and ability to carry out his duties in the Army of Northern Virginia during the upcoming summer campaign; however, the real reason was Lee was not very thrilled with McLaws' generalship. The division commander had missed the Winter 1862–1863 campaign for health reasons, then failed to impress Lee with his performance at the Battle of Chancellorsville in May. In the postwar years, Longstreet informed McLaws that he had made Lee a promise to make sure the division was well-looked after on July 2. In a letter to McLaws, he explained how "I thus became responsible for anything that was not entirely satisfactory in your command from that day." Longstreet further stated that he "was repeatedly told of that fact" by Lee.[10]

13

Longstreet's Wave Rolls Forward

"Wait a little, we are all going in presently"
—James Longstreet

Under the revised attack plan, Hood's division was given the responsibility for beginning Longstreet's assault. Likely sometime between 4 and 4:30 p.m., Brigadier Generals Jerome Robertson and Evander Law's brigades of Hood's division lunged forward from Warfield Ridge (the southern extension of Seminary Ridge) toward some of the now most infamous areas of the Gettysburg battlefield—Devil's Den, the Slaughter Pen, the Triangular Field, and Little Round Top. Just before the assault commenced, one Texan soldier spotted Longstreet behind E.P. Alexander's formidable artillery line of 36 guns posted on Warfield Ridge. Alexander's guns spewed a barrage of fire at Sickles' protruding salient, positioned only a few hundred yards in his front. Longstreet was said to have been "sitting on his horse like an iron man with his spyglass to his eye.... Limbs of trees fell and crashed around him, yet he sat as unmoved as a statue."[1]

According to Robertson, before Hood was wounded by a shell about twenty minutes into the fight, he told his subordinate to "keep my right well closed on Brigadier General Law's left, and to let my left rest on the Emmitsburg Pike." However, in trying to both execute his orders and acknowledge the developing real-time situation, Robertson's brigade split in two. Later, Robertson described how the Emmitsburg Road "bears sharply to the left ... while Law on my right bore to the right." Understanding the gap between the two brigades was too large for his command to cover, Robertson decided to allow two regiments to keep contact with the left of Law, whose own brigade drifted right toward Big Round Top and the saddle between the Round Tops. The other half of Robertson's command advanced toward Houck's Ridge and the Triangular Field, while trying its best to abide by orders and maintain a semblance of a connection to the Emmitsburg Road. The result was that between about 4:45 and 5:30 p.m., three regiments from Law's brigade and two regiments from Robertson's brigade tangled, ultimately unsuccessfully, with Federal forces in a desperate contest for control of Little Round Top. At the same time, Law's 44th and 48th Alabama regiments and Robertson's two other regiments, supported by Brigadier Generals Henry Benning and George "Tige" Anderson's brigades assaulted the Federals positioned west of Little Round Top, across Plum Run Valley on Houck's Ridge. As the Union position eventually crumbled on the south side of Houck's Ridge, the fight spilled northward into the Rose Woods, Wheatfield, and Stony Hill sectors.[2]

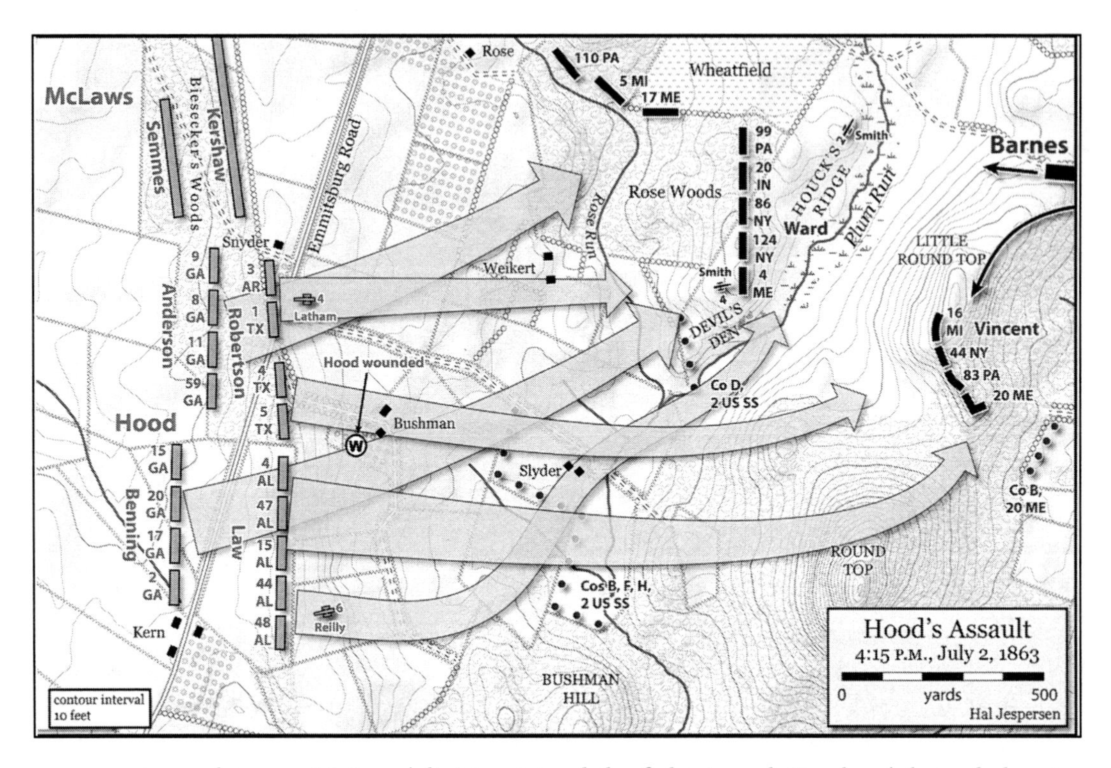

Around 5 p.m., McLaws' division joined the fight. Joseph Kershaw's brigade leapt over the stone wall in their immediate front and moved forward. Kershaw's left rested on the Emmitsburg Road, and the brigade collectively advanced slightly northeast toward the Peach Orchard, while its right pressed in the direction of the Rose Woods and Stony Hill, where "Tige" Anderson's brigade of Hood's division was then engaged. Kershaw later said of his orders, "I was directed to commence the attack as soon as General Hood became engaged, swinging around toward the Peach Orchard, and at the same time establishing connection with Hood on my right, and cooperating with him." He had also been told that William Barksdale's brigade would "conform to my movement; that [Paul] Semmes would follow me, and Wofford follow Barksdale." Longstreet was said to have watched Hood's division attack from a post near Kershaw's brigade and it appears both he and McLaws were insistent that Kershaw understand his orders to the utmost. "These instructions," Kershaw recalled, "I received in sundry messages from General Longstreet and General McLaws, and in part by personal communication with them." Shortly thereafter, Longstreet led by personal example, with Kershaw noting he "accompanied me in this advance on foot, as far as the Emmitsburg Road."[3]

As the battle continued to rage in the Wheatfield, ultimately changing hands between Confederate and Federal forces six times, William Barksdale's brigade of Mississippians advanced left of Kershaw, heading directly toward the Peach Orchard salient at the intersection of the Emmitsburg and Wheatfield Roads. Barksdale had been itching to get into the fight. He sent messages to both McLaws and Longstreet, begging them to allow him to advance. "Wait a little," Longstreet replied, "we are all going in presently." Shortly before 6 p.m., Longstreet himself gave the order for Barksdale to advance. With most of McLaws' division then operational, Longstreet later stated, "Then was fairly

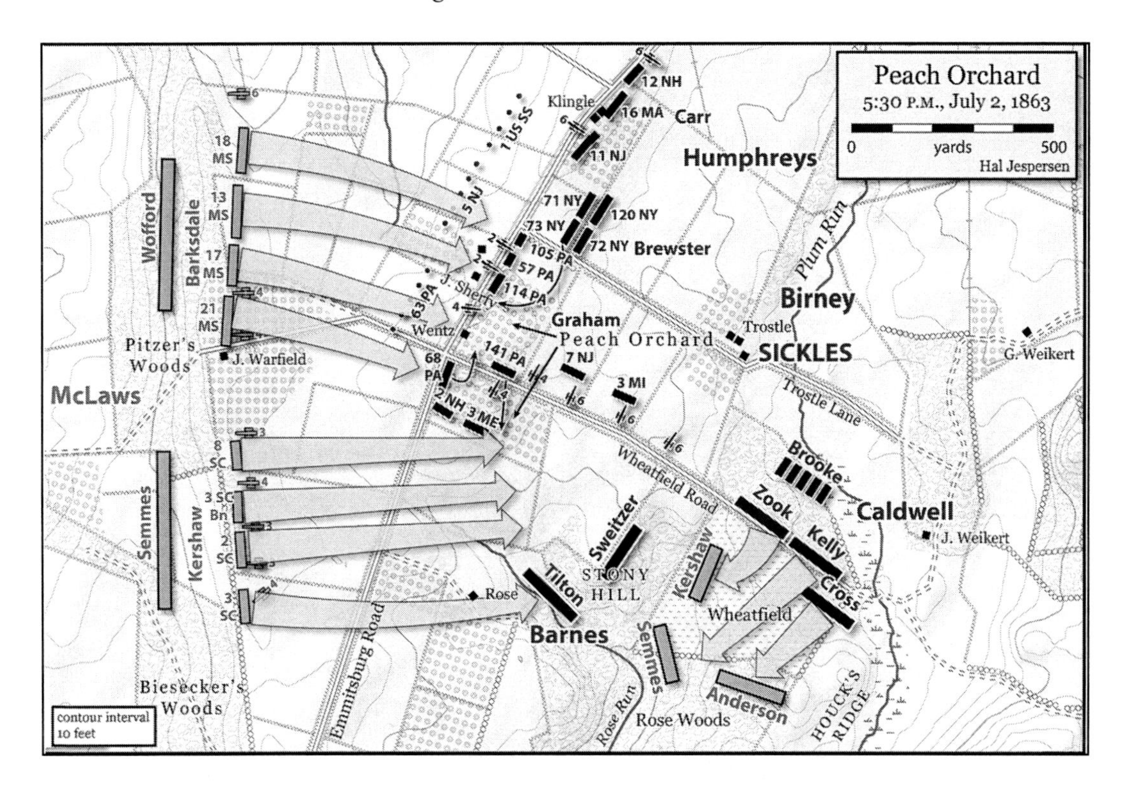

commenced what I do not hesitate to pronounce the best three hours' fighting ever done by any troops on any battle-field." Barksdale's men were "yelling at the top of their voices, without firing a shot, the brigade sped swiftly across the field and literally rushed the goal," one soldier recollected. "Directly in front of us," the First corps commander later described, "occupying the peach orchard, on a piece of elevated ground General Lee desired me to take and hold for his artillery, was the Third Corps of the Federals." With pressure from Kershaw along the Wheatfield Road front, Barksdale crushed the Peach Orchard salient within fifteen minutes, and wheeling left with three regiments, advanced up the Emmitsburg Road toward Trostle Lane and the withdrawing Federals beyond.[4]

Like Kershaw's brigade, Longstreet personally directed Wofford's brigade of McLaws' division into the battle less than a half hour after Barksdale. Lee's Warhorse rode forward with the Georgian brigade and upon hearing cheering from the men, he called out "Cheer less, men, and fight more." Longstreet conducted his corps in such a manner only a few times during the war and his actions demonstrated how emotionally engaged he was on July 2. Fremantle wrote of this dramatic scene, "Every one deplores that Longstreet *will* expose himself in such a reckless manner. To-day he led a Georgian regiment in a charge against a battery, hat in hand, and in front of everybody." When Wofford's command swept forward, it initially filled a gap between Kershaw's and Barksdale's brigades, but instead of following the latter, proceeded down the Wheatfield Road to join in the First Corps' bloodbath in the Wheatfield. Kershaw later said of Wofford that "On his approach the enemy retreated across the wheatfield, where, with the regiments of my left wing, [he] attacked with great effect, driving the Federals upon and

Longstreet directing his attack, July 2, 1863 (Library of Congress).

near to Little Round Top." North of Wofford and after taking the Peach Orchard, Barksdale's left made contact as intended with the right two brigades of A.P. Hill's corps under Brigadier Generals Cadmus Wilcox and David Lang, whose combined force collectively finished off the Federal's advanced position along the Emmitsburg Road shortly after 7 p.m. Colonel Lang recalled the gruesome scene along the road as his men swept forward: "I do not remember having seen anywhere before the dead lying thicker than where the Yankee infantry attempted to make a stand in our front." As Barksdale set his sights on Cemetery Ridge, E.P. Alexander was swept up in the excitement of the moment and limbered up his battalion. The young artillerist moved his guns from Warfield Ridge to the recently captured Sherfy Peach Orchard, intending to provide close-in artillery support for the infantry advance. Indeed, his men were "in great spirits, cheering & straining every nerve to get forward in the least possible time," ripping down any fence that stood in their way, while Alexander's adrenaline was firing on all cylinders. "[We'll] finish the whole war this afternoon," he exclaimed to his gunners. Unbeknownst to Alexander at such an exhilarating moment was that it was not to be so.[5]

14

Lee Watches Hill's Partial Assault

"Ewell and Hill were to afford him vigorous co-operation"
—Armistead Long

"In the fight that ensued, General Longstreet was vastly outnumbered, and yet he made his way over all obstacles of ground and superiority of numbers, and pushed back the heavy masses that confronted him," Cadmus Wilcox, typically a postwar critic of Longstreet's actions at Gettysburg, said emphatically of the First Corps' attack on July 2. Yet, many historians have since downplayed the success of Longstreet's attack during the second day's battle, which served to smash two Federal corps and seriously maim another despite receiving little to no support from the rest of the army. In diminishing Longstreet's success on July 2, many scholars have neglected to make it clear Lee's objective was not Little Round Top, but rather Cemetery Ridge. Indeed, we can say today with a great degree of certainty that Little Round Top commanded the Ridge position and had Lee made a more concerted effort in seizing it, the Federal position would probably have become untenable; however, based on the intelligence Lee had on hand leading up to Longstreet's July 2 attack, Little Round Top was not the designated objective. As Lee stated most clearly in his first after-battle report, and as Longstreet recounted candidly for the rest of his life, "Our attack was to progress in the general direction of the Emmetsburg [*sic*] road," while "The importance of Round Top, as a point d' appui, was not appreciated until after my attack." Lee's focus was first the Peach Orchard, then Cemetery Ridge, and finally Cemetery Hill.[1]

Longstreet achieved the first objective by 6:30 p.m., at the latest. As his attack sprawled northward, Longstreet's two divisions became increasingly spread thin. Hood's early discovery that the Federal left flank was nowhere near the Emmitsburg Road and the subsequent dedication of resources against that reality, coupled with McLaws' attack, as ordered, up the Emmitsburg Road and away from Hood, effectively guaranteed such attenuation. In short, Hood (and later, Law) reacted to the Federal threat to the First Corp's right flank and as a result became bogged down in a fight for Little Round Top and its surrounding environs, while Barksdale's brigade of McLaws' division joined the right of Hill's corps and advanced its attack toward the Federal Cemetery Ridge position. "These two movements of extension so drew my forces out," Longstreet later recalled, "that I found myself attacking Cemetery Hill with a single line of battle against no less than fifty thousand troops." The end result of this separation was that Longstreet's two-division attack became more diluted over a much broader front than

Confederate leadership initially expected, and therefore, in even greater need of support from Anderson's division of Hill's corps to continue the assault. Despite how Longstreet's attack wound up progressing, this support had always been expected. Armistead Long, secretary to Lee and postwar Longstreet critic, recollected years later that "Ewell and Hill were to afford him [Longstreet] vigorous co-operation." Similarly, in an 1876 letter to Jubal Early, Long wrote, "I understood the plan of battle to be, that Longstreet, on the right, should commence the attack, while Hill, in the center, and Ewell, on the left, should cooperate by vigorous support." Of note in both accounts was Long's use of the terms, "vigorous co-operation" and "vigorous support."[2]

Lee provided Longstreet with Anderson's division, albeit under the command of A.P. Hill, in light of George Pickett's absence. Initially, Anderson did carry out Longstreet's attack. After aiding Barksdale's brigade in finishing off the Federal's advanced position along the Emmitsburg Road, and while Wofford's, Kershaw's, and portions of Hood's division were fighting to seize the elusive Wheatfield, Wilcox's and Lang's brigades of Anderson's division pressed on with the Mississippians due east toward Cemetery Ridge around 7:15 p.m. Ambrose Wright's brigade of Anderson's division concurrently made an unsupported attack against the Federal line further north. Significantly, right around this time, Longstreet shot off a message to Lee, reporting that "we are doing well." One would think that such positive news would have energized Lee to seize the moment and be poised to send in whatever units he had on hand to support an attack against his objective, or at the very least, ensure Hill, one of his green corps commanders, fully employed Anderson's division as he had intended. After all, Lee had ordered Hill to "threaten the enemy's center, to prevent re-enforcements being drawn to either wing, and co-operate with his right division in Longstreet's attack."[3]

The next logical question is: given Longstreet's message informing Lee that "we are doing well" and Hill's unambiguous orders, why did Lee then not ensure the entirety of Anderson's division fully press the attack? Much more often than not, historians have focused less on providing an answer to that critical question, and more on their critique of Longstreet's pre-attack actions. For example, Robert Krick has sought to find out why an allegedly frustrated Lee did not "insist on greater organization and speed of movement" on Longstreet's front during the morning hours. Krick neglects to mention Lee was present with or near Longstreet for the majority of the hours leading up to the Confederate attack, and that he consented to almost every one of the First Corps commander's requests. John Fairfax, one of Longstreet's staff officers confirmed this reality in an 1877 letter to Longstreet about a discussion he had recently had with William Pendleton. Fairfax wrote that he informed Pendleton "that you and General Lee were together the greater part of the day up to about three o'clock or later." If Lee was actually upset with Longstreet about the way he was conducting his corps during the hours leading up to attack, he was often present, and as commanding general could have easily insisted that conduct be changed.[4]

Krick then pivots to argue Lee was too busy dealing with the army's two new corps commanders to address any concerns with his senior lieutenant, Longstreet, and that anyway, once a tactical plan had been decided, his typical mode of command was hands-off. In this regard, Krick semi-mirrors the arguments of Clifford Dowdey, who wrote, "Trying to supervise everything, he [Lee] actually led nowhere, and the army felt the lack of a strong hand at the controls." Krick differs from Dowdey in that he seemingly believes Lee did lead when it came to overseeing the actions of Ewell and Hill. "He had already had cause to be deeply concerned about Ewell," Krick contends, "and Hill's inaugural attempt at corps command at Gettysburg had very little impact on the battle. It must have been easy for Lee to decide to stay near the sectors of his two tyros while leaving his one veteran to operate with greater independence, as was Lee's preferred system." Not only does Krick conveniently use Ewell and Hill's fresh status to state Lee could not have been more hands-on with Longstreet (even if desired), but he also neglects to recognize Lee was never hands-on with his two new corps commanders either. Throughout Longstreet's successful attack, Lee never demonstrated being "deeply concerned about Ewell," and never made an attempt to shake Ewell out of his inactivity to relieve some pressure on the Confederate right. And as Longstreet's attack spread northward to Hill's sector, where Lee was physically present, the commanding general never pushed Hill to fully engage Anderson's entire division in the attack on Cemetery Ridge. Contrary to Krick's opinion, on this subject, even life-long Longstreet critic Douglas Southall Freeman admitted, "It is scarcely too much to say that on July 2 the Army of Northern Virginia was without a commander."[5]

Indeed, Anderson's partial three-brigade support of Longstreet's attack, carried out right in front of Lee, created some opportunities for success, but ultimately proved only mildly successful. Along Plum Run, Barksdale's, Wilcox's, and Lang's disorganized brigades tangled with Lieutenant Colonel Freeman McGilvery's patchwork artillery line, scattered remnants of the Federal Third Corps, Colonel George Willard's Second Corps brigade, and two additional regiments, the 19th Maine and 1st Minnesota, who collectively checked the Confederates' advance after 8 o'clock. The advance of Wright's brigade to Lang's left proved more promising for the Confederates, whereby the four Georgia regiments reached the summit and secured a brief lodging on Cemetery Ridge. But looking back to his left for support, Wright saw no one. Carnot Posey's brigade never crossed the Emmitsburg Road and William Mahone's brigade failed to budge at all. Bewilderingly, Lee allegedly told Hill later that evening "It is all well, General. Everything is well," but undoubtedly little had gone well or as planned for Hill's corps on July 2.[6]

So what happened? Why had Hill not fully employed Anderson's division at such an opportune moment? In one of his accounts, Longstreet failed to explain properly what he meant when writing that McLaws' left flank was "not protected by the brigades that were to move en echelon with it." Wilcox's, Lang's, and Wright's brigades of Anderson's division, to McLaws' left, did in fact support and continue Longstreet's attack, but what he was actually referring to was a lack of total support from Anderson's division, including Posey's and Mahone's brigades, and potentially even more extensive support from Hill's corps, namely Pender's division. In the same account, Longstreet clarified his meaning when writing he had been "assured that my flank would be protected by the brigades of Wilcox, [Edward] Perry, Wright, Posey, and Mahone, moving en echelon." All things considered, Longstreet charged that "Hill made no move whatever, save of his brigades of his right division that were covering our left." Interestingly, for the first few years after the battle, the South largely blamed A.P. Hill and J.E.B. Stuart for the Confederate loss at Gettysburg. Just days after the battle, the *Richmond Enquirer* summed up the Confederate army's performance on July 2 by describing how Longstreet

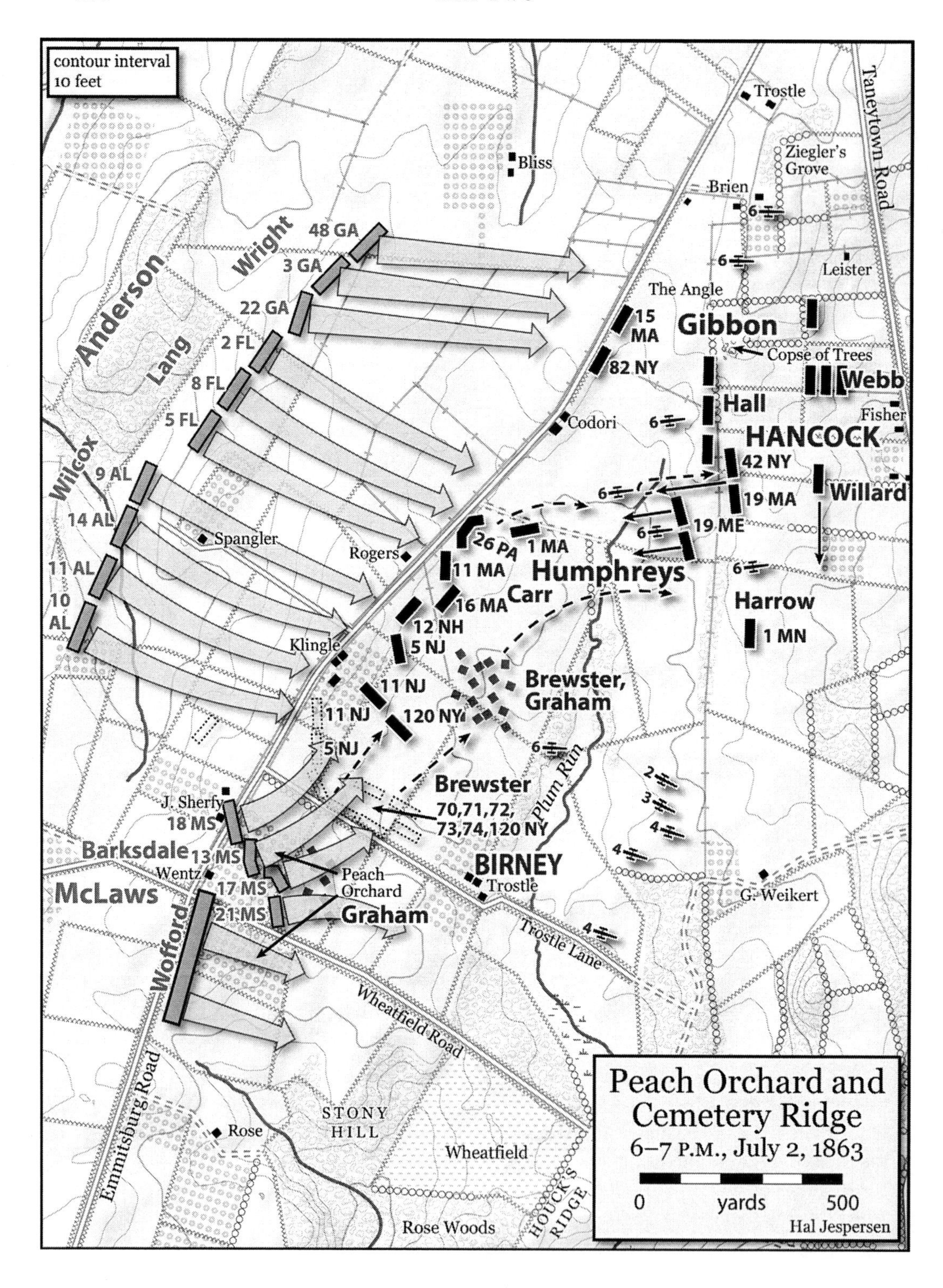
contour interval
10 feet
Peach Orchard and
Cemetery Ridge
6–7 P.M., July 2, 1863
0
yards
500
Hal Jespersen
Trostle
Taneytown Road
Bliss
Ziegler's
Grove
Brien
Leister
The Angle
Gibbon
Copse of Trees
Webb
Hall
Fisher
HANCOCK
Willard
Harrow
1 MN
Humphreys
Carr
Codori
Rogers
Spangler
Klingle
Brewster,
Graham
Brewster
70,71,72,
73,74,120 NY
BIRNEY
Trostle
Plum Run
G. Weikert
Trostle Lane
Wheatfield Road
Peach
Orchard
Graham
J. Sherfy
Wentz
Barksdale
McLaws
Wofford
Emmitsburg Road
Rose
STONY
HILL
Wheatfield
Rose Woods
HOUCK'S
RIDGE
Anderson
Wright
Lang
Wilcox
48 GA
3 GA
22 GA
2 FL
8 FL
5 FL
9 AL
14 AL
11 AL
10
AL
18 MS
13 MS
17 MS
21 MS
15
MA
82 NY
42 NY
19 MA
19 ME
26 PA
1 MA
11 MA
16 MA
12 NH
5 NJ
11 NJ
11 NJ
120 NY
5 NJ

essentially had the battle won, but then Hill failed to continue the attack with any sense of determination. "It was now apparent that the day was lost—lost after it was won—lost, not because our army fought badly, but because a large portion did not fight at all," they wrote, in reference to Hill's limited support. Indeed, one is left wondering why historians have spilt so much ink in nitpicking Longstreet's actions at Gettysburg, trying to identify exactly where he was and what he was doing at every hour, while much less has been written about how and why Hill blatantly failed to act at a critical moment on July 2 when the day "was won" by Longstreet. James McPherson offers little answers in his *Battle Cry of Freedom*, now a mainstay in college-level courses on the war, writing only of Hill's actions on July 2, "Part of Hill's fresh division finally joined Longstreet's assault." On the other hand, Glenn Tucker aptly described the two new corps commanders' poor performances during the second day's battle in comparison to Longstreet's: "Whether from lack of experience in high command or lack of innate ability, the shortcomings of Ewell and A.P. Hill were critical; compared with them, the deficiencies of Longstreet were indeed venial."[7]

Anderson's after-battle report left much to be desired as to an explanation for his division's partial attack on July 2. Perhaps Gilbert Moxley Sorrel's assessment of Anderson was accurate when suggesting "His courage was of the highest order, but he was indolent. His capacity and intelligence excellent, but it was hard to get him to use them." Anderson claimed in his report that "The advance of Mc-Laws' [*sic*] division was immediately followed by the brigades of mine, in the manner directed." He then described how, in obvious reference to Wright's brigade, "They drove the enemy from his first line, and possessed themselves of the ridge and of much of the artillery with which it had been crowned." Anderson also cited his reasoning for why "the brigades were compelled to retire," which included reference to a "second line" of battle; "artillery upon both our front and flanks," and, "strong reinforcements pressed upon our right flank." Anderson held that Wilcox, Lang, Wright, and Posey had advanced; however, he was mistaken about Posey, who failed to support Wright's left, and never mentioned Mahone's brigade, which remained inactive throughout the entire fight. Oddly, during the assault, Mahone repeatedly told anyone who came asking for support "I have my orders from General Anderson himself to stay here"; in one case at least, the brigade commander repeated this statement to an adjutant from Wilcox's brigade whom Anderson had permitted to request assistance from Mahone.[8]

Hill's after-battle report was more accurate in its attention to which of Anderson's brigades had actually participated in the attack. "Soon after McLaws moved forward," Hill wrote, "General Anderson moved forward the brigades of Wilcox, Perry, and Wright, en echelon." Hill then absolved himself of all responsibility for properly employing Anderson's division in the attack, stating "The enemy threw forward heavy re-enforcements, and no supports coming to these brigades, the ground so hardly won had to be given up, and the brigades occupied their former positions in line of battle." Perhaps Hill thought someone else was responsible for ensuring support was provided to his brigades of Wilcox, Lang, and Wright. The new corps commander also never mentioned having thought of utilizing Pender's idle division, positioned to the left of Anderson, in support of the attack.[9]

Colonel William Allan of Ewell's staff and a postwar Longstreet critic recalled years

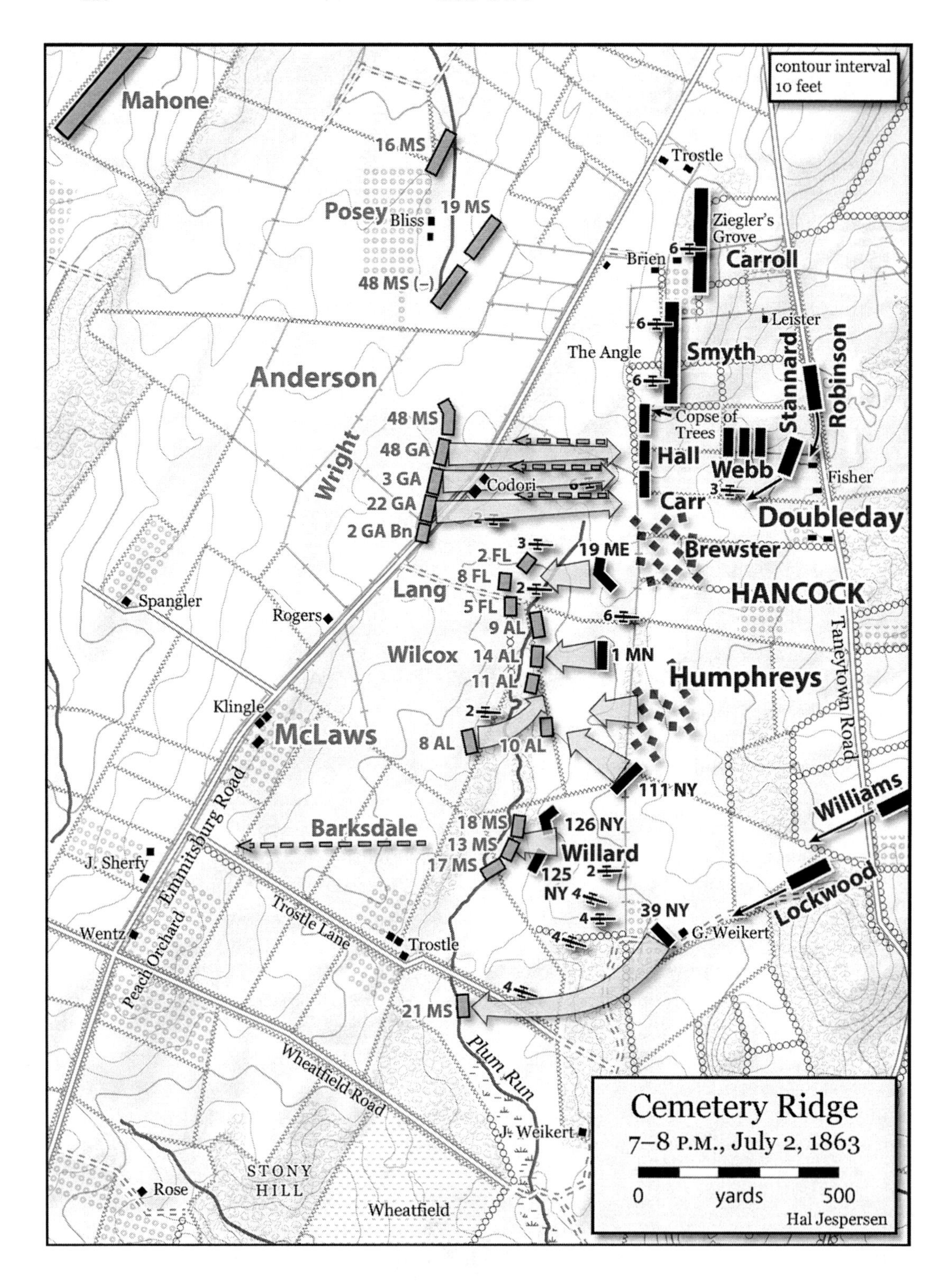
contour interval
10 feet
Mahone
16 MS
Trostle
Posey
Bliss
19 MS
Ziegler's
Grove
6
Brien
Carroll
48 MS (–)
6
Leister
The Angle
Smyth
Stannard
Robinson
6
Anderson
48 MS
Copse of
Trees
48 GA
Hall
Webb
3 GA
Codori
Fisher
Wright
22 GA
3
Carr
2 GA Bn
2
Doubleday
3
2 FL
19 ME
Brewster
8 FL
2
Lang
HANCOCK
5 FL
Spangler
Rogers
6
9 AL
Taneytown Road
Wilcox
14 AL
1 MN
Humphreys
11 AL
Klingle
2
McLaws
8 AL
10 AL
111 NY
Williams
Emmitsburg Road
18 MS
126 NY
Barksdale
13 MS
Willard
J. Sherfy
17 MS
125
NY
2
4
Lockwood
4
39 NY
Wentz
Trostle Lane
Peach Orchard
Trostle
G. Weikert
4
21 MS
Wheatfield Road
Plum Run
J. Weikert
Rose
STONY
HILL
Wheatfield
Cemetery Ridge
7–8 P.M., July 2, 1863
0
yards
500
Hal Jespersen

later that Longstreet's attack "was not promptly seconded by Hill and Ewell when made. Ewell's divisions were not made to act in concert—Johnson, Early, Rodes attacking in succession." Yet Allan was not about to point out the elephant in the room: Who was to ensure Hill and Ewell acted in concert with Longstreet? "It is difficult to decide where the weight of responsibility for these failures rests," Allan wrote, "and I shall not attempt it." Allan did not want to mention the commanding general's name. Furthermore, if Robert Krick's opinion that Lee was busy watching over his two new corps commanders throughout the battle is to be considered, why did both generals fail to carry out their attack orders on July 2?[10]

Lee did not acknowledge the lack of support to the left flank of Wright's brigade in his own after-battle reports. Instead, he described the situation in the Third Corps' front similarly to how Anderson and Hill had done in theirs, writing, "Wilcox reached the foot and Wright gained the crest of the ridge itself, driving the enemy down the opposite side; but having become separated from McLaws and gone beyond the other two brigades of the division, they were attacked in front and on both flanks, and compelled to retire." Like Hill, Lee only mentioned Wright and "the other two brigades of the division," neglecting to acknowledge Anderson had two additional brigades that contributed only marginal support to the attack. Significantly, Lee was present with or near A.P. Hill throughout the majority of the July 2 attack. Lieutenant Colonel Arthur Fremantle, the English officer and observer, provided critical details on Lee's location during the fight, writing, "So soon as the firing began, General Lee joined Hill just below our tree, and he remained there nearly all the time, looking through his field-glass—sometimes talking to Hill and sometimes to Colonel Long of his staff. But generally he sat quite alone on the stump of a tree. What I remarked especially was, that during the whole time firing continued, he only sent one message, and only received one report." Another observer noted similarly that Lee's "countenance betrayed no more anxiety than upon the occasion of a general review." Clifford Dowdey, while never explicitly placing any blame on Lee, admitted Wright's success on Cemetery Ridge took place "directly opposite Lee's command post and under the eye of the Old Man," and that the brigade's assault "had been seen by the general through his field glasses. He had watched his men storm the crest, silence the Union guns, and then fall back from want of support." Knowing this reality, it seems that the only thing more consequential than Hill and Ewell's inactivity for the Confederate army on July 2 was their Chief's apparent inability to recognize this inactivity and apply necessary pressure to ensure Longstreet's attack was properly supported. Indeed, during the late afternoon hours of July 2, Robert E. Lee exhib-

A.P. Hill, wartime (Library of Congress).

ited little leadership initiative and was ostensibly a non-entity. In Longstreet's memoirs, admittedly his most defensive and bitter postwar account, he wrote resentfully but truthfully on this topic, "So it looks as if the commander of the First Corps was easier to move than any one in his [Lee's] army, rather than harder, and his chief left him to fight the battles alone," in reference to his performance as compared to Ewell and Hill, and Lee's lax handling of his new corps commanders on July 2.[11]

Writing in summary of Longstreet's successful attack, Arthur Fremantle declared that "Longstreet carried every thing before him for some time, capturing several batteries, and driving the enemy from his positions; but when Hill's Florida brigade and some other troops gave way, he was forced to abandon a small portion of the ground he had won, together with all the captured guns, except three." Longstreet accomplished all that could have been expected of his two divisions against the formidable Federal position on July 2, even without the proper and intended support. Further, given the Confederates' general misunderstanding of Meade's position for hours leading up to Longstreet's attack, it is fairly astounding that the First Corps was able to accomplish as much as it did. With that said, it is clear when Longstreet's attack transitioned northward into Hill's sector, none of the Confederate leadership present was ready or willing to give Anderson's division the necessary attention, ultimately leaving the seizure of the Peach Orchard, the Wheatfield, and Devil's Den to show for the day's bloody work.[12]

15

The Idleness of the Second Corps

"Who had been all day under orders to attack at the sound of Longstreet's guns"
—E.P. Alexander

Even as early as 1863, Lee's Chief of Artillery William Pendleton exhibited a knack for exaggeration. Gilbert Moxley Sorrel aptly described Pendleton during the war as "a well-meaning man, without qualities for the high post he claimed." Writing in his after-battle report on the effect of the Third Corps batteries on July 2, Pendleton mistakenly believed they produced "a deliberate fire during the whole afternoon," and proved "useful in preventing full concentration by the enemy on either flank." Likewise, he was equally convinced Ewell's corps played a similarly effective role on the Confederate left, alleging their "attack was delayed till afternoon," when in actuality it was made in the late evening hours against East Cemetery Hill. Pendleton was inaccurate on both counts. On the contrary, the ineffective use of Hill's and Ewell's corps on July 2 allowed Meade to more easily shuffle Federal troops from his right flank to his left throughout the late afternoon hours. William Swinton, in his book written shortly after the war ended, summarized Ewell's shortcomings: "Now the plan of battle contemplated that, while Longstreet attacked, Ewell should make vigorous demonstrations against the forces on Cemetery and Culp's Hill, to prevent re-enforcements being drawn from that flank to increase the opposition to be encountered in the real assault against the Union left." Swinton remained puzzled by Ewell's actions on July 2: "For some reason, however, Ewell's demonstrations were much delayed, and it was sunset before he got to work."[1]

As has been proven, Hill's inactivity squashed a potential opportunity for Confederate success on July 2. Likewise, Ewell was equally to blame in neglecting to carry out "a simultaneous demonstration" in support of Longstreet's attack. Ewell's "delay," contrary to Pendleton's assertion, did not end in the afternoon hours, but continued until around 8 p.m. By that time, the First Corps attack had nearly fizzled out. The Second Corps commander's inactivity effectively allowed Meade to focus his attention entirely on stopping Longstreet.

Both Ewell's and his division commander Jubal Early's after-battle reports lack explanation as to why the Second Corps failed to attack to the sound of Longstreet's guns, which opened fire sometime between 4 and 5 p.m. Ewell wrote very plainly that "orders had come from the general commanding for me to delay my attack until I heard General Longstreet's guns open on to the right." He further defined this order a few sentences later, writing that Lee "wished me, as soon as their guns opened, to make a diversion in their favor, to be converted into a real attack if an opportunity offered." Ewell described how he heard Longstreet's guns open "about 5 p.m.," and shortly thereafter "commenced a heavy cannonade" of his own. Despite Douglas Southall Freeman's brief admission of "Ewell's failure to co-ordinate his attacks" with Longstreet, he very blithely described Ewell's artillery demonstration, as if it and a subsequent Second Corps infantry attack would have mattered little to the Confederates' overall effort on July 2: "Evidently Ewell had heard Longstreet's guns and was making the demonstration required by his orders; but of the effect of his cannonade Lee could tell nothing. No infantry was audible from that direction." Yet, Ewell alleged that just an hour later his "guns were overpowered by the greater number and superior position of the enemy's batteries," and so every gun was withdrawn except for one, "which he kept to repel any infantry advance." Ewell's description makes it clear that while Meade was busy stripping his right to reinforce his left against Longstreet's two divisions, Ewell thought it best to proceed with an ineffective cannonade, and worry Meade might advance infantry units against him. Ewell then recollected that "just before sundown, General Johnson ordered forward his division to attack the wooded hill in his front, and about dusk the attack was made," all well after Longstreet's attack had effectively ended. It is reasonable to assume Ewell's minimal support efforts were not what Lee had in mind.[2]

Early's account provides much of the same detail, with the exception of how he described Lee's intended plan for July 2. Early wrote that he was under the impression "the enemy's position would be attacked on the right and the left flanks very early next morning" on July 2, then went on to claim, "The attack did not begin in the morning, as was expected." But as shown, Lee had no such early morning attack plan. He spent the majority of the morning hours reconnoitering, contemplating the details of his attack scheme, deciding where to initiate the attack, and on a more fundamental level, deliberating the best position for Ewell's corps—keep them over on the left or move them around to the right.[3]

Early's acknowledgment that Lee wanted to attack the Federal position on both the right and left flanks leaves much to be desired of the Second Corps' inactivity on July 2, regardless of when Longstreet's attack commenced. Based on Lee's orders to Hill and Ewell, as outlined in his after-battle reports, it was clear he intended for some concert of action. Yet, the Second Corps delivered no supporting or simultaneous movement against the Federal right flank. Essentially, Early echoed Ewell's recollections of that uneventful afternoon: "The fire from the artillery having opened on the right and left at 4 o'clock, and continued for some time, I was ordered by General Ewell to advance upon Cemetery Hill with my two brigades ... as soon as General Johnson's division ... on my left ... should become engaged at the wooded hill on the left ... information being given to me that the advance would be general." It was not until the following paragraph that Early revealed this "general advance" was executed "a little before dusk," again, nowhere near the time Lee had specifically directed. Obfuscation of Ewell's inactivity during Longstreet's assault on July 2 was continued after the war. Walter Taylor summarized the Confederate Army's activity on the afternoon of July 2, writing that "The two divisions of Longstreet's Corps gallantly advanced, forced the enemy back a considerable distance, and captured some trophies and prisoners. Ewell's Divisions were ordered forward, and likewise gained additional ground and trophies." Taylor neglected to point out Ewell never attacked to the sound of Longstreet's guns, and Lee failed to enforce his own order throughout the entire course of the First Corps' assault. Of course, Longstreet critics like Douglas Southall Freeman contend Lee could not possibly have known about anything happening on Ewell's front after Longstreet's attack began. "In the din of the action," Freeman declared, "it had been impossible to tell whether the infantry of the Second Corps had been engaged." If Lee did not want to personally check on the Second Corps' progress after the battle began, would it not be reasonable to assume he could have sent a member of his staff to ensure Ewell was active?[4]

Later, in the postwar years, Early tried to spin Lee's order directing the Second Corps to attack in concert with Longstreet's guns when he contended that "Ewell was to make a demonstration upon the enemy's right, to be converted into a real attack should opportunity offer—that is, should success attend the attack on the enemy's left." Early went on to argue that because Longstreet attacked "late in the afternoon ... there could not be that co-operation that would have taken place had the attack been promptly made at the expected time." Early's argument is, put bluntly, dubious and unconvincing. Early would have students of the war believe Lee directed Ewell to attack only if he found out success had been gained on the Confederate right, in contrast to Lee's clear order as written in his after-battle report stating Ewell was to "make a simultaneous demonstration upon the enemy's right." Even more absurd was Early's claim that since Longstreet attacked in the afternoon, and not the morning, the Second Corps was somehow absolved of all need and responsibility to abide by orders to synchronize its efforts with the First Corps' attack.[5]

E.P. Alexander began his analysis of Longstreet's initial success without proper reinforcement very frankly: "One is tempted to pause for a moment to contemplate the really hopeless situation of the Confederate battle." He explained further, writing, "Already Sickles's six brigades had been reinforced by 10 brigades which had been defeated one, two, or three at a time.... As the 11th and 12th brigades of the Federal reenforcements approach, the Confederate need of at least a fresh division is great. There are not only no reenforcements on the way, but none within two miles." In contrast to the Confederate situation, Meade continually made great use of his interior lines and shifted brigades to his left to check Longstreet's progress. Alexander made it clear that this shuffling was made possible by Ewell's inactivity until dusk: "Besides the reenforcements of 12 brigades already mentioned (including Crawford's Pa. reserves), Meade had followed them with Robinson's and Doubleday's divisions of the 1st corps, five brigades (taken from the lines in front of Hill's corps), and with Williams's division, three brigades of the 12th Corps." The former artillerist further underscored that Meade stripped the 12th Corps of Candy's and Cobham's brigades, moving them from "the intrenchments upon Culp's Hill ... to the left.... These withdrawals left of the 12th corps but a single brigade, Greene's, holding.... Culp's Hill in front of Johnson's division of Ewell's corps, who had been all day under orders to attack at the sound of Longstreet's guns."[6]

Alexander explicitly called out Hill and Ewell for their near-total inactivity on July 2, writing that they "have orders to cooperate with Longstreet's battle, but they are limiting their cooperation to ineffective cannonading of the enemy's intrenchments in their front, while the enemy is stripping these of infantry and marching fresh divisions to concentrate upon Hood and McLaws, and the three brigades of Wilcox, Perry, and Wright, which had supported them." Just a few pages later in one of his postwar accounts, Alexander could not help but restate his assessment of Hill and Ewell on July 2 in even franker terms, declaring that "Longstreet's attack between 4 p.m. and darkness by the other two corps was confined to an artillery duel by 32 guns of Ewell and 55 of Hill, mostly at extreme ranges. But the value of this duel as assistance to Longstreet was absolutely nothing, for it did not prevent the enemy from withdrawing troops from every corps in his line to repel our assault."[7]

Alexander's commentary in his *Military Memoirs*, a work dubbed by one historian as an "exercise in dispassionate analysis," was in lockstep with Longstreet's postwar statements about the lack of support he received from Hill and Ewell on July 2. "If General Ewell had engaged the army in his front at that time (say four o'clock)," Longstreet asserted, "he would have prevented their massing their whole army in my front, and while he and I kept their two wings engaged, Hill would have found their centre weak, and should have threatened it while I broke through their left and dislodged them." Further, Longstreet explicitly underscored "Ewell's non-compliance with General Lee's orders" to "make a simultaneous demonstration upon the enemy's right," as the commanding general wrote in his after-battle report. Longstreet placed great emphasis on the same point numerous times in his writings, namely that Ewell failed to attack until dark when the First Corps offensive was already over. "Ewell did not advance until I had withdrawn my troops.... Ewell did not move until about dusk (according to his own report).... He was to hold himself in readiness to support my attack when it was made.... His orders were to hold himself in readiness to cooperate with my attack when it was made," Longstreet stressed over and over.[8]

Richard Ewell, wartime (Library of Congress).

In yet another postwar account, Longstreet included Hill's and Ewell's "non-compliance" as the sixth of eight critical mistakes he listed for why the Confederates failed at Gettysburg. "Sixth, when I attacked the enemy's left on the 2d, Ewell should have moved at once against his right, and Hill should have threatened his centre, and thus prevented a concentration of the whole Federal army at the point I was assaulting," he maintained. This sixth mistake, like the other seven, he affirmed with great confidence to be "supported with the most particular proof. Not a single one of them has been controverted. Very few of them have been questioned—none of them overthrown." In another section of the same account, Longstreet wrote even more bluntly of the lack of support he received from the rest of the army on July 2, insisting that "It is impossible that any sane man should believe that two of my divisions, attacking at any hour or in any manner, could have succeeded in dislodging the Army of the Potomac." Since the time of Longstreet's writing in the late nineteenth century, most historians have agreed Hill and Ewell performed poorly on July 2; however, the overwhelming bulk of scholarship has remained consistently and puzzlingly focused on Longstreet's performance on that day. Hill's and Ewell's failures are mentioned and explained, but they are never harped on to the degree that historians have focused on Longstreet's actions between sunup and 4 p.m. What are objective students of the war to make of this persistent trend?[9]

Considering the success Longstreet achieved on the afternoon of July 2 without any help from Ewell and minimal support from Hill, it is more than tempting to consider what might have been had both corps supported Longstreet's afternoon assault as Lee had ordered. Writing on the Confederate's limited success on July 2, Joseph Kershaw contended that "Every attack was magnificent and successful, but failed in the end for want of cooperation.... The want of cooperation, or, as the Comte de Paris terms it, the want of 'coordination,' caused the loss of Gettysburg to the Confederates." Similarly, E.P. Alexander concluded, "If the whole fighting force of our army could have been concentrated & brought to bear together upon that of the enemy I cannot doubt that we would have broken it to pieces." Longstreet believed that "It will be proved that the battle made by my men could not have been so improved, in plan or execution, as to have won the day," but "The only amendment that would have ensued, or even promised victory, was for Ewell to have marched in upon the enemy's right when it was guarded by a single brigade, run over their works and fall upon their rear while I engaged them in front, and while Hill lay in a threatening position in their centre." The First Corps commander echoed Kershaw's and Alexander's sentiments about the Confederates' need for coordination between corps on that day, contending that "Had this co-operative movement been made the battle would, in all probability, have been ours." Longstreet then finished his thought most pointedly, declaring, "As it was, no disposition of the men under my charge, no change in the time, or method, or spirit of the assault, could have changed the result for the better."[10]

16

The Attack Fizzles Out

"My seventeen thousand against the Army of the Potomac!"
—James Longstreet

The end of Longstreet's assault came rather quickly in the early evening hours. As the battle sprawled northward from Longstreet's two divisions to Anderson's division of Hill's corps, William Wofford's brigade and remnants of "Tige" Anderson, Kershaw, and Paul Semmes' brigades advanced southeast along the Wheatfield Road toward fresh Federal reinforcements from Major General George Sykes' Fifth Corps. Colonels Joseph Fisher's and William McCandless' brigades of Pennsylvania Reserves under the overall direction of Major General Samuel Crawford stabilized the Federal line just north of Little Round Top. In the meantime, Meade continued to streamline additional units to this part of the battlefield, including Colonel David Nevin's brigade from Major General John Newton's division, and Brigadier General Joseph Bartlett's brigade from Brigadier General Horatio Wright's Sixth Corps division. In contrast to Lee's hands-off battlefield demeanor on July 2, Meade was seemingly everywhere once the battle commenced trying to bolster his left against Longstreet's attack by stripping units from his center and right. This newly formed Federal line met just one advancing Confederate brigade under Wofford, which had already seen plenty of action for the day, and the remnants of three more.[1]

Nevin and McCandless, with support from Bartlett met the Confederates just east of the Wheatfield along Plum Run. By 8 p.m., just fifteen minutes before Ewell initiated his infantry attack against East Cemetery Hill, the Wofford-led coalition was stopped and thrown back. Longstreet later described the First Corps' last ditch effort for the day: "While Meade's lines were growing my men were dropping; we had no others to call to their aid, and the weight against us was too heavy to carry. The extreme left of our lines was only about a mile from us across the enemy's concentric position, which brought us within hearing of that battle, if engaged, and near enough to feel its swell, but nothing was heard or felt but the clear ring of the enemy's fresh metal as he came against us." With obvious pride in his men's accomplishments against the great odds they had faced, he then added, "No other part of our army had engaged! My seventeen thousand against the Army of the Potomac! The sun was down, and with it went down the severe battle." In another account, Longstreet summed up the July 2 battle more succinctly, writing simply, "This was an unequal battle."[2]

Indeed, by that hour, Longstreet determined this "unequal battle" had gone far

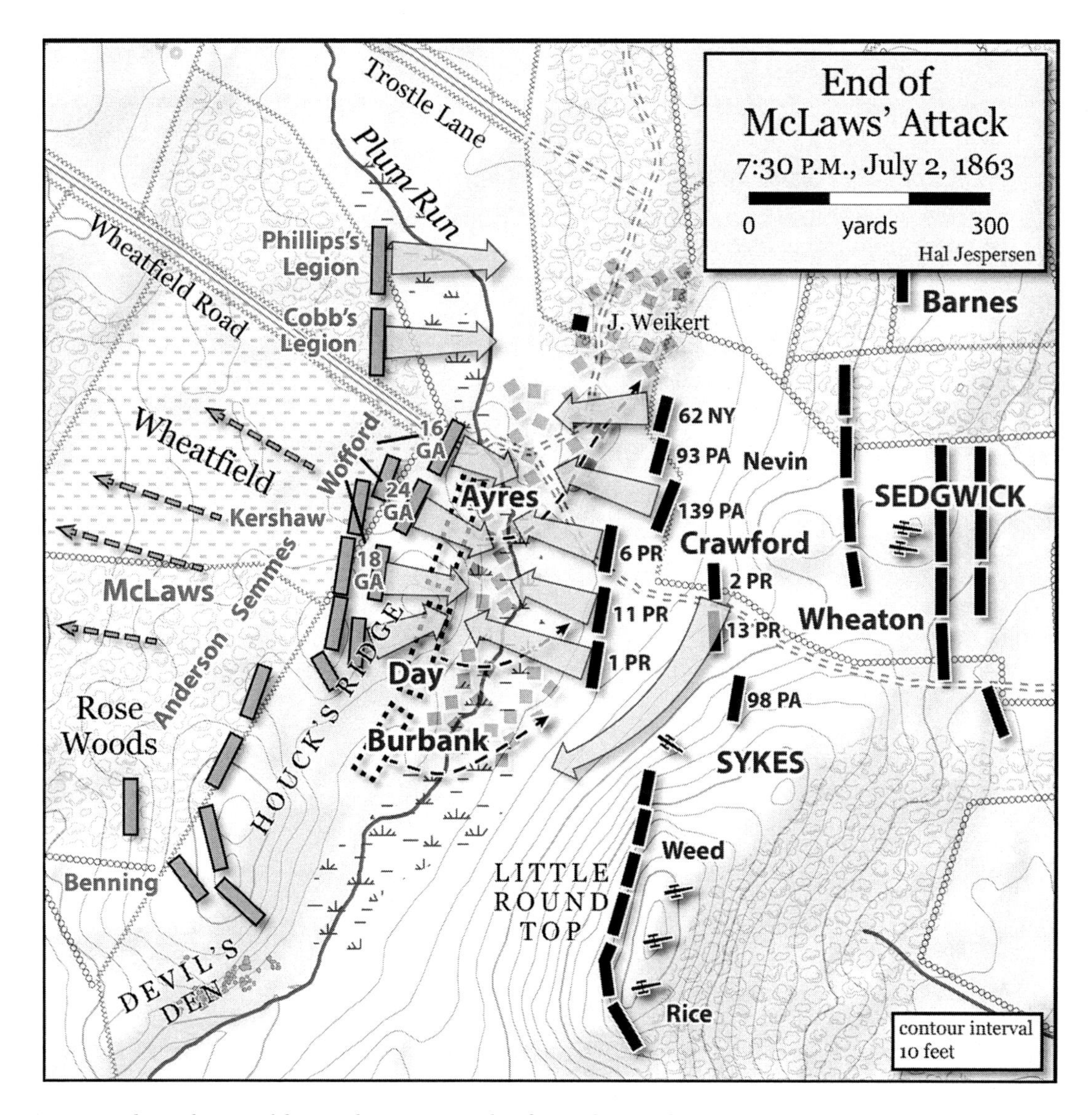

enough without additional support. The frontal assault by Longstreet's two divisions and part of Anderson's division cost the Confederates another 6,500 casualties with little gained besides footholds along the Emmitsburg Road. "We received no support at all," he recollected of this moment, "and there was no evidence of co-operation on any side. To urge my men forward under these circumstances would have been madness, and I withdrew them in good order to the peach orchard that we had taken from the Federals early in the afternoon." Longstreet directed McLaws' men to hold their position at the Peach Orchard and in the woods south of the Wheatfield, while Hood's division was ordered to occupy the ground around Devil's Den.[3]

Over the years, historians have exalted Stonewall Jackson's flank attack at the Battle of Chancellorsville. Undoubtedly, it turned out to be an audacious and ultimately brilliant tactical move; however, historians must also acknowledge that the attack was, like James Longstreet's July 2 assault at Gettysburg, launched late in the day and hindered by the onset of night. Despite the many challenges and delays the First Corps faced leading up to its attack at Gettysburg on July 2, Longstreet was still able to crush two Federal corps and an entire division from another. Even so, in writing about Longstreet's July 2 assault, historians are often much more critical than they are of Jackson's Chancellorsville attack, and often describe it as a failure, largely blaming the First Corps commander for the result. Further, some analyses of Longstreet's actions on July 2 not only stray into nitpicking, but actually harp on Longstreet's every alleged thought and movement. Allen Guelzo has called out many historians' double standard in their handling of Jackson and Longstreet's attacks, and has argued Longstreet's attack on July 2 "was, by any standard, a greater achievement than Stonewall Jackson's more famous flank march at Chancellorsville two months before." In comparison to what most other historians have mustered over the years, Guelzo has come to a more balanced and objective conclusion about Longstreet's attack, which is worth quoting in full:

> In the first place, although James Longstreet's corps failed to turn Dan Sickle's collapse into a complete route, this was no more of a failure than Stonewall Jackson's famous flank attack at Chancellorsville on May 2nd. Jackson, like Longstreet, achieved a great initial success; but Jackson's attack, also like Longstreet's, fell far short of dislodging the entire Federal army (that work had to be completed by Lee on May 3rd). Jackson, again like Longstreet, had begun his attack so late that darkness forced him to halt substantially short of that goal. Yet no one has ever suggested that Jackson's descent on the Union right flank at Chancellorsville was a failure—or at least not in the way Longstreet's descent on the Union left at Gettysburg would be described.[4]

17

The Night of the Second Day Controversy

"In fact, however, Longstreet received no orders during the night"
—E.P. Alexander

Longstreet's "other boot," Major General George Pickett's division spent the majority of July 2 marching from Chambersburg to Gettysburg. They had started out around 2 a.m. and advanced 27 miles to reach the vicinity of the battlefield sometime in the mid-to-late afternoon hours. According to Henry Thweatt (H.T.) Owen of the 18th Virginia Regiment, Richard Garnett's brigade, Pickett's division arrived around the time Hood commenced the First Corps attack. Once they reached the battlefield—about three to four miles from the main Confederate line—Owen recollected hearing rumors that Longstreet needed Pickett immediately and had ordered him to "Bring your division around to the right at once. Hood is about to attack and I want you to support him." This claim should not be immediately discarded considering it was still early in Longstreet's assault and the corps commander had specifically informed Hood during the morning hours, "I never like to go into battle with one boot off," in reference to Pickett's division.[1]

Pickett, with his aide Captain Edward Baird in tow, immediately reported to Longstreet for orders and for a few minutes watched the battle raging in front of him. One account of this moment alleges Pickett informed his Chief that his "men are exhausted and must have rest before going any further." On the contrary, 1st Virginia infantryman Charles Loehr of James Kemper's brigade contended that the men of his regiment "were in fine condition. The march from Chambersburg did not fatigue them at all." Loehr believed they "could have gone into battle ... when they reached Gettysburg." H.T. Owen expressed similar sentiments: "Pickett's Division was silent, within sight and perhaps the opportunity to change the course of history was lost. For had Pickett's Division, upon its arrival on the field ... been led straight to battle, or had it supported the assault of Hood and McClaws [*sic*] at any time after an hour's rest, it is possible the battle of Gettysburg would have ended there." Captain Robert Bright, another member of Pickett's staff who reported to Longstreet during these moments, told the corps commander the division was in shape to fight for an hour or two, but like Pickett, indicated the men were tired. Bright alleged that Longstreet said, "Tell Pickett I will have work for Him tomorrow."[2]

As Pickett arrived at the front, he also told Major Walter Harrison of his staff to report to General Lee for orders. Harrison claimed he told Lee something very similar to what Bright told Longstreet, namely that even though the division was tired, they could be counted on to fight. Then, while Pickett was still in the presence of Longstreet, Harrison rode up after meeting with Lee and reported the commanding general's orders: "Tell General Pickett I shall not want him this evening, to let his men rest, and I will send him word when I want him." Longstreet assented. Oddly, even after Harrison reported Lee's orders to Pickett, the division commander left Longstreet and rode over to see Lee himself, who again reiterated, "I am glad you have come. I shall have work for you tomorrow."[3]

Like Lee's directive to Lafayette McLaws in the morning hours, Lee seemed to be taking personal control of Pickett's division. Having told Pickett, "I will send him word when I want him," there is no evidence Lee provided any subsequent clarification or direction as to what he had in mind for Pickett's division, and therefore it seems neither Longstreet nor his subordinate took any special, out-of-the-ordinary actions on the night of July 2 or the early morning of July 3. In addressing this controversy, Shelby Foote aptly described Lee's indecisive actions in the very early morning hours of July 3: "Lee not only had not sent Pickett or his corps commander any word of his intentions; he did not even do so now. Perhaps, on second thought, he had reasoned that more deliberate preparations were required for so desperate an effort, including another daylight look at the objective, which the enemy might have reinforced or otherwise rendered impregnable overnight."[4]

Addressing what has become a very controversial evening in Civil War history, Longstreet recalled simply "I did not see General Lee that night." Indeed, it is clear Lee did not see Longstreet, or Ewell for that matter, and only sent the Second Corps commander a note instructing him to reopen his attack on the Federal right at daybreak. Sometime after the battle came to a close on July 2, Longstreet informed Austrian observer Fitzgerald Ross that "we have not been so successful as we wished." Longstreet then provided Lee with a brief written report of the day's battle and established his corps headquarters at a small schoolhouse near where his men launched their assault only hours before.[5]

Despite what many historians have contended over the years, there is absolutely no record of Longstreet receiving attack orders that night. George Stewart, in his classic account on Pickett's Charge, wrote plainly that in the postwar years "no one proved that he [Longstreet] had" received orders, and that still holds true today. None of Longstreet's aides, or Lee's for that matter, many of whom wrote abundantly after the war and would have been aware of such orders, ever made mention of Longstreet receiving any attack plan from Lee that evening. Evidence suggests that at Lee's headquarters, the night was much quieter than the previous evening had been, and the commanding general formulated whatever arrangements he had in mind without consulting any of his principal subordinates. One person at headquarters claimed that Lee was "not in good humor over the miscarriage of his plans and his orders" during the July 2 battle. Yet, if Lee was upset with the lack of coordination between corps on July 2, he expended little effort overnight in remedying the situation and ensuring he and his principal subordinates were on the same page for July 3. Unlike Meade, Lee called no council of war and only saw Hill that evening. This solitary behavior was curious coming from Lee, who according to his after-battle report believed the only thing lacking on July 2 was "proper concert of action."[6]

Over the years, Longstreet critics have paid increasing attention to the morning of July 3. They claim with certainty that during the overnight hours Lee sent Longstreet orders instructing him to attack the same part of the Federal line at daylight, except this time it would be led by the battered divisions of Hood and McLaws, and supported by Pickett's three fresh brigades. Typically, historians who support this claim first cite Lee's after-battle report as evidence, where the commanding general stated of the July 2 battle, "The results of this day's operations induced the belief that, with proper concert of action, and with the increased support that the positions gained on the right would enable the artillery to render the assaulting columns, we should ultimately succeed, and it was accordingly determined to continue the attack." In several postwar accounts, Longstreet confirmed Lee's assessment of July 2, as presented in his after-battle report, was truthfully how the commanding general interpreted that day's achievements. In other words, Lee believed it to be a near victory. "When the battle of the 2d was over," Longstreet recalled, "General Lee pronounced it a success, as we were in possession of ground from which we had driven the Federals and had taken several field-pieces." Longstreet, however, made it consistently clear he did not agree with his commander's appraisal of the July 2 battle: "The conflict had been fierce and bloody, and my troops had driven back heavy columns and had encountered a force three or four times their number, but we had accomplished little toward victorious results."[7]

Following Lee's after-battle report statement about being "determined to continue the attack" on July 3, he then outlined what he initially had in mind for a renewed attack: "The general plan was unchanged. Longstreet, re-enforced by Pickett's three brigades, which arrived near the battle-field during the afternoon of the 2d, was ordered to attack the next morning, and General Ewell was directed to assail the enemy's right at the same time." In short, Lee essentially planned for a repeat of the July 2 fight, except this time, Longstreet would use the remnants of Hood's and McLaws' divisions and Pickett's fresh division to again strike the Federal left, while Ewell simultaneously struck their right. As events turned out, the Federals disrupted this general plan almost immediately. Ewell's corps was attacked in the very early morning hours of July 3, resulting in a five-hour fight between Major General Edward Johnson's Confederate division and the Federal Twelfth and First Corps near Culp's Hill, which ultimately culminated in Federal retention of that position.[8]

Even so, Longstreet critics—arguing under the assumption the First Corps commander undoubtedly received orders that night—question why the General was unable to attack sometime during that five-hour timeframe when Ewell was engaged. They draw attention to Lee's after-battle report statement that "General Longstreet's dispositions were not completed as early as was expected," as concrete proof of the First Corps commander's continued disobedience and dereliction of duty. In short, they believe Lee issued Longstreet orders sometime during the night of July 2 and the First Corps commander deliberately ignored them. Douglas Southall Freeman contended in clear reference to Lee's report, "Although Lee wrote later that he gave Longstreet on the second orders 'to attack the next morning,' Longstreet was either slow or else he was resolved to oppose to the last a plan he believed dangerous." Likewise, Clifford

Dowdey wrote that "on the night of the 2nd, Lee had sent Longstreet orders for early action involving those fresh troops," referring to Pickett's division. "The one certainty is that Longstreet had not executed the orders Lee sent him the night before," Dowdey concluded confidently.[9]

Even William Garrett Piston, who has regularly evaluated Longstreet much more fairly and objectively, has questioned Longstreet's actions on the morning of July 3 with respect to Pickett's division being in position near Seminary Ridge "no earlier than 9:00 A.M. ... almost four hours after daylight." Piston has called this alleged oversight "inexplicable" and "Longstreet's great failing in connection with the third day at Gettysburg." Such an omission *would* be a noteworthy blunder *if* Lee had indeed ordered Longstreet to have Pickett ready to lead or support an early morning attack at daylight. The non-urgent nature and pace of the division's movements during the early morning hours of July 3 suggest that either Lee never gave such a specific order or Pickett was not made aware of this order until much later than expected. Since the afternoon of July 2, Pickett's division was located only four miles west of Gettysburg and only began moving out from camp at 3 a.m. on July 3. Given Longstreet and Lee met for their morning meeting at 4:30 a.m. on the 3rd, it can be ruled out that their conference and subsequent discussion roused Longstreet from some momentary bout of ignorance, insubordination, or forgetfulness and was the impetus for Pickett's forward movement. Major Walter Harrison alleged that the division arrived near Seminary Ridge "by about seven o'clock" and Major Charles S. Peyton of the 19th Virginia Infantry indicated the division reached the Emanuel Pitzer farm, less than a half mile west of the main Confederate battle line, "about 9 a.m." If Lee had ordered Longstreet to have Pickett ready by daylight and the order was not carried out, there are numerous potential and unverifiable reasons for this oversight, all ranging in legitimacy, and none of them, as Piston underscores "absolv[ing] him [Longstreet] entirely of culpability for this error."[10]

As early as Longstreet's July 1873 letter to Lafayette McLaws, he disputed any allegation that Lee sent him attack orders on the night of July 2. "The position proving so strong on the 2d," Longstreet recalled, "I was less inclined to attack on the 3d, in fact I had no idea of attacking until Gen. Lee came to me just before Pickett's division arrived" at the front on the morning of July 3. In his 1895 memoirs, Longstreet again challenged these claims and directly addressed what Lee wrote in his after-battle report: "This is disingenuous. He did not give or send me orders for the morning of the third day, nor did he reinforce me by Pickett's brigades for morning attack." It is reasonable to assume for the second part of that statement, Longstreet was referring to Lee's "I will send him [Pickett] word when I want him" comment made on the afternoon of July 2. Shelby Foote expressed concurrence with Longstreet's claims: "No orders reached Longstreet, however; nor was Pickett alerted for the night march he would have to make if he was to have any share in the daybreak assault. Perhaps this was an oversight, or perhaps Lee had decided by then to attack at a later hour." Foote argued with obvious tongue-in-cheek that Lee "did not get in touch with Longstreet at all, apparently being satisfied that ... his old warhorse would know what was expected of him without being told." Despite Freeman, Dowdey, and others' absolute certainty Longstreet lied in the postwar years and had undoubtedly received and ignored attack orders from Lee sometime during the night, upon what actual evidence have their assertions been based?[11]

Some modern historians have taken up the question. Jeffry Wert has gone beyond simply citing Lee's statement about Longstreet not being ready "as early as expected" and actually tries to prove the First Corps commander received orders. To make this argument, Wert uses commentary from one of E.P. Alexander's postwar accounts, where the young artillerist alleged he met with Longstreet sometime late that evening and "I was told that we would renew the attack in the morning. That Pickett's division would arrive and would assault the enemy's line. My impression is the exact point for it was not designated, but I was told it would be to our left of the Peach Orchard." Wert's follow-on narrative about Alexander's alleged experience at First Corps headquarters on the night of July 2 suggests he believes the case is now closed. The historian concludes, "Sometime after dark the orders came from Lee for the resumption of the attack at first light on Friday morning. In his memoirs, Longstreet denied that he received such a directive from Lee, but he either forgot or deliberately lied when he wrote that thirty years after the battle. Porter Alexander's version of events makes it clear that Longstreet had been informed." Another modern historian, Glenn LaFantasie, also draws significant attention to this one account by Alexander, writing in similar fashion to Wert, "Longstreet ... later pretend[ed] never to have received orders from the commanding general at all. But Porter Alexander ... described riding to Longstreet's bivouac that night and learning that 'we would renew the attack early in the morning.'" Likewise, Stephen Sears guesses that "Lee's orders for July 3 reached Longstreet probably about 10 o'clock that Thursday night," "they were probably delivered verbally," and "the best description of their content is artillerist Porter Alexander's."[12]

On this topic, Wert, LaFantasie, and Sears would have been supported by General John B. Gordon, a Second Corps brigade commander at Gettysburg and, by the mid–1880s, a fervent Longstreet critic. Gordon claimed it as absolute fact that Lee ordered Longstreet to attack at daylight on the third day. He actually called it "an established fact," and declared "that General Lee ordered Longstreet to attack at daylight on the morning of the third day, and that the latter did not attack until two or three o'clock in the afternoon, the artillery opening at one."[13]

The fact of the matter is that this case is far from being closed. Beginning with Lee's report, penned only half a year after the battle, the commanding general mentioned nothing remotely close to a specific order. Most Longstreet critics extol Lee to be an extremely gifted general, and in this situation, they should give him much more credit than to assume he issued vague orders to Longstreet in the middle of the night on July 2, telling him the "general plan was unchanged," and now with only one fresh division he should attack over the same ground the "next morning" at some indefinite hour. Lee certainly made no mention of orders for an attack "at daylight," as Gordon contended. The former Georgian officer also vehemently believed that time was of the essence on July 3, writing, "With every moment of delay, Lee's chances are diminishing with geometrical progression." What would Lee's line of reasoning have been to issue such an order for the morning of July 3? As Helen Longstreet astutely pointed out, "Time was not an essential element in the problem of the 3d. The Federal army was then all up." Shelby Foote echoed Helen Longstreet's analysis, characterizing the assault to come as a "one-shot endeavor; late was as good as early, and maybe better, since it not only would permit a more careful study of all the problems, but also would lessen the time allowed the Federals for mounting and launching a counterattack in event of a Confederate repulse." Foote thought the rationale might have even been "simpler than that," arguing that "perhaps Lee merely wanted time for one more talk with" Longstreet.[14]

Realistically, it would have been absurd for Lee to direct Longstreet to attack over the same ground as he had during the previous day's battle, only this time with one fresh division instead of two, and especially without taking time to examine the Federal line in the morning for changes in position and strength. If Lee did, without a doubt, issue orders stating "the general plan was unchanged," he was blindly and irresponsibly assuming the Federal army would return the favor and ensure that their position remained unchanged and not strengthened. Evidence suggests that this assumption would have been unwise. Indeed, Longstreet confirmed the Federal army's activity during the night, writing, "That the enemy was there looking for us, as we heard him during the night putting up his defences." William Pendleton echoed Longstreet's observation when he asserted in his after-battle report, "Thus stood affairs at nightfall, the 2d ... the enemy strengthening himself in position naturally formidable and everywhere difficult to approach." Stephen Sears most aptly describes Lee's alleged plan on the night of July 2, calling it "barren, "uninformed," and "utterly divorced from reality." In sum, Sears contends that "Lee chose this course reflexively, without consulting his lieutenants, without a survey of the battlefield, without an appraisal of the enemy, apparently without consideration of any alternatives. Robert E. Lee felt obliged to demonstrate to his lieutenants that his way was the right way, and the only way."[15]

Jeffry Wert further argues that Longstreet either "forgot or deliberately lied" when he wrote in his memoirs "thirty years after the battle" that he received no orders from Lee on the night of July 2. Stephen Sears also seems to buy into this particular judgment, suggesting Lee's Warhorse deliberately ignored attack orders on the night of July 2 and directed his efforts elsewhere: "James Longstreet could be a remarkably stubborn man, and the receipt of these attack orders did not dissuade him from again building a case against them." Sears also advances an even more serious charge that Longstreet was "stretching a corps commander's discretion to its limit and beyond." On the contrary, in his report written just thirty days after the battle, Longstreet never reported having received orders. The First Corps commander never wrote, as he does numerous times elsewhere in the report, "I was ordered to" or "I received instructions from the commanding general to" anywhere in the section about that evening. Rather, Longstreet described how "On the following morning our arrangements were made for renewing the attack by my right; with a view to pass around the hill occupied by the enemy on his left, and to gain it by flank and reverse attack." Indeed, the absence in Longstreet's after-battle report of any reference to receiving attack orders during the overnight hours is in itself most telling, for as Helen Longstreet penned, "As Longstreet's report passed through Lee's hands, the superior would most certainly have returned it to the subordinate for correction if there were errors in it. This he did not do, neither did Lee indorse upon the document itself any dissent from its tenor." Longstreet's after-battle report clearly shows he was aware of Lee's expectation that offensive operations be resumed on July 3. However, it is equally clear he was neither provided with a specific timeline, nor given direction for how he was expected to carry out that offensive, other than understanding it was to be recommenced. In the absence of those specifics from Lee, Longstreet sought to find the best way to get at the Federal left flank.[16]

On this topic, a number of other modern historians seemingly support these arguments; however, their interpretation sometimes becomes mired in inconsistencies and contradictions. Earl Hess reasonably concludes that during the overnight hours Longstreet received only a "broad directive to resume offensive operations" on July 3. Similarly, Noah Trudeau describes Lee's overnight plan as a "broad directive," "nonspecific," and one that was "open to—perhaps even begged—misinterpretation." Hess contends Longstreet looked further south and to the right of his Peach Orchard-Devil's Den position on the morning of the third because he "wanted to take the offensive but not with a frontal assault," which Longstreet had already tried on July 2 with more men and against a less established Federal position. Yet, shortly thereafter, Earl Hess contradicts himself and asserts that "Pickett's division was ready, but quite a bit later than Lee had anticipated. He had assumed the night before that the Virginians could spearhead an assault by dawn of July 3." Hess seems to have forgotten his earlier statement about how during the overnight hours of July 2, Longstreet only received general guidance to resume the offensive on July 3. Further, Hess' claim that Lee "assumed" Pickett could "spearhead an assault" is dubious, since initially, the commanding general never planned for Pickett to lead a renewed attack. On the contrary, Lee suggested McLaws and Hood's divisions resume the assault, supported by Pickett.[17]

On the use of sources, Jeffry Wert injudiciously chooses to rely on just one of E.P. Alexander's postwar accounts, *Fighting for the Confederacy*, to prove his case that Longstreet received specific orders to attack "at first light on Friday morning." In doing so, Wert neglects Alexander's additional writings and other key participants' accounts. Indeed, Alexander made absolutely no mention of visiting First Corps headquarters in his other major work, *Military Memoirs*. Are we to assume Alexander had temporary amnesia after the war? In fact, if historians selectively choose *Fighting for the Confederacy* as the only account to be taken seriously, they must at the very least admit Alexander's pen could be very inconsistent at times and his portrayal of events occasionally differed significantly from one account to the next. Regarding the events on the night of July 2, *Military Memoirs* is completely at odds with *Fighting for the Confederacy*.[18]

In verifying Longstreet's claim that no orders were given to him that evening, Alexander wrote explicitly in *Military Memoirs*, "[Johnson] had been ordered by Ewell to attack at daylight, under the impression that Longstreet would attack at the same hour. In fact, however, Longstreet received no orders during the night, and the troops required for his attack could not be gotten into their positions before noon." Alexander then described, in very general terms, the purpose of the artillery preparations in the Peach Orchard: "During the night the Washington artillery was brought up and disposed with the rest of Longstreet's guns about the Peach Orchard, with the intention of resuming the battle in the morning." Other than "in the morning," Alexander provided no additional information on when or where the battle would be resumed. In *Fighting for the Confederacy*, his recollections were decidedly altered, whereby he claimed that sometime during the evening he "was told that we would renew the attack early in the morning" and even though the "exact point" for the attack "was not designated," he was

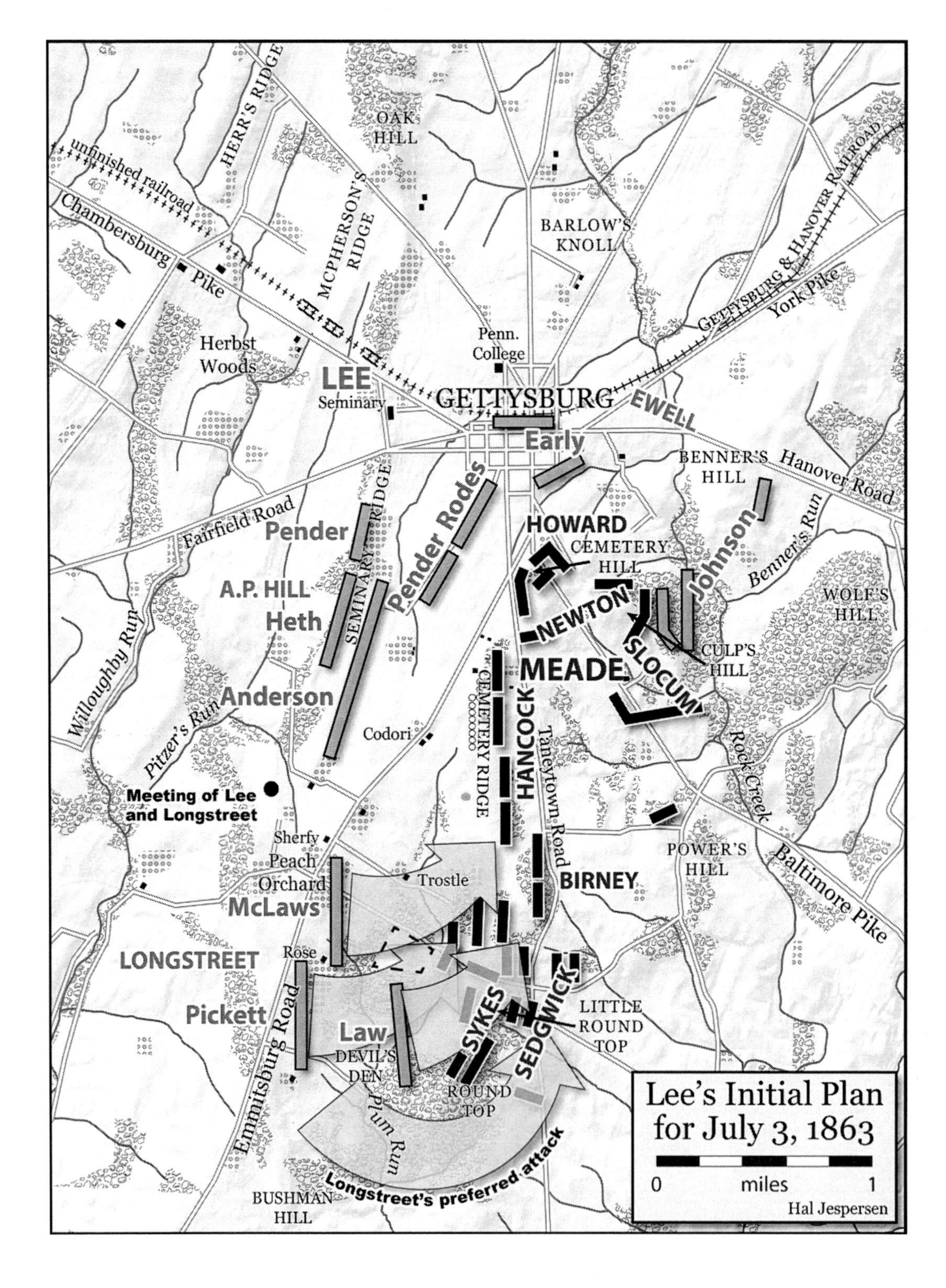

Lee's Initial Plan for July 3, 1863
0 miles 1
Hal Jespersen
HERR'S RIDGE
OAK HILL
unfinished railroad
Chambersburg Pike
MCPHERSON'S RIDGE
BARLOW'S KNOLL
GETTYSBURG & HANOVER RAILROAD
York Pike
Penn. College
Herbst Woods
LEE
Seminary
GETTYSBURG
EWELL
Early
BENNER'S HILL
Hanover Road
Fairfield Road
SEMINARY RIDGE
Pender Rodes
Pender
HOWARD
CEMETERY HILL
Johnson
Benner's Run
WOLF'S HILL
A.P. HILL
Heth
NEWTON
SLOCUM
CULP'S HILL
MEADE
Willoughby Run
Anderson
Pitzer's Run
CEMETERY RIDGE
HANCOCK
Taneytown Road
Codori
Rock Creek
Meeting of Lee and Longstreet
Sherfy
Peach Orchard
Trostle
POWER'S HILL
BIRNEY
Baltimore Pike
McLaws
LONGSTREET
Rose
Pickett
Emmitsburg Road
Law
DEVIL'S DEN
SYKES
SEDGWICK
LITTLE ROUND TOP
ROUND TOP
Plum Run
Longstreet's preferred attack
BUSHMAN HILL

also "told it would be to our left of the Peach Orchard." He also recalled hearing "Pickett's division would arrive and would assault the enemy's line."[19]

In contrast, Alexander stated outright in *Military Memoirs* that Longstreet received no orders that evening, and went on to present an entirely different sequence of events. First, it is worth reiterating that in *Memoirs* Alexander never mentioned riding to Longstreet's headquarters on the night of July 2. Second, he only stated there existed an "intention of resuming the battle in the morning," not "early in the morning." Though nuanced, a morning intention greatly differs from a definitive early morning order for the attack to be renewed at a particular time and location with specific units. Third, in *Memoirs,* Alexander indicated that Lee only made Longstreet aware he wanted the attack made "to our left of the Peach Orchard" after the commanding general consulted with the corps commander in-person on the morning of July 3, or as he wrote, "Lee joined him and proposed an assault upon the enemy's left centre by Longstreet's three divisions." Fourth, Alexander's claim that he was told during the overnight hours the attack was expected to resume to the left of the Peach Orchard fails to size up with what is known about Lee's initial "unchanged" battle plan for July 3, which would have been executed at or to the right of the Peach Orchard.

Similar to *Military Memoirs,* in an 1877 letter, Alexander again wrote only in generalities about Lee's plans to resume the offensive sometime during the morning of July 3. "Before daylight on the morning of the 3d," he recollected, "I received orders to post the artillery for an assault upon the enemy's position, and later I learned that it was to be led by Pickett's division and directed on Cemetery Hill." In this instance, Alexander claimed he only possessed a very general knowledge during the overnight hours it was intended to renew the attack on the Federal position. It was not until an unspecified number of hours later he discovered the designated target of the attack and which unit would be leading the assault.[20]

In *Memoirs,* Alexander also described how before Lee and Longstreet's morning meeting, the latter had been exploring the possibility of a flank attack against the Federal left and was planning to deploy Pickett's division not in the Peach Orchard sector but further off to the right of his line. "During the night," Alexander declared, "Longstreet had sent scouts in search of a way by which he might turn the enemy's left and believed he had found one with some promise of success. Soon after sunrise, while Longstreet awaited the arrival of Pickett's division with [James] Dearing's battalion of artillery, intending then to extend his right" Lee arrived and expressed his desire to use the First Corps to attack the Federal left-center. These details corroborate the notion Longstreet was aware he was expected to resume offensive operations on July 3, but details as to how that resumption should take place had not been forthcoming until Lee rode up in the morning. In the absence of those specifics overnight, Longstreet explored his options by conducting reconnaissance work to find "a way by which he might turn the enemy's left." Oddly, all discussion of Longstreet's scouting for other options on the night of July 2 is completely absent from *Fighting for the Confederacy.*[21]

In Longstreet's own memoirs, he provided a few additional details on this overnight reconnaissance work and his intentions for offensive action on July 3, writing, "In the absence of orders, I had scouting parties out during the night in search of a way by which we might strike the enemy's left, and push it down towards his centre. I found a way that gave some promise of results, and was about to move my command, when he [Lee] rode over after sunrise and gave his orders." On this topic, Clifford Dowdey charged Longstreet with severe insubordination for being ready to set his flank attack plan in motion and again suggesting Lee alter his tactical approach. "At this point he was neither would-be collaborator nor resentful subordinate; indeed, his attitude reflected no accountable military relationship with Lee," Dowdey declared. The Virginian historian then claimed Stonewall Jackson would have had Longstreet arrested and Napoleon would have had him shot, concluding that the only reason Lee did not replace him was because he simply had no one else. Yet, Dowdey neglects to mention Longstreet provided very similar commentary on his flank plan in his after-battle report for Lee to read, where he also added "This would have been a slow process, probably, but I think not very difficult. A few moments after my orders for the execution of this plan were given, the commanding general joined me, and ordered [an] ... assault to be made directly at the enemy's main position, the Cemetery Hill." Again, Lee would have read Longstreet's report and certainly contested any gross inaccuracies in content or references to blatant insubordination. If Lee had indeed ordered Longstreet to be ready to attack early in the morning, he certainly would not have allowed the corps commander to get away with implying that he received no orders until "the commanding general joined me" in the morning. Lee approved the report as written, alleged insubordination and all.[22]

In the postwar years, Lafayette McLaws also wrote at length about the night of July 2. If Longstreet's entire corps had indeed been ordered to attack at daylight on the morning of July 3, McLaws knew absolutely nothing of it. If we are to believe without question the accuracy and truthfulness of Alexander's *Fighting for the Confederacy* account, why would Longstreet have been so quick to inform his artillery commander that Pickett would renew the attack early in the morning to the left of the Peach Orchard, but never provide any of those details to his division commander who was currently holding the line in that sector of the field? Writing about what he knew in the overnight hours, McLaws declared, "What the next move was to be was unknown to me.... I was not notified that it was in contemplation even to make any further attack by either Hood's or my division, nor was I informed that it was the intention to assault the enemy's centre with Pickett's division, with the assistance of troops from other corps." McLaws' commentary makes it clear that Longstreet said nothing to him about plans for an early morning attack and nothing about using Pickett's division to assault the Federal left-center. McLaws knew nothing whatsoever of any plan to attack at daylight. Now if we are to believe E.P. Alexander's one account which described how he was told the First Corps would renew the attack in the early morning with Pickett's division to the left of the Peach Orchard, would not Lafayette McLaws, a division commander in that corps, know something about such a movement, especially considering his battered unit would probably be taking an active role? It would be inexplicable for Longstreet to tell a young artillery officer about such plans, but leave all of his division commanders in the dark. Yet, McLaws did not stop there. Beyond stating that the "next move was ... unknown to me" on the night of July 2, McLaws also directly addressed the claims Lee made in his after-battle report. Referring to Lee's statement about the "the general plan" being "unchanged" and how Pickett would arrive and "was ordered to attack the next morning," McLaws simply contended that "I never heard that such was even contemplated."[23]

The division commander also touched on another important aspect of this topic, specifically how Lee initially intended to use McLaws and Hood's divisions on July 3. "If General Longstreet did not attack early on the 3d, as General Lee says he was ordered to do so," he explained, "his reasons for not doing so appear to have been perfectly satisfactory to General Lee." The fact of the matter is Lee came to Longstreet on the morning of July 3 with a far-fetched plan, which was almost immediately discarded once the commanding general spoke with his principal subordinate. Longstreet later described what happened, writing, "His plan was to assault the enemy's left centre by a column to be composed of McLaws's and Hood's divisions reinforced by Pickett's brigades. I thought that it would not do; that the point had been fully tested the day before, by more men, when all were fresh." He then cited the objections he expressed to Lee about this plan: "That the divisions of McLaws and Hood were holding a mile along the right of my line against twenty thousand men, who would follow their withdrawal, strike the flank of the assaulting column, crush it, and get on our rear towards the Potomac River."[24]

Numerous participants confirmed and agreed with Longstreet's analysis of Lee's ill-conceived plan, specifically the intended use of McLaws and Hood in a renewed attack. E.P. Alexander wrote, "Longstreet pointed out to Lee the enemy's position on the Round Tops and the danger of withdrawing Hood and McLaws from our right flank, which would be necessary if they were to take part in the attack upon the enemy's left centre. Lee recognized the necessity and substituted six brigades from Hill's corps." In another account, Alexander was even more frank in his narrative about the intended use of McLaws' and Hood's divisions on July 3. "For awhile, Longstreet's critics tried to make it appear that he disobeyed an order to put McLaws's & Hood's divisions also in the storming column with Pickett, " he wrote, "But it has been pointed out, in Gen. Lee's report, that *although there had been at first a desire*, on his part, to use some of these troops in Pickett's charge, *it had been abandoned*, & Heth's division under [Johnston] Pettigrew ... & some other of Hill's troops were substituted for them." Lafayette McLaws himself weighed in on Lee's initial plan to use his division and Hood's with support from Pickett, writing, "It is not to be disputed that General Lee could not have expected Longstreet's two right divisions to take part in that charge." Evidence suggests Lee realized upon speaking with Longstreet that the plan he formulated during the overnight hours was not in the best interest of his army's flank and rear. As a result, Lee completely changed the assaulting column to include units from Hill's corps. Pickett's division would now be the only First Corps unit, and Longstreet would be "re-enforced by Heth's division and two brigades of Pender's, to the command of which Major-General Trimble was assigned."[25]

Astoundingly, Earl Hess puts the majority of the blame on Longstreet for Lee's initial plan to use McLaws' and Hood's divisions supported by Pickett in a renewed assault. He also lays blame on Longstreet for Lee's "apparently ... not fully appreciate[ing] the terrain difficulties on this part of the field." Hess writes that the cause for Lee's oversight on these two issues was "partly because Longstreet chose not to report in person on the results on the fighting the night before." These charges generate several critical questions that have regularly gone unanswered: specifically, was Lee not actively watching the battle on July 2 from his perch on Seminary Ridge near A.P. Hill? If he was not watching, why did Lee not choose to hold a conference with Longstreet and his two new corps commanders to get everyone on the same page? Was Lee not aware of how extensively McLaws and Hood had been engaged on July 2? Did Lee not understand McLaws and Hood represented the Confederates' right flank on the morning of July 3? Had Lee yet to grasp the true strength of the Federal position? Was it necessary that Longstreet tell Lee these things during the overnight hours of July 2, when the Confederates had just shed a lot of blood on that same "terrain" just a few hours ago?[26]

In short, it took only a matter of minutes during his morning meeting with Longstreet for Lee to discard his initial plan to use all three First Corps divisions in an assault on the Federal left-center; however, he remained insistent on carrying out a direct attack. Even an ardent Lee supporter like Clifford Dowdey questioned Lee's tactical perspective at this moment in the battle. "The nature of the attack was determined after Longstreet was overruled," Dowdey contended, "and it was then that Lee showed himself to be no longer in possession of his full faculties as a military commander." Dowdey seemingly found Lee's instant pivot away from using McLaws and Hood, and his immediate call for a complete change in the attack's focus from the Federal left-center to the center uncharacteristically erratic. Lee's second plan would also include units from two different Confederate corps under Longstreet's overall tactical direction. Most significantly, when Lee changed his plan and modified which units would take part in the renewed attack, he effectively sealed the deal for a lengthy delay in operations, as preparations would now involve coordination between two corps. In sum, for those who have seen fit to criticize Longstreet for not attacking at daylight on July 3, there is no evidence Lee issued such an order. No Confederate participant in the battle ever recorded the alleged attack order was given to the corps commander on the night of July 2. No one on Lee's staff left a record of who conveyed instructions, or what the level of detail was. Moreover, there was no logical reason for such an order to be issued. Unlike July 2, time was no longer an issue for the Confederates, as the Federal army was then fully up and present on the battlefield. Further, Lee came to Longstreet with a flawed operational plan on the morning of July 3 that, after a brief discussion with his subordinate, was almost immediately discarded for a new one requiring more time and preparation.[27]

18

Lee and Longstreet Prepare for a Last-Ditch Effort

"The morning was occupied in necessary preparations"
—Robert E. Lee

Around 4:30 a.m. on July 3, Lee and Longstreet met for a conference along Seminary Ridge. Unlike the rather dramatic way historians have described this meeting over the years, George Stewart portrayed the encounter most aptly, calling it "merely a brief meeting, between the commanding general and his senior corps-commander—an interchange of views, followed by the giving of some orders." In contrast to Stewart's reasonable judgment, Clifford Dowdey contended Longstreet showed up to the meeting possessed by an "inner turmoil," a "surliness," and a "recalcitrance"—an unsubstantiated claim seemingly based on a mysterious ability to know how Longstreet felt at this controversial moment in the battle.[1]

Longstreet wrote extensively on his meeting with Lee, now one of the most famous moments in Civil War history. In his after-battle report, Longstreet said he informed Lee he had made "arrangements ... for renewing the attack by my right, with a view to pass around the hill occupied by the enemy on his left, and to gain it by flank and reverse attack." He recollected in a postwar account, "On the next morning he came to see me, and, fearing that he was still in his disposition to attack, I tried to anticipate him, by saying 'General, I have had my scouts out all night, and I find that you still have an excellent opportunity to move around to the right of Meade's army, and maneuver him into attacking us.'" In another postwar writing, he asserted "I stated to General Lee that I had been examining the ground over to the right, and was much inclined to think the best thing was to move to the Federal left." In Longstreet's eight "Mistakes of Gettysburg," number seven read "On the morning of the 3d we should have moved to the right, and maneuvered the Federals into attacking us." And finally, in his memoirs, Longstreet recalled of his flank plan on the morning of July 3, "In the absence of orders, I had scouting parties out during the night in search of a way by which we might strike the enemy's left and push it down towards his centre. I found a way that gave some promise of results, and was about to move my command when he [Lee] rode over after sunrise and gave his orders."[2]

Longstreet critics have often dwelled on the subtle differences between all of these accounts, charging that, in some, Longstreet wrote that he intended to make a flank attack, while in others he alluded to a broader maneuver around the Federal left for purposes of receiving the enemy's attack. Even though there undoubtedly exists a difference between the two proposals, the general theme of Longstreet's proposal remained consistent, which was to draw off the Federal left, dashing any thoughts of resuming the frontal attack against the Federal position. Historians can usually place more trust in participants' accounts written closer to the actual event, which in this case was Longstreet's after-battle report, drafted less than a month after the battle and undoubtedly read and reviewed by General Lee. In that report, Longstreet explicitly stated he planned to renew the attack, passing around the Federal left "to gain it by flank and reverse." Therefore, Longstreet clearly advocated for a resumption of offensive operations; however, he in no way supported another direct attack on the Federal position. In an 1883 account, he provided more explanation for his reasoning: "The position of the Federals was quite strong, and the battle of the 2d had concentrated them so that I considered an attack from the front more hazardous than the battle of the 2d had been. The Federals were concentrated, while our troops were stretched out in a long, broken—and thus a weak—line." In contrast, Lee's immovable resolve to attack "from the front" was made quite apparent on July 3: "General Lee hoped to break through the Federal line and drive them off." Longstreet recalled. The First Corps commander then admitted to being "disappointed when he came to me on the morning of the 3d and directed that I should renew the attack against Cemetery Hill, probably the strongest point of the Federal line."[3]

In response to Longstreet's suggestion that the Confederates should draw around and gain the Federal left, Lee allegedly "replied, pointing with his fist at Cemetery Hill: 'The enemy is there, and I am going to strike him.'" Lee ordered Longstreet to attack the Federal left-center with Hood and McLaws' divisions, supported by Pickett's division. Longstreet then proceeded to express his reservations. According to Lee's after-battle report, Longstreet "deemed it necessary to defend his flank and rear with the divisions of Hood and McLaws." By this point in the conversation, Generals A.P. Hill and Harry Heth, the British observer Colonel Fremantle, and various staff officers had joined Lee and Longstreet while they examined the battlefield from a point somewhere northwest of the Peach Orchard. Fremantle recalled that "As we formed a pretty large party, we often drew upon ourselves the attention of the hostile sharpshooters, and were two or three times favored with a shell." Soon thereafter, Lee shared Longstreet's concerns about the use of Hood and McLaws, but then immediately declared that "Heth's division and two brigades of Pender's" could instead join Pickett in an attack on the Federal center. Although perhaps never stated at the time, this attack would be aimed at a copse of oak trees on Cemetery Ridge near where Wright's brigade had advanced on July 2. In a mere matter of minutes, Lee had changed both the point of attack and the units that were to compose the attack column. Heth had been wounded on July 1 and Pender on July 2, so their commands would instead be led by Johnston Pettigrew and James Lane (replaced by Isaac Trimble during preparations). That settled, Lee and Longstreet then turned to discussing the distance the assaulting column would have to traverse between Seminary and Cemetery Ridge, a distance which Longstreet wrote about very candidly in his after-battle report: "The distance to be passed over under the fire of the enemy's batteries, and in plain view, seemed too great to insure great results, particularly as two- thirds of the troops to be engaged in the assault had been in a severe battle two days previous, Pickett's division alone being fresh."[4]

Another topic Longstreet broached with Lee pertained to how many men would be in this revised assaulting column, to which Lee allegedly replied fifteen thousand men. That number made sense given that three divisions, typically 5,000 men per division, would be involved, Pickett, Pettigrew, and Trimble; however, the most accepted modern estimate of the number of Confederates that actually made the march toward Cemetery Ridge on July 3 is closer to 12,500 men. Whatever the number, in later years, Longstreet wrote that he thought "that thirty thousand men was the minimum of force necessary for the work." That Longstreet thought such a large amount of men was necessary for the attack was confirmed by Arthur Fremantle when the British officer and observer recalled how the General had told him on July 4 that "the mistake they had made was in not concentrating the army more, and making the attack yesterday with 30,000 men instead of 15,000." In fact, still totally convinced his commander was gravely erring, Longstreet expressed his concerns to Lee one last time before carrying out his duties in preparing the attack: "'General, I have been a soldier all my life. I have been with soldiers engaged in fights by couples, by squads, companies, regiments, divisions, and armies, and should know, as well as any one, what soldiers can do. It is my opinion that no fifteen thousand men ever arrayed for battle can take that position,' pointing to Cemetery Hill." According to Longstreet, "General Lee, in reply to this, ordered me to prepare Pickett's Division for the attack." Longstreet recollected he strongly considered "saying a word against the sacrifice of my men" at that moment, but instead simply "said no more, however, but turned away." In another account, the corps commander alleged Lee "seemed a little impatient at my remarks, so I said nothing more. As he showed no indication of changing his plan, I went to work at once to arrange my troops for the attack."[5]

* * *

In describing what happened on Longstreet's front on the morning of July 3, Robert E. Lee wrote in his first official report of the battle, published that same month, "The morning was occupied in necessary preparations and the battle recommenced in the afternoon of the 3d." Later, Longstreet succinctly summarized those necessary preparations as consisting of "Pickett [being] put in position and receiv[ing] directions for the line of his advance as indicated by General Lee. The divisions of the Third Corps were arranged along his left with orders to take up the line of march, as Pickett passed before them, in short echelon. We were to open with our batteries, and Pickett was to move out as soon as we silenced the Federal batteries."[6]

Pickett's 5,830-man division filtered in to the left of McLaws' division in the mid-morning hours, taking position on the eastern fringe and in front of Sprangler's Woods, located on the southern end of Seminary Ridge proper. Due to their order of march to the field, Pickett positioned his leading brigades of Richard Garnett and James Kemper in front, with Lewis Armistead approximately 100–200 yards behind Garnett in support. While Pickett's troops filed into their muster position, Longstreet instructed Pickett's aide Walter Harrison to inform Armistead "to remain where he is for the present, and he can make up the distance when the advance is made." Before Pickett's arrival, Wilcox and Lang's brigades of Anderson's division, 1,600 men, vacated Sprangler's Woods and moved out toward Alexander's artillery line posted on the west side of the Emmitsburg Road. A sizable gap of 400 yards existed between Richard Garnett's left and the right of Pettigrew's Third Corps division, which was supported by Isaac Trimble's two brigades. Collectively, Pettigrew and Trimble numbered another 7,300 men. On the western slope of Seminary Ridge and behind Trimble was placed the rest of Anderson's division, Wright, Posey, and Mahone's brigade, another 3,350 troops, who were not a part of the assaulting column.[7]

Longstreet critics often expend a lot of ink and paper in writing about what they believe the First Corps commander did and did not do on the morning of July 3. George Stewart accurately characterized this stripe of historian as one who made "implicit in [their] explanations ... the idea that a different result would have been assured if the writer's ideas had been followed." Stewart correctly pointed out that this tendency had passed "from those who had been at Gettysburg ... to the historians." Such historians claim the following about Longstreet's actions on the morning of the third day: Longstreet never bothered to notice or simply ignored the significant gap between the divisions of Pickett and Pettigrew; Longstreet erred in placing Trimble's two brigades behind the right of Pettigrew's division, leaving John Brockenbrough and Joseph Davis' brigades without ample support on the left; and, Longstreet focused all of his attention on Pickett's three brigades, and almost completely neglected the other six Third Corps brigades. Earl Hess is one modern historian who advances these contentions, asserting in one instance that "all of these weaknesses fall into the category of lapses of thought, not deliberate attempts to sabotage the assault"; however, just two paragraphs later, he tacks on an additional, more disparaging accusation to his first charge, writing, "Longstreet's deliberate attempts to limit the chances of success and thereby limit the loss of valuable manpower also hamstrung the operation." These inconsistencies aside, Hess is confident in his judgment that "for the first time in his career Longstreet was organizing an attack across corps lines and utterly failed to meet the new challenge."[8]

On the matter of the gap between Pickett and Pettigrew, the latter's orders, according to Lieutenant Louis Young of his staff, were to "place the division under the nearest cover to the left of Pickett's Division, with which it would advance in line." The fact of the matter was that the nearest cover to the left was the woods just behind the crest of Seminary Ridge, and so Pettigrew deployed his brigades there from left to right, Brockenbrough, Davis, James Marshall, and Birkett Fry. Fry commanded the brigade that was to connect with Pickett's left, and he, Pickett, and Richard Garnett coordinated efforts prior to the attack, discussing how they would maneuver during the assault so as to close the gap that separated the divisions. Fry recollected that "it was agreed that he [Garnett] would dress on my command.... It was then understood that my command should be considered the centre and that both divisions should align themselves by it." Therefore, it would seem Longstreet and Lee were aware of the space between the divisions and addressed it by instructing Pickett to "dress left" during the march toward Cemetery Ridge to close the gap. Generals in Pettigrew's division similarly noted they were aware of the need to dress to the right. Major John Jones of the 26th North Carolina, Marshall's brigade, recollected that "it had been ordered to close in on the right on Pickett's Divi-

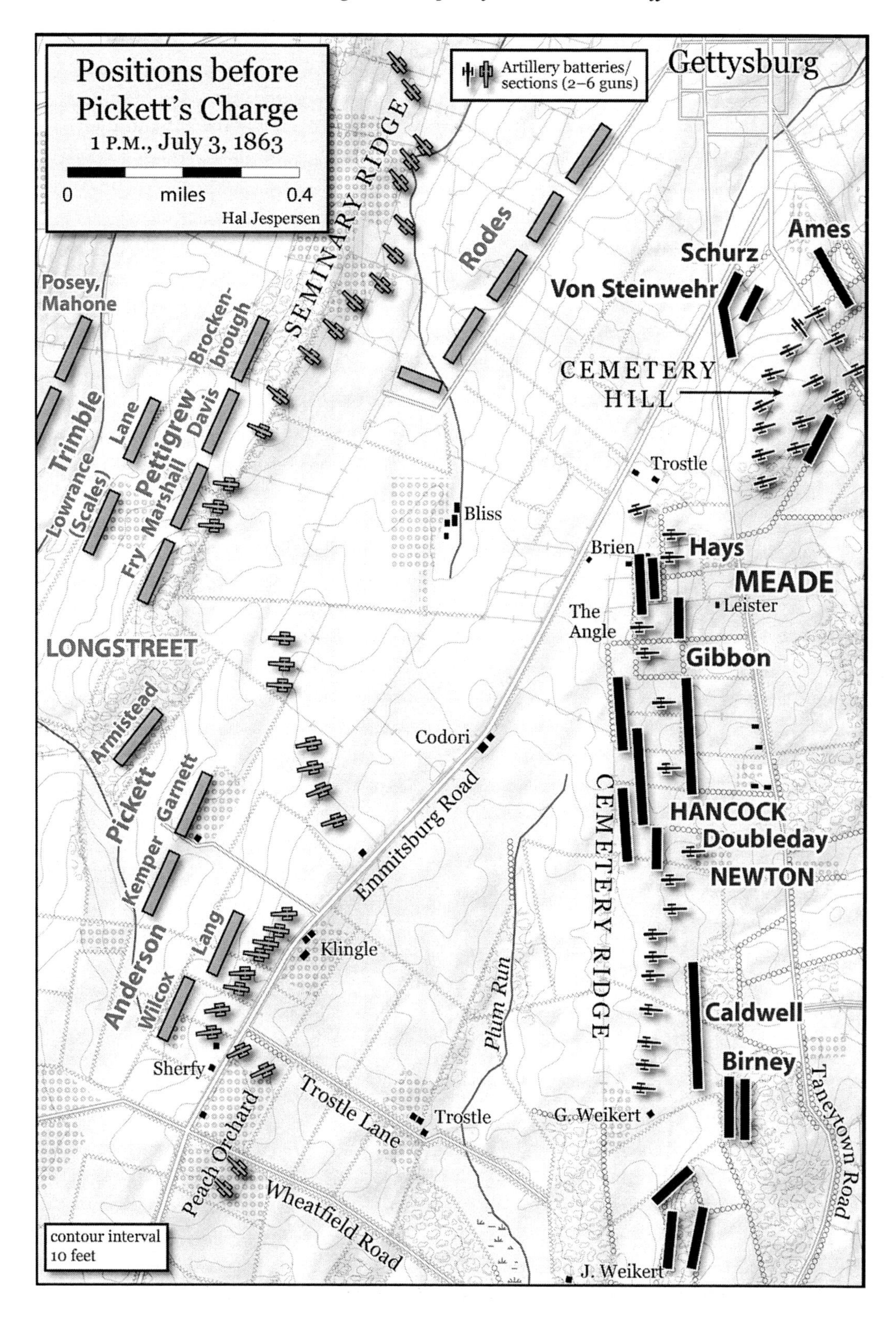
Positions before
Pickett's Charge
1 P.M., July 3, 1863
0
miles
0.4
Hal Jespersen
Artillery batteries/
sections (2–6 guns)
Gettysburg
SEMINARY RIDGE
Rodes
Ames
Schurz
Von Steinwehr
CEMETERY
HILL
Posey,
Mahone
Brocken-
brough
Trimble
Lane
Pettigrew
Davis
Lowrance
(Scales)
Marshall
Fry
Trostle
Bliss
Brien
Hays
MEADE
Leister
The
Angle
Gibbon
LONGSTREET
Armistead
Pickett
Garnett
Codori
Emmitsburg Road
HANCOCK
Doubleday
NEWTON
CEMETERY RIDGE
Kemper
Anderson
Lang
Wilcox
Klingle
Plum Run
Caldwell
Birney
Sherfy
Peach Orchard
Trostle Lane
Trostle
G. Weikert
Taneytown Road
Wheatfield Road
contour interval
10 feet
J. Weikert

sion, while that command gave way to the left." The evidence that Longstreet or Lee made their plan for closing the gap well known to both divisions contradicts Earl Hess' blanket assertion that "[Longstreet] failed to communicate effectively with anyone outside the First Corps."[9]

Evidence suggests that Pickett took strides to ensure Garnett and Fry were aware of the gap separating their brigades and how it would be addressed during the advance. As George Stewart related twice on the matter in his analysis of Pickett's Charge, "Since steps were taken to solve this problem, we can only suppose that the two generals [Lee and Longstreet] recognized it," and "We must assume that the plan was worked out in advance." It is a reasonable assumption given that soon after the forward march began, Pickett ordered his brigades to execute left oblique marching, which essentially meant each brigade made a 45-degree pivot to the left. Also during the meeting between Pickett, Fry, and Garnett, it was established that Fry's brigade "should be considered the centre" of the assault. Given this understanding, it was likely Longstreet's tactical rationale in placing Trimble's two brigades behind and in support of Fry and Marshall, instead of behind Brockenbrough and Davis on the flank, was done with the intent to create a more powerful attack in depth at its critical center point.[10]

With respect to the preparation of the six Third Corps brigades, it is clear Lee entrusted Longstreet with overall tactical control of the attack. Though Lee almost certainly realized Longstreet opposed the attack plan, the commanding general wanted no one else leading the assault. George Stewart aptly wrote that Lee would have "preferred Longstreet, recalcitrant, to Hill, cooperative." With that said, was nothing expected of A.P. Hill? During the July 2 battle, Hill was a ghost, and although again physically present on July 3, he continued to act as an absentee corps commander. Hill oddly allowed for Pettigrew and Trimble to lead the attack's left wing, even though the former had never commanded a division before, and the latter had not commanded an infantry unit in battle for ten months. Furthermore, Trimble was strangely chosen to lead Pender's two brigades while preparations for the assault were already underway. James Lane initially held that position in the morning and had carried out Longstreet's orders to form in the right rear of Pettigrew's division. Then, a bizarre command swap ensued, where Lane was relegated to his brigade command, while Isaac Trimble, who had been tethered to Ewell's corps as a senior officer without a command for the first two days of the battle, took control of the half-division. Trimble readily admitted Pender's men were "entire strangers" to him. Realistically, there were other more seasoned and familiar brigade commanders to choose from to replace Heth and Pender.[11]

Even though Earl Hess hoists blame on Longstreet for "fail[ing] to understand, mostly due to his lack of contact with the Third Corps ... the weakened condition of Pettigrew's and Trimble's units," that responsibility more appropriately rested with Lee and the Third Corps commander. During his early morning meeting with Longstreet, was it not Lee who specifically chose Heth's and Pender's division to join Pickett simply due to their physical position in the Confederate battle line? Further, why had Hill not protested when Lee went on to select depleted and mauled Third Corps units to take part in the assault? Even fervent Longstreet critic Clifford Dowdey admitted on this topic, "The responsibility for conveying this information to Lee was A.P. Hill's." Tellingly, when Lee rode over to examine Trimble's line, he looked at the men in Alfred Scales' (now commanded by Colonel William Lowrance) depleted brigade and remarked, "Many of these poor boys should go to the rear; they are not able for duty." Indeed, George Stewart reasonably described the poor condition of Pettigrew's division on July 3: "The division as a whole had suffered losses of at least forty percent. In most armies, such a battered unit would have been sent to the rear for reorganization, but here it was being selected for a climactic attack!" Similarly, Colonel Robert Mayo of the 47th Virginia described Pettigrew's flank, Brokenbrough's brigade as "nothing more than a line of skirmishers," with reports the brigade only mustered between 200 and 600 men on the morning of July 3.[12]

Lastly, it is reasonable to assume Hill probably did not appreciate Lee temporarily putting several of his brigades under Longstreet's tactical control. Just a year earlier, Hill and Longstreet had engaged in a heated dispute over whose men received newspaper acclaim for engaging or driving back the Federals at the Seven Days Battles of Mechanicsville, Gaines' Mill, and Glendale. The quarrel escalated to the point Hill requested to be "relieved from the command of Major-General Longstreet," refused to comply with any orders originating from Longstreet or his staff, challenged Longstreet to a duel, and ultimately was placed under arrest by Lee's Warhorse. Unsurprisingly, Hill engaged in subsequent feuds with Stonewall Jackson after he was transferred to that command. By July 1863, relations between Hill and Longstreet had cooled enough to work together on a professional level; however, they were not close or intimate friends.

At some point during the morning hours on July 3, Hill allegedly "begged" Lee to allow him to use his whole corps in the attack, perhaps in an attempt—from his principled perspective—to reclaim the Third Corps brigades that had been seemingly handed over to Longstreet, or perhaps more simply to break out of his bystander role. Lee refused the request, telling Hill his corps represented the only reserve the army had left if the assault were to fail. Hill's subsequent actions suggest he made it a point to leave everything to the First Corps commander, including deployment and placement of his Third Corps units. Writing on this matter, Stephen Sears has judged that Longstreet "gave more attention to Pickett than to Pettigrew and Trimble, but in this regard he apparently (and properly) expected A.P. Hill to at least do his duty by his own troops." Overall, Sears aptly characterizes Hill as "the same elusive figure he had been on Wednesday and Thursday," and concludes that "Hill ... resumed his bystander role." In fact, Hill explicitly told James Lane, who commanded one of the two brigades which made up Trimble's division to take his direction from Longstreet. Therefore, on the morning of July 3, Lane's, and Alfred Scales' dilapidated brigade, now commanded by Colonel William Lowrance, acted on Longstreet's orders to "form in rear of the right of Heth's division, commanded by General Pettigrew."[13]

* * *

Perhaps above all else, Longstreet critics neglect to address, or totally ignore, the clear implications of Lee's "the morning was occupied in necessary preparations" statement, expressed just days after the battle. Clifford Dowdey exemplified the critics' erroneous perspective on this topic: "At ten o'clock, when Ewell's action was beginning to dwindle.... Longstreet was no more ready to attack than he had been when Lee left him at six. As is true of Old Pete's inanition during the forenoon of the second day, no one knows what he did during those hours." Remarkably, Dowdey expressed his belief that Longstreet actually duped Lee into thinking the Confederates were engaged "in necessary preparations" on the morning of July 3. "Believing that Longstreet was supervising the charge," Dowdey alleged, "he [Lee] assumed that the passing hours were being spent in preparation." The fact of the matter is Longstreet's preparations and general planning for the assault on July 3 were completed throughout the morning hours, under Lee's eye, and often physically right next to Lee. Indeed, the commanding general was present with Longstreet for a good portion of the morning. Even Douglas Southall Freeman admitted as much, writing, "Lee was determined that nothing should be lacking in infantry preparation. Twice he rode the length of the line with Longstreet and then went over it again without him. Later, Lee rode out in front of the right of Pettigrew's command with Longstreet and with Hill to arrange the last tactical details." The picture of Lee and Longstreet working together on the morning of July 3 to plan the assault stands in stark contrast to many historical analyses of the battle, which often seem to suggest Lee and Longstreet had their meeting in the early morning, both men parted angrily, and then Longstreet rode off to half-heartedly plan an assault with little follow-on input from Lee. Gilbert Moxley Sorrel's comment on the preparations made for Longstreet's July 3 attack exemplified this mistaken belief. Of the Confederate's inability to mount an attack during the morning hours, Sorrel contended that "Indeed, the delay in attacking which undoubtedly hurt us was apparently caused by his [Longstreet's] objections made known to the Commander-in-Chief." Yet, the historical record suggests this and similar viewpoints are fictitious.[14]

George Pickett, wartime (Library of Congress).

First-hand accounts of Lee and Longstreet's collaboration on the morning of July 3 were numerous. Writing later about his artillery preparations, which likely commenced around the 8 a.m. hour, E.P. Alexander recalled that "after Gen. Pendleton's visit I saw & conversed with both Gen. Lee & Longstreet, & most of their staff officers, & got more exact ideas of where Pickett was to direct his march." Arthur Fremantle recollected that sometime just after 6 a.m., he "joined Generals Lee and Longstreet's Staff: they were reconnoitring and making preparations for renewing the attack." Likewise, Fitzgerald Ross, an Austrian observer, wrote "the morning was spent in riding over the battlefield of yesterday, the Generals holding a long consultation, and reconnoitring the position to be attacked to-day." Gart Johnson, a private in the 18th Mississippi, noticed Lee and Longstreet out by the Confederate skirmish line in the Peach Orchard sector, not anywhere near the safest place on the field at the time. Johnson recollected both generals were walking some distance apart, and Lee called out to Longstreet, "Mass your artillery behind that hill, and at the signal bring your guns to the top of the ridge and turn them loose."[15]

John H. Moore, a soldier in the 7th Tennessee of Fry's brigade—the unit positioned directly left of Pickett's division—remembered seeing Longstreet with Lee and Pickett riding in front of the Confederate line "several times—at least three times; if not more—observing our alignment, but principally with field-glasses observing the position and movements of the Federals." Lieutenant John Dooley of the 1st Virginia also saw the same trio of Lee, Longstreet, and Pickett. Longstreet later explained how he "took Pickett to the crest of Seminary Ridge and explained where his troops should be sheltered, and pointed out the direction General Lee wished him to take and the point of the Federal line where the assault was to be made." Gilbert Moxley Sorrel described the extent to which Longstreet made Pickett aware of the objective and how the attack was to be carried out: "While Longstreet by no means approved the movement, his soldierly eye watched every feature of it. He neglected nothing that could help it and his anxiety for Pickett and the men was very apparent." Colonel Fry himself noticed the First Corps commander being joined by many other generals, including Lee. At one point, he wrote, Longstreet rode with Lee and A.P. Hill toward his line, where they all dismounted and sat together on a large tree trunk. "After an apparently careful examination of a map, and a consultation of some length, they remounted and rode away," Fry recalled. When Major Walter Harrison of Pickett's staff sought out Longstreet in the morning hours to seek out an answer concerning the position of Lewis Armistead's brigade on Seminary Ridge, he also found Longstreet present with Lee.[16]

During the morning hours, Longstreet reassured Lee he "had been more particular in giving the orders than ever before," had met with each unit commander who was to take part in the attack, and explained to them their objective and point of attack. The corps commander later wrote on this topic, "Division commanders were asked to go to the crest of the ridge and take a careful view of the field, and to have their officers there to tell their men of it, and to prepare them for the sight that was to burst upon them as they mounted the crest." Longstreet also claimed he alone "rode once or twice along the ground between Pickett and the Federals, examining the positions and studying the matter over in all its phases so far as we could anticipate."[17]

Toward the late hours of the morning—"before the artillery opened fire"—General Wofford of McLaws' division also encountered Longstreet with Lee, whereby the latter asked the brigade commander if he thought the Confederates could once again reach the crest of Cemetery Ridge, as a small portion of the army had done on July 2. Wofford allegedly replied, "No, General, I think not.... The enemy have had all night to entrench and reinforce. I had been pursuing a broken enemy and the situation is now very different." Similar to Wofford's statement, A.P. Hill told Colonel Birkett Fry that after examining the Federal line he thought the position "entirely too strong to attack in front." Likewise, Brigadier General William Mahone recollected later that he told his division commander, Richard Anderson, "No troops ever formed a line of battle that could cross the plain of fire to which the attacking force would be subjected, and ... that I could not believe General Lee would insist on such an assault after he had seen the ground." In the meantime, other accounts of the Lee-Longstreet collaboration abounded. "Gens. Lee and Longstreet [were] on foot, no aides, orderlies or couriers, fifteen or twenty steps apart, field glasses in hand ... stopping now and then to take observations ... arranging, as we soon found out, for the famous charge of Pickett's division," another testimony went. And still in another recollection, others viewed Lee and Colonel Walter Taylor riding "near our lines," where they soon "spread out a map on a stump and were looking over it when Gen'l Longstreet joined them and ... appeared to be holding a council of war as they had sentinels thrown around the group of officers."[18]

Collectively, all of these accounts confirm what Longstreet contended in the postwar years, namely that all preparations for the July 3 assault were done under Lee's eye and therefore stamped with his approval. Longstreet recalled that Lee rode along the line with him multiple times during the morning hours "to see that everything was arranged according to his wishes." Longstreet also described how "the commanders had been sent for and the point of attack had been carefully designated and that the commanders had been directed to communicate to their subordinates, and through them to every soldier in the command, the work that was before them, so that they should nerve themselves for the attack and fully understand it." E.P. Alexander confirmed Longstreet's recollections:

> Then, it must be remembered that the preparations for this charge were made deliberately, & under the observation of Gen. Lee himself, & of all his staff. From sunrise to 1:30 p.m. was nine hours, all devoted to this business, & within a few hundred acres of land. It seems to me impossible to believe that Gen. Lee did not know quite accurately the location of every brigade he had upon that battlefield, hours before the cannonade opened. Certainly he & his staff officers also were all about in my vicinity, during the morning.[19]

19

The Artillery Support Plan for the Grand Charge

"Fire a few rounds before Pickett's men passed on forward between my guns"
—E.P. Alexander

E.P. Alexander also made reference to "troops which were to support the charge" in his comments about Confederate preparations on the morning of July 3, another controversial topic involving Longstreet. Beyond the assertion made by many postwar Longstreet critics that he was to use his entire corps in the attack, specifically referring to the non-use of Hood's and McLaws' divisions, they and some modern historians have also held that Lee intended for the assault to be supported by additional units from Hill's corps, or at the very least, Cadmus Wilcox's and David Lang's brigades, which were positioned to the right of Pickett's division. On these dubious support theories, Walter Taylor wrote that Longstreet "was to be reinforced by Heth's division and two brigades of Pender's, of Hill's corps. These, with his three divisions, were to attack.... Hood and McLaws were not moved forward. There were nine divisions in the army; seven were quiet, while two assailed the fortified line of the enemy." Taylor further alleged, "Had Hood and McLaws followed or supported Pickett, and Pettigrew and Anderson have been advanced, the design of the Commanding-General would have been carried out." Similarly, John B. Gordon believed, "Had Lee's orders been promptly and cordially executed, Meade's centre on the third day would have been penetrated and the Union army overwhelmingly defeated." More specifically, Gordon contended: "General Lee ... ordered Longstreet to make the attack on the last day, with *the three divisions* of his corps, and two divisions of A.P. Hill's corps, and that instead of doing so he sent fourteen thousand men to assail to Meade's army in his strong position." Likewise, Jubal Early argued, "You will observe from General Lee's report ... that the attack was to have been made by the whole of Longstreet's corps." Cadmus Wilcox also stated similarly in the postwar years, "General Longstreet made the attack on the third day with only three brigades of his corps, when it should have been made by his entire corps, and this to have been supported by Hill's corps.... I did not know that he had failed to attack as ordered." Even E.P. Alexander claimed to know what Lee had intended or wanted for the July 3 attack: "And the battle failed of being fought as Gen. Lee expected and wished, when Pickett's advance had traversed 400 yards, & Wilcox and Anderson were not moving under orders to close up on him & go with him to the bitter end." Alexander then followed with the hypothetical question, "If Anderson & Wilcox had been welded into the column from the first & all 14 brigades launched together; or, in other words, if Pickett had had the support which Gen. Lee expected; would those five brigades have saved the day?" Alexander would not be alone in posing such questions. In the twentieth century, George Stewart wrote that these kinds of speculative inquiries were not only advanced during the postwar years "from those who had been at Gettysburg," but also by "historians" since. Earl Hess demonstrates this tendency on the topic of supports when alleging that "[Longstreet's] decision not to use reserve troops to right and left of the attackers, which Lee had clearly authorized him to do, was a serious mistake." Hess further advances the conjecture that "Longstreet should have planned to move Anderson's division forward on both flanks of the attacking column within minutes after Pickett, Pettigrew, and Trimble started."[1]

Unsurprisingly, the theories have not ended there. A more extensive support theory has been dubbed "the second wave," which is not worthy of extensive coverage as it has been disproven and discarded by most of the historical community. Earl Hess aptly concludes of the second wave theory, "Contrary to the assertion of a modern writer, there never was a 'second wave planned for Pickett's Charge.' That is, no one contemplated a large force following directly behind the attackers to provide additional weight of numbers at a key point in the assault." On this topic, A.P. Hill alleged that after the battle he told his adjutant William H. Palmer, "I begged General Lee to let me take in my whole Army corps. He refused, and said what remains of your corps will be my only reserve, and it will be needed if Gen'l Longstreet's attack should fail." Quite simply, Lee never mentioned or insinuated anything to support an intended second wave assault in his after-battle reports. Of A.P. Hill's corps, he wrote, "General Hill was directed to hold his line with the rest of his command, afford General Longstreet further assistance, if required, and avail himself of any success that might be gained." Lee's statement suggested it was at Longstreet's discretion to deploy additional units from Hill's corps, other than those already designated for the attack—Heth's division under Pettigrew and two of Pender's brigades under Trimble. Further, Lee noted the use of additional support units hinged on the assaulting columns achieving "any success" against the Federal center. Walter Taylor, despite his confusing criticism of how Longstreet handled alleged support units for Pickett's Charge, echoed Lee's after-battle report assertions, writing that "A.P. Hill had orders to be prepared to assist Longstreet further if necessary." Similarly, A.P. Hill wrote in his own after-battle report that "Anderson had been directed to hold his division ready to take advantage of any success which might be gained by the assaulting column, or to support it, if necessary. To that end, Wilcox and Perry were moved forward to eligible positions." Likewise, Richard Anderson contended, "I received orders to hold my division in readiness to move up in support, if should become necessary." As events turned out, there was little evidence of success gained by the assaulting column beyond a few hundred men piercing the Federal forward line at "the Angle." Therefore, with the exception of Wilcox's and Lang's brigades, Longstreet, as was intended and ordered, did not think it fit to forward more units from Anderson's division. Additionally, on the use of Hood's and McLaws' divisions as support units, Lafayette McLaws refuted Walter Taylor's claim that they were to have "followed or supported Pickett," asserting, "I therefore do not think that it was ever expected by General Lee that Hood's and my division should take part in the charge unless we had been moved round and enveloped the enemy's left." Helen Longstreet confirmed McLaws' statement and drew upon Lee and Longstreet's after-battle reports:

> There was every reason to believe that the position was much stronger on the final day than when Longstreet attacked it on the 2d. The troops of Hood and McLaws, in view of their enormous losses, were in no condition to support Pickett effectively, even had they been free for that purpose. But it has been shown ... by the testimony of both Lee and Longstreet that they were required to maintain the position they had won in the desperate struggle of the evening previous to prevent the twenty-two thousand men of the Union Fifth and Sixth Corps from falling en masse upon Pickett's right flank, or their own flank and rear had they moved in unison with Pickett.[2]

The only other references Lee made in his after-battle reports to supporting units were twofold; namely that "the batteries were directed to be pushed forward as the infantry progressed, protect their flanks, and support their attacks closely," and "Wilcox's brigade marched in rear of Pickett's right, to guard that flank." As on July 2, Longstreet relied heavily on E.P. Alexander to handle the placement and movements of the First Corps batteries. Alexander's role on July 3 was, in short, to provide a steady, crushing artillery barrage of the Federal center once Pickett was formed for the attack, with the purpose of driving off some of the Federal artillery positioned there. Briefly stated by one Confederate officer, the artillery barrage was to "damage and dismount their guns and demoralize their troops."[3]

That said, Alexander patched together other initiatives to try and support the assault. He later wrote, "While forming for the attack, I borrowed from General Pendleton, General Lee's chief of artillery, seven 12-pounder howitzers, belonging to the Third Corps, under Major [Charles] Richardson, which I put in reserve in a selected spot, intending them to accompany Pickett's infantry in the charge." In two other accounts, he put the number of howitzers at nine. Alexander noted that he personally came up with this idea for Richardson's guns and neither consulted nor told Pendleton his intended use for them. Further, he asserted he thought the guns might serve to "follow Pickett's infantry in the charge, more promptly, & also, perhaps more safely than guns out of the firing line could do." Alexander explained his rationale for using these mobile howitzers, writing, "I say more safely, because one function of a firing line of artillery ... is to cover the retreat of the storming column in case it fails to make a lodgment upon the enemy's line. If the guns from the firing line advance prematurely, & are caught in a repulse, they may not only be lost, but turned on their former owners." Perhaps unknowingly, Alexander's warnings here turned out to be a check on the soundness of Lee's after-battle report assertion that the firing line "batteries were directed to be pushed forward as the infantry progressed, protect their flanks, and support their attacks closely." Lee's statement was also curious considering Alexander's guns were not the only ones present on the field. What of the Second and Third Corps guns? Were they told to move? If so, did they move once the attack began? There is no evidence William Pendleton, Lee's Chief of Artillery, told any artillery officers in the Second and Third Corps to advance their guns as the infantry progressed. As a result, Ewell's guns never once moved and Major William Poague, an artillery officer in Hill's corps wrote, "Not a word was said about following the infantry as they advanced to the attack."

Poague only interpreted his instructions to mean he should move the guns forward if, and only if, the assaulting column achieved success against the Federals on Cemetery Ridge.[4]

Alexander cut to pieces the suggestion that it would be viable for the main artillery line to advance in close support with the infantry during the July 3 assault. He wrote blatantly, "The proposition of Gen. Longstreet's critics is that a considerable force of his artillery should have charged along with his infantry. But that general suggestion does not go into detail, & there are many important details to be considered." Of those "important details," Alexander pointed out it was very rarely desirable for Confederate artillery "to fire over the heads of our infantry." On this subject, Alexander was very clear. "We were always liable to premature explosions of shell & shrapnel, & our infantry knew it by sad experience, & I have known of their threatening to fire back at our guns if we opened over their heads," he wrote. On the solid shot option, Alexander emphasized it was "the least effective ammunition, & the infantry would not know the difference & would be demoralized & angry all the same." Lest critics advance the opinion General Lee instead intended for the guns to advance on the Confederate infantry's flank, Alexander covered that suggestion, as well. "It scarcely needs to be pointed out," he advanced, "that if any guns were advanced entirely out upon the flank of the assaulting column, they would be exposed, not only to the enemy's artillery, but also to rifle musketry of his sharpshooters and infantry ... which would bring it to a stand still in a few minutes & soon destroy every horse and man."[5]

Nevertheless, Alexander's orders for the 75 guns in his firing line were abundantly clear, which suggests Longstreet or Lee discussed it with him sometime during the morning hours. Despite Earl Hess' critique of Longstreet asserting "he neglected to develop and implement detailed plans to push the guns forward in close support of the attackers," Alexander claimed to have received unambiguous orders from Longstreet. "All the batteries in the firing line had similar orders—to limber up & follow any success, as promptly as possible," he recalled. Like the standard for additional infantry support, Alexander made it clear that follow-on, advance support from the main artillery line was dependent on infantry success. Further, the effectiveness of this advanced artillery support hinged on how rapidly it could be repositioned to contribute to the exploitation of that success. Beyond what was expected of the main line, Alexander thought a great deal about those nine 12-pound howitzers. Initially, he intended the guns to "follow behind Pickett's infantry," getting as close as possible without moving into Federal infantry range. Then, he intended to "halt and unlimber," so as to either cover a retreat or move forward to support a potential success. With that said, Alexander admitted he altered his plan later to have the guns moved out in front of Pickett's men, "instead of behind them." From there, Alexander wanted the guns to be moved forward past the Confederate infantry line and short of the Federal musket fire to "fire a few rounds before Pickett's men passed on forward between my guns." Alexander then concluded by admitting frankly "the change proposed cut no essential figure, but it avoided a possible delay in the guns getting out."[6]

Orders directing Alexander to have the main artillery line ready to "follow any success," along with his personal plan to move out nine howitzers to "fire a few rounds" were two tactical schemes undoubtedly filled with good intentions; however, it is reasonable to assume they were impractical and would have yielded little to no consequential results. Alexander understood and articulated the myriad of issues hampering any plan to advance artillery behind or on the flank of an infantry column. Further, the orders directing Alexander to advance the firing line, if the infantry achieved some success "as promptly as possible," were essentially unrealistic. The artillery would not only have had to deal with physical conditions, namely "fences, ditches & wheatfields," but also the obstacles of distance, and ultimately, time, to support whatever fleeting success the nearly 13,000-man assault might realize against the Federal position. Lastly, regarding Alexander's intended use of the mobile howitzers, one is simply left wondering what nine advanced guns would actually have accomplished if they had been able to "fire a few rounds" at the Federals and let Pickett pass.

20

The Alexander-Longstreet Pre-Attack Dialogue

"The order ... would have been revoked had I felt that I had that privilege"
—James Longstreet

Just after 1 p.m., Longstreet signaled for the massive Confederate cannonade to open on the Federal center by firing two guns from the Washington Artillery, positioned near the Peach Orchard. He dispatched a quick note to his First Corps artillery chief, Colonel James Walton, ordering him to "let the batteries open. Order great care and precision in firing. When the batteries at the Peach Orchard cannot be used against the point we intend to attack, let them open on the enemy's on the rocky hill." With the signal from Walton, Alexander's batteries exploded. His artillery line stretched north from the Peach Orchard along the west side of the Emmitsburg Road before bending back toward Rogers Farm near Sprangler's Woods. Colonel Lindsay Walker of A.P Hill's corps extended the artillery line northward along Seminary Ridge. Guns from Ewell's corps, positioned northeast and northwest of Cemetery Hill near Oak Hill and on Benner's Hill, had also been instructed to take part in the bombardment, but much to Alexander's disappointment, several remained largely inactive. Adding insult to injury, Chief of Artillery William Pendleton ineffectively placed the Confederate artillery to the left of Alexander's guns, positioned at too great a range to do much, if any, damage to the Federals before or during the assault. Even the Confederate's two long-range and rather accurate Whitworth Rifles, positioned northeast of town nearly two and a half miles away, had their line of sight hindered by the great cloud of smoke that enveloped the battlefield once the cannonade and assault commenced.[1]

Around the time the artillery barrage started another controversial moment for James Longstreet began. Alexander recalled how Longstreet "instructed me to take position whence I could see best, & I was to determine the moment & give Pickett the order when to charge." Alexander admitted he only intended for the cannonade to continue for "some 20 to 30 minutes," since "I had no expectation whatever of seeing anything special happen in the enemy during the cannonade, either to make me lengthen or shorten this period." In fact, the artillery commander further disclosed that the only reason he felt "cheerful & sanguine" at that moment was because "Gen. Lee had planned" the assault; otherwise, he confessed he had thought "very seriously on the subject & figured up that the enemy had as good & as many guns as we; & great advantage in position & ammunition over us."

After sending his order off to Colonel Walton to let the signal batteries open, Longstreet sent a message to Alexander:

> Colonel. If the artillery fire does not have the effect to drive off the enemy, or greatly demoralize them, so as to make our efforts pretty certain, I would prefer that you should not advise Gen. Pickett to make the charge. I shall rely a great deal on your good judgment to determine the matter & shall expect you to let Gen. Pickett know when the moment offers.[2]

With that, Longstreet "rode to a woodland hard by, to lie down and study for some new thought that might aid the assaulting column." Alexander later thought Longstreet's first note to him, just before the cannonade began, "presented the whole business to me in a new light," as he thought the commanders were now relying upon his "cold judgment" to determine if or when to send Pickett forward. Alexander consulted briefly with Brigadier General Ambrose Wright, commander of the brigade that made a brief lodgment on Cemetery Ridge on July 2, about the message and then scribbled off his own note to Longstreet. Longstreet later summarized Alexander's note: "In a few minutes report came from Alexander that he would only be able to judge the effect of his fire by the return of that of the enemy, as his infantry was not exposed to view, and the smoke of the batteries would soon cover the field. He asked, if there was an alternative, that it be carefully considered before the batteries opened, as there was not enough artillery ammunition for this and another trial if this should not prove favorable." At the end of his note, Alexander also tacked on a very telling judgment of his thoughts on the assault plan, writing, "And even if this is entirely successful it can only be so at a very bloody cost." Longstreet immediately replied:

> Colonel. The intention is to advance the infantry, if the artillery has the desired effect of driving the enemy's off or having other effect such as to warrant us in making the attack. When the moment arrives advise Gen. Pickett, and of course advance such artillery as you can use in aiding the attack.[3]

Longstreet made it clear there was no alternative to this attack plan and the artillery was being heavily relied upon to soften the Federal center. Longstreet's wording, "if the artillery has the desired effect," very much implied the "intention ... to advance the infantry" was dependent on the results of the massive cannonade. If the cannonade was deemed ineffective by Alexander's watchful eye, the intended infantry advance might still be reconsidered. Longstreet also reiterated that part of the assault plan hinged on support from advanced artillery, or as he put it, "advance such artillery as you can use in aiding the attack." At the time, Alexander thought he had that last task covered, as just before Pickett would advance, he was ready to roll out his nine howitzers in front of the assaulting column and "fire a few rounds" at the Federals.

Alexander later stated that upon reading Longstreet's second note, he handed it to Wright, who allegedly asserted "He has put the responsibility back upon you." Alexander recollected thinking for a short moment about how to handle this situation and then "decided in my own mind that I could see nothing during the cannonade upon which any safe opinion could be founded." Alexander's commentary is telling. No one, including Alexander, who Longstreet had specifically tasked with the job of determining the cannonade's effects on the Federal center, possessed any clear line of sight to ascertain if the bombardment was having the desired effect. Alexander then alleged that his thoughts turned back to General Lee to assure himself that everything had been thought through. "Gen. Lee had originally planned it," Alexander reminded himself, "& half the day had been spent in preparation. I determined to cause no loss of time by any decision on my part." Alexander decided he would advise Pickett when to advance, but nothing more; however, he then proceeded to ride over to see Pickett himself "before deciding" on the issue "absolutely." Alexander found Pickett was "in excellent spirits & sanguine of success," so he dispatched another small note to Longstreet, which read, "General. When our artillery fire is at its best I shall order Gen. Pickett to charge."[4]

Over the years, some historians have overanalyzed Longstreet and Alexander's pre-bombardment dialogue to advance some dubious assumptions. Clifford Dowdey wrote in dramatic psychological terms, "The depth of Longstreet's disturbance was indicated by his willingness to shift such a responsibility onto a young gunner." Similarly, Earl Hess believes Longstreet's notes to Alexander signified "Longstreet had deftly shifted a good deal of the burden of conducting this assault onto Alexander's young shoulders." Hess further argues that during those moments Longstreet was hatching a scheming plot to hoist blame on the artilleryman. "Longstreet hoped to create a situation where the attack would be called off by someone else; thus the lives of the infantry would be saved, and he would avoid the primary blame. This is probably why he communicated with the gunner ... by letter rather than consult with him verbally. It enabled Longstreet to create a paper trail of responsibility leading toward Alexander," Hess speculates, only to continue with more conjecture. "A face-to-face meeting between the two men would have allowed Alexander to press Longstreet for more detailed instructions, which the corps leader did not want to give. Alexander's resolution aborted Longstreet's plans, for good or ill," Hess concludes.[5]

Hess' theories about Longstreet's plans do not hold up upon close examination of the messages between Longstreet and Alexander. First, Longstreet, like Lee, regularly gave his subordinates and staff officers extensive leeway when it came time to executing tactical operations under his overall purview. For example, less than a year later at the Battle of the Wilderness, Longstreet gave almost total control of a successful flank attack to his staff officer, Gilbert Moxley Sorrell. Longstreet's regular use of this modus operandi throughout the war could offer some explanation for why he was not physically collocated with Alexander at the Confederate artillery line. It is reasonable to assume Longstreet wanted Alexander's unimpeded judgment without breathing down the young artilleryman's neck. Hess' reference to Longstreet's postwar comment about how he felt unwilling to "'trust myself with the entire responsibility' for sending the men in" is an example of using quotations out of context to fit a narrative. Hess seems to imply Longstreet was actively trying to shirk responsibility and put the burden of the attack and any resulting consequences on Alexander. On the contrary, in this instance, Longstreet was specifically referring to his unwillingness to trust himself with the responsibility for judging when the Confederate artillery had achieved maximum effect and the most opportune time to send Pickett forward. "I had instructed General Alexander," Longstreet recalled in the postwar years, "being unwilling to trust myself with the entire responsibility, to carefully observe the effect of the fire upon the enemy, and when it began to tell to notify Pickett to begin the assault." This statement is corroborated by what Longstreet wrote in one of his notes to Alexander on July 3: "I shall rely a great deal on your judgment to determine the matter, and shall expect you to let Pickett know when the moment offers." Based on this evidence, it is clear Longstreet was simply leaning on Alexander's expertise and trained eye to identify the most opportune moment to commence the assault.[6]

Longstreet's notes to Alexander and his later recollections in no way suggested he was scheming to "avoid the primary blame," or, in other words, trying to place Alexander in a situation where the artilleryman would suggest calling off the attack. Realistically, had Longstreet been desperately looking for any reason to call off the attack prior to Pickett's advance, Alexander actually gave Longstreet ample opportunity to make another such petition to Lee. Indeed, Alexander readily admitted to Longstreet during their exchange of messages that "the smoke will obscure the whole field," therefore inhibiting even his ability to judge the artillery bombardment's effect on the Federal position. Astoundingly, Hess discounts the inevitable loss of visibility and critiques Longstreet on this point too, insisting that "[Longstreet] failed to devise a detailed plan to gauge whether the artillery barrage would damage the Federals enough to justify sending in the infantry."[7]

Another opportunity for Longstreet to petition to call off the attack came when Alexander further suggested that "If ... there is any alternative to this attack, it should be carefully considered." Had Longstreet been scheming, would not the possession of this information been a golden opportunity to cite Alexander's concerns to Lee? Yet, Longstreet did no such thing. Instead he merely informed the young artillerist again of his orders, writing, "The intention is to advance the infantry if the artillery has the desired effect.... When the moment arrives advise General Pickett, and of course advance such artillery as you can use in aiding the attack." Or as Longstreet explained in his postwar memoirs: "He was informed that there was no alternative; that I could find no way out of it; that General Lee had considered and would listen to nothing else; that orders had gone for the guns to give signal for the batteries; that he should call the troops at the first opportunity or lull in the enemy's fire."[8]

Captain Merritt B. Miller's Battery of the Washington Artillery fired its signal rounds from the Peach Orchard just after 1 p.m. and the Confederate artillery line burst into flame. The bombardment included 75 guns from the First Corps, 55 from A.P. Hill's corps, and 33 from Ewell's—a total of 163 artillery pieces in all. Lieutenant John Dooley of the 1st Virginia described the artillery spectacle: "Never will I forgot those scenes and sounds.... The earth seems unsteady beneath this furious cannonade, and the air might be said to be agitated by the wings of death." In the town, Doctor Michael Jacobs, Professor of Mathematics and Chemistry at the local Gettysburg college, wrote that the cannonade was "producing such a continuous succession of crashing sounds as to make us feel as if the very heavens had been rent asunder." But things immediately went awry. First, the effectiveness of the Confederate artillery was almost immediately plagued by faulty fuses and sighting difficulties. Then, the deceptive, undulating nature of the fields between Seminary and Cemetery Ridge, along with the thickening smoke caused extensive overshooting. Most of the Confederate shot and shell sailed over Cemetery Ridge, landing on its eastern slope.[9]

Concurrently, the Federal's return fire took its toll on the momentarily idle Confederate infantry, particularly Pickett's division. Despite this hellish environment,

Brigadier General James Kemper recalled it was during these moments Longstreet rode out in front of the Virginian brigades to reassure and inspire them. Kemper wrote, "Longstreet rode slowly and alone immediately in front of our entire line.... His bearing was to me the grandest moral spectacle of the war. I expected him to fall every instant. Still he moved on slowly and majestically, with an inspiring confidence, composure, self-possession and repressed power." Kemper was so mesmerized he rode out to Longstreet, who asked the brigade commander how his men were holding up. Kemper replied that "a man is cut to pieces here every second while we are talking." Longstreet expressed great empathy for the men, telling Kemper he was "greatly distressed at this; but let us hold our ground a while longer; we are hurting the enemy badly; and will charge him presently." It is reasonable to assume Longstreet did not truly know the extent to which the Confederate artillery was having an effect on the Federal position; however, he likely told Kemper this hyperbole to boost morale at a time when the brigade was regularly being struck by Federal shot. Wilcox later held that Kemper's brigade suffered around 200 casualties due to the Federal artillery fire before they even stepped off toward Cemetery Ridge. Casualty estimates in Pickett's division as a whole while they waited at their jump-off point have varied anywhere from 300 to 500 men, a significant total.[10]

Other descriptions abound of Longstreet at this moment. George Finlay of the 56th Virginia, Garnett's brigade saw the First Corps commander with Gilbert Moxley Sorrel "riding slowly from our right in front of our line and in full view of the enemy skirmishers." Finlay recalled that Longstreet "did not seem to notice the Federal lines at all, but was coolly and carefully inspecting ours." Not surprisingly, he and the men around him "expected him [Longstreet] to be hit any moment. As rifle balls whistled by and a shell now and then ploughed up the ground close to and startled the splendid horse he rode, the general would check him and quietly ride on." Another infantryman described him "as unmoved as a statue," and to yet another, "one of the bravest men I ever saw on the field of battle." An officer recalled "He was as quiet as an old farmer riding over his plantation on a Sunday morning, and looked neither to the right or left." Men along the line shouted for Longstreet "to go to the rear," telling him "We'll fight without you leading us" and that "You'll get your old fool head knocked off." Private Finlay remembered that "not a word fell from his lips, and when he had passed our left he rode into the woods behind us."[11]

While Longstreet was riding in front of Kemper and Garnett's line, E.P. Alexander observed within the first ten minutes of the cannonade that "a force of artillery at work on the enemy's line which I thought it madness to send a storming column out in the face of, for so long a charge under a mid-day July sun." Alexander later recalled how he was very worried about how long he should let the cannonade persist before suggesting Pickett go in. "And so I waited, 15, 20, 25 minutes—I would have liked to have waited longer," he wrote of this desperate moment. Alexander admitted his greatest worry was the "risk [of] getting out of ammunition" to support the charge. And so, with some palpable misgivings, he decided it was time to contact Pickett. "But instead of simply giving the single order 'charge,'" he asserted, "I thought it due to Longstreet and to Pickett to let the exact situation be understood." Therefore, he sent a tense message to Pickett: "If you are coming at all you must come at once, or I cannot give you proper support, but the enemy's fire has not slackened at all. At least 18 guns are still firing from the cemetery itself." It was around this time, only a few minutes into the bombardment that Alexander learned the nine howitzers he had planned to initially advance ahead of Pickett's assault column were nowhere to be found. Alexander later reported that William Pendleton, Lee's Chief of Artillery, had moved "four or five of the guns & disposed of them elsewhere without any notice to me." Additionally, Major Charles Richardson was said to have moved the remaining howitzers because he "found himself in the range of shell from the enemy, thrown at some of A.P. Hill's guns."[12]

With Alexander's howitzer plan scrapped on account of Pendleton and Richardson's actions, he was now unable to abide by Longstreet's directive to "advance such artillery as you can use in aiding the attack." Soon thereafter, Alexander allegedly saw Federal guns being withdrawn and not replaced with fresh ones on Cemetery Ridge. The young artillerist studied the Federal line for five more minutes to be sure new batteries were not moved forward, and then, sensing this moment might be the Confederate infantry's best opportunity for advance, wrote Pickett again, "For God's sake come quick. The 18 guns are gone. Come quick or I can't support you."[13]

Some time between Alexander's first and second notes to Pickett, the First Corps division commander rode over to Longstreet. Pickett handed Longstreet Alexander's first note about the need for him to advance "at once, or I cannot give you proper support." In one of the most dramatic moments of the war, Longstreet allegedly uttered no reply to his subordinate. Pickett queried his Chief, "General, shall I advance?" Longstreet could not find the words, but according to his staff officers, "turned his face aside" and merely nodded. Lee's Warhorse later recollected that "In memory I can see him, of medium height, of graceful build, dark, glossy hair, worn almost to his shoulders in curly waves ... as he gallantly rode from me on that memorable 3d day of July, 1863, saying in obedience to the imperative order to which I could only bow assent, 'I will lead my division forward, General Longstreet.'" Alexander later mentioned Longstreet "himself, told me afterward that he knew the charge must be made, but he could not bring himself to give the order."[14]

While Pickett spurred on to advance his division, Longstreet rode over to see Alexander, who was then located on the left of James Dearing's guns, in front of and on the rise overlooking the First Corps brigades. The artillery commander immediately informed Longstreet that Richardson's nine howitzers had been moved and were no longer available to advance in support of Pickett's infantry. Alexander stated he had not notified Longstreet of the nine howitzers until that moment, as he alleged he was "hoping to give him a little agreeable surprise with them when I ran them out on the field." Because of the howitzers' absence, Alexander admitted to Longstreet that he "feared the support I could give might not be all I wished, & had counted upon." At that very moment, when Pickett was beginning his advance toward Cemetery Ridge, here was Alexander telling Longstreet for the first time that the meager, advanced artillery support he had planned to employ was no longer available. Alexander said nothing to Longstreet about advancing the general artillery line; however, based on his later comments about the feasibility and effectiveness of such a movement, he likely deemed it an impractical and unworkable venture. With that said, subsequently, Alexander did try his best to string together some kind of hodgepodge artillery support for the infantry

Pickett asking for Longstreet's permission to advance his division, July 3, 1863 (Library of Congress).

to make up for the lost howitzers. "In a hurry he [Alexander] got together such guns as he could to move with Pickett," Longstreet later wrote. The young artillerist rode to each battery and "if it had enough long range projectiles left to give some 15 shots..., I ordered it to limber up & move forward after the storming column." Of those guns that had less than 15 shots left, they were "ordered to wait until the infantry had gotten a good distance in front, then, aiming well over their heads, to fire at the enemy's batteries which were [then] firing at our infantry." Alexander's attempt to advance artillery came to naught and was quickly diffused by Federal counter-artillery fire. Underscoring the ineffectiveness of this initiative, the historian for the 5th Massachusetts Light Artillery noted later that "in less than ten minutes not a cannoneer was left to work the guns; all were dead or had 'skedaddled.'"[15]

Alexander dropped a second bombshell on Longstreet at that moment, informing him his guns lacked the ammunition to support the infantry assault. Alexander recalled Longstreet's concern was palpable. "Go & halt Pickett right where he is, & replenish your ammunition," Longstreet ordered. Alexander replied with more bad news: "General, we can't do that. We nearly emptied the trains last night. Even if we had it, it would take an hour or two, & meanwhile the enemy would recover from the pressure he is now under. Our only chance is to follow it up now—to strike while the iron is hot." Alexander was referring to the fact that William Pendleton had disastrously sent the artillery reserve too far to the rear to be of any use. Longstreet was staring at the Federal position through his field glasses, and according to Alexander replied slowly, "I don't want to make this attack—I believe it will fail—I do not see how it can succeed—I would not make it even now, but that Gen. Lee has ordered & expects it." Years later, Longstreet succinctly explained his reasoning in allowing the charge to continue forward at that moment, writing, "The order was imperative. The Confederate commander had fixed his heart upon the work." Longstreet included a candid variation of that same sentiment in his official after-battle report: "I found then that our supply of ammunition was so short that the batteries could not reopen. The order for this attack, which I could not favor under better auspices, would have been revoked had I felt that I had that privilege."[16]

Alexander had presented Longstreet with yet another very last-minute opportunity to petition Lee to call off the attack. If Longstreet had been in some way using Alexander to halt the attack or shift "primary blame," as Clifford Dowdey and Earl Hess have suggested, would not Alexander's disclosures about the non-existence of advanced artillery support and lack of ammunition been opportune for the First Corps commander to make a case for cancelling the assault? But yet again, Longstreet took no such action and carried out his duty, explaining to Alexander that "Gen. Lee has ordered and expects" the assault to be carried out.

21

The Pickett-Pettigrew-Trimble Charge

"Then there was soon nothing to see but volumes of musketry smoke"
—E.P. Alexander

"Up men and to your posts! Don't forget today that you are from Old Virginia!" George Pickett shouted to his men just before his brigades stepped off toward Cemetery Ridge around 3 p.m. Johnston Pettigrew, 400 yards to the left and 200 yards behind Pickett, also advanced soon thereafter with Trimble's two brigades trailing behind. For reasons unknown, portions of Pettigrew's leftmost brigades under Brockenbrough and (to a lesser extent) Davis, were initially delayed in their forward advance with the rest of the division. Curiously, Pettigrew's reaction to this occurrence was to tell one of his aides not to bother with Brockenbrough's brigade, as if little was expected of it anyway. In the 87-degree sun, all nine brigades would have to march about three-quarters of a mile to reach the Federals on Cemetery Ridge, which would require at least 25 to 30 minutes. For the majority of that march, especially once the units reached the Emmitsburg Road, Federal artillery fire would be creating sizable gaps in the Confederate ranks. The attackers, especially those on the left of the assault column, would also have to contend with post-and-plank and post-and-rail fences along the Emmitsburg Road, several of which had not been pulled down because the road in that sector was always well within gunfire range of Federal infantry. Further, the ranks would be staggered and broken up by the physical impediments of the Nicholas Codori and William Bliss farmhouses. But perhaps the most significant challenge was the attacking force had to funnel its mile-and-a-half-wide front to meet the Federals in the narrow space between Ziegler's Grove and the copse of oak trees. Pickett's brigades in particular had to execute a series of left obliques to close the gap with Pettigrew's men.[1]

Almost immediately upon initiating their advance, Pettigrew's division, especially Brockenbrough's brigade on the left, came under deadly fire from some 39 Federal guns. Federal Lieutenant Colonel Franklin Sawyer of the 8th Ohio described how Pettigrew's division was "at once enveloped in a dense cloud of smoke and dust. Arms, heads, blankets, guns and knapsacks were thrown and tossed in to the clear air.... A moan went up from the field, distinctly to be heard amid the storm of battle." Soon thereafter, the 8th Ohio poured musketry fire into Pettigrew's left flank, and coupled with severe Federal artillery fire, routed Brockenbrough's brigade before it even made it to Long Lane or the Bliss Farm. Things did not improve for Pettigrew from there. His division's forward movement was greatly impeded by roadside fencing on both the east and west

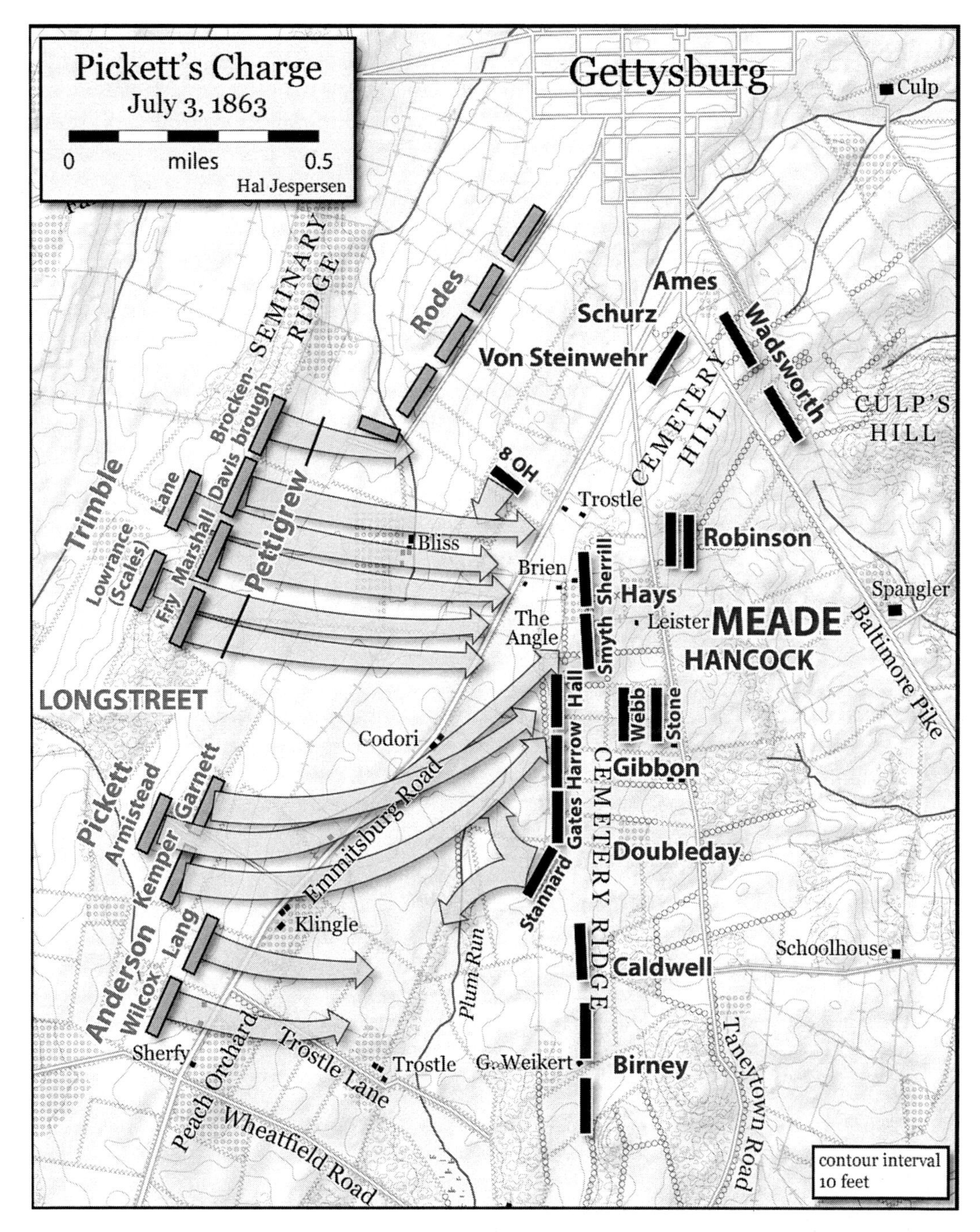

side of the Emmitsburg Road. Another fence extending north from "the Angle" became an additional obstacle for those men who made it beyond the road. As Pettigrew's units neared the road, the Federals started pouring canister and musketry fire into their front, while the 8th Ohio continued to eat away at their flank.[2]

Longstreet viewed the impending threat to Pettigrew and Trimble's flank fairly early in the charge and sent not one, but two staff officers to warn them, in case one did not get through. Sure enough, one staff officer, Major Osmun Latrobe had his horse shot out from under him while en route to the left. The second officer could not find Pettigrew or Trimble in the thick of battle, but did manage to deliver Longstreet's message to James Lane around the time his brigade neared the Emmitsburg Road. After having his own horse shot out from under him, Lane ordered his leftmost brigade, the 33rd North Carolina, to advance against the Federal flanking threat; however, the colonel of the regiment was bewildered at the order and shouted to Lane, "My God! General, do you intend rushing your men into such a place unsupported, when the troops on the right are falling back?" Lane looked to the south and saw Pettigrew's division was buckling, retreating, or staying in the Emmitsburg roadbed. Therefore, he scrapped his attempt to protect the flank, deeming it a hopeless venture.[3]

Indeed, a sizable portion of what remained of Pettigrew's division took meager shelter in the two-foot deep Emmitsburg roadbed. Perhaps around a thousand men from Fry's, Marshall's, and Davis' brigades, most famously the 26th North Carolina and 11th Mississippi, ventured forward from the road toward the Federal line, and many who did so fell in the open, rising ground ahead. Trimble's two brigades added little muscle to Pettigrew's offensive punch, and also were stymied by the 8th Ohio's effective flanking fire. The majority of the men from Lane's and Lowrance's brigades who made it to the Emmitsburg Road mostly joined in with the others from Pettigrew's division to hunker down and take cover, though perhaps a few hundred did advance beyond. Pettigrew's and Trimble's men should be given credit for delivering a stout return fire on the Federals from the road, which over the course of the assault did considerable damage to Alexander Hayes' Federal division massed in their front.[4]

Similarly, on Pickett's front, especially Kemper's brigade on the division's right, came under a murderous hail of Federal artillery fire as it advanced from its muster point. Captain Edwin Dow, a Federal artillerist wrote of the effects of the long-range fire, "I tell you, the gaps we made were simply terrible. But they closed up their lines, and closed up and closed them up." Soon after reaching the crest of the ridge, just about where Alexander's guns were positioned, the First Corps units began executing their first in a series of left obliques. Upon completing the initial oblique, Pickett's division found itself in a low swale of land that allowed for a very brief respite, enough to redress its ranks before resuming the advance. Along with the north-south gap between Pickett and Pettigrew, the left obliques also successfully closed the east-west interval that initially separated them, ensuring Pickett's left met Pettigrew's right about three-quarters of the way into the march. George Stewart aptly described the effect of these movements: "At first, the column [Pettigrew and Trimble] was well behind Pickett. Once his [Pickett's] division had begun its oblique, this interval steadily lessened, since Pickett's men, thus sidling, were forward only about two thirds as fast as Pettigrew's." Stewart held that "the utility of this maneuver" had been "planned in advance" and "had doubtless been considered beforehand, and calculated with some degree of accuracy." Likewise, Edwin Coddington attributed the "convergence of two long battle lines within 1,400 feet of the enemy position" to "a triumph of careful planning on the part of Lee, Longstreet, and other officers."[5]

After Pickett's brigades finished their obliques and finally closed the gap with Pettigrew, they turned eastward toward Federal General John Gibbon's division, positioned behind a low stone wall that ran south from "the Angle," and in front of "the Copse." As Pickett's men made this transition, George Stannard's Vermont brigade initiated and executed the same kind of flanking maneuver the 8th Ohio had done against Pettigrew's division. Stannard moved out from Cemetery Ridge and began to pour flanking fire into the vulnerable Confederates, forcing Kemper to siphon off two regiments to meet the threat. Compounding this issue, Kemper's brigade was also hit in its flank by Federal artillery posted on Cemetery Ridge and Little Round Top. Longstreet later wrote, "The slaughter was terrible, the enfilade fire of the batteries on [Little] Round Top being very destructive. At times one shell would knock down five or six men." By the time Pickett became fully engaged, E.P. Alexander could see nothing from his Confederate artillery line: "Then there was soon nothing to see but volumes of musketry smoke."[6]

Soon thereafter, the remnants of Garnett's and Kemper's brigades pushed up against the Federal's advance line along the low stone wall in front of "the Copse." Armistead's brigade, which drafted behind Garnett during the march, intermixed with what became an indistinguishable mass of Confederate brigades. Armistead pushed what was left of his brigade toward a 50-yard gap in the Federal line, vacated by the left portion of the 71st Pennsylvania regiment. Some 100 men from Armistead's brigade, including the General himself, made it over the stone wall before finding themselves facing gunfire from a combination of the 71st, 72nd, and 69th Pennsylvania to their front and right. After only about ten minutes, the small band of men from Armistead's brigade were either killed, captured, or managed to escape back over the wall. A brief stalemate ensued in front of the stone wall before "Pickett's Charge" entirely collapsed, with its survivors limping or fleeing rearwards toward Seminary Ridge. Many Confederates who remained in the Emmitsburg Road or in front of the stone wall were taken prisoner by the Federals in the minutes after the assault's collapse. Later, Longstreet succinctly described the costly and gruesome end result of the attack: "When the smoke cleared away, Pickett's Division was gone. Nearly two- thirds of his men lay dead on the field, and the survivors were sullenly retreating down the hill." Captain John H. Smith of the 11th Virginia, Kemper's brigade described the scene of the retreat, writing, "We ran out of [musketry] range, shot after shot falling around us until we got over the Emmitsburg road toward our lines.... No organized body of troops did I meet in going back." In his memoirs, Longstreet eulogized his men's conduct during the repulse: "There was no indication of panic. The broken files marched back in steady step." Yet, the assault was technically not over. As Pickett's attack fizzled out, two more brigades advanced toward Cemetery Ridge.[7]

22

The Wilcox and Lang Issue

"Such a reinforcement to Pickett could have availed nothing"
—Cadmus Wilcox

As has already been covered in part, Longstreet critics have expended much ink on the alleged supporting units they believe Lee intended for Longstreet to use during the July 3 assault. Of these supporting units, they focus mostly on the two dilapidated brigades of Brigadier General Cadmus Wilcox and Colonel David Lang, positioned to the right of Pickett's division prior to the attack. In 1887, Colonel William Allan alleged Longstreet misused Wilcox on July 3, contending that the brigade "was sent forward too late to be of use, and where he was too weak to have effected much at best." Similarly, Lee's military secretary, Armistead Long, wrote in 1877, that the attack would have succeeded "had Pickett's division been promptly supported when it burst through Meade's center." Many historians have echoed Allan and Long's criticism. They contend Wilcox and Lang were supposed to protect Pickett's right flank from the get-go and advance in concert with that division. They further argue that these weakened brigades, both of which had been badly cut up during the July 2 battle, would have made a sizable difference in helping the Confederate assault achieve success.[1]

Longstreet critics have once again cut their teeth on trivialities. The fact of the matter is Lee himself, based on a close reading of his after-battle reports, gave very little thought as to the importance of infantry support on Pickett's right. He never once suggested Wilcox and Lang were to have advanced simultaneously with Pickett's column. The only thing he wrote about Wilcox was a short blurb about how "Wilcox's brigade marched in rear of Pickett's right, to guard that flank…." He then very quickly transitioned to how the assault failed and why he thought it failed, none of which mention lack of infantry support to Pickett, Pettigrew, or Trimble. Lee's fixation was on the lack of artillery support, especially advanced artillery support. He stated that the Confederate batteries "nearly exhausted their ammunition in the protracted cannonade that preceded the advance of the infantry" and therefore were "unable to reply, or render the necessary support of the attacking party." He then described the effect this absence of advanced artillery support had on the assaulting column's left flank, namely that "Owing to this fact, which was unknown to me when the assault took place, the enemy was enabled to throw a strong force of infantry against our left, already wavering under a concentrated fire of artillery from the ridge in front, and from Cemetery Hill, on the left." Of the assault's right flank, Lee described how "after penetrating the enemy's lines, entering his advance works, and capturing some of his artillery, was attacked simultaneously in front and on both flanks, and driven back with heavy loss." Indeed, Lee never attributed the absence of infantry support as causation for the Federal's ability to flank the column's left and right, or in an even more general sense, the assault's failure, but focused entirely on the lack of artillery support.[2]

In the postwar years, Cadmus Wilcox himself pointed out what little effect his brigade would have had on the overall result of the attack: "But with this conviction of useless sacrifice of his men, [Longstreet] ordered my brigade, about a thousand or eleven-hundred men, to advance. Such a reinforcement to Pickett could have availed nothing, could only be sacrificed." Wilcox was reasonable in his appraisal of the meager support his and Lang's brigade could afford the assaulting column. Both brigades had been engaged on July 2 and would only have been able to contribute an additional 1,700 men to the July 3 assault. In addition to making little difference in the outcome of the charge, Lee's supposed intent to have them advance simultaneously with Pickett begs the question: who was to support Wilcox and Lang's right flank? As discussed, Lee and Longstreet had agreed Hood's and McLaws' divisions were not to be part of the assaulting column, and therefore not available to aid Wilcox and Lang. Considering the Federal line extended well south and right of the Confederate attack point on July 3, Wilcox and Lang would have undoubtedly experienced the same threat to their flank that Pickett's units ultimately did.[3]

Besides there being no evidence Lee intended for Wilcox and Lang to advance with Pickett, there is also no evidence Longstreet intended to advance Wilcox and Lang unless Pickett either expressly requested their support, or the division commander achieved some kind of observable or reported success. In fact, in the postwar years, Longstreet even admitted that "If Pickett had shown signs of getting a lodgment, I should, of course, have pushed the other divisions forward to support the attack," referring to McLaws' and Hood's divisions. If Longstreet had been willing to use those two divisions to support any significant success achieved by Pickett, it stands to reason he would likely have pushed Wilcox and Lang forward, as well. Yet, Longstreet recognized the futility of this entire topic given "I saw that he [Pickett] was going to pieces at once."[4]

The account of Captain Robert Bright, a member of Pickett's staff, is critical in understanding how events and decisions unfolded on this issue. As Pickett advanced on the Federal center, the division commander sent Bright to find Longstreet and report "the position against which we had been sent would be taken, but he could not hold it unless reinforcements be sent to him." As Bright rode toward the vicinity of where he thought Longstreet was located, he "passed small parties of Pettigrew's command going to the rear." Bright found Longstreet "sitting on a fence alone; the fence ran in the direction we were charging," and he could see "Pickett's column had passed over the hill on our side of the Emmettsburg [*sic*] road, and could not then be seen." The staff officer later described his verbal exchange with Longstreet: "I delivered the message as sent by General Pickett. General Longstreet said: 'Where are the troops that were placed on your flank?' and I answered: 'Look over your shoulder and you will see them.' He looked and saw the broken fragments."[5]

A close reading of this passage reveals that when Longstreet asked Bright about the troops placed on Pickett's flank, he was not referring in surprise to the absence of

Wilcox and Lang, but rather Pettigrew and Trimble. This contention is first confirmed when Bright told Longstreet to look over his shoulder, whereby the commander only saw "broken fragments" of Pettigrew's command "going to the rear." Longstreet was not referring to "troops that were placed" on Pickett's right flank, but rather his left; in other words, Pettigrew and Trimble. This argument is verified again during Longstreet's extended exchange with Bright and Colonel Fremantle, who at that very moment arrived on the scene. On his own journey to join Longstreet, Fremantle not only reported "passing General Lee and his staff," but also recollected seeing "many wounded men retiring from the front." The assault was already crumbling, particularly on the left. According to the British observer, members of Brockenbrough's brigade were then "flocking through the woods in numbers as great as the crowd in Oxford street in the middle of the day." Even so, after finding Longstreet, Fremantle looked out at the advancing Confederates and remarked to the corps commander, "I wouldn't have missed this for anything." Contrary to how many historians characterize Longstreet's temperament at this moment, Fremantle observed a "perfectly calm and unperturbed" Longstreet. The First Corps commander was said to have responded, "The devil you wouldn't! I would have liked to have missed it very much; we've attacked and been repulsed: look there!" Longstreet was again referring to those "broken fragments" on Pickett's left. Bright gave a very similar account of Longstreet's response, recollecting that the General said, "I would, Colonel Fremantle, the charge is over. Captain Bright, ride to General Pickett, and tell him what you have heard me say to Colonel Fremantle." As Bright began to ride away, Longstreet called him back and informed the Captain to "Tell General Pickett that Wilcox's Brigade is in that peach orchard (pointing), and he can order him to his assistance." Longstreet's statement demonstrated he was cognizant of Wilcox's location and the brigade's then idle state.[6]

After Bright rode back to Pickett, the division commander ordered him and two additional staff officers to request Wilcox's assistance. Bright spurred toward Wilcox, but he was not the first to arrive. "When I rode up to Wilcox he was standing with both hands raised and waving and saying to me 'I know, I know.' I said, 'But, General, I must deliver my message,'" Bright recollected of the exchange. Wilcox was visibly annoyed by all the sudden attention, but he was probably most irritated by the fact he had to advance at all. Wilcox was not sanguine of success, and he admitted to those around him he would only advance under protest. Lang had told him he was sure Pickett's assault would fail and that "as we were confident that what Anderson's division had failed to do on the 2nd, Pickett could not do 24 hours later when the enemy had reinforced his line." Lang also queried Wilcox about his thoughts on being ordered to take any part in the July 3 assault: "He replied, in substance, that he would not again lead his men into such a deathtrap. But, said I, suppose your orders are imperative and admit of no discretion in the matter? Then, said he, I will do so under protest." Likewise, one lieutenant in Lang's Florida brigade wrote tellingly, "Knowing what we had to encounter, the order to advance was not obeyed with the same alacrity" as on July 2.[7]

Like Wilcox and Lang, Bright was equally discouraged by the situation and did not believe the two depleted brigades would make any difference in the overall outcome of the assault. When Bright returned to Pickett, the staff officer saw Stannard's Federal troops moving out to flank the division's right. At the time, he was very impressed with the size of this Federal force and estimated its size around 7,000 men, much more than the modest 1,700 Wilcox and Lang could muster. Observing this flanking movement, Bright "advised the General [Pickett] to withdraw his command before" the Federal troops were able to "come into line of battle, sweep around our flank, and shut us up." Pickett's reaction was curious. Instead of replying that Wilcox and Lang would address Stannard's men, he told Bright that Dearing's artillery battalion would protect that flank. "They have orders to follow up the charge and keep their caissons filled; order them to open with every gun and break that column and keep it broken," Pickett directed. The division commander's order again lends credence to the assertion that the principal means of support for the charge was intended to be advanced artillery, not infantry. Bright never found Dearing, but he did run into Captain William Marshall of Battery A, 38th Virginia Battalion, who told the staff officer he had no ammunition except for three solid shots. When asked about his ammunition not remaining filled as ordered, Marshall said the caissons had been away for almost an hour and blamed William Pendleton for sending the "reserve artillery ammunition more than a mile in rear of the field." Marshall went on to fire his three solid shots, and then his guns fell silent.[8]

In the meantime, Wilcox and Lang proceeded forward with grave doubts. The brigades were almost immediately targeted by close to 60 Federal batteries. Lang advanced to the left of Wilcox, and the latter soon realized the heavy smoke coupled with his ignorance of Pickett's left-oblique marching left him uncertain as to where the First Corps division was located. Once Wilcox and Lang passed the Emmitsburg Road, the situation only worsened. Federal artillery shells started raining down on them, making large gaps in their lines. Further, Wilcox and Lang advanced straight ahead, which put them well south of Stannard's Vermont men, who were then delivering flanking fire into Pickett's right. Noticing the Confederate infantry movement in his rear, Stannard simply about-faced and employed the same strategy against Lang's left. Soon thereafter, Lang, desperate for help, asked for artillery support, but was told long-range ammunition had run out. Hearing this, Lang decided he had already had enough and called an end to the advance without even conferring with Wilcox on his right. Like Lang, Wilcox also tried to drum up some artillery support without any success. With no help from the batteries, and no sign of Pickett anywhere, the brigade commander gave the order to retreat. "My small force could do nothing save to make a useless sacrifice of themselves," Wilcox recalled of this futile advance. In the meantime, Richard Anderson alleged that during the very late stages of the charge, he "was about to move forward Wright's and Perry's brigades, when Lieutenant-General Longstreet directed me to stop the movement, advising that it was useless, and would only involve unnecessary loss, as the assault had failed." Robert Rodes who commanded the brigades of Brigadier Generals Stephen Ramseur, Alfred Iverson, George Doles, and the 5th Alabama regiment posted to the left of Thomas' and Perrin's Third Corps brigades in Long Lane north of the Bliss Farm—collectively judged by the division commander to total a scant 1,800 additional men—also reported having received a similar notice "that the attack had already failed," which he admitted "was apparent to me."[9]

For decades, historians have gnashed their teeth over Longstreet's alleged misuse of Wilcox and Lang on July 3. They say these brigades were supposed to advance simultaneously with Pickett. If not, then surely they should have been ordered forward shortly after Pickett's column began its march. They say it was too little, too late when Wilcox and Lang finally stepped off to try and reinforce Pickett. These historians have neglected the broader picture. Indeed, Wilcox and Lang were too little, but even more importantly, they were simply the wrong choice for potential "supporting" units. And in this respect, historians have laid blame at the feet of the wrong general. Rather, they should try to decipher the complete mystery as to why Lee would have considered Wilcox and Lang a reasonable choice for infantry support. Wilcox and Lang had been heavily engaged on July 2 in the same sector. Similarly, when Longstreet requested additional support to Pettigrew's sector of the attack, Wright and Posey's brigades were offered up. Yet, both of these brigades had also seen action during the previous day's battle, and in Wright's case, quite severely. If Lee was unaware of the condition of Wilcox, Lang, Wright, and Posey on July 3, then surely Anderson and A.P. Hill would have known and reported their condition. As it turned out, either no one knew the battered state of these brigades, or no one thought it fit to communicate their status. Compare this negligent generalship to Longstreet's, who in his early morning conference with Lee had notified his superior that Hood and McLaws were then occupying a critical part of the Confederate line, and were in no condition to lead, or even support another assault on the Federal position. A.P. Hill took no such initiative. Likewise, Lee apparently never saw fit to ask Hill which Third Corps brigades had been least utilized to provide support for the assault. Indeed, because of this miscommunication or lack of communication, Hill and Lee wound up choosing the least disposed units from Anderson and Pender's divisions of Hill's corps.

Tellingly on this issue, Pickett's aide, Captain Robert Bright, recollected that just prior to the charge he witnessed a conversation between Pickett and Lieutenant Colonel George T. Gordon of the 34th North Carolina, Scales' brigade of Trimble's division. Gordon frankly told Pickett, "Pickett, my men are not going up to-day." Pickett allegedly replied "But, Gordon, they must go up; you must make them go up." Gordon was not swayed and retorted, "You know, Pickett, I will go as far with you as any other man ... but for the last day or two they have lost heavily under infantry fire and are very sore, and they will not go up to-day." Believe Bright's account or not, it does serve to demonstrate the state of dismay among the more depleted units on the Confederate assault's left that had already seen significant action during the first two days of the battle. Years later, Longstreet told Harry Heth he believed the fact that Heth's division under the command of Pettigrew "with bloody noses, after its severe fight of the 1st, was put in to do a great part in the assault of the 3d was a grievous error."[10]

If Anderson's brigades of Wilcox, Lang, Wright, and Posey, along with Scales' brigade from Pender's division, had seen ample action on July 1 and 2, Mahone's, Perrin's, and Thomas' brigades had seen little to none. These latter three brigades, along with Posey's, which had really only been engaged in severe skirmishing for the first two days of the battle, would have been more reasonable choices for primary or supporting units on July 3. But it was not to be. In the carnival of Confederate errors that came to be somewhat common occurrence on July 3, Lee and Hill picked the units that were in the worst shape to take part in or support Pickett and Pettigrew's assault. Considering Lee's seemingly thoughtless choices for infantry units in several instances, is it really too much to advance the presumption that he probably gave little thought to how and when to employ infantry supports during the charge? Judging by the total absence of post-battle commentary by Lee about lack of infantry support on July 3, coupled with Longstreet's actual employment of some brigades as almost an afterthought during the assault, it is only fitting to conclude that Lee believed advanced artillery support would be most critical to the charge's success, not additional infantry, and that artillery support would be available not only from the get-go, but as requested.

* * *

With the attack repulsed and the remnants of the Confederate column streaming back toward Seminary Ridge, Longstreet recognized how extremely vulnerable the army's center was to Federal counterattack. "When this charge had failed, I expected that, of course, the enemy would throw himself against our shattered ranks and try to crush us," Longstreet later wrote. He described how he directed his staff officers to rally the men and ready themselves for a Federal attack on Seminary Ridge. "With shells screaming over my head and ploughing the ground under my horse," Longstreet rode to the Confederate artillery line because he "knew if the army was to be saved, those batteries must check the enemy." Fremantle observed of Longstreet at that tense moment, "No person could have been more calm or self-possessed than General Longstreet under these trying circumstances, aggravated as they now were by the movements of the enemy, who began to show a strong disposition to advance." Longstreet's demeanor impressed the Englishman, who admitted that "I could now thoroughly appreciate the term bulldog, which I had heard applied to him by the soldiers. Difficulties seem to make no other impression upon him than to make him a little more savage." Fremantle described how at about that time, Longstreet encountered General Pettigrew who reported "'he was unable to bring his men up again.'" Longstreet responded, "'Very well; never mind, then, General; just let them remain where they are: the enemy's going to advance and spare you the trouble.'"[11]

Observing a line of Federal skirmishers pressing forward, "which I thought was the advance of their charge," Longstreet watched as the Confederate batteries "opened again and their fire seemed to check at once the threatened advance." A few moments later, "the line of skirmishers disappeared," and Longstreet admitted that his "mind was relieved of the apprehension that Meade was going to follow us." As Longstreet came to that realization, he later described dramatically how "Our men passed the batteries in quiet walk, and would rally, I knew, when they reached the ridge from which they started."[12]

23

Lee's Costly Decision

"'It is all my fault,' meant just what it said"
—James Longstreet

Lee's decision to assault the Federal center on July 3 cost his army another 7,500 casualties. Multiple first-hand accounts claimed that immediately after the attack Lee took responsibility for the tactical decision and its poor outcome, saying "It is all my fault" as his men straggled back toward Seminary Ridge. Of course, Lee was realistic about what had happened at Gettysburg, writing in a letter just nine days after Pickett's Charge, "You will, however, learn before this reaches you that our success at Gettysburg was not so great as reported." He also offered his resignation to Confederate President Jefferson Davis on August 3, 1863, writing, "No one, is more aware than myself of my inability for the duties of my position. I cannot even accomplish what I myself desire. How can I fulfill the expectations of others?"; however, just half a month earlier, on July 15, Lee tried to cast the campaign in a more favorable light, writing that his "return is rather sooner than I had originally contemplated, but having accomplished what I proposed on leaving the Rappahannock, viz., relieving the Valley of the presence of the enemy & drawing his army north of the Potomac, I determined to re-cross the latter river." Further, when George Pickett, who went on to harbor a life-long resentment toward Lee over the decimation of his division, submitted his after-battle report to the commanding general it was rejected and ordered rewritten. The commanding general wrote to Pickett, explaining his decision: "We have the enemy to fight, and must carefully, at this critical moment guard against dissensions which the reflections in your report would create." Pickett never resubmitted; however, the division commander's complaints apparently addressed lack of support on July 3, and may have reflected poorly on Lee.[1]

For years after the war, Lee's devoted supporters were keen on spinning his post-charge "it is all my fault" statements. What better strategy than to turn an alleged moment of weakness into one of boundless strength and dignity? Indeed, Lost Cause sympathizers characterized Lee's post-charge admission as yet another example of his greatness. John Early Jones, formerly of Jubal Early's staff described a Christ-like Lee in 1880, believing he "would crucify, on self-erected cross, his own illustrious name" and made a "vicarious sacrifice for his lieutenants and his men." In short, Jones held that "the Divinity in his [Lee's] bosom shone translucent through the man, and his spirit rose up to the Godlike." In 1903, John B. Gordon wrote similarly and with palpable arrogance, "To those who knew General Lee well, the assumption by him of entire responsibility for the failure at Gettysburg means nothing except an additional and overwhelming proof of his almost marvelous magnanimity." Later in the twentieth century, Clifford Dowdey married all the major pillars of the Lost Cause belief system together in just three sentences. Dowdey first expressed the traditional, "Lee the Marbleman" belief: "General Lee could not conceivably have believed that the failure of the three-day battle was all his fault." He then pivoted to a minor concession, followed by the typical Jackson rhetoric: "He [Lee] had made mistakes in judgment, of which the most fundamental was to attempt Jacksonian tactics without Stonewall Jackson." Then finally, Dowdey again professed, without any evidence, to know what Lee thought in the months and years following Gettysburg: "At some time after the battle he recognized this." In contrast, Longstreet never subscribed to these grandiose assertions. "This remark, made just after the battle, 'It is all my fault,' meant just what it said," Lee's Warhorse wrote matter-of-factly. Longstreet proved he was aware of and familiar with the Lost Cause rhetoric; however, he rejected its conclusions outright. To Longstreet, Lee's admission to the battle's outcome being his fault "adds to the nobility and magnanimity of that remark, when we reflect that it was the utterance of a deep-felt truth, rather than a mere sentiment."[2]

In 1868, Lee briefly discussed the main reasons why he thought the Confederates lost the battle. He cited Stuart's absence and that success would probably have been achieved had "one determined and united blow been delivered by our whole line." What is most noticeably missing from Lee's analysis was his assuming any blame for the loss, and the fact that during the battle he had a great deal of control over facilitating a "determined and united blow." Indeed, historian William C. Davis, typically a staunch Lee supporter, has pointed out, "What he did not say was that he was ultimately responsible. He let Stuart go, and his own laissez-faire management helped bungle the attacks on July 1 and 2.... Every general has his worst battle. Gettysburg was Lee's." Davis could also have included July 3 in his assessment of Lee's actions at Gettysburg.[3]

Longstreet's 1877 article outlined what he believed to be eight major mistakes made during the battle. The final mistake he mentioned was "the assault by Pickett, on the 3d, should never have been made, as it could not have succeeded by any possible prodigy of courage or tactics, being absolutely a hopeless assault." He continued on to call "the charge of that day ... a forlorn hope." In his *Battles and Leaders* account, Longstreet wrote similarly, "With my knowledge of the situation, I could see the desperate and hopeless nature of the charge and the cruel slaughter it would cause." In essence, Longstreet boiled all of the often intricate analysis of the July 3 attack down to a succinct assessment, which held the Pickett-Pettigrew assault as a complete and utter failure before it even began, with no chance for success. "It is conceded by almost, if not quite, all authority on the subject, that Pickett's charge, on the 3d, was almost hopeless," he argued, and then made sure to underscore that "we had tested the enemy's position thoroughly on the day before, and with a much larger force than was given to Pickett. We had every reason to believe that the position was much stronger on the 3d than it was on the 2d."[4]

Longstreet was not alone in his assessment. Just before the charge commenced, Richard Garnett and Lewis Armistead discussed the prospects for Confederate success.

Garnett told Armistead, "This is a desperate thing to attempt," wherein Armistead replied candidly, "the slaughter will be terrible." Major Walter Harrison of Pickett's staff recalled Longstreet "seemed to be in anything but pleasant humor at the prospect 'over the hill,'" referring to the strength of the Federal position and the Confederate attack point on Cemetery Ridge. Harrison expressed concurrence and described the objective as "frightful to look at." A few days after the battle, Walter Taylor informed his sister that "their [the Federals'] last position was impregnable to any such force as ours." General Fitzhugh Lee, not a Longstreet supporter by any stretch of the imagination, wrote years after the war, "I am inclined to believe that after the 2d no assault we could have made would have succeeded, however wisely the dispositions for it were executed—however gallantly performed." Helen Longstreet wrote similarly just after her husband's death, "It is admitted by almost if not quite all authority on the subject that Pickett's charge was hopeless," and then tagged on, "The addition of McLaws and Hood would not have increased the chances of success." E.P. Alexander argued without reservation of the third day, "Thus ended the second day, and one is tempted to say that thus ended the battle of Gettysburg. For of the third (lay it must be said, as was said of the charge of the Six Hundred at Balaklava, 'Magnificent, but not war.'" Alexander believed the entire plan, particularly its objective being the area near "the Angle" on Cemetery Ridge, was completely foolhardy. He wrote bluntly on how a larger attack with more men would have only served to increase the casualty count: "No formation, however, could have been successful and the light one doubtless suffered fewer casualties than one more compact and deeper would have had." On another occasion, Alexander provided specific details for why he thought the attack, as conceived, was doomed: "Our advance was exposed to the fire of the whole length of that shank some two miles. Not only that, that shank is not perfectly straight, but it bends forward at the Round Top end, so that rifled guns there, in secure position, could & did enfilade the assaulting lines." Additionally, he recollected how "the advance must be over 1,400 yards of open ground, none of it sheltered from fire, & very little from view, & without a single position for artillery where a battery could get its horses & caissons under cover." In this regard, Alexander sounded very much like Longstreet, when the latter wrote similarly in his memoirs, "Forty thousand men, unsupported as we were, could not have carried the position at Gettysburg.... It is simply out of the question for a lesser force to march over broad, open fields and carry a fortified front occupied by a greater force of seasoned troops."[5]

Alexander further thought Lee demonstrated his imprudence on July 3 in going so far as to completely overlook the weakest point in the Federal line, Cemetery Hill. "The point of greatest connection with this battle," Alexander contended, "is the story of our entire failure to recognize this fact." He defended this claim by stating the approach toward Cemetery Hill would have been the shortest distance for the Confederates to traverse for an attack, and further, would have proven the least dangerous with respect to Federal flanking fire. He believed, in short, that "concentrated artillery fire from the north and assaults from the nearest sheltered ground between the west and northeast" held the greatest chance for Confederate success.[6]

Brigadier General Evander Law of Hood's division very similarly echoed Longstreet's and Alexander's critiques. Referring to Lee's actions on both July 2 and 3, Law wrote that "he made his attack precisely where his enemy wanted him to make it and was most fully prepared to receive it." Law discounted the opinion that the Confederates could have succeeded had all three corps achieved proper concert of action at some point during the battle. "Even had he [Lee] succeeded in driving the Federal army from its strong position by a general and simultaneous assault along the whole front (which was the only possible chance of success in that direction)," Law asserted, "he would have found his army in very much the same condition in which Pyrrhus found his, when after driving the Romans from the field of Asculum, he exclaimed, 'Another such victory, and I am undone!'" Additional negative reactions to Lee's handling of the campaign abounded. Cavalryman Wade Hampton wrote to General Joseph Johnston, calling the campaign a "complete failure." Robert Kean of the Confederate War Department described the Battle of Gettysburg in Longstreet-like terms as "the worst disaster which has ever befallen our arms.... To fight an enemy superior in numbers at such terrible disadvantage of position in the heart of his own territory, when the freedom of movement gave him the advantage of selecting his own time and place for accepting battle, seems to have been a great military blunder.... Gettysburg has shaken my faith in Lee as a general." E.P. Alexander wrote most candidly in assessing Lee's actions at Gettysburg, "Never, never, never did Gen. Lee himself bollox a fight as he did this." On the other hand, in evaluating Longstreet's actions at Gettysburg on July 2 and 3, Alexander advanced a reasonable assessment of Lee's Warhorse: "It is true that he [Longstreet] obeyed reluctantly at Gettysburg, on the 2nd & on the 3rd, but it must be admitted that his judgment in both matters was sound & he owed it to Lee to be reluctant, for failure was inevitable do it soon, or do it late, either day."[7]

Of course, Longstreet critics and Lost Cause partisans in the postwar years regularly stated just the opposite of Longstreet and Alexander's assessment of the Confederate Army's chances for success on July 3. Lost Cause writers typically admitted victory was more of a long shot for the Confederates on July 3, but still attainable had Longstreet only executed Lee's plan as they believed the commanding general had intended. "Victory on the third day was for the Confederates a far more difficult problem than on the second, but it was still within their reach," Colonel William Allan declared. Allan further alleged Longstreet's "hesitation" and "want of confidence and hearty cooperation" were to blame for the attack's failure. Surely Lee's plan was rock solid, Allan contended, writing, "Lee never intended that Pickett, Pettigrew, and Trimble should fight unsupported by the remainder of the army." Allan believed Longstreet was supposed to and directed by Lee to use his whole corps during the attack, including "Hood's and McLaws's divisions to support Pickett"; however, "these divisions were practically idle," he argued, ultimately upsetting "Lee's efforts for a concerted attack." Armistead Long speculated "General Longstreet did not enter into the spirit of it, and consequently did not support it with his wonted vigor." Clifford Dowdey very similarly alleged that early on the morning of July 3 "Lee failed to recognize the balky defeatism implicit in Longstreet's behavior and attitude" and "missed the disturbed state that rendered his senior corps commander unfit to direct the assault." Earl Hess also demonstrates his agreement with Long, believing "[Longstreet] was motivated largely by a desire to reduce casualties in what he assumed would be a hopeless cause, thereby helping to ensure it would remain hopeless." Like Long and Hess' estimation, Jubal Early stated in 1872, "A subordinate who undertakes to doubt the wisdom of his superior's plans, and enters upon their execution with reluctance and distrust, will not be likely to ensure success." Early conjectured that the way in which he believed Longstreet carried out his orders on July 3 "may defeat the best devised schemes." In writing about July 3, Gilbert Moxley Sorrel continued his checkered, hit-or-miss account of the battle, contending "it was apparent" in the morning hours "that a great blow must be delivered to Meade's army.... His [Lee's] army and trains could only be saved by a tremendous strike straight at the enemy." A response to these and similar comments has never been fashioned better than by historian George Stewart who asserted "The idea that ... Longstreet failed in [his] duty on July 3 seem ... on the evidence, to be unfounded, and in fact utterly fantastic."[8]

Going back to the 1870s, Longstreet critics have often expressed abhorrence at one of Longstreet's postwar comments on Lee's decision to attack the Federal center head-on on July 3. Longstreet's controversial statement is represented in one instance as "That he [Lee] was excited and off his balance was evident on the afternoon of the 1st, and he labored under that oppression until enough blood was shed to appease him." Most assuredly, Longstreet had July 3, 1863, most in mind when he wrote that statement in various forms over the years, for he always admitted consistently that "Never was I so depressed as upon that day. I felt that my men were to be sacrificed, and that I should have to order them to make a hopeless charge." In another account, he wrote, "That day at Gettysburg was one of the saddest of my life." To Longstreet, the Confederate assault on July 3, and to a lesser extent July 2, proved to be two very costly attacks that ultimately produced little results, while an alternative and less costly course of action was readily available for the taking. Yet critics ask, how could Longstreet have said such an unsavory thing about Lee? Robert Krick claims to know the answer in writing that Longstreet actually never really liked Lee during the war and preferred Joseph Johnston, and therefore, he concludes that for thirty years after the war, Longstreet harbored a "distaste" for Lee. Longstreet probably did prefer Johnston's tactical approach to waging battle, but going so far as to argue Longstreet disliked Lee during and after the war is complete and utter nonsense. In making such bold statements after the war, Longstreet was simply being honest about how he disagreed with Lee's tactical approach at Gettysburg. Even though Longstreet clearly believed the commanding general's fixation on the tactical offensive proved to contribute significantly to the army's undoing at Gettysburg, he also prefaced such beliefs with deference to Lee. For example, in one account he writes, "Before discussing the weak points of the campaign of Gettysburg, it is proper that I should say that I do so with the greatest affection for General Lee, and the greatest reverence for his memory."[9]

James Longstreet, probably 1864 or 1865 (Library of Congress).

Furthermore, Longstreet's criticism of Lee and the way in which he went about it were actually not unique at the time. Other participants like E.P. Alexander, Gilbert Moxley Sorrel, Arthur Fremantle, and D.H. Hill wrote similarly on Lee's actions at Gettysburg. Alexander contended, "Then perhaps in taking the aggressive at all at Gettysburg in 1863 & certainly in the place & dispositions for the assault on the 3rd day, I think, it will undoubtedly be held that [Lee] unnecessarily took the most desperate chances & the bloodiest road." Likewise, Sorrell maintained, "To succeed, he [Lee] knew battles were to be won, and battles cost blood, and blood he did not mind in his general's work.... He would pour out their blood when necessary or when strategically advisable," and again later in his postwar narrative, "Our general, as it has been said, did not mind blood when it had to be shed." Arthur Fremantle alleged he counseled Lee: "Don't you see your system feeds upon itself? You cannot fill the places of these men. Your troops do wonders, but every time at a cost you cannot afford." D.H. Hill asserted similarly of Lee's often tactically offensive approach, "We were lavish of blood in those days, and it was thought to be a very great thing to charge a battery of artillery or an earth-work lined with infantry.... The attacks on the Beaver Dam intrenchments [Seven Days], on the heights of the Malvern Hill [Seven Days], at Gettysburg, etc., were all grand, but of exactly the kind of grandeur which the South could not afford." Have historians seen fit to equally lambast Alexander, Sorrell, Fremantle, and Hill for their comments about Lee? They have not, and in all truth, should not. Indeed, is it reasonable to single-out and nitpick Longstreet's frank statement about what he judged Lee's mindset to be at Gettysburg; particularly when that mindset cost the Army of Northern Virginia a total of 22,600 casualties, a whopping 30-percent casualty rate, without accomplishing a single noteworthy success?[10]

24

Longstreet Assesses Lee and Gettysburg

"We were not hunting for any fight that was offered"
—James Longstreet

"Lee's weak side was in delivering offensive battle," Longstreet told Captain Leslie Perry in an interview very late in life. Similarly, and as it related specifically to Gettysburg, Longstreet wrote in his memoirs, "The Confederate chief at Gettysburg looked something like Napoleon at Waterloo." Considering the postwar environment in the South where Lee was almost never criticized, Longstreet was undoubtedly bold in making such statements. Longstreet even went so far as to call out the elephant in the room, asserting that "No Southern writer dares to admit that General Lee ever made a military mistake." Longstreet had written many times previously about his love for Lee and his warm professional and personal relationship with the commanding general during and after the war; however, he also stated emphatically that he would not subscribe to the "Southern sentimentality" that he had no weaknesses, and made no mistakes as a general.[1]

Longstreet told Perry, "No Southerner will ever admit that Meade was the superior of Lee. I agree with my people." With that said, Longstreet contended Meade was Lee's equal or superior as a tactician. Longstreet cited Meade's prudence and breadth of experience as qualities that aided his ability as a general, despite him being "just a safe, every-day sort of commander." To Longstreet, Meade's experience as a subordinate only added to his predilection for keen judgment, a quality he thought the Federal general especially displayed at Gettysburg, whereas he noted Lee had little experience as a subordinate officer on the field of battle.[2]

As far as Lee's abilities as an offensive commander, Longstreet did underscore that he "several times won victory," as at Chancellorsville, but largely attributed these victories to luck. Indeed, Longstreet was not one to heap praise on Lee for battles where he employed unfettered offensive tactics. Even with Chancellorsville, Longstreet deemed that victory, ultimately, as a fruitless one that resulted in costing the Army of Northern Virginia 11,100 more casualties—a 19 percent casualty rate. In line with Longstreet's mode of thinking on Chancellorsville, E.P. Alexander underscored a glaring example of Lee's attack at all costs mindset. On May 5–6, 1863, the Army of the Potomac began its retreat northward, a move Alexander considered lucky for the Army of Northern

Virginia, given Lee had planned to execute an all-out assault against a hardened Federal position the following day. On Lee's "audacity," Alexander wrote that he "felt it was already overfulfilled," while the enemy's retreat "saved us from what would have been probably the bloodiest defeat of the war." Alexander described how the Federal army, "some 90,000 infantry, were in the Wilderness, backed against the Rapidan [and the Rappahannock], & had had nearly three days to fortify a short front, from the river above to the river below," and "a line of breastworks could in a few hours make a position absolutely impregnable to assault." With such a strong position to confront, Alexander questioned Lee's headlong predilection to pursue aggressive offensive tactics. "Lee gave orders for a grand assault the next morning by his whole force of about 40,000 infantry.... And how I did thank God when in the morning the enemy were gone!" he exclaimed.[3]

The earlier Seven Days Campaign in the summer of 1862 followed very much the same storyline. Of course, Lee successfully beat back the Federal threat from the gates of Richmond; however, an extremely costly series of battles—21 percent casualty rate—ensued against an inept Federal general, George B. McClellan, whereby in every instance Lee employed offensive tactics and never achieved proper coordination and concert of action to deliver an effective blow. It was during the Seven Days Campaign when the original Lost Cause marble man, Stonewall Jackson, was a near-complete nonentity who failed to execute Lee's orders on several occasions, most especially at Glendale. The Battle of Second Manassas, in Longstreet's opinion, was Lee's greatest semi-offensive achievement, whereby Jackson established a stout defensive line and held off numerous attacks from yet another inept Federal general, John Pope, while Longstreet maneuvered into position on the Federal's left flank and delivered a crushing assault that sent the Army of the Potomac reeling backwards. Gilbert Moxley Sorrel thought "Longstreet was seen at his best during the battle. His consummate ability in managing troops was well displayed that day and his large bodies of men were moved with great skill and without the least confusion."[4]

During Lee's first invasion of the North which resulted in a pitched battle at Sharpsburg, Maryland in September 1862, Lee again employed offensive strategies and tactics throughout the campaign. Lee boldly divided his army in three and when Federal General McClellan was luckily presented with a lost copy of Lee's strategic plans, it forced the Confederate commander to concentrate his forces quickly and prematurely. Lee was compelled to fight the bloodiest single-day battle of the war—23 percent casualty rate—where he was badly outnumbered, and only the cautiousness and incompetence of the Federal General and the saving grace of the last-minute arrival of A.P. Hill's men allowed his army to survive to fight another day.[5]

With all of these examples in mind, Longstreet declared Lee was at his best when he invited defensive battle. "On the defensive Lee was absolutely perfect. Reconciled to the single purpose of defense he was invincible," he emphasized to Perry. In this regard, the battles of Fredericksburg, Cold Harbor, and Petersburg came to mind, along with the already mentioned semi-offensive Second Manassas. When Perry came to ask Longstreet specifically about the second invasion of the North, Longstreet referred to the pitched battle as "the Gettysburg fiasco." Longstreet, as already proven and discussed, came to agree and support Lee in his strategic idea to, yet again, march the

Army of Northern Virginia northward. "General Lee was a large minded man, of great and profound learning in the science of war. In all strategical movements he handled a great army with comprehensive ability and signal success," and the summer 1863 plan was "a large conception promising great results," Longstreet told Perry. He continued, "The result was bad, but mind you, I am not saying the invasion in itself was ill-advised or unwarranted. The grand strategy proposed was good, but the ultimate battle tactics unfortunate." Once the army concentrated at Gettysburg and the Confederates initiated pitched offensive battle for three days, Longstreet believed "a pitiable state of affairs ensued. No two corps fought in concert. It was a piecemeal battle," much like every battle during the Seven Days Campaign. Longstreet once again held that even if proper coordination and concert of action between corps could have been achieved at Gettysburg, it would have mattered little. "The Union position alone defeated us. Besides that, the whole Federal army fought magnificently at all points," he concluded.[6]

During a tour of the Sharpsburg battlefield with Perry, when asked about Gettysburg again, the general perhaps offered his most cogent and coherent summation of the battle:

> We did not invade Pennsylvania merely to fight a battle. We could have gotten a battle anywhere in Virginia, and a very much better one than was offered us at Gettysburg. We invaded Pennsylvania not only as a diversion, to demoralize and dishearten the North and shake off Grant from Vicksburg, but, if possible, to draw the Federals into a battle upon our terms. We were so to maneuver as to outgeneral the Union commander, as we had done in the Second Manassas campaign; in other words, to make opportunities for ourselves and take prompt advantage of the most favorable one that presented itself. I had confidence that this was the purpose of General Lee and that he could accomplish it. We were not hunting for any fight that was offered.[7]

Longstreet held that Lee simply switched his tactical approach on July 1 after the army collided with advance Federal cavalry and infantry at Gettysburg. When the Federals concentrated their forces on the strong Cemetery Ridge line, Longstreet simply believed pursuing offensive tactics against such a strong position was expressly unwise and would never produce the fruitful victory the Confederates had gone into the campaign seeking. Lee's Warhorse described how he approached the Battle of Gettysburg, and any battle for that matter: "It was entirely different with me. When the enemy was in sight, I was content to wait for the most favorable moment to strike—to estimate the chances, and even decline battle if I thought them against me." Longstreet cited Lee's "headlong combativeness," and the commanding general's tendency to "return" an attack by the enemy immediately and "on the spot" as a characteristic that forced Lee into a poor situation at Gettysburg, and as explanation for his repeated use of offensive tactics against the Federals. More specifically, Longstreet stated of Lee that "His impatience to strike, once in the presence of the enemy, whatever the disparity of forces or relative conditions, I consider the one weakness of General Lee's military character." Longstreet then concluded in basic terms, "That is all there is to Gettysburg; we did the best we could; we failed simply because we had undertaken too great a contract, and went about it in the wrong way."[8]

25

Shouldering the Burden of Gettysburg

"No one will then excel you"
—Robert E. Lee

Up until his death, Lee never once expressed displeasure with Longstreet's actions at the Battle of Gettysburg. Responding to Longstreet critics' common argument that the General knowingly disobeyed orders at Gettysburg, Helen Longstreet wrote appropriately, "It is absolutely certain that there is no evidence of any such belief in any of Lee's official utterances during the progress of the war, nor a hint of it in his private correspondence then or afterwards, so far as has been produced." This pronouncement still holds true today. In fact, in September 1863, Lee expressed disappointment at temporarily losing Longstreet to the Western Theater. After the Battle of Chickamauga, less than 90 days after Gettysburg, Lee wrote Longstreet, "My whole heart and soul have been with you and your brave corps in your late battle.... Finish the work before you, my dear general, and return to me. I want you badly, and you cannot get back too soon." Is this how a commanding general would write to someone who supposedly dragged their feet during a major battle just two months ago; someone who was allegedly insubordinate, slow, and prone to sulking? Further, when his Old Warhorse eventually returned to him in April 1864, Lee displayed great happiness. Walter Taylor wrote Longstreet on April 26, informing him, "He [Lee] is anxious to see you, and it will give him much pleasure to meet you and your corps once more. He hopes soon to be able to do this." Again, from May to October 1864, when Longstreet was recovering from a severe wound received at the Wilderness, Lee missed his subordinate's skill and council. And once Longstreet recovered enough to resume command of the First Corps, Lee accepted him with open arms. After the army's surrender at Appomattox, Lee told Longstreet's aide, Thomas Goree, "Captain, I am going to put my old warhorse under your charge. I want you to take good care of him."[1]

In the postwar years, Longstreet continued his warm relationship with Lee. "Our relations were affectionate, intimate, and tender during the whole war," Longstreet held, while contending, "That his confidence in me was never shaken, there is the most abundant proof." In another account, Longstreet claimed "There was never a harsh word between us." The surviving proof comes in the form of a letter from Lee, written just months after the war's end: "If you become as good a merchant as you were a soldier I shall be content. No one will then excel you, and no one can wish you more success and more happiness than I. My interest and affection for you will never cease, and my prayers are always offered for your prosperity." Lee's words not only evoked warmth and friendship, but his statement "No one will then excel you" implied Longstreet, his senior and most trusted corps commander, was never and would never be outshined.[2]

Likewise, despite their difference of opinion at times, Longstreet always held Lee's skills as a military officer and their personal friendship in high regard. Just before Longstreet temporarily left for the West in September 1863, he wrote Lee from Richmond, "If I did not think our move a necessary one, my regrets at leaving you would be distressing to me.... Our affections for you are stronger, if it possible for them to be stronger, than our admiration for you." Again, a few months after Gettysburg and just after Longstreet propelled the Confederacy to a great victory at the Battle of Chickamauga, he wrote to Secretary of War James Seddon requesting Lee be sent west. "Can't you send us General Lee? The army in Virginia can operate defensively, while our operations here should be offensive, until we have recovered Tennessee, at all events. We need some such great mind as General Lee's (nothing more) to accomplish this," Longstreet wrote glowingly of Lee. Considering the unquestionable endurance of the Lee-Longstreet partnership, the logical question to be asked is: if Longstreet had been exceptionally insubordinate at Gettysburg to the point of dereliction—as many postwar Lost Cause writers and historians since have contended—why then did Lee not only retain Longstreet as his senior subordinate until the surrender at Appomattox, but also maintain an extremely warm and cordial relationship with him until his death five years later?[3]

Former Longstreet aide Thomas Goree made a claim on May 17, 1875, that may portend toward some kind of answer. In a letter to Longstreet, Goree reminded his former Chief that in the winter of 1864, when Longstreet's corps was still out west, he "sent me from E. Tennessee to Orange C.H. with some dispatches to Genl. Lee." Goree then described how "upon my arrival there," Lee asked him into his tent where "two or three Northern papers [were] on his table." The rest of Goree's account merits full disclosure:

> He remarked that he had just been reading the Northern official reports of the Battle of Gettysburg, that he had become satisfied from reading those reports that if he had permitted you to carry out your plans on the 3d day, instead of making the attack on Cemetery Hill, we would have been successful. He said that the enemy seemed to have anticipated the attack on their centre, in consequence of which they had withdrawn the larger part of their force from their left flank, and from Round Top Mountain, and that if you had made your flank movement early on the morning of the 3d day as you desired that you would have met with but little opposition. To this conversation I am willing, if necessary, to make affidavit.[4]

Understandably, historians are skeptical of this kind of account and have questioned its trustworthiness, given it originated from one of Longstreet's longtime staff officers. With that said, the mode of reasoning historians have advanced to doubt this specific account's credibility is telling. Earl Hess reminds his readers that "Longstreet and his staff members were by no means unbiased; the general especially was guilty of attempts to manage the historical record." Put simply, such a statement could be advanced about any former Confederate officer who wrote in the postwar years; no exceptions. Many historians typically only feel the need to point out something so patently obvious when it involves Longstreet's postwar correspondence and writings. With respect to Goree's account, the fact is we will never know, but one wonders what the former aide's rationale would be in advancing such a detailed claim about a very specific moment in time. In his response to Goree on May 21, Longstreet brought up "a writer for *Blackwoods' Magazine*, March, 1872," who he said conveyed a very similar account. Longstreet quoted the writer as stating, "'If,' said he [Lee] on many occasions, 'I had taken General Longstreet's advice on the eve of the second day of the battle of Gettysburg and had filed off the left corps of my army behind the right corps in the direction of Baltimore and Washington along the Emmettsburg [*sic*] Road, the Confederates to-day would be a free people.'" Longstreet disagreed with the assertion that a Confederate victory at Gettysburg would have decided the war; however, he expressed to Goree, "I have not a doubt about the result of the battle if he [Lee] could have permitted me to operate as I wished." Curiously, Harry Heth alleged that around the same timeframe, the early spring months of 1864, Lee told him in reference to the July 3 assault in particular, "After it is all over, as stupid a fellow as I am can see the mistakes that were made." Further, Lee supposedly admitted to Heth, "I notice, however, my mistakes are never told me until it is too late, and you, and all my officers know that I am always ready and anxious to have their suggestions."[5]

In one of his first postwar accounts, Longstreet openly wrote about how he and Lee dealt with the subject of Confederate defeat at Gettysburg. Longstreet claimed that "General Lee and myself never had any deliberate conversation about Gettysburg. The subject was never broached by either of us to the other. On one occasion it came up casually, and he said to me (alluding to the charge of Pickett, on the 3d), 'General, why didn't you stop all that thing that day?'" The former First Corps commander alleged he replied to the commanding general by pointing out he "could not, under the circumstances, assume such a responsibility, as no discretion had been left me." No other party ever confirmed or denied this conversation, or similar dialogue, actually transpired between Longstreet and Lee. That said, another member of Longstreet's staff, Captain Erasmus Taylor claimed his Chief showed him a letter Lee had sent him around the winter of 1864 which stated something to the effect of "Oh, General, had I taken your advice, instead of pursuing the course that I did, how different all would have been." Taylor contended he had committed the words to memory.[6]

James Longstreet, probably 1870s (Library of Congress).

In his several postwar accounts, Longstreet regularly expressed his profound desire that the calculated and coordinated attempt to make him the scapegoat for Confederate defeat at Gettysburg had been initiated before Lee's death. He wished Lee was around to answer those "wordy soldiers," who tried to "fix upon me the whole burden of the battle—their rashness carrying them so far as to lead them to put false orders in the mouth of our great captain, and charge me with having broken them." Longstreet contended, "If the charges so vehemently urged against me after his [Lee's] death had been preferred, or even suggested, in his lifetime, I do not believe they would have needed any reply from me." Intertwined with this unrealistic hope was Longstreet's supreme and unconquerable optimism that historians would one day represent him accurately: "General Lee would have answered them himself, and have set history right." The former First Corps commander declared his overarching objective for writing about the battle and answering his critics was born from "a desire on the one hand to have future historians properly informed" about his role at Gettysburg. Concurrently, he believed it "a necessity on the other hand of correcting important mis-statements made ignorantly or maliciously concerning it." Longstreet expressed confidently that he did not "fear the verdict of history on Gettysburg," trusting "Time sets all things right" and "Error lives but a day—truth is eternal," perhaps the most quoted statement he ever made.[7]

Veterans groups' many references to future history and historians immediately after Longstreet's death demonstrated his convictions neither went unheard nor unnoticed. A member of the United Confederate Veterans stated "all true history ... places Longstreet in the very first rank as to ability and generalship among any of Lee's subordinates." Just as Longstreet wrote in the postwar years, the member was sure that "in the generations to come, when passion and prejudice shall vanish like the mists of the morning at the presence of the clear sunlight of truth, Longstreet's name shall receive at the hands of the entire civilized world the praise and honor to which it is justly entitled." David D. Shelby of the United States Circuit Court of Appeals wrote Helen Longstreet on January 5, 1904, expressing similar sentiments: "When history is written after time has modified all passions and prejudices, his career will stand in honorable and distinguished contrast with those of his critics who were 'invisible in war and invisible in peace.'" "Invisible in peace" was a phrase that Geo W. Weir explored further in a letter to Mrs. Longstreet on January 4 as it related to the General's critics in the postwar years. He asked sardonically, "How many ex-Confederates refuse office under the United States government to-day, is a question I would like to have answered. Longstreet was too big a man for his day, that was all. The scribbling of unscrupulous parties can not dim his fame. He was the hardest fighter of the Civil War." From Washington, D.C. on January 5, George Baber also expressed his profound respect not only for Longstreet's military abilities—calling his critics "the narrow minded few"—but also for his being the bigger man after the country had been torn apart in the 1860s. "He was truly great in war as the brilliant leader of gallant armies, but he was greater in peace as the patriotic citizen loyally dedicating his splendid fame to the cause of his country's restoration to an harmonious brotherhood," Baber wrote glowingly of the former General.[8]

About 37 years after interviewing Longstreet, even Hamlin Garland was made fully aware of the General's ongoing predicament with history and historians. In 1933, Garland received a letter from Warren Hastings Miller, another prolific writer at the turn of the twentieth century who wrote over 30 books and was managing editor of

Field & Stream magazine from 1910 to 1918. Miller expressed a profound desire to write a book about Longstreet and Ulysses S. Grant, with the intention of "placing the reader within the minds of both characters as they attacked the problems before them." Miller called Longstreet and Grant the only "two major strategists" of the Civil War and devoted a lengthy paragraph to how history had largely forgotten or shunned Longstreet. Miller never fulfilled his desire to write this book, but his thoughts on Longstreet are worth quoting in full:

> If Longstreet had been in supreme command on the Southern side the whole course of history would have been changed. There would have been no Vicksburg, no Gettysburg, no Wilderness campaign. Lincoln would have gone down in history as the president who failed to keep the Union intact, and Grant would never have had the opportunity to assume command of all our armies. The popular heroes in the South today are Lee and Jackson, both great fellows to win a battle, but neither having the least idea on what to do with a victory when won. Longstreet is never mentioned. He fell out of favor because a friend of Grant's and too lenient about the reconstruction measures. I will have difficulty in getting the material I want about him.... With Longstreet we only have his own, "Bull Run to Appomattox"; the rest critical or biased by later hostility to him.... I marveled, when I went into the Spanish War, that Longstreet, the only man alive in America who had ever commanded as much as thirty thousand men, was neglected, while Joe Wheeler, a second rate cavalry commander, was sent to the front.... I get only coldness and indifference on him from my Southern acquaintances.[9]

It is only very recently that a few historians have advanced a more reasonable assessment of Longstreet's actions at Gettysburg, especially as it pertains to how little Longstreet actually contributed to the Confederate loss. Refreshingly, Allen Guelzo's one-volume history of the battle published in 2013 manages to capture Longstreet's sizable role at Gettysburg without all the Lost Cause and Freeman-Catton-Dowdey residue that beset the overwhelming majority of works throughout the 1990s and early 2000s. The last major biography of Longstreet was written in 1993, and even though it has been touted as a fresh look at the General, it now shows some age in its sometimes conciliatory approach to Longstreet critics' arguments of that time. Discussing the slow but steady trend away from feeling beholden to past dogma when it comes to Longstreet, Douglas Young, a Gainesville State College history professor told the *Gainesville Times* in 2011 that "I really believe that now, the general is far more appreciated than he has ever been. I think there has been a real restoration of his reputation, militarily, politically and personally." It would appear Young is increasingly correct. As New Orleans descended into a fierce debate about the removal of Confederate monuments in January 2016, at least one journalist had the historical awareness to suggest that Lee's "12-foot statue ... atop a 60-foot Doric column" be replaced with one of Longstreet, "whose Reconstruction-era service has never properly been recognized." On the subject of Gettysburg, the journalist further contended that after the war many ex–Confederates "scapegoated Longstreet for the Rebel defeat at Gettysburg," believing he "had to be smeared so Lee could occupy his pedestal." On the reputation, political, and personal front, the journalist identifies what Helen Longstreet dubbed "General Longstreet's Americanism" 112 years ago: "Longstreet risked his life for the worst cause Americans ever espoused, then for the best one. In short, he epitomized this nation's saving grace, and humanity's: the capacity to learn from our mistakes, and to change."[10]

Douglas Young also underscores the lasting obstacle impeding a fair and accurate

Helen Longstreet, probably 1890s (Library of Congress).

evaluation of Longstreet's actions at Gettysburg: "People couldn't blame Lee for the loss at Gettysburg and so they blamed Longstreet." Longstreet's political choices after the war made him an easy target. With this perpetual need to regularly prop up Lee losing its grip in the historical community, Young is accurate in his assessment that historians "are able to take a fresh look" at Longstreet now. Young also reasonably identifies what motivated Longstreet to repeatedly rebut his critics between the 1870s and 1890s: "I do think that Longstreet was sensitive to the charge that he had failed his troops at Gettysburg. That bothered him light years more than charges he was pro-black, pro–Yankee." Indeed, to Longstreet, Gettysburg became a reoccurring battle, fought again and again with each new, deliberate falsification and dubious claim made by the Lost Cause partisans. He would not let such an obvious smear campaign go unanswered, and it is now the responsibility of historians to take their share of the responsibility and confront the fact that they have sometimes subtly and often times blatantly perpetuated the myths of the Lost Cause well into the late twentieth and early twenty-first century.[11]

The degree to which Longstreet was increasingly bitter and sensitive to "the charge that he had failed his troops at Gettysburg" was most poignantly on display in his memoirs, written and published during the last few years of his life. The First Corps commander's piqued bearing was understandable by that point, given his military record, particularly his actions at Gettysburg, had been unfairly assailed for the better part of nearly 30 years, and he had been forced to actively defend his conduct for two decades. Longstreet's writings in the third day at Gettysburg section of his memoirs display just how acidic he had become to his critics' calculated attempt to "work up public opinion as to shift the disaster to my shoulders." "General Early has been a picturesque figure in the combination," Longstreet claimed, "ready to champion any reports that could throw a shadow over its [the First Corps'] record, but the charge most pleasing to him was that of treason on the part of its commander. The subject was lasting, piquant, and so consoling that one is almost inclined to envy the comfort it gave him in his latter days."[12]

When discussing Lee's decision to put him in tactical control of Pickett's Charge and the preparations he made for the assault, a resentful Longstreet lashed out bitterly,

James Longstreet's grave adorned by the American flag, Gainesville, Georgia (author's collection).

unfairly, and falsely in his memoirs. Longstreet held that Lee "should have put an officer in charge who had more confidence in his plan." Of course, Lee would have put no other corps commander in charge of the assault. Not only was Longstreet his most senior subordinate, but he was also his most dependable and seasoned combat commander. Longstreet continued with apparent indignance: "Knowing my want of confidence, he

A statue of James Longstreet by sculptor Gregory Johnson, Gainesville, Georgia (author's collection).

should have given the benefit of his presence and his assistance in getting the troops up, posting them, and arranging the batteries; but he gave no orders or suggestions after his early designation of the point for which the column should march." Yet, the fact was Lee was frequently with Longstreet throughout the preparation stages of the July 3 assault. Longstreet was also well aware that it was not the duty of the commanding general to deploy troops and "arrange the batteries."[13]

In that same chapter of his memoirs, Longstreet's resentful state also seeped through when discussing General Stonewall Jackson. Resultantly, his narrative became bogged down in some inaccurate and petty claims. In responding to allegations made by General Fitzhugh Lee that the commanding general "said that he would have gained the battle [of Gettysburg] if he had had General Jackson with him," Longstreet became paltry and defensive, writing, "But he had Jackson in the Sharpsburg campaign, which was more blundering than that of Gettysburg." Longstreet then included a footnote that falsely alleged Jackson "left the field" at Sharpsburg from 7 a.m. to 4 p.m. Later in the chapter, he briefly and accurately discussed Jackson's failures during the Seven Days Campaign, but then he unfairly downplayed Jackson's notable performance at Second Manassas; again made false claims that "I was at Sharpsburg all day; Jackson only about two and a half hours," and, erroneously alleged that he saved Jackson's command at Fredericksburg by "swing[ing] off from my right and join[ing] in his battle." Longstreet did not have to engage in these kinds of arguments to defend his own military record, and when he had first started defending himself against critics' attacks in the 1870s and 1880s, he largely avoided using such diatribes and was more magnanimous to his fellow corps commander. Writing of Jackson's death after the Battle of Chancellorsville in an 1887 account, he emphasized that "The shock was a very severe one to men and officers, but the full extent of our loss was not felt until the remains of the beloved general had been sent home. The dark clouds of the future then began to lower above the Confederates." Longstreet wrote a similar account of Jackson's death in his memoirs; however, it comes off a bit more stilted and forced than his earlier versions.[14]

Granted, Longstreet's attacks on Jackson and some of his other assertions in his memoirs were largely unfair and erroneous; however, the fact was that by 1895, Longstreet was likely and understandably bitter toward his Lost Cause detractors whose attacks were even more unfair and unnecessary than most anything he could muster toward others. Longstreet also recognized that while they assailed him, the Lost Cause group had concurrently fashioned Jackson and Lee into marble men who never once made a mistake. During an interview late in life, he made mention of this established hero worship: "In all these criticisms of me, you will observe that the merits of the question are carefully avoided. Their only recourses now, in the light of the inside official history of the war, is an appeal to Southern sentimentality by beating the totem of General Lee's great name, undisputed fame and lovable personality. That answers every criticism, hushes all cavillers. No Southern writer dares to admit that General Lee ever made a military mistake." Impartial historians now readily admit what Longstreet understood then and had the courage to vocalize in the late nineteenth century, namely that Jackson and Lee had unsurprisingly made mistakes like any other officer during the war.[15]

Postscript: Reminiscences

"The sorest and saddest reflection of my life for many years"
—Longstreet

As Hamlin Garland finished his interview with Longstreet, he stepped out from the General's "cramped conditions" into the early evening air. In their affable discussion, Garland caused Longstreet to reminisce. "My questions had put him far back in the past, that was evident," Garland observed. From his lifelong friendship with Ulysses S. Grant to his actions as a young soldier "fifty years ago" in the Mexican War, from his "[winning] his way by leaps and bounds to a foremost place in the battleline of '65 to a position second to none in patriotism when the war was over," Longstreet's life appeared "epic in its contrasts." Besides the hardships Longstreet suffered daily as a result of his throat wound reminding him of his frontline role in many major battles of the Civil War, Garland wondered whether "the past does not all seem a dream to him?"[1]

Before Garland set his sights on "the winding street toward the village," Longstreet shook the novelist's hand and bade him a good night. In that moment, from Garland's point of view, the General "loomed above me with a hulking stoop in his massive frame, and his eyes peered down at me, sad and penetrating, but his broad face was inscrutably placid." Longstreet seemed unquestionably the Confederacy's "greatest living representative." Yet, with the benefit of historical hindsight, surely Garland was mistaken in saying the past seemed but a dream to Longstreet, as the postwar controversy over his actions at Gettysburg had by then spanned decades and seemingly rendered the General's life permanently fixed in time to three days in July 1863. As early as 1868, Longstreet was said to have regarded Gettysburg and specifically the third day's attack as "where I came to grief." Twenty years later at the 25th anniversary of the battle, Longstreet was said to have stood near the Angle and Copse of Trees and "gazed long and intently at the gloomy woods of Seminary Ridge from which Pickett and his thousands had dashed to make the memorable charge." After silent reflection, Longstreet predictably held that "Both God and reason were against it. The latter I then saw. The former I now devoutly and greatly recognize."[2]

Conversely, Garland proved very discerning in his awareness of Longstreet's overall placid manner. As Longstreet neared the end of his life in the late 1890s and early 1900s, his anger and frustration slowly turned toward indifference and composure toward his detractors' charges. He began saying things like, "I'm used to it. This is mild as a summer shower. Thirty years ago I was pilloried." In 1902, just before his death, Longstreet frankly admitted to Federal General Daniel Sickles, his foe on July 2 at Gettysburg and close postwar friend, that the July 1863 battle became "the sorest and saddest reflection of my life for many years." As Garland turned away and waved affably to Lee's former

A statue of James Longstreet by sculptor Gary Casteel, Gettysburg, Pennsylvania (author's collection).

Warhorse, Longstreet was again peering through his binoculars, examining the Federal position on Cemetery Ridge for the first time on July 1; trying to convince his commanding general to move the army off the Federal left flank in the early morning hours of July 2; and, sitting on the rail fence as George Pickett rode up to ask if he should advance his division on July 3. In that sense, Garland was more correct than he probably knew as he walked away from Longstreet that evening saying to himself, "I have seen the ghost of the Confederacy." Indeed, now in the year 2019, it is well beyond time for historians to lay Longstreet's embattled and scapegoated ghost at Gettysburg to rest.[3]

Chapter Notes

Prologue

1. Hamlin Garland's article was published in the *Pittsburgh Leader* and then reprinted in Edward Jewitt Wheeler, ed., *Current Literature*, Volume 22, Volumes 689–702 of American Periodical Series, 1850–1900 (Current Literature Publishing Company, 1897), 415; No date of publication is provided for this article; however, according to "Who Is Hamlin Garland?" *The Hamlin Garland Society*, http://www.garlandsociety.org/biography.html (accessed January 21, 2018), Garland "received a commission in 1896 from Samuel S. McClure to write a biography of Ulysses S. Grant which, after two years of exhaustive research, was serialized in *McClure's Magazine* before appearing in book form in 1898." Given that a significant portion of the article discusses Longstreet's thoughts on and relationship with Grant, it is very likely Garland visited Longstreet sometime between 1896, when he received his commission, and 1897, when this *Current Literature* volume was published. By that time, Longstreet would have been 75 or 76. As for where Garland traveled from to reach Gainesville in 16 hours by Pullman Car, Keith Newlin, an English professor at the University of North Carolina Wilmington and author and editor of several books on Garland, stated he "moved from Boston to Chicago in April 1894. It is hard to track down his movements, for as a bachelor and lecturer, he was on the move all the time. He also had settled his parents in West Salem, Wisconsin, so he visited there frequently, especially in the summers. In the summers of 1895–97, he visited a number of Indian reservations, spent time in New York City, and of course in 1896 began traveling to interview people who knew Grant." See: Keith Newlin, e-mail message to author, January 22, 2018.

2. Gilbert Moxley Sorrel, *At the Right Hand of Longstreet: Recollections of a Confederate Staff Officer* (Lincoln: University of Nebraska Press, 1999), 116; Thomas J. Goree, *Longstreet's Aide: The Civil War Letters of Major Thomas J. Goree*, ed. Thomas W. Cutrer (Charlottesville: University Press of Virginia, 1995), 98.

3. William Garrett Piston, *Lee's Tarnished Lieutenant: James Longstreet and His Place in Southern History* (Athens: University of Georgia Press, 1987), 97; Allen C. Guelzo, *Gettysburg: The Last Invasion* (New York: Alfred A. Knopf, 2013), 21–22; Goree, *Longstreet's Aide*, 60; Sorrel, *At the Right Hand of Longstreet*, 23–24, 37–38.

4. Wheeler, *Current Literature*, Volume 22, 415; Sorrel, *At the Right Hand of Longstreet*, 274; Goree, *Longstreet's Aide*, 157, 172; James A. Hessler and Wayne E. Motts, *Pickett's Charge at Gettysburg: A Guide to the Most Famous Attack in American History* (El Dorado Hills, CA: Savas Beatie, 2015), 266.

5. Wheeler, *Current Literature*, 415; Helen Dortch Longstreet, *Lee and Longstreet at High Tide: Gettysburg in the Light of the Official Records* (Gainesville, GA: Published by the author, 1904), 123; Piston, *Lee's Tarnished Lieutenant*, 151–152.

6. Wheeler, *Current Literature*, 415; Ulysses S. Grant, *The Personal Memoirs of Ulysses S. Grant* (New York: Konecky & Konecky), 388; Jeffry D. Wert, *General James Longstreet: The Confederacy's Most Controversial Soldier* (New York: Touchstone, 1993), 421–422; Piston, *Lee's Tarnished Lieutenant*, 152, 153.

7. Wheeler, *Current Literature*, 415; Piston, *Lee's Tarnished Lieutenant*, 153.

8. Edward Alfred Pollard, *Lee and His Lieutenants: Comprising the Early Life, Public Services, and Campaigns of General Robert E. Lee and His Companions in Arms, with a Record of Their Campaigns and Heroic Deeds* (University of Iowa: E. B. Treat & Company, 1868), 419; James D. McCabe Jr., *Life and Campaigns of General Robert E. Lee* (Atlanta, GA: National Publishing Company, 1870), 461; Piston, *Lee's Tarnished Lieutenant*, 102.

9. *New Orleans Times*, June 8, 1867; *Chicago Tribune*, June 10, 1867; Piston, *Lee's Tarnished Lieutenant*, 106.

10. John Donald Wade, *Augustus Baldwin Longstreet: A Study of the Development of Culture in the South*, ed. M. Thomas Inge (Athens: University of Georgia Press, 2010), 355; *Chicago Tribune*, June 10, 1867; Piston, *Lee's Tarnished Lieutenant*, 106, 108–112, 123, 137–139, 167; Wert, *General James Longstreet*, 413–419, 425; Helen Dortch Longstreet, *Lee and Longstreet at High Tide*, 17–18.

11. Piston, *Lee's Tarnished Lieutenant*, 110–111.

12. Piston, *Lee's Tarnished Lieutenant*, 106; Goree, *Longstreet's Aide*, 160, 175; Robert K. Krick, "'If Longstreet Says So...It Is Most Likely Not True': James Longstreet and the Second Day at Gettysburg," in *The Second Day at Gettysburg: Essays on Confederate and Union Leadership*, ed. Gary W. Gallagher (Kent, OH: Kent State University Press, 1993), 64.

13. Krick, "'If Longstreet Says So...It Is Most Likely Not True,'" 64; Glenn Tucker, *Lee and Longstreet at Gettysburg* (Dayton, OH: Morningside Bookshop, 1982), 38–39.

14. George R. Stewart, *Pickett's Charge: A Microhistory of the Final Attack at Gettysburg, July 3, 1863* (Boston: Houghton Mifflin, 1959), 285.

15. John Brown Gordon, *Reminiscences of the Civil War* (New York: Charles Scribner's Sons, 1903), 161,

169; William Swinton, *Campaigns of the Army of the Potomac: A Critical History of Operations in Virginia, Maryland and Pennsylvania, from the Commencement to the Close of the War, 1861–1865* (New York: Charles Scribner's Sons, 1882), 340.

16. Piston, *Lee's Tarnished Lieutenant,* 117–120, 130–131; See all of these letters in: James Longstreet, "Lee in Pennsylvania," in *Annals of the War,* originally published in the *Philadelphia Weekly Times,* republished (Edison, NJ: Blue & Grey, 1996), 437–441; Krick, "'If Longstreet Says So...It Is Most Likely Not True,'" 72; William Garrett Piston, "Marked in Bronze: James Longstreet and Southern History," in *James Longstreet: The Man, the Soldier, the Controversy,* ed. R.L Dinardo and Albert A. Nofi (Cambridge, MA: Da Capo, 1998), 209.

17. James Longstreet, *From Manassas to Appomattox* (Philadelphia: J.B. Lippincott Company, 1895, republished Cambridge, MA: Da Capo, 1992), 377; Stewart, *Pickett's Charge,* 286; Piston, *Lee's Tarnished Lieutenant, 168–169;* Wert, *General James Longstreet,* 426–427; Four days earlier on January 2, Longstreet succumbed to a sudden bout of pneumonia at the age of eighty-two, which caused him to hemorrhage violently, and resultantly, led not only to the reopening of his Wilderness throat wound, but also delirium, and finally loss of consciousness before the end. For the past year or two, Longstreet had also suffered from a bout of cancer in his right eye, and more chronic ailments like rheumatism and severe weight loss, shrinking from 200 pounds to 135.

18. Helen Dortch Longstreet, *Lee and Longstreet at High Tide,* 219, 231–232, 242.

19. *Ibid.,* 234.

20. Stephen Sears, *Gettysburg* (Boston, New York: Houghton Mifflin, 2003), 57, 6; Wert, *General James Longstreet,* 205–206; Glenn W. LaFantasie, *Twilight at Little Round Top: July 2, 1863—The Tide Turns at Gettysburg* (New York: Vintage, 2005), 20; Sorrel, *At the Right Hand of Longstreet,* 32, 76; Goree, *Longstreet's Aide,* 126; Stewart, *Pickett's Charge,* 17.

21. Helen Dortch Longstreet, *Lee and Longstreet at High Tide,* 236, 242, 250, 262.

22. *Ibid.,* 280, 278, 319, 321, 323.

23. *Ibid.,* 292, 327, 293, 296.

24. Longstreet, *From Manassas to Appomattox,* xii.

Chapter 1

1. Daniel M. Laney, "Wasted Gallantry: Hood's Texas Brigade at Gettysburg," *Gettysburg Magazine,* Volume 16 (1997), 27; Swinton, *Campaigns of the Army of the Potomac,* 340.

2. Gary W. Gallagher, *Lee and His Generals in War and Memory* (Baton Rouge: Louisiana State University Press, 1998), 47, 58, 60; James Longstreet, *From Manassas to Appomattox,* x; Jeffry D. Wert, "'No 15,000 Men Can Take that Hill': Longstreet at Gettysburg," in *James Longstreet: The Man, the Soldier, the Controversy,* ed. R.L Dinardo and Albert A. Nofi (Cambridge, MA: Da Capo, 1998), 92; Sorrel, *At the Right Hand of Longstreet,* xii; Krick, "'If Longstreet Says So...It Is Most Likely Not True,'" 57; Clifford Dowdey, *Lee and His Men at Gettysburg: The Death of a Nation* (Lincoln: University of Nebraska Press, 1958), 169; Robert Alonzo Brock, ed., *Southern Historical Society Papers,* Volume 6 (Richmond: Virginia Historical Society, 1878), 124.

3. Piston, *Lee's Tarnished Lieutenant,* 132; Tucker, *Lee and Longstreet at Gettysburg,* 51; For an example of such "pettifoggery," see: Paul Clark Cooksey, "'I Still Desired to Save My Men'...Lieutenant General James Longstreet on July 3, 1863," *Gettysburg Magazine,* Volume 34 (2006), 51–63.

4. Earl J. Hess, *Pickett's Charge: The Last Attack at Gettysburg* (Chapel Hill: The University of North Carolina Press, 2001), 7, 12; Edwin B. Coddington, *The Gettysburg Campaign: A Study in Command* (New York: Simon & Schuster, 1968), 361.

5. James Longstreet, "Lee in Pennsylvania," in *Annals of the War,* 415–417; Wert, *General James Longstreet,* 243–244; Sears, *Gettysburg,* 5–9.

6. Helen Dortch Longstreet, *Lee and Longstreet at High Tide,* 64–65.

7. Swinton, *Campaigns of the Army of the Potomac,* 340.

8. Richard Rollins, "'The Ruling Ideas' of the Pennsylvania Campaign: James Longstreet's 1873 Letter to Lafayette McLaws," *Gettysburg Magazine,* Volume 17 (1997), 14–16.

9. Longstreet, "Lee in Pennsylvania," in *Annals of the War,* 417.

10. James Longstreet, "Lee's Invasion of Pennsylvania," in *Battles and Leaders of the Civil War: The Tide Shifts,* Volume III (New York: Castle), 246–247.

11. Longstreet, *From Manassas to Appomattox,* 331.

12. Krick, "'If Longstreet Says So...It Is Most Likely Not True,'" 61, 69; Brock, *Southern Historical Society Papers,* Volume 6, 107–108; Dowdey, *Lee and His Men at Gettysburg,* 170; Piston, *Lee's Tarnished Lieutenant,* 131, 145, 153; Interestingly, in the case of Longstreet's first lengthy 1877 article, William Garrett Piston has pointed out that since the general's "wound from the Wilderness made penmanship painful and difficult," he employed Henry W. Grady, an Atlanta journalist, "to copy, edit, and polish" his "rough drafts." Apparently, Grady sent his polished draft directly to the *Philadelphia Weekly Times* without approval from Longstreet. Grady likely took some liberty in adding his own flair to Longstreet's writing, which may have created such stilted statements as, for instance, "Upon this understanding my assent was given." Again, when composing his *Battles and Leaders of the Civil War* articles from 1884 to 1887, Longstreet selected Uncle Remus stories author Joel Chandler Harris and Josiah Carter, a journalist for the *Atlanta Constitution,* as ghost writers and editors. The writing process consisted of Longstreet sending a rough draft to Carter to look over. Carter would then meet with Longstreet in person or send him a list of questions to answer. The journalist would then rewrite Longstreet's draft and return it to the former general. Longstreet would make any necessary corrections and suggestions before sending it back to Carter, who would make some final edits and pass the manuscript to the editors of the collection of articles, Robert Underwood Johnson and Clarence C. Buel. Though Longstreet had his draft returned to him several times during this process for review, one can assume that some of the language choice and writing style was not genuinely Longstreet's. In fact, it appears Longstreet gave his editors a considerably free hand in rewriting and editing. In one case, he told Carter to "touch up" the ar-

ticle on the Battle of Sharpsburg specifically, directing him to add "as much pathos as you may be pleased to apply." For his last major manuscript, his 1895 memoirs, Longstreet employed *Atlanta Constitution* journalist Pascal J. Moran to help him with the writing and editing process. Then an elderly man in poor health and nearly twenty years after composing his first salvos against the anti-Longstreet faction, it is only logical to presume that Longstreet probably leaned on Moran more so than any of the previous ghost writers, very likely allowing him significant latitude in language and style.

13. Wert, *General James Longstreet*, 244–246; Wert, "'No 15,000 Men Can Take that Hill,'" 81–82.

14. Coddington, *The Gettysburg Campaign: A Study in Command*, 10.

15. Tucker, *Lee and Longstreet at Gettysburg*, 51; Allan's account of his interview of Lee can be found in Charles Marshall, *Lee's Aide De Camp*, Frederick Maurice, ed. (Lincoln: University of Nebraska Press, 2000), 252.

16. Robert Nicholson Scott, ed., *The War of the Rebellion: A Compilation of the Official Records of the Union and Confederate Armies*, Volume 27, Part 2 (Washington: U.S. Government Printing Office, 1889), 318; Douglas S. Freeman, *Lee's Lieutenants: A Study in Command* (New York: Simon & Schuster, 1998), 574.

17. Marshall, *An Aide De Camp Of Lee*, 250.

18. Wert, *General James Longstreet*, 246; Sears, *Gettysburg*, 8; LaFantasie, *Twilight at Little Round Top*, 6.

19. Edward Porter Alexander, *Fighting for the Confederacy: The Personal Recollections of General Edward Porter Alexander*, ed. Gary W. Gallagher (Chapel Hill: University of North Carolina Press, 1989), xxii–xxiii; Gallagher, *Lee and His Generals in War and Memory*, 60; Wert, "'No 15,000 Men Can Take That Hill,'" 93.

20. Edward Porter Alexander, *Military Memoirs of a Confederate: A Critical Narrative* (New York: Charles Scribner's Sons, 1907), 365–366; Alexander, *Fighting for the Confederacy*, 277.

21. Robert Alonzo Brock, ed., *Southern Historical Society Papers*, Volume 4 (Richmond: Virginia Historical Society, 1877), 98–100.

22. Walter Taylor, "The Campaign in Pennsylvania," in *Annals of the War*, 305–307; Brock, *Southern Historical Society Papers*, Volume 4, 82; Longstreet, "Lee's Right Wing at Gettysburg," in *Battles and Leaders of the Civil War: The Tide Shifts*, Volume III (New York: Castle), 350.

Chapter 2

1. Longstreet, "Lee in Pennsylvania," in *Annals of the War*, 420.

2. Bradley M. Gottfried, *The Maps of Gettysburg: An Atlas of the Gettysburg Campaign, June 3-July 13, 1863* (New York: Savas Beatie, 2013), 2–7; Wert, *General James Longstreet*, 250–251; Sears, *Gettysburg*, 59–62; Guelzo, *Gettysburg: The Last Invasion*, 48–49, 56; Robert Alonzo Brock, ed., *Southern Historical Society Papers*, Volume 37 (Richmond: Virginia Historical Society, 1909), 81; Eric J. Wittenberg, *The Battle of Brandy Station: North America's Largest Cavalry Battle* (Charleston: History, 2010), 198.

3. Gottfried, *The Maps of Gettysburg*, 14–21; Wert, *General James Longstreet*, 251–252; Sears, *Gettysburg*, 94–99; Guelzo, *Gettysburg: The Last Invasion*, 58; Arthur J.L. Fremantle, *Three Months in the Southern States: April-June 1863* (Lincoln: University of Nebraska Press, 1991), 273, 237; Robert Nicholson Scott, ed., *The War of the Rebellion: A Compilation of the Official Records of the Union and Confederate Armies*, Volume 27, Part 3 (Washington: U.S. Government Printing Office, 1889), 932.

4. On June 22, Lee wrote Stuart a letter, asking him if he knew the current location of the Federal army "and what [Hooker] is doing?" Even after Lee openly admitted that "I fear he [Hooker] will steal a march on us and get across the Potomac before we are aware," he caved to Stuart's proposal; Scott, ed., *The War of the Rebellion*, Volume 27, Part 2, 692; Longstreet, "Lee in Pennsylvania," in *Annals of the War*, 435; Guelzo, *Gettysburg: The Last Invasion*, 94; Scott, *The War of the Rebellion*, Volume 27, Part 3, 913.

5. Scott, *The War of the Rebellion, Volume 27, Part 3*, 913; Robert Alonzo Brock, ed., *Southern Historical Society Papers*, Volume 40 (Richmond: Virginia Historical Society, 1915), 258.

6. Scott, *The War of the Rebellion*, Volume 27, Part 3, 915; Guelzo, *Gettysburg: The Last Invasion*, 95.

7. Scott, *The War of the Rebellion*, Volume 27, Part 3, 915.

8. Scott, *The War of the Rebellion*, Volume 27, Part 3, 923; Marshall, *Lee's Aide De Camp*, 208; Longstreet, *From Manassas to Appomattox*, 343.

9. Guelzo, *Gettysburg: The Last Invasion*, 96–98; Sears, *Gettysburg*, 105–106.

10. Longstreet, *From Manassas to Appomattox*, 343; Scott, *The War of the Rebellion*, Volume 27, Part 3, 927–928; Sears, *Gettysburg*, 139–140; Henry B. McClellan, *I Rode with Jeb Stuart: The Life and Campaigns of Major General J.E.B. Stuart* (Cambridge, MA: Da Capo, 1994), 336–337.

Chapter 3

1. Gottfried, *The Maps of Gettysburg*, 28–33; Wert, *General James Longstreet*, 253; Guelzo, *Gettysburg: The Last Invasion*, 113–114; Sears, *Gettysburg*, 123–124; Sorrel, *At the Right Hand of Longstreet*, 161; Freeman, *Lee's Lieutenants*, 551; Scott, ed., *The War of the Rebellion*, Volume 27, Part 2, 316.

2. Longstreet, "Lee in Pennsylvania," in *Annals of the War*, 419–420.

3. Longstreet, *From Manassas to Appomattox*, 351–352; Sears, *Gettysburg*, 160–225, 257; Guelzo, *Gettysburg: The Last Invasion*, 139–241; Gottfried, *The Maps of Gettysburg*, 60–141.

4. Armistead Lindsay Long and Marcus Joseph Wright, *Memoirs of Robert E. Lee: His Military and Personal History* (London: S. Low, Marston, Searle, and Rivington, 1886), 275; Alexander, *Fighting for the Confederacy*, 231–232; Longstreet, "Lee in Pennsylvania," in *Annals of the War*, 420.

5. James Longstreet, "The Mistakes of Gettysburg," in *Annals of the War*, originally published in the *Philadelphia Weekly Times*, republished (Edison, NJ: Blue & Grey, 1996), 620; Robert Alonzo Brock, ed., *Southern Historical Society Papers*, Volume 5

(Richmond: Virginia Historical Society, 1878), 174; Scott, *The War of the Rebellion,* Volume 27, Part 2, 607, 317–318.

6. Scott, *The War of the Rebellion,* Volume 27, Part 2, 317, 607, 445; Longstreet, *From Manassas to Appomattox,* 358.

7. Brock, *Southern Historical Society Papers,* Volume 5, 174.

8. Guelzo, *Gettysburg: The Last Invasion,* 215.

9. Robert E. Lee, *The Recollections & Letters of Robert E. Lee* (New York: Konecky and Konecky, 1992), 102; Guelzo, *Gettysburg: The Last Invasion,* 456; Longstreet, "The Mistakes of Gettysburg," in *Annals of the War,* 619; Longstreet, *From Manassas to Appomattox,* 351; Brock, *Southern Historical Society Papers,* Volume 5, 167; Brock, *Southern Historical Society Papers,* Volume 6, 122; Justus Scheibert, *Seven Months in the Rebel States During the North American War, 1863,* ed. W. Stanley Hoole (Tuscaloosa: University of Alabama Press, 2009), 113; Sorrel, *At the Right Hand of Longstreet,* 163; Alexander, *Fighting for the Confederacy,* 232.

Chapter 4

1. Longstreet, *From Manassas to Appomattox,* 358; Longstreet, "Lee in Pennsylvania," in *Annals of the War,* 421.

2. Dowdey, *Lee and His Men at Gettysburg,* 116–117.

3. Bruce Catton, *Never Call Retreat* (London: Phoenix, 1965), 184.

4. Gordon, *Reminiscences of the Civil War,* 154.

5. Longstreet, "The Mistakes of Gettysburg," in *Annals of the War,* 627; Edward H. Bonekemper, *The Myth of the Lost Cause: Why the South Fought the Civil War and Why the North Won* (Washington: Regnery History, 2015), 189.

6. Scheibert, *Seven Months in the Rebel States,* 118; Longstreet, "The Mistakes of Gettysburg," in *Annals of the War,* 627; Swinton, *Campaigns of the Army of the Potomac,* 337.

7. Longstreet, *From Manassas to Appomattox,* 358; Rollins, "'The Ruling Ideas' of the Pennsylvania Campaign: James Longstreet's 1873 Letter to Lafayette McLaws," 15; Glenn Tucker, *High Tide at Gettysburg: The Campaign in Pennsylvania* (Gettysburg: Stan Clark Military Books, 1958, reprint 1995), 6–8; Stewart, *Pickett's Charge,* 16–17; Helen Dortch Longstreet, *Lee and Longstreet at High Tide,* 311; Alexander, *Fighting for the Confederacy,* 277–278.

8. Scott, *The War of the Rebellion,* Volume 27, Part 2, 318; Swinton, *Campaigns of the Army of the Potomac,* 340–341.

9. Alexander, *Fighting for the Confederacy,* 233–234; William Calvin Oates, *The War Between the Union and the Confederacy, and Its Lost Opportunities* (New York and Washington: Neale, 1905), 224, 231.

10. Longstreet, "Lee in Pennsylvania," in *Annals of the War,* 421; Noah Andre Trudeau, *Gettysburg: A Testing of Courage* (New York: HarperCollins, 2002), 252; Fremantle, *Three Months in the Southern States,* 249.

11. Longstreet, "Lee in Pennsylvania," in *Annals of the War,* 421; Longstreet, "Lee's Right Wing at Gettysburg," in *Battles and Leaders of the Civil War:* Volume III, 340; Longstreet, *From Manassas to Appomattox,* 358–359.

12. Douglas Southall Freeman, *Lee: An Abridgement in One Volume,* ed. Richard Harwell (New York: Touchstone, 1997), 326; Shelby Foote, *The Civil War, A Narrative: Fredericksburg to Meridian* (New York: Random House, 1963), 480; Scott, *The War of the Rebellion,* Volume 27, Part 2, 317–318.

13. Longstreet, *From Manassas to Appomattox,* 358; Longstreet, "Lee in Pennsylvania," in *Annals of the War,* 421; Fitzgerald Ross, *A Visit to the Cities and Camps of the Confederate States* (Edinburgh: William Blackwood and Sons, 1865), 80–81.

14. Scott, *The War of the Rebellion,* Volume 27, Part 2, 318; Robert Alonzo Brock, ed., *Southern Historical Society Papers,* Volume 33 (Richmond: Virginia Historical Society, 1905), 145; Maj. J. Coleman Alderson, "Lee and Longstreet at Gettysburg" in *Confederate Veteran,* Volume 12 (S.A. Cunningham, 1904), 488.

15. Sears, *Gettysburg,* 183; Guelzo, *Gettysburg: The Last Invasion,* 174; Coddington, *The Gettysburg Campaign: A Study in Command,* 370, 732.

16. Gallagher, *Lee and His Generals in War and Memory,* 66–67.

17. *The Gettysburg Campaign: A Study in Command,* 320; Scott, *The War of the Rebellion,* Volume 27, *Part 2,* 318, 445; Sears, *Gettysburg,* 232–234.

18. Sears, *Gettysburg,* 230, 228; Tucker, *High Tide at Gettysburg,* 183, 220; Alexander, *Military Memoirs of a Confederate,* 386.

19. Gallagher, *Lee and His Generals in War and Memory,* 67; Tucker, *Lee and Longstreet at Gettysburg,* 209.

Chapter 5

1. Coddington, *The Gettysburg Campaign: A Study in Command,* 730; Longstreet, "The Mistakes of Gettysburg," in *Annals of the War,* 628; Gallagher, *Lee and His Generals in War and Memory,* 68.

2. Alexander, *Fighting for the Confederacy,* 234; *The War of the Rebellion,* Volume 27, Part 2, 446; Tucker, *High Tide at Gettysburg,* 211–215; Sears, *Gettysburg,* 230–231; Guelzo, *Gettysburg: The Last Invasion,* 220.

3. Alexander, *Fighting for the Confederacy,* 234; Alexander, *Military Memoirs of a Confederate,* 386–387; Bonekemper, *The Myth of the Lost Cause,* 171.

4. Gallagher, *Lee and His Generals in War and Memory,* 68.

5. Marshall, *Lee's Aide De Camp,* 231–232; Sears, *Gettysburg,* 231–233; Tucker, *High Tide at Gettysburg,* 219–220.

6. Longstreet, "Lee in Pennsylvania," in *Annals of the War,* 421.

7. Wert, *General James Longstreet,* 258; Gallagher, *Lee and His Generals in War and Memory,* 69.

8. Gallagher, *Lee and His Generals in War and Memory,* 68; William Allan, "A Reply to General Longstreet," in *Battles and Leaders of the Civil War:* Volume III (New York: Castle), 355.

9. Allan, "A Reply to General Longstreet," in *Battles and Leaders of the Civil War,* Volume III, 356; Brock, *Southern Historical Society Papers,* Volume 6, 112.

10. Freeman, *Lee: An Abridgement in One Volume,* 327–328.

11. Harry W. Pfanz, *Gettysburg: The Second Day* (Chapel Hill: University of North Carolina Press, 1987), 21–22, 28; Armistead Long is quoted in Tucker, *High Tide at Gettysburg*, 219, 216–217.

12. Longstreet, "Lee in Pennsylvania," in *Annals of the War*, 422; Alexander, *Military Memoirs of a Confederate*, 388; Coddington, *The Gettysburg Campaign: A Study in Command*, 369.

13. Gallagher, *Lee and His Generals in War and Memory*, 62; Freeman, *Lee's Lieutenants*, 575; Piston, *Lee's Tarnished Lieutenant*, 174–178.

14. Longstreet, "Lee in Pennsylvania," in *Annals of the War*, 439; Fremantle, *Three Months in the Southern States*, 256;

15. Longstreet, "Lee's Right Wing at Gettysburg," in *Battles and Leaders of the Civil War:* Volume III, 349–350.

16. Longstreet, "Lee in Pennsylvania," in *Annals of the War*, 421; Scheibert, *Seven Months in the Rebel States*, 118.

Chapter 6

1. Longstreet, *From Manassas to Appomattox*, 362; Freeman, *Lee: An Abridgement in One Volume*, 328; Dowdey, *Lee and His Men at Gettysburg*, 159, 167; David L. Schultz and Scott L. Mingus Sr., *The Second Day at Gettysburg: The Attack and Defense of Cemetery Ridge, July 2, 1863* (El Dorado Hills, CA: Savas Beatie, 2015, 2016), 94–95, 140.

2. Longstreet, "Lee in Pennsylvania," in *Annals of the War*, 422; Longstreet, "Lee's Right Wing at Gettysburg," in *Battles and Leaders of the Civil War:* Volume III, 340; Brock, *Southern Historical Society Papers*, Volume 5, 179; Wert, *General James Longstreet*, 295.

3. Schultz and Mingus, *The Second Day at Gettysburg*, 228; Kevin O' Brien, "'Stubborn Bravery': The Forgotten 44th New York at Little Round Top," *Gettysburg Magazine*, Volume 15 (1996), 37; Longstreet, "Lee in Pennsylvania," in *Annals of the War*, 422; Longstreet, *From Manassas to Appomattox*, 364; Sorrel, *At the Right Hand of Longstreet*, 167.

4. Guelzo, *Gettysburg: The Last Invasion*, 235; Sears, *Gettysburg*, 252–254; Pfanz, *Gettysburg: The Second Day*, 105–106; Wert, *General James Longstreet*, 261; Freeman, *Lee: An Abridgement in One Volume*, 328; Coddington, *The Gettysburg Campaign: A Study in Command*, 376; Longstreet, *From Manassas to Appomattox*, 363; Longstreet, "Lee in Pennsylvania," in *Annals of the War*, 422, 438.

5. Coddington, *The Gettysburg Campaign: A Study in Command*, 371; Robert Alonzo Brock, ed., *Southern Historical Society Papers*, Volume 7 (Richmond: Virginia Historical Society, 1879), 68.

6. Brock, *Southern Historical Society Papers*, Volume 7, 68; Pfanz, *Gettysburg: The Second Day*, 110–111; Guelzo, *Gettysburg: The Last Invasion*, 238.

7. Brock, *Southern Historical Society Papers*, Volume 7, 68–69.

8. Brock, *Southern Historical Society Papers*, Volume 5, 92; John Bell Hood, *Advance and Retreat: Personal Experiences in the United States and Confederate States Armies* (Cambridge, MA: Da Capo, 1993), 57; Longstreet, "Lee in Pennsylvania," in *Annals of the War*, 421; Tucker, *Lee and Longstreet at Gettysburg*, 26.

9. Coddington, *The Gettysburg Campaign: A Study in Command*, 361–362; Krick, "'If Longstreet Says So...It Is Most Likely Not True,'" 70.

10. Sears, *Gettysburg*, 254; Sorrel, *At the Right Hand of Longstreet*, 167.

11. Sorrel, *At the Right Hand of Longstreet*, 167–168.

12. Guelzo, *Gettysburg: The Last Invasion*, 238.

Chapter 7

1. David A. Powell, "A Reconnaissance Gone Awry: Capt. Samuel R. Johnston's Fateful Trip to Little Round Rop," *Gettysburg Magazine*, Volume 23 (2000), 91.

2. Freeman, *Lee's Lieutenants*, 600–601; Guelzo, *Gettysburg: The Last Invasion*, 238, 242–243, 245; Sears, *Gettysburg*, 253, 255, 264; Pfanz, *Gettysburg: The Second Day*, 62, 107.

3. Brock, *Southern Historical Society Papers*, Volume 40, 278; Alexander, *Military Memoirs of a Confederate*, 389.

4. Scott, *The War of the Rebellion*, Volume 27, Part 3, 350.

5. Alexander, *Fighting for the Confederacy*, 235–236; Alexander, *Military Memoirs of a Confederate*, 390–391.

6. Alexander, *Military Memoirs of a Confederate*, 391; Longstreet, *From Manassas to Appomattox*, 363, 380; Pfanz, *Gettysburg: The Second Day*, 112.

7. Wert, "No 15,000 Men Can Take that Hill," 86; Brock, *Southern Historical Society Papers*, Volume 7, 76.

8. Sears, *Gettysburg*, 256–257; Pfanz, *Gettysburg: The Second Day*, 111–112; Longstreet, "Lee in Pennsylvania," in *Annals of the War*, 422; Longstreet, *From Manassas to Appomattox*, 363.

9. Pfanz, *Gettysburg: The Second Day*, 112; Freeman, *Lee: An Abridgement in One Volume*, 330; Coddington, *The Gettysburg Campaign: A Study in Command*, 376.

10. Brock, *Southern Historical Society Papers*, Volume 4, 68.

11. Brock, *Southern Historical Society Papers*, Volume 4, 59; Tucker, *Lee and Longstreet at Gettysburg*, 46.

12. Gallagher, *Lee and His Generals in War and Memory*, 51.

13. Gallagher, *Lee and His Generals in War and Memory*, 61; Alexander, *Fighting for the Confederacy*, 278; Helen Dortch Longstreet, *Lee and Longstreet at High Tide*, 67, 76; Bonekemper, *The Myth of the Lost Cause*, 147.

Chapter 8

1. Longstreet, "Lee in Pennsylvania," in *Annals of the War*, 422; Scott, *The War of the Rebellion*, Volume 27, Part 3, 358, 318, 614, 608; Hood, *Advance and Retreat*, 57; Pfanz, *Gettysburg: The Second Day*, 113.

2. Scott, *The War of the Rebellion*, Volume 27, Part 3, 318–319.

3. Tucker, *Lee and Longstreet at Gettysburg*, 34; Tucker, *High Tide at Gettysburg*, 243; Guelzo, *Gettysburg: The Last Invasion*, 237, 254–255; Longstreet, "The Mistakes of Gettysburg," in *Annals of the War*,

626; Helen Dortch Longstreet, *Lee and Longstreet at High Tide*, 27–28.

4. Sears, *Gettysburg*, 257; Freeman, *Lee: An Abridgement in One Volume*, 330.

5. Krick, "'If Longstreet Says So...It Is Most Likely Not True,'" 70; Walter H. Taylor, *Four Years with General Lee* (New York: D. Appleton and Company, 1877), 98; John William Jones, *Life and Letters of Robert Edward Lee: Soldier and Man* (New York and Washington: The Neale Publishing Company, 1906), 275; Alexander, *Military Memoirs of a Confederate*, 392.

6. Krick, "'If Longstreet Says So...It Is Most Likely Not True,'" 70–71; Coddington, *The Gettysburg Campaign: A Study in Command*, 378; Schultz and Mingus, *The Second Day at Gettysburg*, 229; Brock, *Southern Historical Society Papers*, Volume 4, 65.

7. Pfanz, *Gettysburg: The Second Day*, 113–114; Dowdey, *Lee and His Men at Gettysburg*, 193.

8. Scott, *The War of the Rebellion*, Volume 27, Part 3, 350; Trudeau, *Gettysburg: A Testing of Courage*, 312.

9. Scott, *The War of the Rebellion*, Volume 27, Part 3, 350.

10. Long and Wright, *Memoirs of Robert E. Lee*, 281–282; Tucker, *Lee and Longstreet at Gettysburg*, 27; Guelzo, *Gettysburg: The Last Invasion*, 246; Robert Nicholson Scott, ed., *The War of the Rebellion: A Compilation of the Official Records of the Union and Confederate Armies*, Volume 27, Part 1 (Washington: U.S. Government Printing Office, 1889), 515.

Chapter 9

1. Brock, *Southern Historical Society Papers*, Volume 7, 69; Scott, *The War of the Rebellion*, Volume 27, Part 3, 358; Longstreet, "Lee in Pennsylvania," in *Annals of the War*, 422; Longstreet, "Lee's Right Wing at Gettysburg," 340; Longstreet, *From Manassas to Appomattox*, 365–366; Allan, "A Reply to General Longstreet," in *Battles and Leaders of the Civil War*, Volume III, 356; Brock, *Southern Historical Society Papers*, Volume 5, 184; Freeman, *Lee's Lieutenants*, 578; Dowdey, *Lee and His Men at Gettysburg*, 196.

2. Brock, *Southern Historical Society Papers*, Volume 5, 183; Trudeau, *Gettysburg: A Testing of Courage*, 312; Krick, "'If Longstreet Says So...It Is Most Likely Not True,'" 71.

3. Krick, "'If Longstreet Says So...It Is Most Likely Not True,'" 65; Tucker, *Lee and Longstreet at Gettysburg*, 20, 31.

4. Brock, *Southern Historical Society Papers*, Volume 5, 183; Tucker, *Lee and Longstreet at Gettysburg*, 20; Bill Hyde, "Did You Get There? Capt. Samuel Johnston's Reconnaissance at Gettysburg," *Gettysburg Magazine*, Volume 29 (2003), 87; Krick, "'If Longstreet Says So...It Is Most Likely Not True,'" 71; Trudeau, *Gettysburg: A Testing of Courage*, 312.

5. Tucker, *Lee and Longstreet at Gettysburg*, 30–31; Brock, *Southern Historical Society Papers*, Volume 7, 69.

6. Dowdey, *Lee and His Men at Gettysburg*, 194.

7. Longstreet, "Lee in Pennsylvania," in *Annals of the War*, 423; Guelzo, *Gettysburg: The Last Invasion*, 240; Longstreet, *From Manassas to Appomattox*, 402; Scott, *The War of the Rebellion*, Volume 27, Part 3, 358.

8. Guelzo, *Gettysburg: The Last Invasion*, 239–240; Sears, *Gettysburg*, 258; Pfanz, *Gettysburg: The Second Day*, 119; Krick, "'If Longstreet Says So...It Is Most Likely Not True,'" 72; Brock, *Southern Historical Society Papers*, Volume 7, 69; Sorrel, *At the Right Hand of Longstreet*, 168.

9. Brock, *Southern Historical Society Papers*, Volume 7, 69.

10. Brock, *Southern Historical Society Papers*, Volume 4, 68; Guelzo, *Gettysburg: The Last Invasion*, 240.

11. Alexander, *Fighting for the Confederacy*, 236–237.

12. Alexander, *Fighting for the Confederacy*, 236; Alexander, *Military Memoirs of a Confederate*, 392.

13. Krick, "'If Longstreet Says So...It Is Most Likely Not True,'" 72; Laney, "Wasted Gallantry," *Gettysburg Magazine*, Volume 16, 33; Wert, *General James Longstreet*, 270; Alexander, *Fighting for the Confederacy*, 236.

14. Alexander, *Military Memoirs of a Confederate*, 392; Pfanz, *Gettysburg: The Second Day*, 118.

15. Freeman, *Lee: An Abridgement in One Volume*, 331; Wert, *General James Longstreet*, 270; Brock, *Southern Historical Society Papers*, Volume 5, 184; Brock, *Southern Historical Society Papers*, Volume 4, 101.

16. Joseph B. Kershaw, "Kershaw's Brigade at Gettysburg," in *Battles and Leaders of the Civil War*: Volume III (New York: Castle), 331.

17. Wert, *General James Longstreet*, 270.

Chapter 10

1. Brock, *Southern Historical Society Papers*, Volume 7, 69; Gottfried, *The Maps of Gettysburg*, 142–143; Sears, *Gettysburg*, 261; Guelzo, *Gettysburg: The Last Invasion*, 239; Brock, *Southern Historical Society Papers*, Volume 5, 198.

2. Kershaw, "Kershaw's Brigade at Gettysburg," in *Battles and Leaders of the Civil War*: Volume III, 332; Brock, *Southern Historical Society Papers*, Volume 7, 70.

3. Kershaw, "Kershaw's Brigade at Gettysburg," in *Battles and Leaders of the Civil War*: Volume III, 332.

4. Alexander, *Fighting for the Confederacy*, 278; Brock, *Southern Historical Society Papers*, Volume 7, 84; Sears, *Gettysburg*, 252; Guelzo, *Gettysburg: The Last Invasion*, 248–251; Helen Dortch Longstreet, *Lee and Longstreet at High Tide*, 29.

5. Brock, *Southern Historical Society Papers*, Volume 7, 70.

6. Brock, *Southern Historical Society Papers*, Volume 7, 72; Pfanz, *Gettysburg: The Second Day*, 152–153.

7. Dowdey, *Lee and His Men at Gettysburg*, 201; James M. McPherson, *Battle Cry of Freedom: The Civil War Era* (New York: Ballantine, 1988), 657; Schultz and Mingus, *The Second Day at Gettysburg*, 276, 283.

8. Krick, "'If Longstreet Says So...It Is Most Likely Not True,'" 75.

9. Brock, *Southern Historical Society Papers*, Volume 7, 72; Wert, *General James Longstreet*, 272; Ross, *A Visit to the Cities and Camps of the Confederate States*, 54–55; John C. Oeffinger, ed., *A Soldier's General: The Civil War Letters of Major General Lafayette McLaws* (Chapel Hill: University of North Carolina Press, 2002), 40; Coddington, *The Gettysburg Campaign: A Study in Command*, 381.

Chapter 11

1. Hood, *Advance and Retreat,* 57.
2. *Ibid.,* 58–59.
3. Hood, *Advance and Retreat,* 58; Evander M. Law, "The Struggle for Round Top," in *Battles and Leaders of the Civil War:* Volume III (New York: Castle), 321–322; Alexander, *Military Memoirs of a Confederate,* 394.
4. Hood, *Advance and Retreat,* 58–59.
5. Brock, *Southern Historical Society Papers,* Volume 6, 108; Bonekemper, *The Myth of the Lost Cause,* 147.
6. LaFantasie, *Twilight at Little Round Top,* 49; Dowdey, *Lee and His Men at Gettysburg,* 207; Foote, *The Civil War, A Narrative: Fredericksburg to Meridian,* 499; Emory M. Thomas, *Robert E. Lee: A Biography* (New York: W.W. Norton, 1995), 302; Laney, "Wasted Gallantry," *Gettysburg Magazine,* Volume 16 (1997), 34; Krick, "'If Longstreet Says So...It Is Most Likely Not True,'" 75.
7. H. J. Eckenrode and Bryan Conrad, *James Longstreet: Lee's War Horse* (Chapel Hill: University of North Carolina Press, 1936, 1986), 367; Ben Ames Williams, *House Divided* (Chicago: Chicago Review, 1947, 1974, 2006); Dowdey, *Lee and His Men at Gettysburg,* 180; Krick, "'If Longstreet Says So...It Is Most Likely Not True,'" 75, 72.
8. Helen Dortch Longstreet, *Lee and Longstreet at High Tide,* 26.
9. Freeman, *Lee: An Abridgement in One Volume,* 332; Ross, *A Visit to the Cities and Camps of the Confederate States,* 54.
10. Sorrel, *At the Right Hand of Longstreet,* 167; Scott, *The War of the Rebellion,* Volume 27, Part 2, 308; Helen Dortch Longstreet, *Lee and Longstreet at High Tide,* 39.
11. Allan, "A Reply to General Longstreet," in *Battles and Leaders of the Civil War,* Volume III, 356; Brock, *Southern Historical Society Papers,* Volume 4, 80, 72, 122; Brock, *Southern Historical Society Papers,* Volume 6, 115; Brock, *Southern Historical Society Papers,* Volume 7, 76; Jubal A. Early, *The Campaigns of Gen. Robert E. Lee* (Baltimore: John Murphy & Co., 1872), 34; Gordon, *Reminiscences of the Civil War,* 161; Sorrel, *At the Right Hand of Longstreet,* 168.
12. Alexander, *Fighting for the Confederacy,* 237; Scheibert, *Seven Months in the Rebel States,* 114.
13. Wert, *General James Longstreet,* 279; McPherson, *Battle Cry of Freedom,* 656–657.
14. Freeman, *Lee's Lieutenants,* 578, 600; Foote, *The Civil War, A Narrative: Fredericksburg to Meridian,* 498.
15. Goree, *Longstreet's Aide,* 158.
16. Wert, *General James Longstreet,* 279; Helen Dortch Longstreet, *Lee and Longstreet at High Tide,* 21; Alexander, *Military Memoirs of a Confederate,* 390.
17. Tucker, *High Tide at Gettysburg,* 392; Coddington, *The Gettysburg Campaign: A Study in Command,* 445.
18. Alexander, *Fighting for the Confederacy,* 278.

Chapter 12

1. Oeffinger, *A Soldier's General: The Civil War Letters of Major General Lafayette McLaws,* 197, 41; Krick, "'If Longstreet Says So...It Is Most Likely Not True,'" 77.
2. Oeffinger, *A Soldier's General: The Civil War Letters of Major General Lafayette McLaws,* 197; Pfanz, *Gettysburg: The Second Day,* 116.
3. Brock, *Southern Historical Society Papers,* Volume 7, 74.
4. *Ibid.,* 75.
5. *Ibid.,* 75–76.
6. *Ibid.,* 75.
7. *Ibid.,* 76.
8. *Ibid.,* 72.
9. Pfanz, *Gettysburg: The Second Day,* 155, 497.
10. Wert, *General James Longstreet,* 249–250.

Chapter 13

1. Guelzo, *Gettysburg: The Last Invasion,* 256, 262–274; Sears, *Gettysburg,* 265–281; Gottfried, *The Maps of Gettysburg,* 144–159; Pfanz, *Gettysburg: The Second Day,* 165.
2. Scott, *The War of the Rebellion,* Volume 27, Part 2, 404; Gottfried, *The Maps of Gettysburg,* 146–153, 156–169; Sears, *Gettysburg,* 272; Guelzo, *Gettysburg: The Last Invasion,* 265.
3. Gottfried, *The Maps of Gettysburg,* 166–169; Sears, *Gettysburg,* 284–287; Guelzo, *Gettysburg: The Last Invasion,* 282–288; Kershaw, "Kershaw's Brigade at Gettysburg," in *Battles and Leaders of the Civil War:* Volume III, 333–334.
4. Gottfried, *The Maps of Gettysburg,* 182–191; Sears, *Gettysburg,* 297–302; Guelzo, *Gettysburg: The Last Invasion,* 307–317; Longstreet, "Lee in Pennsylvania," in *Annals of the War,* 424; Franklin Lafayette Riley, ed., *Publications of the Mississippi Historical Society,* Volume 14 (Mississippi Historical Society, 1914), 236.
5. Gottfried, *The Maps of Gettysburg,* 176–181, 192–197; Sears, *Gettysburg,* 302–305; Guelzo, *Gettysburg: The Last Invasion,* 296–300; Fremantle, *Three Months in the Southern States,* 261; Kershaw, "Kershaw's Brigade at Gettysburg," in *Battles and Leaders of the Civil War:* Volume III, 337; Kevin E. O'Brien, "'To Unflinchingly Face Danger and Death': Carr's Brigade Defends Emmitsburg Road," *The Gettysburg Magazine,* Volume 12 (1995), 19; Alexander, *Fighting for the Confederacy,* 240.

Chapter 14

1. Brock, *Southern Historical Society Papers,* Volume 6, 116; Longstreet, "Lee in Pennsylvania," in *Annals of the War,* 425.
2. Longstreet, "Lee in Pennsylvania," in *Annals of the War,* 425; Brock, *Southern Historical Society Papers,* Volume 4, 122, 67.
3. Gottfried, *The Maps of Gettysburg,* 200–211; Sears, *Gettysburg,* 313–321; Guelzo, *Gettysburg: The Last Invasion,* 317–334; Fremantle, *Three Months in the Southern States,* 260; Scott, *The War of the Rebellion,* Volume 27, Part 2, 318.
4. Krick, "'If Longstreet Says So...It Is Most Likely Not True,'" 73; Longstreet, *From Manassas to Appomattox,* 380.
5. Dowdey, *Lee and His Men at Gettysburg,* 202; Krick, "'If Longstreet Says So...It Is Most Likely Not

True,'" 73; Douglas Southall Freeman, *R.E. Lee, A Biography:* Volume 3 (New York: Charles Scribner's Sons, 1935), 150.

6. Gottfried, *The Maps of Gettysburg,* 200–211; Sears, *Gettysburg,* 313–321; Guelzo, *Gettysburg: The Last Invasion,* 317–334; Bradley M. Gottfried, "Mahone's Brigade: Insubordination or Miscommunication?" in *The Gettysburg Magazine,* Volume 18 (1998), 67–76; James I. Robertson and Robert H. Rhodes, *General A.P. Hill: The Story of a Confederate Warrior* (New York: Vintage, 1987), 220; Tucker, *High Tide at Gettysburg,* 318.

7. Longstreet, "Lee in Pennsylvania," in *Annals of the War,* 425, 424; Longstreet, "Lee's Right Wing at Gettysburg," in *Battles and Leaders of the Civil War:* Volume III, 341; Tucker, *Lee and Longstreet at Gettysburg,* 8; McPherson, *Battle Cry of Freedom,* 657, 659; Tucker, *High Tide at Gettysburg,* 394.

8. Sorrel, *At the Right Hand of Longstreet,* 136; Scott, *The War of the Rebellion,* Volume 27, Part 2, 614; Foote, *The Civil War, A Narrative: Fredericksburg to Meridian,* 510; Tucker, *High Tide at Gettysburg,* 289.

9. Scott, *The War of the Rebellion,* Volume 27, Part 2, 608.

10. Brock, *Southern Historical Society Papers,* Volume 4, 79.

11. Scott, *The War of the Rebellion,* Volume 27, Part 2, 319; Fremantle, *Three Months in the Southern States,* 259–260; Coddington, *The Gettysburg Campaign: A Study in Command,* 444; Dowdey, *Lee and His Men at Gettysburg,* 228, 240; Longstreet, *From Manassas to Appomattox,* 408.

12. Fremantle, *Three Months in the Southern States,* 260–261.

Chapter 15

1. Sorrel, *At the Right Hand of Longstreet,* 121; Scott, *The War of the Rebellion,* Volume 27, Part 2, 351; Swinton, *Campaigns of the Army of the Potomac,* 354; Tucker, *High Tide at Gettysburg,* 300.

2. Scott, *The War of the Rebellion,* Volume 27, Part 2, 446–447; Freeman, *Lee: An Abridgement in One Volume,* 334, 332.

3. Scott, *The War of the Rebellion,* Volume 27, Part 2, 470.

4. Scott, *The War of the Rebellion,* Volume 27, Part 2, 470; Walter Taylor, "The Campaign in Pennsylvania," in *Annals of the War,* 310; Freeman, *Lee: An Abridgement in One Volume,* 333.

5. Brock, *Southern Historical Society Papers,* Volume 4, 59–60.

6. Alexander, *Military Memoirs of a Confederate,* 405–406.

7. Alexander, *Military Memoirs of a Confederate,* 405, 409.

8. Alexander, *Fighting for the Confederacy,* xxii–xxiii; Longstreet, "Lee in Pennsylvania," in *Annals of the War,* 428.

9. Longstreet, "The Mistakes of Gettysburg," in *Annals of the War,* 620, 626.

10. Kershaw, "Kershaw's Brigade at Gettysburg," in *Battles and Leaders of the Civil War:* Volume III, 338; Alexander, *Fighting for the Confederacy,* 242; Longstreet, "The Mistakes of Gettysburg," in *Annals of the War,* 624.

Chapter 16

1. Gottfried, *The Maps of Gettysburg,* 212–215; Sears, *Gettysburg,* 321–322; Guelzo, *Gettysburg: The Last Invasion,* 298–303.

2. Longstreet, *From Manassas to Appomattox,* 373; Longstreet, "Lee's Right Wing at Gettysburg," in *Battles and Leaders of the Civil War:* Volume III, 341.

3. Longstreet, "Lee in Pennsylvania," in *Annals of the War,* 425.

4. Guelzo, *Gettysburg: The Last Invasion,* 460, 351.

Chapter 17

1. Sears, *Gettysburg,* 349; Hess, *Pickett's Charge: The Last Attack at Gettysburg,* 47; Guelzo, *Gettysburg: The Last Invasion,* 380; Tucker, *Lee and Longstreet at Gettysburg,* 69.

2. Scott Bowden and Bill Ward, *Last Chance for Victory: Robert E. Lee and the Gettysburg Campaign* (Cambridge, MA: Da Capo, 2003), 387; Robert Alonzo Brock, ed., *Southern Historical Society Papers,* Volume 32 (Richmond: Virginia Historical Society, 1903), 40; *Lee and Longstreet at Gettysburg,* 69; Hess, *Pickett's Charge: The Last Attack at Gettysburg,* 47.

3. Sears, *Gettysburg,* 349; Bowden and Ward, *Last Chance for Victory,* 387.

4. Foote, *The Civil War, A Narrative: Fredericksburg to Meridian,* 526.

5. Longstreet, "Lee in Pennsylvania," in *Annals of the War,* 429; Sears, *Gettysburg,* 347; Guelzo, *Gettysburg: The Last Invasion,* 376; Ross, *A Visit to the Cities and Camps of the Confederate States,* 59.

6. Stewart, *Pickett's Charge,* 4; Henry Kyd Douglas, *I Rode With Stonewall* (Chapel Hill: University of North Carolina Press, 2000), 249.

7. Scott, *The War of the Rebellion,* Volume 27, Part 2, 320; Longstreet, "Lee's Right Wing at Gettysburg," in *Battles and Leaders of the Civil War:* Volume III, 341.

8. Scott, *The War of the Rebellion,* Volume 27, Part 2, 320; Sears, *Gettysburg,* 360–371; Guelzo, *Gettysburg: The Last Invasion,* 383–387.

9. Scott, *The War of the Rebellion,* Volume 27, Part 2, 320; Freeman, *Lee's Lieutenants,* 587; Dowdey, *Lee and His Men at Gettysburg,* 251, 253.

10. William Garrett Piston, "Cross Purposes: Longstreet, Lee, and Confederate Attack Plans for July 3 at Gettysburg," in *The Third Day at Gettysburg and Beyond,* ed. Gary W. Gallagher (Chapel Hill: University of North Carolina Press, 1994), 45–46; Hessler and Motts, *Pickett's Charge at Gettysburg,* 44–45; Alexander, *Military Memoirs of a Confederate,* 429. Piston's assertion about Longstreet and the movements of Pickett's division on the morning of July 3 when he states, "Incredibly, Longstreet failed during the night to order the division into a position where it would be ready at dawn to support either an attack on Cemetery Ridge, a movement around Little Round Top to attack the Federal rear, or, for that matter, a strategic maneuver to force Meade to do the costly attacking," again, largely hinges on if Lee actually ordered Longstreet to have Pickett's division ready for an attack on Cemetery Ridge at dawn (or some other specific time around the daylight hour), and also on if Lee and Longstreet would have agreed, as they did

almost immediately upon meeting in-person at 4:30 a.m., to not use Hood and McLaws' divisions at all in an attack. Any frontal attack on Cemetery Ridge on the morning of July 3 without the assistance of Hood and McLaws would have necessitated pulling units from another corps, which would have significantly delayed any assault plan well beyond the dawn hour. The latter half of Piston's point is more unique and thought-provoking since the question of how Longstreet intended to use Pickett in a flank attack or turning movement (presumably carried out sometime in the morning hours), and how the division's mid-morning arrival would have affected the execution of those plans has rarely, if ever, been posed. Given Longstreet stated in his after battle report on his flank attack plan, "A few moments after my orders for the execution of this plan were given, the commanding general joined me," which would have been around 4:30 a.m., and Pickett did not arrive near Seminary Ridge until 7 a.m. at the earliest, it is unknown what Pickett's role would have been in the attack or Longstreet's prospective timeline for carrying out such an attack. To make this issue even more opaque, it is unclear what stage of execution Longstreet's plan was actually in when Lee joined him.

11. Rollins, "'The Ruling Ideas' of the Pennsylvania Campaign," *The Gettysburg Magazine*, Volume 17, 15; James Longstreet, *From Manassas to Appomattox*, 385; Foote, *The Civil War, A Narrative: Fredericksburg to Meridian*, 523.

12. Wert, *General James Longstreet*, 282; LaFantasie, *Twilight at Little Round Top*, 232; Sears, *Gettysburg*, 346–347.

13. Piston, *Lee's Tarnished Lieutenant*, 141; Helen Dortch Longstreet, *Lee and Longstreet at High Tide*, 45.

14. Gordon, *Reminiscences of the Civil War*, 164; Helen Dortch Longstreet, *Lee and Longstreet at High Tide*, 46; Foote, *The Civil War, A Narrative: Fredericksburg to Meridian*, 526.

15. Longstreet, *From Manassas to Appomattox*, 386; Scott, *The War of the Rebellion*, Volume 27, Part 2, 351; Sears, *Gettysburg*, 348–349.

16. Wert, *General James Longstreet*, 282; Sears, *Gettysburg*, 347, 349; Scott, *The War of the Rebellion*, Volume 27, Part 2, 358–360.

17. Hess, *Pickett's Charge: The Last Attack at Gettysburg*, 5; Trudeau, *Gettysburg: A Testing of Courage*, 436, 526; Helen Dortch Longstreet, *Lee and Longstreet at High Tide*, 47; *The War of the Rebellion*, Volume 27, Part 2, 320.

18. William Garrett Piston offers some explanation for the differences in Alexander's two major accounts in: "Cross Purposes: Longstreet, Lee, and Confederate Attack Plans for July 3 at Gettysburg," in *The Third Day at Gettysburg and Beyond*, ed. Gary W. Gallagher (Chapel Hill: University of North Carolina Press, 1994). Piston indicates Alexander was in Nicaragua when he wrote *Fighting for the Confederacy* in 1897, "lacked access to printed sources, such as Longstreet's memoirs, published the year before," and was "relying entirely on memory." It was only after returning to the United States, Piston points out, that Alexander "revised his recollections," which were published in 1907 work, *Military Memoirs of a Confederate*.

19. Alexander, *Military Memoirs of a Confederate*, 415; Alexander, *Fighting for the Confederacy*, 244.

20. Alexander, *Military Memoirs of a Confederate*, 415; Brock, *Southern Historical Society Papers*, Volume 4, 102.

21. Alexander, *Military Memoirs of a Confederate*, 415.

22. Longstreet, *From Manassas to Appomattox*, 25–26; Dowdey, *Lee and His Men at Gettysburg*, 253; Scott, *The War of the Rebellion*, Volume 27, Part 2, 359.

23. Brock, *Southern Historical Society Papers*, Volume 7, 79, 82.

24. Brock, *Southern Historical Society Papers*, Volume 7, 82; Longstreet, *From Manassas to Appomattox*, 386; Editors of Stackpole Books, *Gettysburg: The Story of the Battle With Maps* (Mechanicsburg, PA: Stackpole, 2013), 95.

25. Alexander, *Military Memoirs of a Confederate*, 416; Alexander, *Fighting for the Confederacy*, 252; Brock, *Southern Historical Society Papers*, Volume 7, 82; Scott, *The War of the Rebellion*, Volume 27, Part 2, 320.

26. Hess, *Pickett's Charge: The Last Attack at Gettysburg*, 7.

27. Dowdey, *Lee and His Men at Gettysburg*, 257.

Chapter 18

1. Stewart, *Pickett's Charge*, 18; Dowdey, *Lee and His Men at Gettysburg*, 259,

2. Longstreet, "Lee in Pennsylvania," in *Annals of the War*, 429; Longstreet, "Lee's Right Wing at Gettysburg," 342; Scott, *The War of the Rebellion*, Volume 27, Part 2, 359; Longstreet, "The Mistakes of Gettysburg," in *Annals of the War*, 620; Longstreet, *From Manassas to Appomattox*, 385.

3. Longstreet, "Lee's Right Wing at Gettysburg," 342.

4. Longstreet, "Lee in Pennsylvania," in *Annals of the War*, 429, 432; Scott, *The War of the Rebellion*, Volume 27, Part 2, 320, 359; Fremantle, *Three Months in the Southern States*, 262.

5. Longstreet, *From Manassas to Appomattox*, 386; Hessler and Motts, *Pickett's Charge at Gettysburg*, 58; Fremantle, *Three Months in the Southern States*, 274; Longstreet, "Lee in Pennsylvania," in *Annals of the War*, 429; Longstreet, "Lee's Right Wing at Gettysburg," 343.

6. Scott, *The War of the Rebellion*, Volume 27, Part 2, 308; Longstreet, "Lee's Right Wing at Gettysburg," 343.

7. Sears, *Gettysburg*, 383, 392; Hess, *Pickett's Charge: The Last Attack at Gettysburg*, 233; Hessler and Motts, *Pickett's Charge at Gettysburg*, 45, 51–53, 58; Richard Rollins, *Pickett's Charge: Eyewitness Accounts at the Battle of Gettysburg* (Mechanicsburg, PA: Stackpole, 1994, 2005), 76; Gottfried, *The Maps of Gettysburg*, 250–251.

8. Stewart, *Pickett's Charge*, 282; Hess, *Pickett's Charge: The Last Attack at Gettysburg*, 32.

9. Rollins, *Pickett's Charge: Eyewitness Accounts at the Battle of Gettysburg*, 269; Stewart, *Pickett's Charge*, 89–90; Sears, *Gettysburg*, 383–384, 386, 389; Hessler and Motts, *Pickett's Charge at Gettysburg*, 72; Hess, *Pickett's Charge: The Last Attack at Gettysburg*, 32.

10. Stewart, *Pickett's Charge*, 89–90.

11. Stewart, *Pickett's Charge*, 23; Hessler and Motts, *Pickett's Charge at Gettysburg*, 32–34; Hess, *Pickett's Charge: The Last Attack at Gettysburg*, 65–67.

12. Hess, *Pickett's Charge: The Last Attack at Gettysburg*, 32, 59; Dowdey, *Lee and His Men at Gettysburg*, 279; Hessler and Motts, *Pickett's Charge at Gettysburg*, 28, 36; Stewart, *Pickett's Charge*, 39, 108.

13. Paul Clark Cooksey, "When an Officer Orders a Disregard of His Superiors: The Jackson-A.P. Hill Feud and its Effect on the Gettysburg Campaign," *Gettysburg Magazine*, Volume 25 (2001), 10–11; Hessler and Motts, *Pickett's Charge at Gettysburg*, 32; William W. Hassler, *A. P. Hill: Lee's Forgotten General* (Chapel Hill: University of North Carolina Press, 1957, 1962, 2000), 164; Sears, *Gettysburg*, 503, 385; Scott, *The War of the Rebellion*, Volume 27, Part 2, 666.

14. Dowdey, *Lee and His Men at Gettysburg*, 263, 280; Freeman, *Lee: An Abridgement in One Volume*, 335; Sorrel, *At the Right Hand of Longstreet*, 171–172.

15. Alexander, *Fighting for the Confederacy*, 253; Fremantle, *Three Months in the Southern States*, 262; Ross, *A Visit to the Cities and Camps of the Confederate States*, 60; Hess, *Pickett's Charge: The Last Attack at Gettysburg*, 22; Stewart, *Pickett's Charge*, 30–31; Guelzo, *Gettysburg: The Last Invasion*, 381.

16. Hess, *Pickett's Charge: The Last Attack at Gettysburg*, 21; Joseph T. Durkin, ed., *John Dooley, Confederate Soldier: His War Journal* (University of Notre Dame Press, 1963), 102; Longstreet, "Lee's Right Wing at Gettysburg," 343; Sorrel, *At the Right Hand of Longstreet*, 173; Brock, *Southern Historical Society Papers*, Volume 7, 92; Rollins, *Pickett's Charge: Eyewitness Accounts at the Battle of Gettysburg*, 76.

17. Longstreet, "Lee in Pennsylvania," in *Annals of the War*, 432; Longstreet, *From Manassas to Appomattox*, 390; Longstreet, "Lee's Right Wing at Gettysburg," 343.

18. Tucker, *High Tide at Gettysburg*, 337; Hess, *Pickett's Charge: The Last Attack at Gettysburg*, 20; George Morley Vickers, ed., *Under Both Flags: A Panorama of the Great Civil War, as Represented in Story, Anecdote, Adventure, and the Romance of Reality* (People's Publishing Company, 1896), 69; Guelzo, *Gettysburg: The Last Invasion*, 381.

19. Longstreet, "Lee in Pennsylvania," in *Annals of the War*, 432; Alexander, *Fighting for the Confederacy*, 280.

Chapter 19

1. Brock, *Southern Historical Society Papers*, Volume 4, 63, 84–85; Gordon, *Reminiscences of the Civil War*, 160–161; Brock, *Southern Historical Society Papers*, Volume 5, 120; Alexander, *Fighting for the Confederacy*, 282; Stewart, *Pickett's Charge*, 282; Hess, *Pickett's Charge: The Last Attack at Gettysburg*, 32–33.

2. Hess, *Pickett's Charge: The Last Attack at Gettysburg*, 15; See, Richard Rollins, "The Second Wave of Pickett's Charge," *Gettysburg Magazine*, Volume 18 (1998), 96–113, for extensive commentary on this theory; Robert Alonzo Brock, ed., *Southern Historical Society Papers*, Volume 41 (Richmond: Virginia Historical Society, 1916), 40; Scott, *The War of the Rebellion*, Volume 27, Part 2, 320, 608, 614; Brock, *Southern Historical Society Papers*, Volume 4, 84; Brock, *Southern Historical Society Papers*, Volume 7, 83; Helen Dortch Longstreet, *Lee and Longstreet at High Tide*, 55.

3. Scott, *The War of the Rebellion*, Volume 27, Part 2, 320; Stewart, *Pickett's Charge*, 119.

4. Brock, *Southern Historical Society Papers*, Volume 4, 103; Alexander, *Fighting for the Confederacy*, 247; Alexander, *Military Memoirs of a Confederate*, 418–419; Hessler and Motts, *Pickett's Charge at Gettysburg*, 21.

5. Alexander, *Fighting for the Confederacy*, 248.

6. Hess, *Pickett's Charge: The Last Attack at Gettysburg*, 32; Alexander, *Fighting for the Confederacy*, 249.

Chapter 20

1. Longstreet, *From Manassas to Appomattox*, 390; Gottfried, *The Maps of Gettysburg*, 252–253; Hessler and Motts, *Pickett's Charge at Gettysburg*, 20–25; Alexander, *Fighting for the Confederacy*, 249–251; Stewart, *Pickett's Charge*, 98.

2. Alexander, *Fighting for the Confederacy*, 254.

3. Longstreet, *From Manassas to Appomattox*, 391; Alexander, *Fighting for the Confederacy*, 254–255.

4. Alexander, *Fighting for the Confederacy*, 255.

5. Dowdey, *Lee and His Men at Gettysburg*, 290; Hess, *Pickett's Charge: The Last Attack at Gettysburg*, 29.

6. Sorrel, *At the Right Hand of Longstreet*, 240–242; Longstreet, "Lee in Pennsylvania," in *Annals of the War*, 430.

7. Alexander, *Fighting for the Confederacy*, 254; Hess, *Pickett's Charge: The Last Attack at Gettysburg*, 32.

8. Alexander, *Fighting for the Confederacy*, 254–255; Longstreet, *From Manassas to Appomattox*, 391.

9. Another account has put the total at 159 guns; Hessler and Motts, *Pickett's Charge at Gettysburg*, 60, 66; Sears, *Gettysburg*, 383, 396–398; Stewart, *Pickett's Charge*, 120, 159–161; Guelzo, *Gettysburg: The Last Invasion*, 396–402.

10. Sears, *Gettysburg*, 404; Wert, *General James Longstreet*, 289–290; Stewart, *Pickett's Charge*, 139–140.

11. Mauriel P. Joslyn, "Gettysburg and the Immortal Six Hundred," *Gettysburg Magazine*, Volume 12 (1995), 114.

12. Alexander, *Fighting for the Confederacy*, 249, 258.

13. Of course, Alexander only possessed the line of sight to see Brown's Federal battery withdraw; however, he had seen some guns retire, and therefore believed that if Pickett was to advance, his opening had arrived; Alexander, *Fighting for the Confederacy*, 259; Stewart, *Pickett's Charge*, 158.

14. Alexander, *Fighting for the Confederacy*, 260; Longstreet, "Lee in Pennsylvania," in *Annals of the War*, 430–431; Longstreet, "Lee's Right Wing at Gettysburg," 344–345; Longstreet, *From Manassas to Appomattox*, 392; Hessler and Motts, *Pickett's Charge at Gettysburg*, 47.

15. Stewart, *Pickett's Charge*, 177; Alexander, *Fighting for the Confederacy*, 261–262; Longstreet, "Lee's Right Wing at Gettysburg," 345; Rollins, *Pickett's Charge: Eyewitness Accounts at the Battle of Gettysburg*, 244.

16. Unknown to Longstreet at the time, Lee later hinted in one of his after-battles reports that he might have called off the attack had he known about the inability of the Confederate artillery to adequately re-

spond to the resumption of the Federal's cannon fire soon after Pickett and Pettigrew started forward, along with their incapacity to "render the necessary support to the attacking party"—a reasonably clear reference to his desire for advanced artillery support; Alexander, *Fighting for the Confederacy,* 261; Sears, *Gettysburg,* 407; Longstreet, *From Manassas to Appomattox,* 392; Scott, *The War of the Rebellion,* Volume 27, Part 2, 321, 360.

Chapter 21

1. Hessler and Motts, *Pickett's Charge at Gettysburg,* 72, 130; Guelzo, *Gettysburg: The Last Invasion,* 408–410; Sears, *Gettysburg,* 415–419; Stewart, *Pickett's Charge,* 180–183; Hess, *Pickett's Charge: The Last Attack at Gettysburg,* 78–79; Gottfried, *The Maps of Gettysburg,* 254–255.

2. Sears, *Gettysburg,* 421–425, 429–433; Stewart, *Pickett's Charge,* 189; Guelzo, *Gettysburg: The Last Invasion,* 421–423; Edmund Rice, "Repelling Lee's Last Blow at Gettysburg," in *Battles and Leaders of the Civil War: The Tide Shifts,* Volume III (New York: Castle), 392; Hess, *Pickett's Charge: The Last Attack at Gettysburg,* 182–193; Gottfried, *The Maps of Gettysburg,* 256–257.

3. Rollins, *Pickett's Charge: Eyewitness Accounts at the Battle of Gettysburg,* 254; Hessler and Motts, *Pickett's Charge at Gettysburg,* 285–286; Hess, *Pickett's Charge: The Last Attack at Gettysburg,* 254; Longstreet, *From Manassas to Appomattox,* 393–394.

4. Sears, *Gettysburg,* 433–435; Guelzo, *Gettysburg: The Last Invasion,* 423–425; Hess, *Pickett's Charge: The Last Attack at Gettysburg,* 201–209, 248–258; Hessler and Motts, *Pickett's Charge at Gettysburg,* 90–102; Gottfried, *The Maps of Gettysburg,* 258–261.

5. Stewart, *Pickett's Charge,* 184–188; Hess, *Pickett's Charge: The Last Attack at Gettysburg,* 170–178, 196, 219–227; Guelzo, *Gettysburg: The Last Invasion,* 410–417; Sears, *Gettysburg,* 435–442; Coddington, *The Gettysburg Campaign: A Study in Command,* 504; Gottfried, *The Maps of Gettysburg,* 256–259.

6. Hess, *Pickett's Charge: The Last Attack at Gettysburg,* 227–233; Sears, *Gettysburg,* 442–443; Longstreet, "Lee's Right Wing at Gettysburg," 346; Alexander, *Fighting for the Confederacy,* 262–263.

7. Hess, *Pickett's Charge: The Last Attack at Gettysburg,* 260–271, 307–315; Sears, *Gettysburg,* 444–458; Guelzo, *Gettysburg: The Last Invasion,* 417–421; Longstreet, "Lee in Pennsylvania," in *Annals of the War,* 431; Longstreet, *From Manassas to Appomattox,* 394; Gottfried, *The Maps of Gettysburg,* 260–263.

Chapter 22

1. Allan, "A Reply to General Longstreet," in *Battles and Leaders of the Civil War,* Volume III, 356; Brock, *Southern Historical Society Papers,* Volume 4, 123.

2. Scott, *The War of the Rebellion,* Volume 27, Part 2, 320–321.

3. Brock, *Southern Historical Society Papers,* Volume 6, 119; Hess, *Pickett's Charge: The Last Attack at Gettysburg,* 72; Guelzo, *Gettysburg: The Last Invasion,* 393.

4. Longstreet, "Lee in Pennsylvania," in *Annals of the War,* 432.

5. Rollins, *Pickett's Charge: Eyewitness Accounts at the Battle of Gettysburg,* 156.

6. Fremantle, *Three Months in the Southern States,* 264–266; Rollins, *Pickett's Charge: Eyewitness Accounts at the Battle of Gettysburg,* 156.

7. Rollins, *Pickett's Charge: Eyewitness Accounts at the Battle of Gettysburg,* 157; Hess, *Pickett's Charge: The Last Attack at Gettysburg,* 73; Hessler and Motts, *Pickett's Charge at Gettysburg,* 57.

8. Rollins, *Pickett's Charge: Eyewitness Accounts at the Battle of Gettysburg,* 157.

9. Hess, *Pickett's Charge: The Last Attack at Gettysburg,* 226–227, 296–307; Sears, *Gettysburg,* 454–455; Hessler and Motts, *Pickett's Charge at Gettysburg,* 54–58; Scott, *The War of the Rebellion,* Volume 27, Part 2, 557, 620; Rollins, *Pickett's Charge: Eyewitness Accounts at the Battle of Gettysburg,* 265; Hessler and Motts, *Pickett's Charge at Gettysburg,* 79–83.

10. Robert Alonzo Brock, ed., *Southern Historical Society Papers,* Volume 31 (Richmond: Virginia Historical Society, 1903), 229; Hess, *Pickett's Charge: The Last Attack at Gettysburg,* 374.

11. Longstreet, "Lee in Pennsylvania," in *Annals of the War,* 431; Longstreet, *From Manassas to Appomattox,* 395; Fremantle, *Three Months in the Southern States,* 266–267.

12. Longstreet, "Lee's Right Wing at Gettysburg," 347; Longstreet, *From Manassas to Appomattox,* 395.

Chapter 23

1. Bonekemper, *The Myth of the Lost Cause,* 184; Sears, *Gettysburg,* 457–458; Guelzo, *Gettysburg: The Last Invasion,* 428–429; Robert Edward Lee, *Recollections and Letters of General Robert E. Lee,* 101; McPherson, *Battle Cry of Freedom,* 665; Robert E. Lee, *The Wartime Papers of Robert E. Lee,* ed. Clifford Dowdey (Boston: Little, Brown for the Virginia Civil War Commission, 1961), 551; Hessler and Motts, *Pickett's Charge at Gettysburg,* 49.

2. Piston, *Lee's Tarnished Lieutenant,* 143; Gordon, *Reminiscences of the Civil War,* 166; Dowdey, *Lee and His Men at Gettysburg,* 340; Rollins, *Pickett's Charge: Eyewitness Accounts at the Battle of Gettysburg,* 35.

3. Lee, *Recollections and Letters of General Robert E. Lee,* 102; Bonekemper, *The Myth of the Lost Cause,* 187.

4. Longstreet, "The Mistakes of Gettysburg," in *Annals of the War,* 620, 627; Longstreet, "Lee in Pennsylvania," in *Annals of the War,* 441; Longstreet, "Lee's Right Wing at Gettysburg," 343.

5. Wert, *General James Longstreet,* 287; Rollins, *Pickett's Charge: Eyewitness Accounts at the Battle of Gettysburg,* 76–77; Walter Taylor, *Lee's Adjutant: The Wartime Letters of Colonel Walter Herron Taylor, 1862–1865,* ed. R. Lockwood Tower and John S. Belmont (Columbia: University of South Carolina Press, 1995), 59; Brock, *Southern Historical Society Papers,* Volume 4, 73; Helen Dortch Longstreet, *Lee and Longstreet at High Tide,* 55; Alexander, *Military Memoirs of a Confederate,* 412, 420; Alexander, *Fighting for the Confederacy,* 252, 404.

6. Alexander, *Military Memoirs of a Confederate,* 417.

7. Law, "The Struggle for Round Top," in *Battles and Leaders of the Civil War:* Volume III, 322;

Bonekemper, *The Myth of the Lost Cause,* 186; Sears, *Gettysburg,* 504–505; Wert, *General James Longstreet,* 296.

8. Allan, "A Reply to General Longstreet," in *Battles and Leaders of the Civil War,* Volume III, 356; Brock, *Southern Historical Society Papers,* Volume 4, 123, 285; Dowdey, *Lee and His Men at Gettysburg,* 257; Hess, *Pickett's Charge: The Last Attack at Gettysburg,* 386; Sorrel, *At the Right Hand of Longstreet,* 171; Stewart, *Pickett's Charge,* 286.

9. Longstreet, *From Manassas to Appomattox,* 384; Longstreet, "Lee in Pennsylvania," in *Annals of the War,* 430; Krick, "'If Longstreet Says So...It Is Most Likely Not True,'" 62; Rollins, *Pickett's Charge: Eyewitness Accounts at the Battle of Gettysburg,* 34.

10. Alexander, *Fighting for the Confederacy,* 92; Sorrel, *At the Right Hand of Longstreet,* 80, 171; Robert Alonzo Brock, ed., *Southern Historical Society Papers,* Volume 13 (Richmond: Virginia Historical Society, 1885), 211; Daniel Hill, "Lee's Attacks North of the Chickahominy," in *Battles and Leaders of the Civil War: The Struggle Intensifies,* Volume II (New York: Castle), 352; Bonekemper, *The Myth of the Lost Cause,* 188.

Chapter 24

1. Tucker, *Lee and Longstreet at Gettysburg,* 226, 228; Longstreet, *From Manassas to Appomattox,* 405.

2. Tucker, *Lee and Longstreet at Gettysburg,* 228.

3. Tucker, *Lee and Longstreet at Gettysburg,* 228; Bonekemper, *The Myth of the Lost Cause,* 190; Alexander, *Fighting for the Confederacy,* 92.

4. Bonekemper, *The Myth of the Lost Cause,* 189; Stephen Sears, *To The Gates of Richmond: The Peninsula Campaign* (Boston, New York: Houghton Mifflin, 1992), 193–200, 234–236, 277–278, 279, 283–293; Tucker, *Lee and Longstreet at Gettysburg,* 233; Sorrel, *At the Right Hand of Longstreet,* 98.

5. Bonekemper, *The Myth of the Lost Cause,* 189.

6. Helen Dortch Longstreet, *Lee and Longstreet at High Tide,* 83; Tucker, *Lee and Longstreet at Gettysburg,* 228, 229, 232, 234; Longstreet, *From Manassas to Appomattox,* 330.

7. Tucker, *Lee and Longstreet at Gettysburg,* 233.

8. Wert, *General James Longstreet,* 296; Helen Dortch Longstreet, *Lee and Longstreet at High Tide,* 83–84; Tucker, *Lee and Longstreet at Gettysburg,* 234.

Chapter 25

1. Helen Dortch Longstreet, *Lee and Longstreet at High Tide,* 77–78; Long and Wright, *Memoirs of Robert E. Lee,* 628; Longstreet, "The Mistakes of Gettysburg," in *Annals of the War,* 631; Goree, *Longstreet's Aide,* 167.

2. Longstreet, "The Mistakes of Gettysburg," in *Annals of the War,* 628; Longstreet, "Lee in Pennsylvania," in *Annals of the War,* 433; Longstreet, *From Manassas to Appomattox,* 654–655.

3. Long and Wright, *Memoirs of Robert E. Lee,* 626; Sorrel, *At the Right Hand of Longstreet,* 306.

4. Goree, *Longstreet's Aide,* 158.

5. Hess, *Pickett's Charge: The Last Attack at Gettysburg,* 373–374; Goree, *Longstreet's Aide,* 160.

6. Longstreet, "Lee in Pennsylvania," in *Annals of the War,* 432.

7. Longstreet, "The Mistakes of Gettysburg," in *Annals of the War,* 632–633.

8. Helen Dortch Longstreet, *Lee and Longstreet at High Tide,* 316, 334, 340, 343.

9. "Camp Craft, Modern Practice and Equipment... Free Book," posting to Outdoor Self Reliance Blog, June 18, 2014, http://outdoorselfreliance.com/camp-craft-modern-practice-equipment-free-book/ (accessed January 22, 2018); Warren Miller to Hamlin Garland, May 17, 1933, Box 26, Folder 55, Hamlin Garland checklist no. 2840, Hamlin Garland Papers, Correspondence, 1860–1940, USC Libraries Special Collections, University of Southern California Libraries, http://digitallibrary.usc.edu/cdm/compoundobject/collection/p15799coll81/id/23479/rec/2.

10. Jeff Gill, "Civil War at 150: Longstreet Left His Mark on Gainesville," *Gainesville Times,* April 17, 2011, http://www.gainesvilletimes.com/m/archives/49185/; Charles Lane, "The Forgotten Confederate General Who Deserves a Monument," *The Washington Post,* January 27, 2016, https://www.washingtonpost.com/opinions/the-forgotten-confederate-general-who-would-make-a-better-subject-for-monuments/2016/01/27/f09bad42-c536-11e5-8965-0607e0e265ce_story.html; Helen Dortch Longstreet, *Lee and Longstreet at High Tide,* 85.

11. Jeff Gill, "Civil War at 150."

12. Longstreet, *From Manassas to Appomattox,* 397, 401.

13. *Ibid.,* 388.

14. *Ibid.,* 401, 407, 332; James Longstreet, "Lee's Invasion of Pennsylvania," in *Battles and Leaders of the Civil War:* Volume III, 245.

15. Tucker, *Lee and Longstreet at Gettysburg,* 226.

Postscript

1. Wheeler, Current Literature, Volume 22, 415.

2. Wheeler, Current Literature, Volume 22, 415; Hessler and Motts, *Pickett's Charge at Gettysburg,* 199, 266

3. Wheeler, Current Literature, Volume 22, 415; Tucker, *Lee and Longstreet at Gettysburg,* 226; Wert, *General James Longstreet,* 296; About two years after visiting Longstreet in Gainesville, Garland sent the general a copy of his biography on Ulysses S. Grant, *Ulysses S. Grant: His Life and Character,* to which Longstreet replied, "I write to thank you for remembering me with a copy of your book...and for the pleasure the interesting and clever story of the great General has given me." See: James Longstreet to Hamlin Garland, June 14, 1899, Box 23, Folder 55, Hamlin Garland checklist no. 2596, Hamlin Garland Papers, Correspondence, 1860–1940, USC Libraries Special Collections, University of Southern California Libraries, http://digitallibrary.usc.edu/cdm/compoundobject/collection/p15799coll81/id/21939/rec/1.

Bibliography

Alderson, Maj. J. Coleman. "Lee and Longstreet at Gettysburg." In *Confederate Veteran*, Volume 12. S.A. Cunningham, 1904.

Alexander, Edward Porter. *Fighting for the Confederacy: The Personal Recollections of General Edward Porter Alexander*, ed. Gary W. Gallagher. Chapel Hill: University of North Carolina Press, 1989.

Alexander, Edward Porter, *Military Memoirs of a Confederate: A Critical Narrative*. New York: Scribner's, 1907.

Annals of the War. Originally published in the *Philadelphia Weekly Times*, republished, Edison, NJ: Blue & Grey, 1996.

Battles and Leaders of the Civil War: The Struggle Intensifies, Volume II. New York: Castle.

Battles and Leaders of the Civil War: The Tide Shifts, Volume III. New York: Castle.

Bonekemper III, Edward H. *The Myth of the Lost Cause: Why the South Fought the Civil War and Why the North Won*. Washington: Regnery History, 2015.

Bowden, Scott, and Ward, Bill. *Last Chance for Victory: Robert E. Lee and the Gettysburg Campaign*. Cambridge, MA: Da Capo, 2003.

Brock, Robert Alonzo, ed. *Southern Historical Society Papers*, Volume 4. Richmond: Virginia Historical Society, 1877.

Brock, Robert Alonzo, ed. *Southern Historical Society Papers*, Volume 5. Richmond: Virginia Historical Society, 1878.

Brock, Robert Alonzo, ed. *Southern Historical Society Papers*, Volume 6. Richmond: Virginia Historical Society, 1878.

Brock, Robert Alonzo, ed. *Southern Historical Society Papers*, Volume 7. Richmond: Virginia Historical Society, 1879.

Brock, Robert Alonzo, ed. *Southern Historical Society Papers*, Volume 13. Richmond: Virginia Historical Society, 1885.

Brock, Robert Alonzo, ed. *Southern Historical Society Papers*, Volume 31. Richmond: Virginia Historical Society, 1903.

Brock, Robert Alonzo, ed. *Southern Historical Society Papers*, Volume 32. Richmond: Virginia Historical Society, 1903.

Brock, Robert Alonzo, ed. *Southern Historical Society Papers*, Volume 33. Richmond: Virginia Historical Society, 1905.

Brock, Robert Alonzo, ed. *Southern Historical Society Papers*, Volume 37. Richmond: Virginia Historical Society, 1909.

Brock, Robert Alonzo, ed. *Southern Historical Society Papers*, Volume 40. Richmond: Virginia Historical Society, 1915.

Brock, Robert Alonzo, ed. *Southern Historical Society Papers*, Volume 41. Richmond: Virginia Historical Society, 1916.

"Camp Craft, Modern Practice and Equipment... Free Book." Posting to Outdoor Self Reliance Blog, June 18, 2014, http://outdoorselfreliance.com/camp-craft-modern-practice-equipment-free-book/. Accessed January 22, 2018.

Catton, Bruce. *Never Call Retreat*. London: Phoenix, 1965.

Chicago Tribune. June 10, 1867.

Coddington, Edwin B. *The Gettysburg Campaign: A Study in Command*. New York: Simon & Schuster, 1968.

Cooksey, Paul Clark. "'I Still Desired to Save My Men'...Lieutenant General James Longstreet on July 3, 1863." *Gettysburg Magazine*, Volume 34 (2006).

Cooksey, Paul Clark. "When an Officer Orders a Disregard of His Superiors: The Jackson-A.P. Hill Feud and its Effect on the Gettysburg Campaign." *Gettysburg Magazine*, Volume 25 (2001).

Dinardo, R.L, and Albert A. Nofi. *James Longstreet: The Man, the Soldier, the Controversy*. New York: Cambridge, MA: Da Capo, 1998.

Douglas, Henry Kyd. *I Rode with Stonewall*. Chapel Hill: University of North Carolina Press, 2000.

Dowdey, Clifford. *Lee & His Men at Gettysburg: The Death of a Nation*. Lincoln: University of Nebraska Press, 1958.

Durkin, Joseph T., ed. *John Dooley, Confederate Soldier: His War Journal*. University of Notre Dame Press, 1963.

Early, Jubal A. *The Campaigns of Gen. Robert E. Lee*. Baltimore: John Murphy & Co., 1872.

Eckenrode, H.J., and Conrad, Bryan. *James Longstreet: Lee's War Horse*. Chapel Hill: University of North Carolina Press, 1936, 1986.

Editors of Stackpole Books. *Gettysburg: The Story of the Battle with Maps*. Mechanicsburg, PA: Stackpole, 2013.

Foote, Shelby. *The Civil War, A Narrative: Fredericksburg to Meridian*. New York: Random House, 1963.

Freeman, Douglas Southall. *Lee: An Abridgement in One Volume*, ed. Richard Harwell. New York: Touchstone, 1997.

Freeman, Douglas Southall. *Lee's Lieutenants: A Study in Command*, ed. Stephen W. Sears. New York: Simon & Schuster, 1998.

Freeman, Douglas Southall. *R.E. Lee, A Biography: Volume 3*. New York: Scribner's, 1935.

Fremantle, Arthur J.L. *Three Months in the Southern States: April-June 1863*. Lincoln: University of Nebraska Press, 1991.

Gallagher, Gary W. *Lee and His Generals in War and Memory*. Baton Rouge: Louisiana State University Press, 1998.

Gallagher, Gary W., ed. *The Second Day at Gettysburg: Essays on Confederate and Union Leadership*. Kent, OH: Kent State University Press, 1993.

Gallagher, Gary W., ed. *The Third Day at Gettysburg and Beyond*. Chapel Hill: University of North Carolina Press, 1994.

Gill, Jeff. "Civil War at 150: Longstreet Left His Mark on Gainesville." *Gainesville Times*, April 17, 2011, http://www.gainesvilletimes.com/m/archives/49185/.

Gordon, John Brown. *Reminiscences of the Civil War*. New York: Scribner's, 1903.

Goree, Thomas J. *Longstreet's Aide: The Civil War Letters of Major Thomas J. Goree*, ed. Thomas W. Cutrer. Charlottesville: University Press of Virginia, 1995.

Gottfried, Bradley M. "Mahone's Brigade: Insubordination or Miscommunication?" *Gettysburg Magazine*, Volume 18 (1998).

Gottfried, Bradley M. *The Maps of Gettysburg: An Atlas of the Gettysburg Campaign, June 3–July 13, 1863*. New York: Savas Beatie, 2013.

Greezicki, Roger J. "Humbugging the Historian: A Reappraisal of Longstreet at Gettysburg." *Gettysburg Magazine*, Volume 6 (1992).

Guelzo, Allen C. *Gettysburg: The Last Invasion*. New York: Alfred A. Knopf, 2013.

Hassler, William W. *A.P. Hill: Lee's Forgotten General*. Chapel Hill: University of North Carolina Press, 1957, 1962, 2000.

Hess, Earl J. *Pickett's Charge: The Last Attack at Gettysburg*. Chapel Hill: University of North Carolina Press, 2001.

Hessler, James A., and Motts, Wayne E. *Pickett's Charge at Gettysburg: A Guide to the Most Famous Attack in American History*. El Dorado Hills, CA: Savas Beatie, 2015.

Hood, John Bell. *Advance and Retreat: Personal Experiences in the United States and Confederate States Armies*. Cambridge, MA: Da Capo, 1993.

Hyde, Bill. "Did You Get There? Capt. Samuel Johnston's Reconnaissance at Gettysburg." *Gettysburg Magazine*, Volume 29 (2003).

Jones, John William. *Life and Letters of Robert Edward Lee: Soldier and Man*. New York and Washington: Neale, 1906.

Joslyn, Mauriel P. "Gettysburg and the Immortal Six Hundred." *Gettysburg Magazine*, Volume 12 (1995).

Knudsen, LTC Harold M. *General James Longstreet: The Confederacy's Most Modern General*, revised edition. Girard, IL: USA, 2007.

LaFantasie, Glenn W. *Twilight at Little Round Top: July 2, 1863—The Tide Turns at Gettysburg*. New York: Vintage, 2005.

Lane, Charles, "The Forgotten Confederate General Who Deserves a Monument." *The Washington Post*, January 27, 2016, https://www.washingtonpost.com/opinions/the-forgotten-confederate-general-who-would-make-a-better-subject-for-monuments/2016/01/27/f09bad42-c536-11e5-8965-0607e0e265ce_story.html.

Laney, Daniel M. "Wasted Gallantry: Hood's Texas Brigade at Gettysburg." *Gettysburg Magazine*, Volume 16 (1997).

Lee, Robert E. *The Recollections & Letters of Robert E. Lee*. New York: Konecky and Konecky, 1992.

Lee, Robert E. *The Wartime Papers of Robert E. Lee*, ed. Clifford Dowdey. Boston: Little, Brown, for the Virginia Civil War Commission, 1961.

Long, Armistead Lindsay, and Marcus Joseph Wright. *Memoirs of Robert E. Lee: His Military and Personal History*. London: S. Low, Marston, Searle, and Rivington, 1886.

Longstreet, Helen Dortch. *Lee and Longstreet at High Tide: Gettysburg in the Light of the Official Records*. Gainesville, GA: Published by the author, 1904.

Longstreet, James. *From Manassas to Appomattox*. Philadelphia: J.B. Lippincott Company, 1895, reprinted Cambridge, MA: Da Capo, 1992.

Longstreet, James, to Hamlin Garland. June 14, 1899. Box 23, Folder 55, Hamlin Garland checklist no. 2596, Hamlin Garland Papers, Correspondence, 1860–1940, USC Libraries Special Collections, University of Southern California Libraries, http://digitallibrary.usc.edu/cdm/compoundobject/collection/p15799coll81/id/21939/rec/1.

Marshall, Charles. *Lee's Aide De Camp*, Maurice, Frederick, ed. London and Lincoln: University of Nebraska Press, 2000.

McCabe, James D., Jr. *Life and Campaigns of General Robert E. Lee*. Atlanta, GA: National Publishing Company, 1870.

McClellan, Henry B. *I Rode with Jeb Stuart: The*

Life and Campaigns of Major General J.E.B. Stuart. Cambridge, MA: Da Capo, 1994.
McPherson, James M. *Battle Cry of Freedom: The Civil War Era.* New York: Ballantine, 1988.
Miller, Warren, to Hamlin Garland, May 17, 1933. Box 26, Folder 55, Hamlin Garland checklist no. 2840, Hamlin Garland Papers, Correspondence, 1860–1940, USC Libraries Special Collections, University of Southern California Libraries, http://digitallibrary.usc.edu/cdm/compoundobject/collection/p15799coll81/id/23479/rec/2.
New Orleans Times. June 8, 1867.
Newlin, Keith. "Who Is Hamlin Garland?" *Hamlin Garland Society,* http://www.garlandsociety.org/biography.html. Accessed January 21, 2018.
Oates, William Calvin. *The War Between the Union and the Confederacy, and Its Lost Opportunities.* New York and Washington: Neale, 1905.
O'Brien, Kevin. "'Stubborn Bravery': The Forgotten 44th New York at Little Round Top." *Gettysburg Magazine,* Volume 15 (1996).
O'Brien, Kevin. "'To Unflinchingly Face Danger and Death': Carr's Brigade Defends Emmitsburg Road." *Gettysburg Magazine,* Volume 12 (1995).
Oeffinger, John C., ed. *A Soldier's General: The Civil War Letters of Major General Lafayette McLaws.* Chapel Hill: University of North Carolina Press, 2002.
Pfanz, Harry W. *Gettysburg: The First Day.* Chapel Hill: University of North Carolina Press, 2001.
Pfanz, Harry W. *Gettysburg: The Second Day.* Chapel Hill: University of North Carolina Press, 1987.
Piston, William Garrett. *Lee's Tarnished Lieutenant: James Longstreet and His Place in Southern History.* Athens: University of Georgia Press, 1987.
Pollard, Edward Alfred. *Lee and His Lieutenants: Comprising the Early Life, Public Services, and Campaigns of General Robert E. Lee and His Companions in Arms, with a Record of Their Campaigns and Heroic Deeds.* University of Iowa: E. B. Treat & Company, 1868.
Powell, David A. "A Reconnaissance Gone Awry: Capt. Samuel R. Johnston's Fateful Trip to Little Round Rop." *Gettysburg Magazine,* Volume 23 (2000).
Riley, Franklin Lafayette, ed. *Publications of the Mississippi Historical Society, Volume 14.* Mississippi Historical Society, 1914.
Robertson, James I., and Robert H. Rhodes. *General A.P. Hill: The Story of a Confederate Warrior.* New York: Vintage, 1987.
Rollins, Richard. *Pickett's Charge: Eyewitness Accounts at the Battle of Gettysburg.* Mechanicsburg, PA: Stackpole, 1994, 2005.
Rollins, Richard. "'The Ruling Ideas' of the Pennsylvania Campaign: James Longstreet's 1873 Letter to Lafayette McLaws." *Gettysburg Magazine,* Volume 17 (1997).
Rollins, Richard. "The Second Wave of Pickett's Charge." *Gettysburg Magazine,* Volume 18 (1998).
Ross, Fitzgerald. *A Visit to the Cities and Camps of the Confederate States.* Edinburgh: William Blackwood and Sons, 1865.
Sawyer, Gordon. *James Longstreet: Before Manassas and After Appomattox,* second edition. Alpharetta, GA: BookLogix, 2005, 2014.
Scheibert, Justus. *Seven Months in the Rebel States During the North American War, 1863,* ed. W. Stanley Hoole. Tuscaloosa: University of Alabama Press, 2009.
Schultz, David L., and Scott L. Mingus, Sr. *The Second Day at Gettysburg: The Attack and Defense of Cemetery Ridge, July 2, 1863.* El Dorado Hills, CA: Savas Beatie, 2015, 2016.
Scott, Robert Nicholson, ed. *The War of the Rebellion: A Compilation of the Official Records of the Union and Confederate Armies, Volume 27, Part 1.* Washington: U.S. Government Printing Office, 1889.
Scott, Robert Nicholson, ed. *The War of the Rebellion: A Compilation of the Official Records of the Union and Confederate Armies, Volume 27, Part 2.* Washington: U.S. Government Printing Office, 1889.
Scott, Robert Nicholson, ed. *The War of the Rebellion: A Compilation of the Official Records of the Union and Confederate Armies, Volume 27, Part 3.* Washington: U.S. Government Printing Office, 1889.
Sears, Stephen W. *Gettysburg.* Boston, New York: Houghton Mifflin, 2003.
Sears, Stephen W. *To the Gates of Richmond: The Peninsula Campaign.* Boston, New York: Houghton Mifflin, 1992.
Sorrel, Gilbert Moxley. *At the Right Hand of Longstreet: Recollections of a Confederate Staff Officer.* Lincoln: University of Nebraska Press, 1999.
Stackpole, Edward J., and Wilbur S. Nye. *The Battle of Gettysburg: A Guided Tour,* Bradley M. Gottfried, ed. Gettysburg, PA: Americana Souvenirs and Gifts, 1998.
Stewart, George R. *Pickett's Charge: A Microhistory of the Final Attack at Gettysburg, July 3, 1863.* Boston: Houghton Mifflin, 1959.
Swinton, William, *Campaigns of the Army of the Potomac: A Critical History of Operations in Virginia, Maryland and Pennsylvania, from the Commencement to the Close of the War, 1861–1865.* New York: Scribner's, 1882.
Taylor, Walter H. *Four Years with General Lee.* New York: D. Appleton, 1877.
Taylor, Walter H. *Lee's Adjutant: The Wartime Letters of Colonel Walter Herron Taylor, 1862-1865,* ed. R. Lockwood Tower and John S. Belmont. Columbia: University of South Carolina Press, 1995.
Thomas, Emory M. *Robert E. Lee: A Biography.* New York: W.W. Norton, 1995.

Trudeau, Noah Andre. *Gettysburg: A Testing of Courage.* New York: HarperCollins, 2002.

Tucker, Glenn. *High Tide at Gettysburg: The Campaign in Pennsylvania.* Gettysburg, PA: Stan Clark Military Books, 1958, reprint 1995.

Tucker, Glenn. *Lee and Longstreet at Gettysburg.* Dayton, OH: Morningside Bookshop, 1982.

Vickers, George Morley, ed. *Under Both Flags: A Panorama of the Great Civil War, as Represented in Story, Anecdote, Adventure, and the Romance of Reality*. Philadelphia: People's Publishing Company, 1896.

Wade, John Donald. *Augustus Baldwin Longstreet: A Study of the Development of Culture in the South,* ed. M. Thomas Inge. Athens: University of Georgia Press, 2010.

Wert, Jeffry D. *General James Longstreet: The Confederacy's Most Controversial Soldier.* New York: Touchstone, 1993.

Wheeler, Edward Jewitt, ed. *Current Literature,* Volume 22, Volumes 689–702 of American Periodical Series, 1850–1900. Current Literature Publishing Company, 1897.

Williams, Ben Ames. *House Divided.* Chicago: Chicago Review, 1947, 1974, 2006.

Wittenberg, Eric J. *The Battle of Brandy Station: North America's Largest Cavalry Battle.* Charleston, SC: History, 2010.

Index

Numbers in ***bold italics*** indicate pages with illustrations